José Martí

JOE R. AND TERESA LOZANO LONG SERIES IN
LATIN AMERICAN AND LATINO ART AND CULTURE

José Martí

A REVOLUTIONARY LIFE

By Alfred J. López

University of Texas Press   *Austin*

Requests for permission to reproduce material from this work should be
sent to:
    Permissions
    University of Texas Press
    P.O. Box 7819
    Austin, TX 78713-7819
    http://utpress.utexas.edu/index.php/rp-form

♾ The paper used in this book meets the minimum requirements of
ANSI/NISO Z39.48-1992 (R1997) (Permanence of Paper).

LIBRARY OF CONGRESS CATALOGING-IN-PUBLICATION DATA
López, Alfred J., 1962–
    José Martí: a revolutionary life / by Alfred J. López. — First edition.
        pages   cm. — (Joe R. and Teresa Lozano Long series in Latin
American and Latino art and culture)
    Includes bibliographical references and index.
    ISBN 978-0-292-73906-2 (cloth : alk. paper)
    1. Martí, José, 1853–1895.   2. Revolutionaries — Cuba — Biography.
    3. Statesmen — Cuba — Biography.   4. Cuba — History — 1878–1895.   I. Title.
    F1783.M38L5769   2014
    972.91′05092 — dc23
    [B]

                                       2014012771

doi:10.7560/739062

For Susan, wife, best friend, and honorary Cuban

Contents

Part *Three*: THE GREAT WORK (1881–1895)

Preface

I T IS INDICATIVE OF NORTH AMERICANS' LACK OF INTER-
est in the rest of their hemisphere that José Martí, a giant of Latin
American politics and letters, remains unknown in the United States. Martí
was the founding father of not only Cuban independence but a broader pan-
American vision of freedom and democracy. In all of modern Latin American
history, arguably only the "Great Liberator" Simón Bolívar rivals Martí in stature and legacy. Yet among Americans, most of whom could easily pick Fidel
Castro or Ricky Ricardo out of a line-up, relatively few would even recognize
Martí's name.

Among Latin Americans and U.S. Latinos, however, Martí is a household
name. Since his death on a Cuban battlefield in 1895, his legacy has overtaken
the facts and foibles of his life, rendering the man who lived and died for the
dream of Cuban independence the outsized hero, martyr, "Apostle," and founding father that every Cuban — and Cuban American — boy and girl knows today.

In today's Cuba, Martí is inescapable. His face appears on Cuba's one-
peso note (figure 0.1). An enormous Martí statue originally commissioned by
Castro's predecessor Fulgencio Batista presides over Havana's Plaza de la Revolución, the Castro regime's favorite site for speeches and rallies (figure 0.2).
Martí's name also adorns both Havana's airport and Cuba's national library.
Nor do such displays come at the expense of his written work. Cuba's Centro
de Estudios Martianos (Center for Martí Studies), founded in 1977, is a state-
supported agency dedicated to the study and dissemination of Martí's work.
Tens of thousands have visited such public Martí shrines as his Havana birthplace and the former site of the Spanish prison where the adolescent Martí was
incarcerated.

Beyond these major Martí sites, even the casual observer cannot help noticing the ubiquity of Martí's face, name, and words reproduced in settings from

FIGURE 0.1. *Cuba's one-peso note, with Martí's face prominently displayed.*

FIGURE 0.2. *Fidel Castro delivering a speech in Havana's Plaza de la Revolución at the foot of an enormous statue of Martí. From Fidel Castro,* José Martí: El Autor Intellectual *(Centro de Estudios Martianos. Havana: Editora Política, 1983).*

small-town squares to baseball stadiums to private shrines in people's homes. A similar wealth of Martís awaits the visitor to Miami's Little Havana neighborhood, where Martí busts, photos, and calendars abound. In South Florida's Cuban American community, Martí's name and face adorn everything from grocery stores to Cuban cafeterías, a public park, and even a chain of private schools. The exile community's favorite AM radio station, the top-rated WQBA (La Cubanísima—literally "The Most Cuban"), still features quotations from Martí at the top of every hour, and its talk hosts routinely refer to Fidel Castro as "El Tirano" (The Tyrant). Monuments and statues of Martí and other Cuban heroes abound, as well as parks: Máximo Gómez Park, the Bay of Pigs Memorial, and, of course, José Martí Park, site of its namesake's birthday celebration every year (figure 0.3). The city boasts dozens of codesignated streets named after Cuban heroes: from Ignacio Agramonte to Lolo Villalobos, every Cuban body who was anybody has his or her name prominently displayed on a street sign.[1] Martí himself has two. Miami's Lincoln-Martí Schools are "dedicated to the mission of educating the future of our community, both academically and socially."

Even Martí's most fervent devotees, however, have historically known little of the icon's life beyond the sanitized mythologies disseminated by Cuban governments and the exile communities that jealously guard his legacy. The resulting accretion over more than a century of mythmaking, appropriations, and outright falsehoods has done both Martí and his followers a tremendous disservice. In the process of gilding his legend for their own political purposes, scholars and ideologues have simplified and dehumanized Martí, ironically reducing the man's internal contradictions and complexities even as they have inflated him to his iconic status.

Much of the Martí legend has necessarily grown to fill strategic vacuums in what we know about him. As he was an active revolutionary, it is not surprising that key parts of his private and politically sensitive writings have been destroyed either by his own direction or the initiative of well-meaning supporters. But this alone does not account for the cherry-picking and selective blindness that has plagued Martí scholarship for more than a century. More recently, fifty years of ideological warfare between the Castro regime and the Cuban diaspora have produced two politically incompatible Martís—one an atheist Marxist revolutionary, the other a pro-U.S. capitalist—while colluding in the shared task of concealing the more unsavory aspects of his life from the larger public. Martí's many biographers have only deepened this chasm by hewing faithfully to one side or the other of the Havana-Miami divide. As a result, many of those who today profess to love Martí know little of his life and works beyond official, politically managed versions.

JOSÉ JULIÁN MARTÍ Y PÉREZ (1853–1895) WAS THE FOUNDing hero of Cuban independence and stands among the half-dozen most important Latin Americans of the nineteenth century. Beyond his accomplishments as a revolutionary and political thinker, he was a giant of Latin American letters whose poetry, essays, and journalism rank among the canonical texts of their time. As a poet he pioneered Latin American *modernismo*, with works such as *Ismaelillo* (1882) and *Versos sencillos* (1891) considered masterpieces. His work as a foreign correspondent appeared in South America's most respected newspapers of the 1880s and stand today among the most important journalism of the Gilded Age. Martí published four plays, a novel, and a newspaper, *Patria*, which served as the independence movement's official publication. He worked at various points as an editor and translator, a secondary teacher and university professor, and a diplomat. His collected works fill twenty-six volumes, and previously unknown writings still are emerging.

Martí's life falls into three distinct phases: childhood and adolescence in Cuba (1853–1870); first exile and subsequent life in Spain, Mexico City, and Guatemala (1871–1878); and mature revolutionary period in New York City (1881–1895). Martí's exile from Cuba occurred after his arrest and imprisonment

FIGURE O.3. *Bust of José Martí in Miami Beach.*

for conspiracy against Spain. He spent his first four years abroad in Madrid and Zaragoza, where he earned a law degree. After graduation he rejoined his family in Mexico City but fled the country after the rise of dictator Porfirio Díaz. While in Mexico Martí met Carmen Zayas Bazán and married her in 1877, then took her to Guatemala, where he had immigrated. But political disagreements with President Justo Rufino Barrios forced the couple to leave the country. After an abortive attempt to resettle in Havana after the Ten Years' War (1868–1878),

Martí lived his last fifteen years in New York. By the 1880s New York had a sizable exile community and a history of Cuban activism, making it an ideal base for Martí's revolutionary aspirations.

Although he was virtually unknown in Cuba when he died in battle in 1895, by the 1930s Martí had become Cuba's apostle of independence, his name synonymous with Cuban nationalism. Generations of Cuban governments further burnished his legend, which reached its apogee with the 1959 Cuban Revolution's claim to Martí as its primary inspiration. The emigration of hundreds of thousands of Cubans fleeing the revolution spread Martí's fame to the United States and Europe. Martí is, in fact, perhaps the one subject on which Cuban exiles and Fidel Castro agree, as the Cuban leader long claimed Martí as the crucial inspiration and intellectual author of the revolution. Although Martí was not a Latino in the contemporary sense, his lived experience of exile and life in the United States have since made him a key figure in the history of Latin American immigration to the United States and the forging of Latino/a identities.[2]

ALTHOUGH BOOKS AND ESSAYS ON MARTÍ BEGAN APPEARing shortly after his death in 1895 and continue to abound, most of the published biographies are hagiographies, few attempting serious critical evaluation of his life and work. This is primarily because Martí's biographers generally strive less to examine or critique him than to praise him in the interests of ideologically slanted mythmaking. At least two Martí biographies, Alberto Baeza Flores's *Life of José Martí* (1954) and Luis Toledo Sande's *Basket of Flames: A Biography of José Martí* (1996), were directly subsidized by Cuban administrations, and earlier biographers such as Jorge Mañach and Félix Lizaso held ministerial positions in the Batista government.[3] Other Martí biographies, among them Raúl García Martí's *Family Biography* and Gonzalo de Quesada's *Martí, the Man* (both 1940), are the products of authors with close personal links to Martí.[4] It is worth noting that the first serious scholarly biography of Martí, by Carlos Márquez Sterling, was not published in Havana or the United States but in Argentina.[5]

Decades of ideological warfare between the Cuban government and U.S.-based exiles in the aftermath of the Cuban Revolution have deepened this problem, in effect producing two incompatible versions of Martí to suit their respective ideological imperatives. Much of the posthumous mythology that has grown around Martí is the direct result of such skewed writings, as scholars and ideologues have avoided the internal contradictions and complexities of his writings for their own — or their patrons' — political purposes.

THIS BOOK AIMS TO CHANGE ALL THAT, DESPITE THE FACT that, professionally speaking, I have no business writing a biography of José

Martí. I am a professor of literature, by training neither a biographer nor a historian. My primary academic training is in twentieth-century literature, so I cannot even claim formal expertise in the century during which Martí lived and died. Being Cuban American doesn't necessarily count as a credential either, any more than being born in Virginia would qualify me to write about George Washington. Yet it is precisely my unfamiliarity with the ways I was supposed to have read and interpreted Martí that has enabled me to write this book.

As the son of Cuban exiles, born at the height of the Cuban missile crisis and raised in Miami, once the most culturally Cuban city on earth outside of the island, I have in a sense spent my entire life preparing to write this book. Yet, during much of my adult life, including the crucial years of graduate study, I have lived away from Miami and Cubanness. I now realize this distance was necessary because it has given me the outsider's perspective necessary to do justice to my subject, who was himself an exile. Paradoxically, only because I no longer live or work in Miami can I now write this book.

CUBANS ON THE ISLAND AND IN EXILE CLING TO THE CEN-trality of their shared hero's words and image, making Martí not only a central figure in Cuba's history but a key ideological weapon in the battle over its future. Some myths develop from necessity—for keeping a community and its dreams alive. The myth of Martí has served precisely this function for postrevolution Cuba and the Cuban American community established in its wake. Yet to remain useful, any such myth must withstand scrutiny and more than scrutiny. It must survive its own undoing to show its devotees that they and the truths that bind them together are greater than the lies they have sometimes had to tell for the sake of unity.

For at least a century now, Cubans on the island and across the planet have revered Martí as more than a founding national hero. To them he is a mythic figure, practically a national saint: the intellectually gifted, righteous Apostle of freedom who overcame poverty, colonization, prison, exile, physical duress, mental anguish, and the combined efforts of two empires to achieve the impossible. "My sling is the sling of David," Martí writes in his final, unfinished letter from the Cuban front, a phrase Cubans have used as a rallying cry ever since.[6] Yet perhaps the most remarkable—and overlooked—hallmark of Martí's greatness, of his undeniable status as one of the nineteenth century's greatest political, cultural, and literary minds, is the degree to which he triumphed over his own physical, psychological, and moral limitations as a human being. Through it all—imprisonment, illness, exile, immigration, cultural isolation, emotional estrangement, and his own insecurities and self-perceived shortcomings—José Martí worked, struggled, and prevailed.

This book, then, tells the story of how one brilliant, troubled, flawed man lived and died to free his people from centuries of subjugation and bring them into the light of modernity. It moves chronologically through Martí's life, from the child's burgeoning awareness of Cuba's subjugation to the adolescent's first explicit acts of rebellion, his imprisonment and exile; from the young man's restless travels and eventual arrival in New York to his ascendance as the revolution's preeminent leader; from the last frantic struggle to launch a revolution, to his death on a Cuban battlefield. Beyond these events, which Martí's many biographers have generally recognized as highlights of his life and career, this book also calls attention in five interchapters to some less celebrated, even overlooked moments that I consider crucial ones for Martí. The book focuses on these separately from the main chapters not to marginalize them but precisely to bring them the attention they have not received in earlier biographies.

I hope that you will be generous in your judgment of this volume, not because its author deserves a better fate than any other, but because its subject does. Contrary to the beliefs of those who would whitewash their icons and protect them from scrutiny, I believe that the careful examination of Martí's life can only enhance his stature as one of the nineteenth century's true artistic and intellectual giants. I have written this biography out of a long-standing conviction that the life of José Martí was one deeply worthy not merely of our respect and esteem but of our attention. This biography is not ideologically or otherwise beholden to the imperatives of Havana or Miami; thus it can represent Martí in all of his cultural, political, and personal complexity, a comprehensive portrait that I believe will, at long last, do him justice. This book will no doubt enrage partisans on both sides of the Cuban ideological divide. That, however, is a small price to pay for the chance to reintroduce José Martí to generations of readers who remain unaware of his true stature and worth. They, and he, deserve no less.

Acknowledgments

I PONDERED WRITING THIS BOOK FOR MANY YEARS BE-
fore setting out to actually do it. The first step, although I did not
recognize it at the time, was a chapter on Martí in my dissertation at the University of Iowa. That chapter later appeared as a stand-alone essay in *Cuban
Studies* 33 (2002) and served as the point of departure for my 2006 book *José
Martí and the Future of Cuban Nationalism*. I am thus obliged to many who read
parts or all of that earlier work, including Peter Nazareth, Cheryl Herr, Adriana
Méndez Rodenas, Lisandro Pérez, Jorge Camacho, and Emilio Bejel. The help
and encouragement of Joseph Urgo and Lois Parkinson Zamora became indispensable later, as I took the first fitful (or fateful) steps toward researching and
writing the biography.

I am also deeply indebted to Orlando José Hernández and Lucinda R. Zoe,
directors of the 2005 National Endowment for the Humanities Summer Seminar "Visions of Freedom for the Americas: Eugenio María de Hostos and José
Martí in Nineteenth-Century New York" at Hostos Community College in the
Bronx. My admission to the seminar exposed me to scholars, perspectives, and
resources without which this book would not exist in its present form. It was
at Hostos that summer that I was fortunate to meet Tom Miller, whose erudition, friendship, and good humor have left their indelible mark on these pages.
Among other Martí scholars with whom I have corresponded as I developed
this project, Manuel A. Tellechea and Miguel Fernández especially stand out
for their insight, critical eye, and willingness to share what they know with a
relative newbie.

My agent, Jason Ashlock of Moveable Type Management, saw the importance of a new Martí biography early on and shepherded me through the onerous proposal process. He and his assistant Craig Kayser have been great allies
for this project and my work generally, for which I am deeply grateful.

I am likewise grateful for the generous support of Purdue University's Center for Humanistic Studies that freed me from teaching duties as I researched this project in 2008. A Purdue Library Scholars Grant funded my travel to archives and libraries during this crucial period.

I owe a special debt of thanks to Gustavo Pérez Firmat, whose long-distance mentorship has been invaluable for many years now. His guidance and support as I conceived and developed this biography are a major reason for my success in completing it.

I am also grateful to University of Texas Press manuscript editor Lynne Chapman and freelance copyeditor Tana Silva; thanks to their hard work and diligence, this is a much more readable book than it would otherwise have been.

It will be clear to anyone who has studied or written about Martí that any single account of his life will have to navigate the vast body of work published by hundreds of scholars over the past one-hundred-plus years. This book would have been impossible without the enormous amount of primary research published by Cuban and Cuban American scholars who have delved into every conceivable aspect of Martí's life and times. Astute readers will note one particular name that figures prominently in this book's bibliography. Carlos Ripoll (1922–2011) was the preeminent Martí scholar of his time, a tirelessly prolific researcher whose work on Martí remains unmatched for quality and range of vision. Although I have not always agreed with Ripoll's conclusions regarding certain aspects of Martí's life, I owe him a great debt for the substantial contribution his lifetime of work has made to this book.

But most of all, I owe an unrepayable debt to my wife, Susan, to whom I have dedicated this book. More than anyone, she has shared with me the joys and frustrations of writing it and has been my strength and best counsel throughout.

José Martí

Mariano and Leonor

*In Cuba, the son has received his first counsel on pride
and independence from his Spanish father.*

"NUESTRAS IDEAS" (OUR IDEAS), MARCH 14, 1892

J OSÉ JULIÁN MARTÍ Y PÉREZ WAS BORN IN THE EARLY
morning hours of January 28, 1853, an unseasonably cold day.[1] He
was born on the second floor of the small house his proud parents, Mariano and
Leonor Martí, shared with her sister Rita's family. The house was situated on the
outskirts of Old Havana a few blocks from the sea. There was no heat aside from
a small wood stove in the kitchen. Those present at the birth — his aunt Rita, an
unknown midwife, and the child's parents — kept the windows shuttered against
the damp chill of that January morning.[2] There already would have been significant traffic along Calle Paula even at that early hour: a motley assortment of
clergymen and sailors, clerks, soldiers, and sellers carrying their wares to market. Young *beatas* (devotees) were on their way to the nearby church. Everyone
was bundled up against the biting cold of the damp, seaside winds. None in the
street would have had any way of knowing that a child was being born so close
by. None would have had any reason to remark on the event, as children were
generally born at home. Yet not a single person in the street below would fail to
be touched by the child being born in that unassuming second-story bedroom.

Mariano and Leonor were a fairly typical, if relatively affluent, military
colonial couple; only she was born into the Spanish military life and culture.
Mariano was the first on his side of the family to join the army; Leonor was the
third of five children born to Antonio Pérez, a highly decorated sergeant and
infantryman whose two other daughters married Spanish military men.[3]

Although the new parents were loyal Spaniards, the different regions in which they grew up colored their respective early relationships to their mother country. The Pérezes were a firmly middle-class family, and Antonio Pérez owned various properties in their native Canary Islands. The men of the Pérez family could also read and write—a rarity in a region where nearly 90 percent of the population was illiterate.[4]

The Canary Islands archipelago was one of Spain's oldest colonial possessions and had for centuries been an important outpost for Spanish traffic to the New World. The islands' remoteness and distance from the Iberian Peninsula, however, rendered it little more than a way station for Spanish ships and a convenient source of cheap labor and willing military conscripts. The islands' proximity to northern Africa meant that mainland Spaniards viewed the islanders as racially and culturally inferior. These factors, along with hard times due to Spain's single-crop economic policy for the islands, led to massive migration from the Canary Islands to Cuba and Puerto Rico throughout the nineteenth century.[5]

Young Leonor was by all accounts a respectful, disciplined, and devout child who attended church regularly and who never visibly chafed against the rigors of her strict military and Catholic upbringing. The outwardly compliant daughter, however, harbored a keen and fiercely intelligent mind. Spanish girls of the time were generally forbidden to learn to read and write for fear that they would correspond with undesirable suitors. As a teenager, however, the otherwise obedient Leonor taught herself to read and write without her parents' knowledge, apparently the only one of the female Pérez siblings to do so.[6]

If her father's and brothers' literacy was unusual, Leonor's constituted nothing less than a miracle in a land where few women beyond royalty and the very wealthy ever learned such skills. That she did so on her own, without her parents' support or even approval, demonstrates her natural intelligence. It also suggests a pragmatic and resourceful woman who learned early on the wisdom of working within the limitations placed on young women of her class.

In September 1842, Antonio Pérez requested and received a commission in the artillery brigade of Havana. The Pérez family—including fourteen-year-old Leonor—left the Canary Islands for Cuba in November 1843. Leonor's elder sisters, Joaquina and Rita, had married Spanish artillerymen assigned to Havana and were already raising families there. Although no explicit reason for Pérez's transfer appears in his records, it is likely that the career soldier wished to live closer to his married daughters and grandchildren.[7]

Unlike Leonor, Mariano Martí had no family history of military service. He was the third of six children born to Vicente Martí, a farmer and rope maker, and María Martí Navarro. Mariano enlisted in the Spanish army in 1835 at age twenty, likely as a way to escape the lifelong poverty and lack of opportunity that almost invariably awaited young men of his class. His father and elder brothers displayed no interest in or affinity for the military life, but for Mariano 1835 proved an opportune year for ambitious and able-bodied young men to pursue military careers. By the time of his enlistment the Spanish Empire was in steep decline, its once-vast holdings reduced to Cuba and Puerto Rico in the Caribbean and the Philippines and a handful of smaller possessions in the Pacific.[8] The Spanish economy was still in shambles from the Peninsular War against Napoleon (1808–1814), and Spain now lagged badly behind the rest of Europe, which was rapidly modernizing.[9] Spain was again fighting a war on its own soil as conservative opposition to the liberal rule of Regent Maria Cristina sparked the first of three civil conflicts known as the Carlist Wars. The combination of Spain's tenuous hold on its home front and remaining colonies led to a nearly fourfold increase in its standing army between 1828 and 1838, much of it fueled by forced conscription from the provinces.[10]

Mariano's choice to pursue a military career thus proved a wise decision, as the army provided the young man with a lifestyle, education, and class status his elder brothers were never to achieve. Surely the military held more promise for a young man of the time than the prospect of a lifetime carrying bales of hemp for his father's rope-making business. A tailor by trade, Mariano could have left for the city, as two of his brothers eventually did, in hopes of finding work or opening his own shop.[11] Yet Mariano chose military life for reasons not entirely financial. It is especially telling that Mariano was the only one of six Martí siblings who learned to read and write. Having received by all accounts the same upbringing as his male siblings and given the sorry state of primary education throughout Spain at the time, it is reasonable to speculate that perhaps he became literate only after joining the army.[12]

Whatever his reasons for enlisting beyond the prospect of steady employment, Mariano quickly took to military life and was soon promoted to the rank of corporal. After an initial period in his native Valencia, Mariano was transferred in 1844 to Barcelona, where Spain had put down a second Carlist uprising two years earlier. His performance in the artillery corps led to his promotion to the rank of first sergeant in 1850.[13]

Shortly after his promotion, Mariano's artillery unit joined a larger contingent of four infantry battalions and additional squadrons, and all were then transferred to Havana after the failed invasion of the island in May by Narciso López, a disgruntled former general.[14] As with Mariano's enlistment, the timing of his promotion and transfer had a great deal to do with larger forces at work in Spain and its colonies. For decades the English government had pressured Spain to abolish slavery in its remaining colonies, a move strongly opposed by the island's plantation-owning elite, or plantocracy. The plantocracy depended on slave labor for the economic viability of the sugar industry as well as the relatively smaller tobacco and coffee trades.

For this reason the Spanish government had long been ambivalent about slavery in the colonies, agreeing only reluctantly—and under intense pressure from England—to outlaw the slave trade in 1817.[15] The government's enforcement of the slaving prohibition was half-hearted at best, and slavery itself remained legal in the colonies, yet island elites grew increasingly nervous about their economic future. After two decades of ongoing tension between the plantocracy and the mother country on the subject of slavery, Cuba's official exclusion in 1837 from representation in the Spanish court proved the final straw.

From that point on, the island elites became attracted to the idea of annexation to the United States, where slavery seemed much more likely to survive.[16] The feeling was apparently mutual, as the U.S. government—specifically the successive administrations of James Polk and Zachary Taylor—made direct offers to buy the island outright from Spain.[17] Neither the Cuban nor U.S. plantocracies, however, were content to watch events unfold from the sidelines. Prominent planters from both camps were prepared to finance a private filibustering expedition—essentially a mercenary invasion force—to topple the colonial Cuban government and pave the way for U.S. acquisition. The plantocracies possessed the means and motivation for an invasion, and it did not take long before a suitable candidate emerged to lead it.

General Narciso López was Venezuelan by birth and enlisted in the Spanish army against Simón Bolivar's insurgent forces in 1814 at the age of sixteen. He rose quickly through the ranks, and by the time Bolivar's forces prevailed in 1823, the young man was a colonel. Forced to leave his native country along with the Spanish, he relocated first to Spain, where he fought in the First Carlist War, then to Cuba. For a time López's loyalty to Spain paid ample dividends: he married into a wealthy Cuban family, was promoted to general, and served in a string of government posts. As a liberal, however, he suddenly found himself out of favor with the rise of a center-right, moderate government in 1843. López's sudden estrangement—he retained his rank as general but no longer had any official duties—engendered a deep resentment toward the empire he had served for nearly thirty years. After he suffered a number of failed business ventures, López's dwindling fortunes and lasting bitterness turned him against his erstwhile masters; he fled to the United States in 1848 and sought out parties to bankroll an expeditionary force.[18]

By the time of Mariano's arrival in Havana in the summer of 1850, López had tried and failed twice to capture Cuba. In August of the following year, Mariano would help defend Cuba against López's third and final attempt on the island.[19] His superiors duly noted the valor, energy, and zeal he displayed during the crisis, qualities that would eventually enable Mariano to rise into the officers' ranks.

For now, however, his escape from hunger and poverty and into a promising new life seemed more than enough. First Sergeant Mariano Martí was a thirty-five-year-old career soldier who finally began to glimpse the life he may have envisioned when he enlisted as a young man. An enlisted man's salary in the colonial army was more valuable for its regularity than for its size. Even so, shortly after his arrival in Cuba, Mariano was financially comfortable for the first time in his life, thanks in part to a bonus he received for meritorious service during the last Narciso López filibuster. Mariano displayed an interest in business during this time: aside from his regular salary he enjoyed some income from two businesses he acquired, a barbershop and a small café named La Fuente de la Salud (Fountain of Health).[20]

Given thirty-six-year-old Mariano's newfound affluence and relatively advanced age for a bachelor, he unsurprisingly set about to find himself a wife. Little is known about Mariano Martí's romantic or sexual life before this point in his life. Apparently he made no move toward serious courtship and marriage until he became financially and professionally secure, suggesting a man who wanted to marry well, within the restrictions imposed by his rank and class, and was willing to wait until he could attract a socially appropriate spouse. Such a match would be the crowning achievement of a lifelong struggle to overcome the station of his birth. A wife with social and economic status would be the affirmation of Mariano's material, social, and personal success.

For Mariano, Leonor Perez was the perfect match. Leonor was a young, beautiful, intelligent, and well-mannered woman from a military family whose two elder sisters already were married to career soldiers. Mariano and Leonor met at one of the weekly dances held at a downtown ballroom in the old city that provided a venue for the social debuts of daughters of middle-class colonials before potential suitors. Mariano Martí, a good-looking man splendidly attired in full military-dress uniform, would have made a deep and immediate impression on young Leonor despite his average height and build.[21] Mariano's charms proved as irresistible for the Pérez family as for Leonor. Having secured his commanding officer's permission and Antonio Perez's blessing, the couple became formally engaged on January 19, 1852, and were married less than three weeks later, on the sunny but slightly chilly morning of Saturday, February 7.[22] After the ceremony, the newlyweds retired to their new home on Calle Paula, where less than a year later José Martí was born.

BY THE TIME OF JOSÉ MARTÍ'S BIRTH, CUBA HAD BEEN A Spanish possession for nearly 350 years. As the economic and political center of the island colony, Havana showed little sign of the restlessness that would soon strain its relations with the mother country. The colony's native elites had lost their taste for López-style filibustering, and after his capture and public execution following his third attempt they displayed little appetite for continued agitation. Others on the island who continued to advocate either independence or annexation to the United States had, like López, also been silenced by execution or exile.[23] Despite the independence movements that had swept the Latin American continent earlier in the century and continuing international pressure, especially from England, for Spain to abolish slavery in its remaining colonies, Cuba appeared on the surface every bit the placid, contented "Ever-Faithful Isle" (Siempre-Fidelísima Isla) in an otherwise troubled empire.[24]

In 1853 Havana was a bustling, cosmopolitan city of about 200,000 inhabitants characterized as much by its busy international trade, political clout, and displays of military might as by its lively nightlife and thriving arts and social scene. The vast majority of its population, however, could only enjoy the city's many charms from a distance, as these remained strictly the province of the wealthy plantocracy and merchant classes and to a lesser extent those in the military.

The island's Creole elites continued to suppress the immutable tension between material wealth and political subjugation that defined their class. Their awareness of the recent winds of liberalizing political change that had swept Europe and blown as far as their erstwhile colonial peers on the Latin American continent only heightened their untenable position as affluent but second-class citizens.[25] Thus on the day of Martí's birth, local newspapers could announce on the same page and without any notable sense of contradiction the schedule of theatrical premieres and social balls for carnival season alongside the arrival of vaccinations against cholera, which was still running rampant throughout the island.[26] Into this web of contradictions, of surface gaiety and calm veiling a growing sense of unease, was born the first child and only son of Mariano and Leonor Martí.

Part One

BEFORE THE FALL (1853–1870)

CHAPTER ONE

An Unlikely Prodigy

Well: the times are bad, but your son is good.

LETTER TO LEONOR MARTÍ, 1892

*And from whom did I learn my integrity and my rebelliousness,
or from whom could I have inherited them, if not from my father
and from my mother?*

LETTER TO LEONOR MARTÍ, MAY 15, 1894

JOSÉ MARTÍ'S FIRST DECADE OF LIFE WAS A LARGELY UN-
eventful one, a good thing in a city where one in ten inhabitants —
and a disproportionate number of children — died of yellow fever.[1] The precarious state of the island's sanitation and its nearly nonexistent health-care system were further taxed by the return of cholera, which reached pandemic proportions during the 1850s.[2]

Childhood anecdotes suggest that José was a sensitive, well-behaved child who gave his parents no cause for particular concern. By his tenth birthday, José Martí — or Pepe, as his parents called him — began to show the first signs of his prodigious intellectual and literary talent. Both of his parents had managed to acquire levels of education beyond what was typical — or in Leonor's case, even encouraged — for Spaniards of their respective backgrounds and classes. They grasped the value of enabling Pepe's education as far as their limited means allowed, although they would come to differ sharply over what kinds of learning and how much was best. Neither his parents' education nor their enthusiasm for his own, however, could account for the child's spectacular record of achievement in school or his apparently immense capacity for intellectual work.

Given the class-bound nature of Cuba's and Spain's educational systems and the chronic lack of opportunity of advancement for all but the upper crust of Creole society, a more unlikely origin could hardly be imagined for the child who would become one of Latin America's most revered political and literary figures.

During José Martí's infancy, his father's military career continued to prosper. On February 14, 1855, Mariano was promoted to the rank of lieutenant. This boon was largely due to a personality exceptionally well suited to the requirements of the times: unwavering loyalty to the mother country, boundless energy, and a mental toughness that appealed to his superiors. Spain needed such men to safeguard the precarious colonial situation in Cuba. The landed elites' latent anticolonial feelings never completely dissipated after the López debacle, and the colonial government found itself constantly on guard against new potential uprisings. Given the burgeoning U.S. empire's growing ambitions in the Caribbean and Spain's corresponding decline, many Creoles believed annexation to the United States was inevitable and perhaps even desirable.[3] It was, in short, an opportune time for ambitious and fiercely loyal Spaniards to find their enthusiasm amply rewarded by the Spanish crown.

Yet the events that led to and in fact necessitated Mariano Martí's promotion were far from ideal. The appointment in 1853 of Marqués Juan de la Pezuela, an avowed abolitionist, as captain-general and thus supreme military and civilian authority of Cuba fueled a renewed economic anxiety among the plantocracy, who depended on slavery for their economic and political survival. The planters' fears of economic and political disaster triggered a return to the general unrest and annexationist pressures that had facilitated Mariano's arrival five years earlier. By February 1854 the U.S. government, emboldened by Cuban planters' urgent petitions and Spain's increasingly precarious position, made renewed offers to buy the embattled colony, and Cuban exiles were lobbying powerful U.S. Southern politicians such as Mississippi Governor John A. Quitman to organize a new filibustering effort.[4] The government in Madrid itself was nearly toppled in June but managed to restore order within a few weeks.[5]

Pezuela responded to the rapidly escalating tensions on the island with a sharp increase in military activity. All forces on the island, including Mariano's unit, kept constant vigilance against actual or perceived threats with orders to crush any uprising or invasion.

The birth of a second child, Leonor Petrona, whom the family called Chata, in July put increased financial pressure on the Martí family that Mariano's promotion the following year undoubtedly helped assuage. Yet the new husband and father soon tired of the chronic state of alert in which he lived. The unflagging vigilance and permanent state of readiness demanded of his unit in turn required never-ending rounds of drills and maneuvers that kept Mariano away from Havana and his family for extended periods. News of his mother's death in Valencia in 1855, coupled with Leonor's becoming pregnant with their third child, further taxed the once steadfast, even enthusiastic soldier and family man. He wore slowly but inexorably down under the professional and emotional strain. On December 22 Mariano received an early Christmas present: his request to resign his commission and retire from the army was granted.[6]

Shortly after the birth on June 8, 1856, of the couple's third child, Mariana, whom they called Ana, the Martís moved to a larger house; José Martí was three years old. With the new baby came increased economic pressures on Mariano, prompting the now ex-soldier to seek employment in the civilian ranks. His military experience and lifelong loyalty to the mother country made him a seemingly ideal candidate for a position in the Carabineros, the colonial national police. Despite Mariano's long and meritorious service, his desired position among the *aventajados*, an elite corps of troopers, did not materialize. The family remained hopeful, as Mariano was in line for a much-coveted position as chief inspector of Templete, the city's main commercial district and home of the colonial government offices.[7]

The family soon moved again, this time to a house in Templete. But before Mariano could formally claim the position, his candidacy had to endure the slow grind of Havana's formidable colonial bureaucracy. In the meantime, it became clear that the income from Mariano's café and barbershop, which he only ever meant to supplement his military salary, would not cover the family's needs. To keep the family financially afloat until her husband could start his new job, Leonor began working at home as a seamstress in addition to her household duties. The months that followed were hard ones for the Martí family. But finally, Mariano again received an early Christmas present: an official notice to report to his new post as chief inspector of Templete district.[8]

Although chief inspectors occupied a relatively minor position within the larger civil and military hierarchy, they wielded significant power over the lives of Cuban civilians. Cubans generally considered the local chief inspector as an arm of the colonizer, not an unreasonable view given that inspectors' ranks were almost entirely composed of Spaniards and most of them former soldiers. At least one observer of the time described the chief inspector's power as equal parts bureaucrat and colonial spy:

> Families are obliged to give notice to the *celador* [chief inspector], or alderman of their locality, of the increase or diminution of the family, of the admission of a new inmate, or of a guest, of a change of living, and of whatever reunion or party they may celebrate in their house, thus subjecting the whole country to a complete system of espionage.[9]

Chief inspectors were the first line of enforcement for construction permits and business licenses as well as keeping roadways safe and clear for city traffic.[10] Their most visible function on the streets, however, was to be seen as a deterrent to criminal activity; an effective chief inspector knew that beyond his physical presence in the neighborhood, it was his image in the minds of the civilian population that served to maintain public order and deter potential miscreants. Walking his beat as a Havana chief inspector, Mariano for a time embraced his duties as public officer and private spy, playing his public visuals especially well, as José Martí's childhood friend Fermín Valdés Domínguez would later reminisce:

> [Mariano] was, then, one of those agents of the law who, when he walked the streets with his two bodyguards behind him, would strike fear into the criminals, when these were not themselves collaborating with him in the persecution of some Cuban opposing the despots or an enemy of the slave traders.[11]

Mariano's initial success as a chief inspector gave the Martís hope of better times to come. The new position enabled a return to financial stability for the Martí family, and the Templete district's wealth of potential business and government contacts held the promise of further professional and personal advancement. Unfortunately, Mariano displayed no particular talent for professional or social networking, his successful courtship of Leonor notwithstanding, and had risen through the army ranks more by dint of persistence and sheer ambition than by personal charm. The martial air and personal brusqueness that served him well as a soldier would have made him a very effective chief inspector in a different part of the city but actually proved a hindrance in Templete, where he interacted with government bureaucrats and merchants unfamiliar with the rigidities of military life. It did not take the new chief inspector long to make enemies among both the people he policed and his own colleagues.

Worse, at the age of forty-one the physical robustness that had been one of Mariano's greatest assets began to fail him. Given that life expectancy for Cuban men at this time hovered between thirty-five and forty years, it was not surprising for a man of Mariano's age and work history to experience a decline in health.[12] Unlike other men at his stage of life, however, Mariano had three young children to support and was beginning a new position he could ill afford to lose after a lengthy unemployment. The specific nature of Mariano's malaise is as puzzling as its timing was unfortunate, as Martí biographers have been unable to identify a specific illness or other direct cause for it. Yet Mariano's libido seemed unaffected, as Leonor became pregnant with their fourth child during this period.[13] This and the absence of any identifiable illness or disorder suggest the possibility of a psychological rather than physical cause for his waning health. Whatever the cause, Mariano Martí found himself out of his element not only socially and professionally but now also physically, while his sense of professional and familial duty demanded that he remain at his post until a new opportunity emerged.

With the new year came the opening Mariano had been hoping for if not actively seeking. In January 1857 the couple learned of the death of Antonio Pérez, Leonor's father, who had returned to Spain shortly after Leonor's marriage. Having retired from the army, the Pérez family patriarch then decided to return to the Canary Islands, where he owned land and could live a quieter life away from rising political tensions in Cuba. Upon his death, his estate was to be distributed among his wife and children, a prospect that prompted the Martís to consider following Pérez's lead and relocating to the mother country. The decision could not have been an easy one. A voyage of this magnitude required a significant amount of money that Mariano could likely raise only by selling off most of his business interests, which by now included two slaves he bought as part of a short-lived foray into tobacco farming.[14]

The prospect of staking almost all of their financial resources on the move was an enormous gamble for the family, one made even more daunting by the complexity of planning and undertaking it with three small children. Mariano's own fitness for the transatlantic voyage—an average of ten weeks by sail—must also have given them pause, although Leonor's pregnancy in March suggests that perhaps his physical condition was less of an issue than Martí biographers generally assert.[15]

Despite all of these concerns, the promise of an easier, more affluent life proved irresistible to Mariano. On May 3, after less than six months on the job as chief inspector of Templete, a span shorter than the time it took him to get the position, he submitted his letter of resignation, citing his desire to return to Spain to recover from an unspecified illness.[16]

In June the Martí family—Mariano, Leonor (now four months pregnant), Pepe, Chata, and Ana—boarded the *Magdalena*, a Spanish merchant ship bound for Valencia. Soon after the seventy-five-day voyage they settled into a rented flat on Calle Tapineria where the couple's fourth child, María del Carmen, was born. Despite the substantial expense of the move and perhaps due to an actual or anticipated financial windfall from Leonor's inheritance, the Martís hired a domestic servant they never could have afforded in Cuba.[17] Their all-or-nothing bet on a better life appeared, at least initially, to be paying off.

But before long, the family's situation started going badly. Leonor had spent her entire life in the tropical climates of Cuba and the Canary Islands, and she did not take well to the relative chill of the Valencia winters. Despite Valencia's more temperate weather by Spanish standards, Leonor soon began suffering from chilblains (perniosis) on her hands, a painful itching and swelling associated with exposure to cold, damp conditions.[18] This, along with Leonor's late-pregnancy fatigue and Mariano's diminished physical state, made their first months on the peninsula difficult ones. Leonor began to struggle emotionally after the birth of María del Carmen on December 2. Feeling physically and culturally uprooted, she began to withdraw from her husband's family and even her own children.[19]

The Martís' relations with Mariano's Spanish relatives also may have soured during their stay.[20] His father had remarried since his mother's death, and Mariano had not seen his father or siblings since his departure for Cuba seven years earlier. The retired military officer who greeted them now was a profoundly changed man—physically reduced but no less martial in his manner or unbending in his ways. Leonor failed to establish any lasting bond with Mariano's extended family due perhaps to their resentment of her relatively superior class status and/or education. It is possible that the Spanish colonial cultural logic of the time, according to which peninsula-born Spaniards considered themselves culturally and even racially superior to Creoles, played a significant role in the extended family's disapproval of the island-born Leonor regardless of her class or education.[21]

Aside from María del Carmen's birth, little is known about the Martís' twenty-two-month stay in Valencia.[22] There is no record of Mariano having sought or failed to find work, either in the police or anywhere else, nor is there evidence of his having pursued business interests. It is thus likely that the family supported itself with the funds from Leonor's inheritance along with whatever savings they brought with them. Mariano's health during this time showed significant improvement over his earlier condition; among other indicators, Leonor had become pregnant once again. By the spring of 1859 the money was running out, the Martís tired of Valencia, or both. Whatever the reasons, Mariano and Leonor again staked much of their now-dwindling fortunes on a transatlantic voyage back to Cuba and the promise of employment.

It would be difficult to overstate the impact of the Martís' venture in Valencia on their material well-being and, more ominously, the emotional and psychological ties that bound them. Beyond leaving the family practically penniless, the failed expedition demoralized them. For Mariano it meant the end of his dreams of a comfortable retirement and the grim realization that he would have to spend the rest of his days—or as long as his health and body held out—working for his family's survival. This was enough to light a spark of frustration and resentment that with future setbacks and indignities would grow into the chronic anger and bouts of rage that would eventually render him unemployable. For Leonor, her relief at having escaped an emotionally and physically trying situation in Valencia was tempered by deep concern for her husband's future health and ability to support the family.[23] Although they could not have known it at the time, the Martís' Spanish misadventure marked only the beginning of the family's slow but inexorable decline, neither the last nor the greatest misfortune they would endure.

MARIANO, TRAVELING ALONE, RETURNED TO HAVANA IN June 1859 and wasted no time in seeking employment. Leonor, pregnant once again, and the four children stayed behind in Valencia with the understanding that Mariano would send for them once he found a job and suitable dwelling. Mariano remembered well the anxiety and hardships his family suffered during the long months before he was offered the post at Templete, and he hoped he would not be separated from them for long. Luckily, Mariano's inquiry coincided with the resignation of the chief inspector for the Santa Clara district of Havana; within a month Mariano was selected to assume the post. Leonor arrived in Havana with the children soon afterward, and on November 13 she gave birth to María del Pilar Eduarda, their fifth child.[24]

The Santa Clara district's residents little resembled the affluent, well-connected population of Mariano's previous assignment in Templete. Santa Clara was a solidly working-class neighborhood with a reputation for criminality and hard living. Unlike his previous experience as the chief inspector of Templete, Mariano immediately took to his new post, and his natural rigidity and authoritarian approach proved effective in policing the challenging district. Over time, however, it became clear that he had little taste for the particularities of police procedures or for the necessary internal politicking among his fellow officers and superiors. Mariano remained at Santa Clara for less than a year, but that proved long enough to make enemies in the community and in the police force. He found himself repeatedly reprimanded for a series of real and fictionalized errors and oversights, but his success at containing the district's more unsavory elements made his superiors reluctant to dismiss him. Still, it was only a matter of time before his martial ways and difficulties in controlling his temper resulted in his dismissal.

The events of September 27, 1860, and a wealthy Creole woman's subsequent complaint to the captain-general gave Mariano's enemies the necessary pretext to finally remove him from his post. The incident itself involved a right-of-way dispute between a *carretonero* (cart driver) and a horse-drawn carriage owned by Adelaida de Villalonga, a woman from a wealthy Havana family. Such disputes were quite common in Havana, and at least one commentator of the time has remarked on the difficulty of navigating the city's impossibly narrow streets:

> The streets are so narrow, and the houses built so close upon them, that they seem to be rather spaces between the walls of houses than high-

ways for travel. It appears impossible that two vehicles should pass
abreast; yet they do so. There are constant blockings of the way.[25]

The point on Calle Aguiar where the dispute occurred was even more con-
stricted than the typical Havana street, as construction partly blocked the road,
forcing northbound traffic temporarily to the left. Although the *carretonero*
claimed the right of way, Villalonga's driver was unable to reverse course or
retreat on the narrow, congested road. The *carretonero*, for his part, refused to
yield. The first policeman on the scene proved unable to resolve the impasse
and summoned a chief inspector from another district who happened to be in
the area. He in turn refused to intervene, explaining that he had no jurisdiction
in Santa Clara and that Mariano Martí was the appropriate officer to settle the
matter. By the time Mariano arrived, a crowd of men had gathered on the street,
and the more curious women looked on, as was the custom, from the comfort
and protection of nearby windows.[26]

The chief inspector of Santa Clara wasted no time in resolving the conflict,
nor did he disappoint those hoping for some free entertainment on that hot
September morning. After briefly interviewing both parties and an eyewitness,
Mariano resolved to move the carriage. Seeing no other way to persuade the
animal and tired of the cries of drivers frustrated by the prolonged blockage
and the circus that had sprung up around him, he began to violently beat Villalonga's horse with his cane. The horse quickly relented under the chief inspector's blows and withdrew, ending the confrontation. Villalonga claimed in her
formal complaint that Mariano's assault destroyed her carriage's retractable
canvas top. What the incident more pointedly damaged, though, was her sense
of entitlement: the proud Creole lady had been publicly humiliated by a man
of the lower classes, and a Spaniard to boot, who denied her passage in favor of
a lowly *carretonero*'s. The chief inspector's greatest crime was perhaps not the
violence with which he handled the matter but rather his failure to yield to the
will of his social betters regardless of the rules.

After a cursory investigation following Villalonga's complaint—during
which the *carretonero* was not sought out or interviewed—Mariano was sum-
marily dismissed from his post on October 16, 1860.[27] Although the investigator's failure to include both parties to the dispute betrays the report's lack
of impartiality, further inconsistencies emerge between it and Villalonga's account. Both reports emphasize the coarseness of Mariano's conduct and especially his language, describing his behavior in terms similar to the *carretonero*'s.
The investigator's account asserts that in his words and actions the chief inspector willfully disrespected Villalonga and failed to show proper deference
to a lady of her stature, charges that Villalonga did not specifically make in her
complaint. The report authored by a Nicolás Lobo contrasts Mariano's behav-

ior with that of the chief inspector of another district who arrived on the scene before Mariano did:

> [And] the *carretonero* claimed the same [right], compelling the lady by his bad manners and way of expressing himself to call for the chief inspector, and upon presenting himself the [chief inspector] of San Felipe who lived nearby appealed to the *carretonero* to understand that he had no right to sustain his pretension and that further she was a lady to whom should be given the highest consideration.[28]

Lobo goes on to assert that Mariano's violence against the horse was not merely the heavy-handed execution of a conscious decision but a spontaneous outburst of rage triggered by his confrontation with Villalonga herself:

> The chief inspector of Santa Clara don Mariano Martí . . . rudely ordered the driver to yield; he refused to obey, and at this point was when the lady told the chief inspector that she would teach him his duty, that he was failing to show consideration for a lady whom in this case he should respect; these words made the chief inspector so indignant that he would certainly make her yield, replying that he needed no one to teach him his duty: that with respect to the blows the complainant claims he dealt the horse Chief Inspector Martí is not satisfied that he beat it enough.[29]

In contrast to the first chief inspector, who recognized his duty to defer to Villalonga, Mariano is portrayed as not merely ignorant of her tacit authority but willfully and impulsively insubordinate. Villalonga's complaint, on the other hand, studiously avoids any specific reference to class, couching her outrage in the coded language of "gentlemen" as guardians of "the rule of law." Perhaps she did not think it necessary to assert her class privilege, believing the point would be obvious enough to the captain-general. Further, Lobo's report does not substantiate Villalonga's claim of a damaged carriage, nor does it even mention her assertion of "grave risk" that the horse's sudden retreat would have posed to herself and other onlookers.

Whatever the veracity of these various accounts or the parties' particular claims, what they include and omit tells us a great deal about the respective authors' overlapping objectives. Villalonga sought punishment for the one who disrespected her and failed to defer to her and who by doing so violated the colonial society's strict class hierarchy. Lobo's apparent goal was to portray the chief inspector as a violent, impulsive man unworthy of his position. That he focused on Mariano's socially inappropriate behavior toward Villalonga rather than his violence toward the horse lays bare the unspoken assumption behind the report: that this was a man who did not distinguish between his betters and a common *carretonero*, who was as likely to lash out against one as the other—a man who, in short, did not know his place. Such a man could not be trusted, as Villalonga euphemistically put it, "to safeguard the public order and to prevent the consequences of injustice and injury."[30] Thanks largely to their respective accounts, Villalonga and Lobo got their wish: the captain-general's final report on the incident cites among the reasons for Mariano's dismissal his "lack of good manners, limited capacity, and lack of aptitude for dealing with well-educated persons."[31]

IN THE MONTHS AFTER MARIANO'S DISMISSAL, LIFE IN THE Martí household grew tense and occasionally ugly. Mariano's bitterness over being fired and mounting frustration at his inability to find another position made him more prone than ever to sudden explosions of rage. A man who took pride in his appearance and kept himself fastidiously dressed and groomed, Mariano began to look disheveled. His health continued to decline. The formerly occasional bouts of asthma he experienced toward the end of his tenure at Santa Clara came more regularly now, and a fall he suffered during floods left him with a pronounced limp.

By age seven, young Pepé's dominant impression of his father was of a tired, frail, shabby-looking man with no job and negligible prospects. He watched his mother suffer silently, seldom grumbling about the family's diminished state lest she spark another of her husband's rants. Mariano remained unemployed for eighteen months, repeatedly doomed by a paper trail that followed him everywhere he went in the aftermath of the Villalonga incident. The Martí family, which had never fully recovered from the near-disaster of the Valencia venture, now found itself subsisting on Leonor's sewing for hire and whatever odd jobs Mariano occasionally found. Even their joy at the birth of their sixth child, Rita Amelia, the following year was tempered by their unspoken desperation at having yet another mouth to feed.

It was during this dark period that young Pepe showed the first signs of the intelligence and intellectual curiosity that even then set him apart from his peers. Pepe excelled in virtually every subject at school, although literature was by far his favorite. Due perhaps partly to the utter lack of any other good news and partly to his being the oldest and the only male, Pepe's early successes made him much celebrated in the Martí household.

His parents held very different ideas for how to best develop Pepe's abilities. Leonor longed to enroll him in San Anacleto, a school highly regarded for its academics. From Mariano's perspective, nine-year-old Pepe already had acquired far more formal education than he or his father and siblings could have ever dreamed. For Mariano, Pepe's most important assets were his excellent penmanship and precocious language skills. Once he became more fluent in English, he would be eminently employable as a clerk or translator — skills very much in demand in a society with increasing ties to the United States and where less than 40 percent of the population could claim basic literacy in even one language.[32]

Pepe began during this time to form what would prove an unbreakable lifelong bond with his mother and to grow away from his father. Mariano started taking the boy along on his trips into the provinces to seek work, a habit that only exacerbated Leonor's resentments and Pepe's growing estrangement from Mariano. Mother and son resented the frequent absences from school but were overruled by Mariano, who insisted that he needed the boy along due to his own physical limitations. Leonor implicitly understood that Pepe was valuable for Mariano less as a laborer than as an amanuensis for his father. Mariano Martí, while literate, detested the paperwork that came with police work. He recognized that nine-year-old Pepe's skill and affinity for writing already far surpassed his own. In April 1862 Mariano finally found a post far from home at a significantly reduced salary and even then only because of another man's scandal and sudden dismissal.

The Spanish government had long been ambivalent on the subject of slavery in the colonies, reluctantly bowing to English pressure to ban the slave trade in 1817.[33] However, slave labor was indispensable for the Cuban economy, which depended on the labor-intensive sugar industry for its continued growth. Spanish government officials knew that the Cuban plantocracy, frustrated by decades of disenfranchisement, would vigorously resist any serious move toward abolition.

Trapped in an untenable position between the need to appease Britain and the desire to avoid further political unrest on the island, Spain only halfheartedly enforced the ban against slave trafficking, when it did so at all. For their part, colonial authorities turned a blind eye to the illegal slave trade and often profited indirectly from it through bribes and kickbacks. Meanwhile, traders — often with the help of knowledgeable Cuban officials — played an ongoing cat-and-mouse game with the Royal Navy, which constantly patrolled the Caribbean for the human contraband.[34]

But when on March 31 the British consul filed a formal protest over the disembarkation of more than four hundred slaves at Ciénaga de Zapata on the island's southern coast, the captain-general in Matanzas was forced to act, and the perpetrators were quickly arrested. In the authorities' rush to save face, they inadvertently caught one of their own: Captain Manuel Aragón Quintana was accused of accepting a substantial bribe — five thousand pesos and seven slaves — in exchange for allowing the slave ship to land within his jurisdiction.[35] Quintana served as *juez-pedáneo* (petty judge), the colonial equivalent of a small-town sheriff, of Caimito de la Hanábana, a tiny village near the coast. He was immediately dismissed, which created an opening for a replacement and an unexpected opportunity for Mariano Martí.

As an assignment, Hanábana was hardly comparable in terms of salary and prestige to Mariano's previous posts. It would mean giving up the relative comforts of Havana for a backwater more than a hundred miles away, roughly two days' journey on horseback. Leonor would have to remain in Havana with the children. Mariano insisted that Pepe accompany him to Hanábana, since school was over for the year and the child would be useful to him in his new position. Leonor feared that her husband would not let Pepe return to school in the fall but keep him in Hanábana, thus dashing her dream of sending the boy to San Anacleto. But the disgraced former chief inspector was in no position to decline any offer of regular employment, and his wife was in no position to begrudge him anything that would restore his dignity and raise their family out of poverty.

So on the morning of April 13 Mariano and Pepe set off for Hanábana, arriving late the following day. Upon arrival, the newly minted captain's first official act was to seize the property of all parties involved in the illegal shipment at Ciénaga, including his predecessor Quintana's.[36] After this initial flurry of activity, Mariano found little in Hanábana that required his attention beyond Sunday cockfights and the occasional drunken row. The most onerous duty associated with the position was the constant stream of written reports and other paperwork that even the most insignificant colonial outpost did not fail to generate. This aspect of the job that Mariano loathed posed no problem now that he had Pepe to share the burden.

Now nearly forty-seven years old, with a bad leg and prone to asthma, Mariano grew to appreciate the quiet, rural town with a generally agreeable population and little crime. For his part, Pepe served his father well and showed no sign of missing either the city or his studies. Father and son were getting on well and seemed content with their new surroundings and each other.

Pepe's time in Hanábana also meant closer and more frequent contact with slaves and slavery than he experienced in Havana. Although the capital's residents certainly kept slaves, these were generally household servants or laborers. In this small, agricultural village, Pepe saw firsthand the life of plantation slaves. As the town's top civilian authority, Mariano would have been present at public punishments of slaves such as whippings. Years later, the adult José Martí would recall one such event he witnessed during the months in Hanábana:

> And the Negroes? Who has seen a slave whipped who does not forever after consider himself in his debt? I saw it, I saw it when I was a child,

and still my cheeks burn with shame. For superior spirits who have rejected honors as unnecessary, these anxieties of justice are a matter of
nobility. I saw it and swore myself to his defense ever since.[37]

Nor would that be the last or worst of what nine-year-old Pepe would witness. Two particular events, the unloading of a slave ship and the child's discovery of a dead slave hanged in the woods feature prominently in Poema XXX
of *Versos sencillos*, arguably Martí's best-known volume:[38]

> The lightning the heaven scorches,
> And the clouds are bloodstained patches:
> The ship its hundreds disgorges
> Of captive blacks through the hatches.
>
> The fierce winds and brutal rains
> Beat against the dense plantation:
> In a file the slaves in chains
> Are led naked for inspection . . .
>
> Red as in the desert zone,
> The sun rose on the horizon:
> And upon the dead slave shone,
> Hanged from a tree on the mountain.
>
> A boy saw him there and shook
> With passion for the oppressed:
> And at his feet an oath took
> That this crime would be redressed.[39]

Martí biographers have differed on the question of when Pepe would have
witnessed these scenes and whether they represent a single experience or a
composite of two or more events.[40] Given the image of the child's oath common to the poem and the account of the whipped slave, it is also possible that
Martí somehow conflated multiple events into one memory or distilled them
into a single, powerful poetic expression. Slaves who caused trouble during the
crossings were routinely disciplined in cruel and violent ways, and many died
from being beaten or otherwise punished. But traders generally had no interest in killing slaves unless absolutely necessary, and they considered doing so
akin to destroying valuable merchandise.[41] Thus it is unlikely that Pepe witnessed the spectacle of the hanged slave simultaneously with the slave ship, as
the poem implies, unless the body was left there before the ship landed. Martí

later showed facility for fictionalizing real events in his journalistic writings on the United States and did not mention these experiences elsewhere in his writings, as he did regarding the whipped slave; thus it is possible that the actual experiences were less dramatic or visceral than his portrayal of them in the poem.[42] Regardless of what and how much nine-year-old Pepe actually saw or the particular circumstances surrounding the portrayed events, what is indisputable is that the boy's exposure to the implementation of slave justice and the often sadistic treatment of slaves left a profound and lasting impression on him. Pepe and his father would soon leave the countryside and return to the relative civility of Havana, but he would never again see slaves or slavery in the same way as his schoolmates back home. He had simply seen too much.

For Leonor, her son could not come home soon enough. It became obvious by the fall of 1862 that, as she had suspected, Mariano had no intention of sending Pepe back to school. Her disappointment was somewhat assuaged by her husband's apparent success at his new job and by the family's improved financial situation. Thanks to Mariano's new position they even raised enough money to buy their first home, a transaction completed on October 22 for the price of three thousand pesos.[43] Although she missed her son and worried about her husband, Leonor no doubt was relieved at the family's good fortune and hoped that the worst was behind them.

Unbeknown to Mariano, the illegal trade that indirectly enabled his arrival was resuming under his very nose. On October 6 provincial authorities in the nearby city of Colón received an order from the captain-general in Havana to apprehend a slave ship that would be landing along the southern coast, seize the cargo, and arrest the traders. The lieutenant governor at Colón replied the following week assuring Havana of heightened vigilance and readiness to act. Captain Mariano Martí did not receive orders to that effect, nor was the alleged slave ship ever sighted.[44] The traders — and their conspirators, among them Mariano's superiors in Colón — succeeded in duping the *juez-pedáneo* in what would become a pattern of duplicity, subterfuge, and complicity between traders and the authorities.

Mariano did not succeed in stopping slave shipments from landing in Hanábana, a popular spot from which slaves could easily be transported to inland sugar plantations in Matanzas Province. In the deeply corrupt world of Cuban governance, even Mariano's ineffectual resistance to the continuing slave trade posed an inconvenience for a system used to open collaboration with colonial authorities. However ineffective or superfluous his resistance, Mariano's continued presence in Hanábana became a nuisance to the corrupt authorities who only arrested the parties involved in the March 31 slave-ship incident to appease the English consul. Before the year was out, a Spanish court dismissed the case against the slavers and their government collaborators for lack of evidence, despite a wealth of physical evidence that included the remains of the ship and a mass grave for those who died during the voyage. Numerous eyewitness accounts of the landing as well as the disembarking slaves and their sale to waiting buyers likewise failed to persuade the court, which ordered *juez-pedáneo* Mariano Martí to return to the defendants the property he confiscated during his first day on the job.[45]

However demoralizing the court's rebuke might have been for Mariano, the final indignity was yet to come: shortly after the Christmas holidays, he was dismissed from his post and replaced by Manuel Aragón Quintana, the very man who had resigned the position in shame nine months earlier and whom Mariano had replaced.[46] Once again Mariano failed to hold a job that his family badly needed. Beyond that, this dismissal definitively ended Mariano's last chance to retain his place as head of his household. It would be only a matter of time now before Pepe would seek and find a new hero to replace his tired, defeated father—one better suited to his nascent literary and intellectual ambitions.

A BOY'S FIRST LETTER

IN HINDSIGHT, THE MOST NOTEWORTHY EVENT OF
Pepe's tenth year was neither the scandal of an intercepted slave
ship nor a small-town officer's purchase of a modest house but rather
his first letter to his mother. October 23, 1862, marks the date of
Martí's first known letter, which he sent from Hanábana. Although
short and not particularly substantive, the letter is nevertheless as-
tounding for the eloquence of its nine-year-old author:

> Hanábana, October 23, 1862
> Dear mother:
> Before anything, I hope that you are well along with the girls,
> Joaquina, Luisa, and Mama Joaquina [Leonor's sister and her two
> daughters]. Papa received your letter on the twenty-first, since the
> mail did not run on Saturday the eighteenth, and he did not re-
> ceive it until Tuesday; the mail — according to him — could not
> come across the river called "Sabanilla" that is blocking the way to
> "New Bermeja" as well as here. Papa has no pain from his fall but
> has a rash that keeps him up all night, and he has been like this
> the past three nights.
> I have been taking great care of my horse and feed him like
> a fattened pig, I am teaching him to wear a bridle so that he will
> trot handsomely, every afternoon I ride him around, [and] every
> day he grows more spirited. I have yet another thing to enter-
> tain myself and pass the time; the thing I am referring to is a "fine
> cock" given to me by Dn. [don] Lucas de Sotolongo; he is very
> handsome and Papa takes good care of him. Now Papa is looking
> for someone who will cut off his comb and get him ready to fight

this year, and he says that the rooster is worth more than two ounces [of gold].

Both the river that crosses Dn. Jaime's "farm" and the "Sabanilla" over which the mail must cross were extremely high on Saturday; ours flooded all the way up to Dn. Domingo's fence, but they have come down a lot.

And not having anything else to say, give my regards to Mama Joaquina, Joaquina, and Luisa and the girls and give Pilar a kiss, from your obedient son who loves you deliriously

José Martí[1]

In this briefest of glimpses into Martí's boyhood we can see what occupied his nine-year-old mind: his family back in Havana, especially his mother; the weather; the horse and rooster that were his closest companions; and his father's precarious health.

More importantly, in this brief note we can already glimpse the traits that would distinguish all of the boy's future correspondence as an adult: a serious, respectful tone; a florid, somewhat eccentric writing style; and a sense of absolute devotion to those he loved. All of these traits would soon flourish under the tutelage and mentorship of a very special teacher, a man who would soon eclipse Mariano Martí in the heart and mind of his only son.

CHAPTER TWO

The Teacher Appears

Mother of my soul, beloved mother,
On your birthday, thus I will sing;
Because my soul, swelling with love,
Though very young, never forgets
She from whom I was given life.

"TO MY MOTHER," 1868

Oh Cuba! I bless, enthused,
The crib where I was born beneath your sky.
And this immense torrent you have given me
Of evangelical love and consolation.

RAFAEL MARÍA DE MENDIVE, "THE MUSIC OF THE PALMS"

O N THE COLD FRIDAY MORNING IN 1853 ON WHICH José Martí was born, Havana's daily paper *El Diario de La Habana* published several short literary items, a feature typical in newspapers of the time.[1] The January 28 edition of *El Diario* included the latest chapter of Federico Soulié's serialized novel *El becerro de oro* (The Golden Calf) as well as an announcement of the publication of *Las flores silvestres* (The Wildflowers), the second volume of poems by "well-known bard" José Socorro de León. As an incentive for readers to buy León's book, *El Diario* published a poem from it titled "Las estrellas y las flores" (The Stars and the Flowers), which he composed as a tribute to fellow poet Rafael María de Mendive.[2] For Mendive, it was among the first of many such honors in a long, illustrious career. It would be another decade, however, before Mendive would begin the work for which he is today best remembered: as the teenage José Martí's mentor and teacher.

However ascendant Mariano Martí's fortunes were at the moment of his son's birth, he never achieved the public respect and prominence enjoyed by Mendive, who would eclipse him for a time in his son's heart and mind. José Martí would, as an adult, grow to cherish his father, seek his counsel, and recognize how much of his father's incorruptible nature and moral rectitude colored his own personality and worldview. Yet the three years young Pepe spent under Mendive's tutelage left a formative and lasting impact on the future revolutionary leader. Such was the teacher's sway over the young man that by the time of teenage Pepe's headlong immersion into anticolonial politics, he was intellectually, politically, and emotionally as much Mendive's son as Mariano Martí's.

At the time of León's "Las estrellas y las flores," Mendive was widely respected in the world of Cuban letters as a poet, editor, and educator. Born in 1821 into an affluent Havana family, Mendive as a teenager nevertheless found himself orphaned and impoverished. He was able to continue his education thanks largely to his older brother Pablo, who home-schooled him in Spanish, Italian, and French languages and literatures. Young Rafael took to literary study and by his mid-twenties had completed a decorated university career and joined the ranks of Cuba's most respected teachers and academics. He published his first poems before turning twenty, and in 1846 — at the age of twenty-five — he was appointed head of literature at the prestigious Liceo de La Habana. A year later he published *Pasionarias*, his first volume of poetry. His fame as a poet eventually spread beyond the island as his collected works were published in Madrid and Paris in 1860. By the time Pepe Martí entered the Escuela Superior Municipal de Varones (Municipal Secondary School for Boys) four years later, its new headmaster, Mendive, was among Cuba's most admired and accomplished men of letters.[3] For Pepe, whose intelligence and love of learning only needed a suitable outlet to flourish, the contrast between the brilliant schoolmaster and his father — a man Pepe's closest childhood friend later described as "honest, but of little intelligence and learning" — could not have been clearer.[4]

By the time of Mendive's first appearance in Pepe's life, Mariano Martí's own professional and financial fortunes were decidedly on the wane. Toward the end of 1862, Mariano received permission to return to Havana and rejoin his family for the Christmas holidays, only to be fired shortly into the new year.[5] With his father again unemployed, a significant barrier to Pepe's continued education had lifted only to be substituted by another: the boy could now remain in Havana, but any hope of paying for his education evaporated along with Mariano's job. Nearly fifty years old, having lost his second position in less than two years and with no immediate prospects for a third, Mariano now had to find some way to keep himself, his wife, and their six children out of poverty. Money for schooling, even for an only male child and an undeniably brilliant one at that, was simply not available for a family struggling just to survive.

The year 1863 was a grim one for the Martís. Mariano traveled by ship to British Honduras (today Belize) in search of work and took Pepe with him. British Honduras had just become a British colony after decades under de facto British rule. Since the official abolition of slavery a quarter-century earlier, the territory had faced a difficult labor situation, and the British Honduras Company spent much of the 1860s trying to lure workers and potential investors to the new colony. Mariano's most obvious objective for the journey was thus to find work, but he may have been lured also by the prospect of buying cheap land or even relocating the family as many immigrants did during the 1860s. No correspondence of Mariano's or his son's from this venture exists to confirm the senior Martí's specific intentions.

Pepe accompanied Mariano to British Honduras over Leonor's almost certain objections. Despite her desire to keep Pepe in school, Leonor knew that the boy's skills as a writer and English speaker would have been indispensable to Mariano's prospects for success. Pepe was by now old enough to be sensitive to his family's financial predicament and well acquainted with his father's needs and limitations. Whatever explicit discussion may have taken place in the Martí household on the question of Pepe or whether Leonor relented or was simply overruled by her husband, in the end Pepe did accompany his father to British Honduras. Pepe's presence at Mariano's side says much about the father's dependence on and confidence in his son. The fact that Mariano, a man far past his physical prime, would undertake such a trip on the basis of little more than speculation suggests the family's growing financial desperation.

Mariano's credentials as a retired Spanish officer and former civilian official apparently did not sway prospective employers. The British Honduras Company's primary interest during the 1860s was developing the sugar industry, and Mariano's lack of experience in the sugar trade, not to mention his advanced age and declining health, would have made him less than optimal as a job candidate. His son's only substantive reference to the childhood trip in his writings is a brief vignette of a family of U.S. Southern emigrés building a plantation: "My childhood was not entirely gone when I admired again in British Honduras a wealthy Southern family brought by misfortune to painful scantiness — and raising by its hands, in the thick bosom of forest, a clean, elegant, prosperous sugar plantation."[6]

At least one Martí biographer has speculated that both Martí and his father were employed at this plantation, but no evidence has emerged to support this claim. Mariano's physical frailty and utter lack of familiarity with English and his son's limited English skills would have made them unlikely candidates for either the physical rigors of plantation labor or more sedentary clerical or domestic work.[7] Investing in land, even in the relatively undeveloped interior, would have been all but impossible, as prices in British Honduras were prohibitive. The going rate for arable land during the first years of British rule was five dollars per acre, compared to twenty-two cents per acre in Brazil, and neighboring Spanish Honduras land was offered free to settlers with the means to develop it.[8]

And so Mariano and Pepe soon returned to Havana, having wasted the family's dwindling funds on a trip that produced nothing of substance. Leonor again took charge as she had during Mariano's first experience with postmilitary unemployment. She enlisted eldest daughters Chata and Ana as seamstresses working at home for hire. Mariano, an experienced tailor from his early years in the military, took up his old trade again and managed to contract the family's work out to commercial tailors in the city.

Dissatisfied with this financial arrangement, perhaps because of the implicit blow to his status as head of household, Mariano soon grew restless. The news that Leonor was expecting yet another child, the family's seventh, heightened the pressure on Mariano to find a more substantial source of income for the family. In the spring of 1864, spurred on by some business acquaintances, Mariano became enthusiastic about the prospects of investing in stone quarries, then a growing business in construction-happy Havana. He quickly decided to sell the family home in the Havana district of Peñalver to finance the new business venture. In June Mariano unsuccessfully petitioned to be restored to his former position as a *celador* (chief inspector), likely as a means of securing short-term income while awaiting returns from his new investment.

On October 6, 1864, Leonor gave birth to the Martís' sixth daughter, Antonia Bruna, and baptized the child in January. Antonia's baptismal godfather, Francisco Arazoza, was a neighbor and family friend who around this time also served as godfather at Pepe's confirmation. Arazoza was unique among the Martí children's many baptismal and confirmation sponsors because without his intervention Pepe might not have continued his formal education beyond grade school. More importantly, it was Arazoza — not Mariano or Leonor Martí — who made the pivotal decision to enroll Pepe at the Escuela Superior Municipal, where Rafael María de Mendive served as headmaster. Arazoza recognized both Pepe's abilities and his family's financial plight, but he knew Mariano was too proud to accept money from him directly. Determined to help the boy, Arazoza claimed the right as Pepe's confirmation godfather to take financial responsibility for his schooling. Thus Pepe, now twelve years old, finally began attending Havana's Escuela Superior in March 1865, with his godfather Arazoza paying the school directly for all expenses.[9] This solution enabled Pepe to continue his education while allowing Mariano to save face. It also brought

Pepe under the direct influence of Mendive, who would play a crucial role in shaping the heart and mind of the future revolutionary.

Mendive's influence soon showed its first visible impact on Pepe in the form of a hemp bracelet. Pepe and many of his classmates donned the bracelets during the week of April 16–23 to mourn the assassination of Abraham Lincoln, whom the abolitionist Mendive greatly admired.[10] Pepe's earlier experiences of observing the treatment of slaves in Hanábana and perhaps British Honduras no doubt paved the way for the ready acceptance of his teacher's passionate speeches against the evils of slavery.

The symbolic gesture of the bracelet, an implicit rebuke of the ongoing practice of slavery on the island, was apparently lost on Mariano as he became preoccupied with business matters. Having failed in his bid to regain a position as chief inspector, Mariano needed cash; the situation may have compelled him in March 1865 to unsuccessfully sue his cousin Francisco Martí with whom he still co-owned the café La Fuente de la Salud. In the suit Mariano accused his relative of having removed more than three thousand reales' worth of sweets — equivalent to about $375 — for sale at a competing establishment without compensating him. Although the evidence seemed to weigh in Mariano's favor, he made the mistake of filing his suit during Lent, which enabled the defendant's attorney to cast doubt on Mariano's honesty: What good Christian, after all, would sue a man during Lent, the forty-day period of prayer and penitence preceding Easter? Mariano's argument that the defense's claims were irrelevant to the case apparently did not persuade the court, and he failed to win a judgment against Francisco.[11] This latest in a string of defeats and failed adventures no doubt further diminished Mariano in the eyes of his family, his business associates, and his only son, who was now fully in the thrall of his impressive new teacher.

At the Escuela Superior Pepe was reunited with Fermín Valdés Domínguez, his closest friend from their days at San Anacleto.[12] It would be difficult to overestimate the importance of Pepe's budding friendship with Fermín in shaping his adult political and philosophical views. Fermín, the child of an affluent Havana family, and Pepe forged a lifelong friendship at the school that survived many material and emotional hardships, including the adult Valdés Domínguez's unreliability at crucial moments of the revolutionary struggle. As a grown man organizing a revolution in New York, Martí became notorious for dropping fellow conspirators at the first sign of disloyalty or inconsistency. To the dismay of others in Martí's inner circle, he never turned away his childhood friend or doubted his loyalty to himself or the cause they served. That he did not do so says less about the adult Martí's skill as a judge of character than it does about the power of a bond forged in childhood, a bond soon solidified by the friends' shared experience of danger, suffering, and exile.

Both at San Anacleto and the Escuela Superior, Pepe had to contend with the surprise and resentment of boys from more privileged backgrounds who did not appreciate their poorer classmate's ascent past them to the top of his classes. Pepe overcame the initial resentment of his peers largely through a quiet modesty that belied his obvious intellectual superiority and a generous nature that allowed him to defer to other views and voices in the classroom. Pepe's instinctive deference in the face of class difference and unequal privilege, coupled with his dedication to scholarly work and quiet confidence in his own abilities, endeared him to teachers, who supported the boy's every initiative. These qualities also attracted Fermín, whose overt affection nevertheless unnerved his new classmate at first.

Pepe, for whom the haughtiness and self-interest of the rich was axiomatic, avoided treating upper-class boys as equals as a matter of social survival, as one who had long since internalized the lessons of class difference and power in colonial Cuba. Pepe never forgot how his father had lost his position as chief inspector of Templete for standing up to a wealthy Creole. He was not about to endanger what was perhaps his last, best chance for a better life by forgetting his place now. Only slowly and warily did Pepe warm to Fermín and learn to trust him.

Pepe's friendship with Fermín along with the mentorship of a teacher as prominent and accomplished as Mendive were his first significant encounters with economic, social, and intellectual worlds beyond those typically available to a child of his background and class and without which his eventual blossoming as a thinker and political leader would not have been possible. These relationships, combined with the child's awareness of his family's relatively inferior status, impressed on him early the reality of entrenched socioeconomic differences that had hindered the island's hopes for a better future. Mendive and to a lesser extent Fermín gave Pepe the language and knowledge from which his revolutionary thought grew. But Pepe's early insights at the Escuela Superior led him as an adult to grasp the importance of having people like them on his side if the revolutionary ideals they taught him were ever to succeed.

Much of the two friends' initial bond—one that allowed them to overcome the differences that otherwise would have defined their relationship in advance—was their mutual affection for their teacher. Pepe and Fermín were Mendive's most enthusiastic students, hanging on the master's every word and spreading his political views with an evangelical fervor. That Mendive seemed to favor Pepe made no apparent difference to Fermín, who along with his poorer classmate thrilled to the master's rants against the injustices of colonialism, the arrogance and corruption of the colonial rulers, and the island's increasingly dim future prospects under Spanish rule.

Mendive lectured on these subjects for many years and never made much effort to conceal his political views or veil his distaste for Spanish colonialism.

Although his outspokenness had made him some enemies, these rarely managed to slow his professional ascent or blunt his criticisms of the island's colonial rulers. In his two young disciples Mendive managed to light an emotional and intellectual fire that even he would prove unable to douse.

As was typical for headmasters of the time, Mendive and his family lived on the school grounds at Calle Prado no. 88, an arrangement that made it convenient for the teacher and his preferred students to continue their discussions or pursue further reading in Mendive's personal library. Pepe soon started visiting Mendive's library at every opportunity, immersing himself in his teacher's plethoric collection of great works and authors. His first literary love was Byron, an attraction that an astonished Mendive discovered when he found the boy at work in the library translating "A Mystery."[13] Pepe's nascent attempt at literary translation exceeded Mendive's already high estimation of his student's talents and compelled him to take an even greater interest in the boy's burgeoning career. Pepe would later make an attempt at translating Shakespeare's *Hamlet*, but he confessed in an unpublished fragment to leaving it unfinished: "Since I could not get beyond the scene with the grave diggers and believed at the time that it was beneath the dignity of such a great genius to speak of rats, I contented myself with Byron's incestuous 'A Mystery.'"[14]

The three years that followed were largely uneventful for the Martí family, punctuated at regular intervals by the string of Pepe's academic awards and accomplishments. Mariano, finding no place for himself in his son's intellectual pursuits, immersed himself in various business interests. Although the debate over Pepe's scholastic future seemed settled for the moment, Mariano never embraced or understood his son's love of books and learning, and he never abandoned the idea of removing him from school as soon as he developed sufficient skills for a clerical or other such position. Mendive's wife, Micaela, later observed, "There was an incompatibility of character between the two . . . they were continually fighting because [Mariano] wanted at all costs for him to leave school and start working."[15]

Leonor gave birth to the Martís' seventh daughter, Dolores Eustaquia, on November 2, 1865; less than two weeks later another daughter, six-year-old Pilar, fell ill and died. Deaths of young children due to yellow fever and malaria were not uncommon in Cuba at the time, especially in the more densely populated cities, but the exact cause of Pilar's death is not known.[16]

Having sold their home in Peñalver to bankroll Mariano's investment in the quarries, the Martís moved in September 1866 to the family's seventh address in Havana in a little over twelve years, and they would move again within six months. That September thirteen-year-old Pepe passed the entrance exam and enrolled at a prestigious Havana secondary school thanks in part to his mentor's guidance and his godfather's financial support.[17]

Through 1866 and into the following year, Pepe continued to read and write and to listen and learn. Only when the awards and accolades began piling up in the summer and fall of 1867 did Pepe's family and many others in Havana academic circles discover what his classmates and teacher had known since his first days in school. Pepe was first in his class and won awards in arithmetic, Latin, English, and Spanish grammar, accomplishments duly noted in various publications around the city. Under Mendive's mentorship Pepe expanded his studies into the arts, adding drawing classes to his regular schoolwork.[18]

The awards brought prestige and the promise of advancement not only for the successful student but also for the mentor who had sponsored him, as this typical newspaper story from the June 19, 1867, edition of *El Eco de La Habana* notes:

> BRILLIANT YOUTH.—With the greatest pleasure we have learned that young Mr. José Martí, student at the Escuela Superior Municipal for boys headed by the illustrious Master Don Rafael Ma. de Mendive, has won the prize in competition in the subject of arithmetic at this city's Instituto de Segunda Enseñanza, receiving a mark of "Outstanding" in the final course examination for the same subject. We congratulate for these accomplishments both young Mr. Martí and most especially his teacher, the illustrious don Rafael Ma. de Mendive.

The success of the Escuela Superior under Mendive's leadership led to his being additionally awarded the directorship of the new school, Escuela San Pablo, which was simultaneously designated as part of Havana's prestigious secondary school system. At the end of September 1867, Pepe transferred to the Escuela San Pablo, a high school founded and directed by Mendive and situated at the same Calle Prado location as the Escuela Superior where he had completed his primary education. Both student and mentor were reaping the benefits of their respective achievements until a war and a badly timed laugh brought their successful partnership—and much else—to an untimely end.

Until the onset of the Ten Years' War (1868–1878), Pepe's accomplishments under Mendive's mentorship, which Leonor followed closely and celebrated with considerable enthusiasm, provided the sole source of joy in an otherwise dismal period for the Martís. In September Leonor's mother, Rita Cabrera, died in the Canary Islands, having prepared her will a few weeks earlier. Ailing and bankrupted by the Cabrera family's various transatlantic journeys, the widow's will left little of value for her surviving offspring.[19] Meanwhile, Mariano's failures continued to accumulate. By January 1868 the quarries in which he had invested the family's last reserves, including the entire proceeds from the sale of their home, closed for good. The failure of this venture on which Mariano pinned his hopes for the family left the aging patriarch no choice but to apply once again—unsuccessfully—for work in the civilian police.[20]

During the period leading up to the outbreak of the war in October 1868, Mendive played a crucial role in the formation of Pepe's revolutionary consciousness, which was burgeoning alongside his continuing academic successes. Under Mendive's tutelage the youth's revolutionary ideals and intellectual growth became inextricable from each other as well as from his teacher's growing influence as a mentor and surrogate father. Mendive's bond with Pepe coincided with Mariano Martí's waning influence and fortunes, which suffered even more when set beside Mendive's successes as an educator on the island and his ascendant international reputation as a poet and intellectual.

The death of Mendive's own son, the year-old Miguel Ángel, in mid-April 1868 further cemented the bond between Mendive and Pepe. The teacher's anguished mourning over the death of his first child coincided perfectly with the virtual absence of the student's increasingly irrelevant father. When not in school, Pepe spent most of his waking hours either with Mendive's family or with Fermín at the Domínguez home—substitutes, respectively, for a father and siblings whose interests and affinities did not match his own. From this period came Pepe's first published poem, as the sadness of the death of Mendive's child combined with Pepe's renewed attachment to his mentor to inspire "To Micaela," dedicated to the dead infant's grieving mother:

> When in the night of mourning
> The soul weeps its sorrows,
> And laments its disgrace,
> And condoles its burdens,
> Saddened tears escape
> Like pearls from the seas . . .
> And that is why, Micaela,
> You cry, with none who could
> Your pain console or your
> Sighing alleviate;
> And that is why, Micaela,
> Sad in your mother's pain,
> You cry always, always
> Lamenting the death of
> Miguel Ángel.[21]

This first of the poem's four stanzas only hints at the full-blown sentimentality of the rest, culminating with the speaker urging the grieving mother to watch as angels lift the baby to heaven. Nevertheless, the poem is remarkable for the precocity of its voice and especially for the darkness of its vision. More than anything else Pepe wrote before the onset of the Ten Years' War, "To Micaela" offers a glimpse into the teenager's empathic ability to feel the suffering of those closest to him. The poem, albeit sentimental and self-consciously romantic in its view of death, is a harbinger of the adult Martí's talent for creating art from the deepest pain.

The summer of 1868 brought Pepe's final scholastic achievements before he turned his full attention to more urgent matters. In June he received a mark of "Outstanding" in geometry and in July a perfect score on his geography exam. By September his integration into the Mendive household and estrangement from his biological family was nearly complete as he took up permanent residence in the Mendive's home at the Escuela Superior and began his third year of high school.[22] With Pepe's move to the Mendive household, a besieged Mariano tacitly surrendered to the famed educator his role as the child's primary guardian and male role model.

The immediate pretext for the change was that the Martís were preparing to move to Marianao in anticipation of Mariano finally landing a position as chief inspector of the port city of Batabanó. Mariano did officially assume his inspectorship on November 26, more than two months later.[23] Batabanó's location more than thirty miles south of Havana over difficult terrain at a time when rail travel was neither easy nor cheap made it unfeasible for Pepe to continue his studies from the Martí family home. Given Pepe's ongoing academic success and its singular importance to his own and his family's hopes for a better life, the Martís' decision to leave him with Mendive seems reasonable. Nevertheless, the Martís' permission for Pepe to remain in Havana with the Mendives suggests as much the significance the family now placed on Pepe's studies as it does Mariano's inability to successfully demand that his son again accompany him to a new job. If Mariano did again attempt to argue for Pepe's indispensability, a number of factors would have conspired to overrule him: the importance Leonor placed on Pepe's studies, the unsuccessful trip with Pepe to British Honduras, and Leonor's willingness to relocate and take her son's place as amanuensis for Mariano. Most importantly, the family's physical estrangement was undeniable proof of the waning and growing influence on Pepe, respectively, of Mariano and Mendive.

Outside events would soon forcefully cut short this seeming resolution of the paternal triangle. A coalition of wealthy Cuban planters from the western part of the island, known as the Reformadores (Reformers), offered renewed hope for an arrangement that would preserve the island's ties to Spain while ceding more political and economic power to Cuban Creoles. The Reformadores were motivated largely by their shared disillusionment at the failure of the previous decade's annexationist projects and a common recognition that in the wake of the Union's victory in the U.S. Civil War, Spain was their sole remaining hope for continuing slavery on the island. The wealthy planters found their interests threatened by an increasingly organized and belligerent slave labor force. Thus in early 1865 the Reformadores began their threefold appeal to the Spanish government, for a reform of the tariff system in hopes of stimulating trade with the United States, for Cuban representation in the Spanish court, and for measures to protect the slave trade or at least to have a slow, incremental phasing out that would compensate them for the loss of their slaves.[24]

In the summer of 1866, as thirteen-year-old Pepe was starting his first year of high school, it appeared to a hopeful Cuban population that the Reformadores might succeed in negotiating a degree of autonomy from Spain without acrimony or, as many feared, war. In July the Spanish government received a Cuban delegation for the putative purpose of negotiating these and other requests. By the following spring, however, it became clear that the Spanish government, which during the negotiations had veered sharply to the right due to domestic upheavals in Madrid, was no longer inclined to enact the delegation's desired reforms. After nearly a year of talking, all hopes for change were dashed. Spain's failure to come to terms with the restless plantocracy created an opening for a group of smaller-scale planters from the island's eastern provinces to solve the impasse in their own way: by emancipating their slaves and enlisting them in an armed uprising against Spain. The small-scale planters, led by landowner and lawyer Carlos Manuel de Céspedes, were encouraged by the Spanish government's apparent inability to suppress domestic discontent on the peninsula, a perception seemingly confirmed by the deposing on October 3 of Queen Isabella II in an armed uprising. The time, it seemed, was ripe for Creoles to finally rise up against a weakened, distracted mother country.[25]

In the early morning of October 10, 1868, Céspedes freed his slaves, armed them, and declared a war of independence against Spain. Despite initial setbacks and the decimation of Céspedes's original group, within days the insurgent force swelled to some twelve thousand men, mostly peasants and freed slaves. By October 20, overmatched and surprised by the size and ferocity of the rebellion, Spanish forces defending the city of Bayamo at the island's eastern end surrendered to the insurgents. Céspedes's act, known as the Grito de Yara (Cry of Yara) for the place it originated, marked the onset of the Ten Years' War, over the course of which an estimated two hundred thousand people died.[26] Despite the insurgents' eventual surrender, the Ten Years' War proved the first in a series of events that galvanized Pepe's allegiance to Cuba and sparked his lifelong dedication to Cuban independence.

In early 1869 the Martís were able to return to Havana due to Mariano's assuming the inspectorship of Guanabacoa, a small town roughly three miles southeast of the capital. Leonor and her six surviving daughters moved to a house in the capital, leaving Mariano behind in Batabanó awaiting his replacement. The Martís' return to Havana enabled Pepe to return to his parents' care, but the change did nothing to extinguish his nascent revolutionary ardor. Under Mendive's sway, the teenage Pepe embraced nationalist views considered radical, if not seditious, by many on the island. His political views were in fact the clearest sign that Mendive had won the battle with ardent royalist Mariano for the boy's heart.

With the onset of the war, however, Mendive's young follower began to chart his own course as an advocate for his country's freedom from colonial oppression. Paradoxically, Pepe's burgeoning activism was further fueled by Cuba's newfound—and as it turned out, fleeting—freedom of the press, enacted by decree on January 9, 1869, by the colony's new captain-general, Domingo Dulce y Garay. Spain's embattled liberal government installed Dulce as the island's top military and civilian authority in hopes that a program of moderate reforms would quell rising tensions among civilians and defuse their anger over the repressive tactics of his predecessor Francisco Lersundi. Along with freedom of the press, Dulce's new reforms included freedom of assembly and Cuban representation in the Spanish court. Dulce attempted to begin peace negotiations with Céspedes and decreed a forty-day amnesty period during which rebels could surrender without punishment.[27]

Dulce's gestures did not have the desired effect, as the sudden outlets for long-simmering tensions sparked a surge in public enthusiasm for the rebels. An unintended but eminently foreseeable consequence of Dulce's decree was that news from the front could more readily reach the capital although the war was being fought on the island's eastern extreme, far from Havana. On January 12, only three days after the onset of the islandwide freedom of the press, the talk of Havana was the news that the inhabitants of Bayamo had burned their own city to the ground before Spanish forces could retake it. A flurry of anti-Spanish pamphlets and one-off newspapers followed, most of them published anonymously or under pseudonyms. One of these, the anonymous pamphlet "El diablo cojuelo" (The Mischievous Devil) circulated in Havana, turned out to be the work of Fermín Valdés Domínguez, Pepe's closest friend since their elementary school days.[28] Many years later, Valdés Domínguez asserted Martí's authorship of parts of the pamphlet, although more recent scholarship has disputed this claim.[29] Regardless of Martí's participation in "El diablo cojuelo," Valdés Domínguez would play a crucial role in later events through which the schoolmates would forge a lasting bond of friendship.

THE EVENTS OF JANUARY 1869 BROUGHT THE DISTANT WAR home, giving the would-be revolutionary his first taste of the dangers of identifying with the revolutionary cause. Pepe was hardly alone in his enthusiasm.

The rebels' initial successes awakened widespread feelings of animosity toward Spain that had been simmering at least since the Reformadores' failed attempts to negotiate Cuban autonomy. Emboldened by good news from the east, pro-independence sympathizers now conspired with impunity, meeting in cafés and other public places to denounce Spanish domination and raise money for the rebels.

In an absence of any apparent move by the colonial government to counter the anticolonial groundswell, Spanish loyalists began organizing as well, forming the so-called Voluntarios, a network of right-wing, paramilitary groups backed by wealthy Spanish merchants and others loyal to the mother country. The Voluntarios' immediate objectives were to deter public displays of sympathy with the rebels and to punish those who dared to speak out against Spain. More importantly, their leaders sought to counter what they saw as the government's appeasement of Céspedes, fearing that the openly abolitionist Dulce would eventually agree to emancipate Cuba's slaves. From their inception the Voluntarios were a formidable force, initially numbering more than thirty-three thousand — nearly five times the number of regular Spanish troops on the island. By dint of both sheer numbers and support among the island's Spaniards, the organization posed a significant threat not only to the Cuban population but also to any colonial administration that tried to stand against them. It was not long before the Voluntarios started flexing their collective muscle in the new captain-general's office and on the streets of Havana.[30]

On the evening of January 22, during the performance of a comedy at the Teatro Villanueva, unscripted pro-independence remarks by a cast member sparked a three-day orgy of violence in Havana. By the time authorities restored order, fourteen Cubans were dead, twenty-six injured, and dozens more imprisoned. No charges were brought against the Voluntario mobs that terrorized the capital city, and the Spanish army did little to stop the slaughter.

Posters outside the Villanueva announcing that evening's play, *El perro huevero* (The Egg-Sucking Dog), were more than suggestive of its political content, featuring phrases such as "Viva libertad" and "Se armó la gorda" (roughly, "It's On"). Inside, the performance was being staged in honor of Florinda Campos, a prominent comic known for mocking the Spanish in her performances. The combination of the inflammatory advertising and Campos's association with the show attracted a pro-Cuban crowd that packed the 1,300-seat theater. It was not Campos who provided the spark that lit the powder keg, however, but Jacinto Valdés, another star of the show whom rebel sympathizers persuaded to give onstage huzzahs to their cause. Valdés proved true to his word, shouting "Viva!" for a fellow cast member named Carlos Manuel. The crowd quickly picked up the thinly veiled reference to Carlos Manuel de Céspedes, leader of the Cuban insurrection, and shouts of "Viva Céspedes!" soon filled the theater.[31]

The next morning's newspapers prominently featured the incident, and one columnist actually chastised Spaniards in the audience for not drawing their weapons on the spot. Also appearing on the Havana streets that day was the first and only issue of *La Patria Libre*, Pepe's self-published paper that featured his first play, the fiercely revolutionary *Abdala*.[32] Given the already tense atmosphere in Havana, such provocations gave the Voluntarios all the pretext they needed for the chaos that followed.

Pepe rose early on the morning of January 23 and along with his classmates spent much of the day distributing and selling *La Patria Libre*. Whatever sense of success or revolutionary euphoria the young author may have felt abruptly ceased upon his return home. Far from celebrating Pepe's accomplishment, Leonor Martí was beside herself with anguish and the fear of what would befall her sixteen-year-old son after putting his name to such a publication in the environment of the moment. She insisted that he stop his activities or at least wait until tensions in the city subsided.[33] But neither Leonor's imploring nor the promise of trouble to come deterred Pepe from his commitment to the Cuban cause.

Whatever little thought the teenage Martí seems to have given to the perilous circumstances into which he launched *La Patria Libre*, his play *Abdala* was prescient in its anticipation of Leonor's fears. The play in fact dramatizes an imagined conversation in which the eponymous protagonist's mother, Espirta, struggles between her protective instincts and her son's allegiance to the independence cause:

> Abdala: Please forgive, oh mother! I must leave you
> To depart for the country. Oh! These tears
> Bear witness to my terrible anxiety,
> And the hurricane that roars inside me . . .
> I tremble only for you. And though my tears
> I do not show to my country's warriors,
> See how they run down my face! Oh mother!
> See now how many over my cheeks spill!
> Espirta: And so much love for this corner of dirt?
> Did it protect you in your infancy?
> Did the lover hold you upon her breast?
> Is she who engendered your audacity
> And your strength? Or your mother? Answer me! . . .
> Abdala: The love, mother, to one's country is not,

> Not the ridiculous love of the land,
> Nor of the grass we trample underfoot,
> But invincible hate of her oppressor,
> Eternal hatred of her attacker; —
> And such a love awakens in our breast
> The world of memories that calls us back,
> To life again, when blood, the blood spills forth
> From the wound with the anguish of the soul; —
> The sole image of love that comforts us
> And all the placid memories it keeps!
> Espirta: And this love it wakes is greater than what
> Your breast holds for your mother?
> Abdala: Can you believe
> In anything more sublime than your country?[34]

Although the language of *Abdala* is awkward, its metaphors of land and blood not as finely wrought as in Martí's later writings, the play remains a remarkable example of its young author's prescience of his own future as a revolutionary and the terrible toll his patriotism would take on those he loved.

Leonor's worst fears were soon confirmed. On the evening of January 23, an angry mob of Voluntarios convened outside the Villanueva during a performance of *El perro huevero*. Some of them entered the theater, awaiting any utterance or gesture from the cast that would give the assembled Spaniards a pretext to strike.

They did not have to wait long. Upon hearing a performer utter the line "He has no shame who does not say / 'Long live the land that produces the cane,'" the crowd began shouting "Viva Cuba! Viva Cuba!" The Voluntarios in the crowd raised their own chorus of "Viva España!" which soon spread to the assembled mob outside. Thus provoked into action, the armed Voluntarios outside began to move menacingly toward the unprotected theater. The aggressors got the worst of the initial firefight that night, as Cubans were not only in the majority but had come armed in anticipation of trouble. The Spanish troops that soon surrounded the building were deterred from burning it to the ground only by the realization that a number of Voluntarios remained inside.[35]

For the next two days and nights, gunfire rang through the streets of Havana. Roving mobs of Voluntarios proceeded to shoot up nearby businesses and homes of known rebel sympathizers, while Spanish forces remained conspicuously absent. In the worst of the violence, a group of Voluntarios opened fire on a busy downtown café called the Louvre and wounded an unspecified number of staff and customers. They invaded the homes of prominent pro-Cuba families, shooting anyone in their way. Between specifically targeted locations, anyone they identified or even suspected of supporting the rebels would be shot in the street.[36]

Among their targets on the night of January 24 was the Escuela Superior, which was also the Mendives' home, three blocks from the theater. That same night, Pepe Martí and a group of classmates found themselves inside the Mendive house hard at work on the next issue of *La Patria Libre*.

The din of shouts and gunfire eventually reached the Martí home on San José, about a mile away from Mendive's house. With Mariano still in Batabanó awaiting his replacement, Leonor found herself alone with her daughters, including the newborn Dolores. Quickly realizing that Mendive's school was a likely Voluntario target, Leonor did not waste a second. Her mother's sense of protection perhaps heightened by the recent death of six-year-old Pilar, she left the infant in the care of the older daughters and ran to hail the first carriage she could find that would take her to her imperiled son. This act was remarkable in itself, as the very idea of an unaccompanied woman hailing a carriage, especially at night, was at the time unthinkable. That she could additionally persuade a driver to accept such a perilous assignment at all seems in context nothing short of miraculous and a testament to Leonor's decisiveness and sheer audacity in the face of acute danger. No record survives of how much Leonor paid the unidentified carriage driver to retrieve her only son or of why he agreed to such a fare on such a night.[37]

Leonor's courage did not fail her upon arriving at the by-now besieged Mendive residence. Undaunted by the smell of gun smoke or the sight of the school's bullet-riddled walls, the frightened but determined mother ran and pounded on the front door at Calle Prado no. 88, crying out for her son in the midst of the smoke and noise. It was not long before a visibly blanched Pepe, horrified as much by the assault as by Leonor's reckless disregard for her own safety, leapt into his mother's arms. The Voluntarios, perhaps chastened by the mother's display, momentarily stood down, and together mother and son scrambled to the safety of the waiting carriage. Six years later, the young man would publish his first description of the evening's traumatic events:

> It is not enough that upon a packed, defenseless theater, upon women, and men, and children, would fall at once a flaming wall of gunfire. . . . Nor the horrible days of January that filled with murdered bodies the sidewalks of Jesús del Monte and the streets of Jesús María, and the ones my mother crossed over in search of me, and the bullets flying past her, and the dead falling at her side, the same horrible night of the 22nd [*sic*] on which so many armed men fell upon so many unarmed ones! It

was my mother: She went to find me in the midst of the wounded, and the streets ablaze with crossfire, and above her very head the exploded shells of bullets fired at a woman, there in that place where her vast, immeasurable love sought to find me![38]

Nor did the events of that night recede from his memory over the years. Twenty-two years after the event the adult Martí would commemorate in a poem Leonor's courage that night:

> The brutal enemy
> Fires upon the house:
> His saber lays waste the streets
> Beneath the tropical moon . . .
>
> Among the bullets a carriage passes;
> A dead woman emerges:
> A hand knocks upon the door
> In the blackness of the night.
>
> No bullet but drills through
> The front door: and the woman
> Who calls out has given me life:
> My mother has come for me.
> In the jaws of death,
> The brave Habaneros
> Removed their hats
> Before the brave matriarch.[39]

Martí sent Leonor a first-edition copy of *Versos sencillos*, the volume in which this poem first appeared. He inscribed his mother's copy, "To my brave and most noble mother" and advised her in an accompanying letter to "begin reading it on page 51," where the untitled poem appears.[40]

Mariano Martí received word in Batabanó of trouble in the capital and, fearing for his family's safety, took the first available train back to Havana. In the preceding years Pepe was mostly shielded from his father's episodic outbursts, partly due to his mother's protection but also because of the family's respect and admiration for the boy's scholastic achievements. He had spent the previous several months living with the Mendives and was seldom home even when putatively housed by the Martís. Mariano's temper seemed to have cooled in the months since his renewed employment as a chief inspector. The father's legendary anger was roused, however, by the specter of his only son, the source of the family's greatest pride and hope for a better life, choosing a path that could easily end in tragedy. As a man for whom, as an acquaintance would later lament, "fatherhood was understood as an absolute right to exercise all manner of tyranny," an insubordination of this magnitude required a severe and immediate response.[41]

Endangering the boy's hopes for a future career or a proper life in Cuban society paled compared to the immediate prospect of imprisonment, labor camps, exile, or death, whether executed by the state or at the hands of the belligerent Voluntarios. As a former colonial officer, Mariano was acutely aware of the danger in which his son had heedlessly placed not only himself but the entire family. If the Voluntarios were so bold as to assault the home of a man as respected as Mendive, he reasoned, what would stop them from doing the same to the infinitely more expendable Martís? In fact, Mariano's lingering reputation as a loyal and steadfast Spaniard may have been the main reason bloodshed never darkened the Martís' door. Given the precarious political situation and the ongoing violence in the capital, there was no telling how long the talisman of Mariano's protection would last. Everything depended on Pepe's renunciation of his revolutionary beliefs or at least his willingness to temporarily quiet them.

The young man would not yield. Nor did he yield when Mendive himself, alarmed by the radical turn in Pepe's activism, came to the Martís' home to counsel moderation. The Mendives' relationship with the Martís had never been a warm one, perhaps partly because the families had little in common culturally or politically. Mariano must have managed at some point to offend Mendive's wife, Micaela, who regarded him as "a Spaniard as recalcitrant and rude as can be."[42] With Pepe and Mariano at an impasse and their relationship reaching a crisis point, the Martís turned to the one man they believed could persuade their son to stand down. Mendive agreed to come and talk to Pepe, perhaps as much out of desire to avert a family crisis as to save the boy from Spanish prisons. But the mentor's entreaties, delivered in the presence of Pepe's family, not only failed to curb the young man's fervor but also temporarily severed the bond between them. Shortly after Mendive's unsuccessful intervention, a wounded Pepe rebuked him for his perceived betrayal in a brief, undated note:

> Sr. [Señor] Mendive:
>
> I do not know that a generous father need remind a son who adores him of his duties. This is why your errand so astonished me, when at every instant I would give for you my life, which is yours and only yours, and another thousand if I had them to give. . . .
>
> Your disciple and son
> MARTÍ[43]

It is not known whether Mendive had any further contact with Pepe in the immediate aftermath of receiving his note. Their estrangement might have become permanent had it not been for one unfortunate yet foreseeable event. It is perhaps the first of the many great ironies of José Martí's life that only after Mendive's own arrest and incarceration was his wayward student able to forgive his beloved mentor.

CHAPTER THREE

Trial by Fire

*I deeply lament being behind bars; but my experience in prison will
serve me well. It has given me many lessons for my life, which I augur
will be short, and I will not fail to make the most of them.*

LETTER TO LEONOR MARTÍ, NOVEMBER 10, 1869

*Filiation of the W[hite] prisoner José Martí y Pérez, son of Mariano
and of Leonor Pérez, native of Havana, province of id., domiciled in id.,
by trade a clerk, a single man, 17 years of age, average height, good color,
regular face, mouth id., nose id., grey-brown eyes, brown hair, brows id.,
no beard. Distinguishing features: A scar on the chin and another on the
second finger of the left hand.*

PROCESSING DOCUMENT SIGNED BY COMANDANTE M.
DE PALACIO, PRESIDIO DEPARTAMENTAL DE LA HABANA,
APRIL 4, 1870

MENDIVE'S WARNING TO PEPE THAT HIS REVOLU-
tionary activities would lead to a bad end proved more
immediately prescient for himself.[1] Although the violence in Havana declined somewhat in the days after Leonor's daring rescue of Pepe, Voluntario
leaders opened a new front in their war against the civilian population by successfully pressuring the colonial government into detaining prominent pro-
independence Cubans. On January 28, Mendive was arrested on suspicion of
conspiracy, including the charge that he had been involved in organizing the
program at the Teatro Villanueva that provoked the Voluntarios.[2]

Bereaved at his teacher's detention in prison awaiting trial — and feeling perhaps some guilt over his reproachful note — Pepe devoted himself anew to his fallen mentor. Showing something of his mother's temerity on the night of the Villanueva incident, he successfully petitioned the colonial governor for permission to visit Mendive in prison. In the months leading up to Mendive's trial, Pepe made daily pilgrimages to the Havana prison known locally as El Castillo (the Castle) to visit him, apparently heedless to how an increasingly paranoid Spanish government, not to mention the Voluntarios, might view such acts.[3]

The news on February 6 that a second insurgent force in Las Villas Province near the original site of Céspedes's uprising had joined the rebellion did nothing to quell the now toxic atmosphere that pervaded the capital.[4] This time there were no expressions of joy, at least in public, among rebel supporters, as such news could only mean further Voluntario reprisals. In such an environment, Mendive was less likely than ever to escape the wrath of a besieged empire clinging to the last vestiges of its former glory. Worse still for Pepe, Mendive's arrest meant the shutting down of the school that had been the student's second home and the primary outlet of his intellectual and emotional development. Mariano, who feared what might come of the combination of idleness and emotional anguish in his son, quickly found employment for him in as a clerk at a Havana law firm.[5]

Mourning the loss of his beloved mentor and wounded by his sudden banishment from the life of letters and literature — and politics — that he had come to love, Pepe wrote his first explicitly revolutionary poem, the incendiary "10 de octubre" (October 10), in a student newspaper called *El Siboney*. The poem's opening and closing lines unmistakably announce its author's belief in the righteousness of his cause as well as his defiance of the oppressing force that would destroy it:

> It is not a dream, it is real: A cry of war
> Has the Cuban people hurled, enraged;
> The people that for three centuries has suffered
> All the blackness of an enclosing oppression . . .
>
> Thank God! At last with integrity
> Cuba breaks the yoke that oppressed it
> And proud and free raises up her head![6]

Pepe's pen fell silent for a time after the appearance of "10 de octubre" due largely to Havana's ongoing political crisis. In the aftermath of the Villanueva incident Captain-General Dulce rescinded his decree granting freedom of the press on the island, making it all but impossible to publicly distribute anticolonial writings without swift and severe retribution.[7] The months that preceded Mendive's trial assumed a rhythm of normality for the Martís that belied the perilous environment surrounding them. Pepe remained in Guanabacoa with his family but made regular trips to the city to visit the imprisoned Mendive. He also hoped to return to school in the fall, as Mariano had successfully petitioned for his son's transfer to a different institution after the closure of Mendive's school. Mariano himself was managing to avoid in his position at Guanabacoa the bad luck and judgment that had doomed his previous assignments.

The war dragged on, with the Spanish making little headway against the poorly equipped but tenacious insurgents. Thanks largely to a forty-thousand-strong army—double the most generous estimates of the enemy's numbers—Spain managed to contain the rebellion within the eastern regions and keep the fighting away from the more prosperous western provinces. Even where there was no fighting, Spanish rule was repressive and ruthless. Provincial rulers in the eastern provinces confined women and children to their homes, one general actually ordering that males over the age of fifteen found away from home without cause be shot.[8] In the west, authorities and Voluntarios alike scrutinized citizens' movements ever more closely, to the point that Mendive compelled Pepe to suspend his daily visits to him in prison for fear that Pepe himself would be detained.

On April 25 Mendive was found guilty of conspiracy and sentenced to four years' exile. Exactly twenty days later he boarded a ship bound for Spain but soon found his way to New York, where he continued to write and work for Cuban independence.[9] Mendive returned to Cuba after the insurgents surrendered in 1878, under the terms of a general amnesty, and by all accounts succeeded in reestablishing his former career as a respected teacher and poet. He also carefully avoided politics in both the classroom and in public for the rest of his life. There is no way of knowing what Pepe's childhood mentor would have thought of his adult fame as a poet and revolutionary, as he did not live to see its fullest flowering: Rafael María de Mendive died in Havana on November 24, 1886, at the age of sixty-five.[10]

Despite the failure of the Ten Years' War to definitively establish either Cuba as a sovereign state or Spain's hold on the island, it accomplished what Mariano Martí, by his initial resistance to Pepe's scholastic ambitions, and Mendive himself, by his disapproval of his student's activism, could not: it severed the relationship between Pepe and the man whose guidance set the course for his future life.

Losing his mentor was merely the first of many separations and heartaches awaiting the young revolutionary, each of which would test his devotion to the cause he embraced. This first loss, however, proved the primal blow through which he would view all future hardships.

MARTÍ NEVER LOST THE SENSE OF OUTRAGE AND REVOLU-
tionary fervor forged during those early months of 1869. He could not have
anticipated, however, how utterly and irrevocably the events of the next few
months would transform his life. By the end of the year, a teenage José Martí
would find his mettle severely tested and would experience hardships and suffering beyond anything he had ever imagined.

The spring of 1869 saw a reduction in violence in Havana and a relative return to normalcy. The city's long history of unrest and upheaval had engendered
its capacity to settle down relatively quickly after January's traumatic events. Yet
the mood in the capital was more taut than calm, a stillness born of unresolved
tensions awaiting a later moment of reckoning.

In the eastern provinces the war hobbled along, the action more political
than military. Cubans in the field outnumbered the Spanish, but their lack of
firepower limited them to guerrilla tactics. The island plantocracy, fearful of independence if it meant abolition, was hesitant to support the rebellion without
assurances that its leaders would maintain the status quo. The Cuban leadership
remained divided on both slavery and independence, an ambivalence that was
costing them the landowners' support. But with Spanish forces concentrated in
the cities and valuable plantations of the western provinces, the army could not
capitalize on the rebels' relative weakness.

In Havana, Captain-General Dulce was quickly becoming irrelevant. With
his reformist policies discredited, generals in the field disregarding his calls for
moderation, and no reinforcements coming any time soon, Dulce lost control of the war and the government. All that remained was for the Voluntarios,
who had opposed him from the start, to finish him off. That happened soon
enough, and in dramatic fashion: before the end of May, a Voluntario mob invaded Dulce's home and demanded his resignation.[11]

The besieged captain-general bowed to the inevitable. By June 5 he was
gone, not even awaiting his successor's arrival before quitting the island. The interim of several weeks between Dulce's departure and the new captain-general's
arrival turned out to be his parting gift to the Voluntarios, who proceeded to
set themselves up as the island's de facto rulers. The new captain-general's
more Voluntario-friendly orientation assured that they would remain Cuba's
supreme civilian and military authority.[12]

The political tumult in the capital had little immediate impact on the Martí
household. Anxious to restore a sense of normalcy and routine to his son's
life — and to improve the household's always tenuous finances — Mariano Martí
got his son a clerical job in the office of Felipe Gálvez Fatio not far from the
Martí home. The younger Martí spent most of his waking hours for the next six
months in that second-story office above Fatio's home, arriving at 6 a.m. and
often working until 7 or 8 p.m. For a time, the regular routine and long work-

days seemed to settle him down, if only out of exhaustion and the sheer tedium of his job as a *dependiente de diligencias*—basically a clerk who ran errands and did whatever other small tasks needed to be filled. Mariano was too busy with his official duties in Guanabacoa to personally ensure Pepe's compliance with the new household rules, so he entrusted Leonor with that task. Fearful that her son would fall back into his former revolutionary activities, Leonor kept a close watch on the boy, enforcing his father's strict curfew.[13]

So diligent was Leonor that the events that led to her son being arrested, imprisoned, and eventually exiled would never have occurred but for an accident of geography. It happens that Fatio's offices on the corner of Virtudes and Industria in Old Havana stood only two blocks from the home of Pepe's best friend, Fermín Valdés Domínguez. The junior Martí had always been welcome in Fermín's house, and the convenience of the Domínguez residence so near his workplace made it a logical place for his afternoon siesta. Although we do not know for certain whether the Martís knew of their son's visits to the Domínguez home, it is reasonable to presume that they did not. As Fermín was a former student of Mendive who also published anti-Spanish papers, Pepe's parents would have been much troubled about their continued friendship.

Over time, the Martís' fears dissipated, due to Pepe's apparent acclimation to his new circumstances. He worked at Fatio's office through the summer and into the fall, and his visits to the Domínguez household likewise continued without incident.

The Martís tended to focus disproportionately on Pepe at the expense of his sisters. Now Leonor's heightened attention to her son's daily activities necessarily reduced the already limited time she could devote to her daughters. It is not clear how Chata, second oldest of the Martí children and the oldest daughter, met Manuel García y Álvarez, much less how she managed to begin a relationship with him under her parents' noses. By August 1869, however, Mariano and Leonor had to face their fourteen-year-old daughter's engagement to a nineteen-year-old man without their consent. True to his history of violent eruptions, Mariano became especially virulent in his opposition. His demands and threats only redoubled his daughter's resolve to marry. Chata abandoned the Martí home on August 19 after an exasperated Mariano administered a brutal beating. The formal complaint she filed the next day at the Guadalupe district's inspector's office specifically refers to "the unmistakable marks on her face and other parts of her body."[14]

Faced with the threat of civil or even criminal charges and burdened with an erratic employment history, Mariano understood that his inspectorship in Guanabacoa could not survive such a public scandal. He thus had little choice but to accede to the Guadalupe inspector's recommendation that his daughter live with a "neutral" third party—her boyfriend's uncle—until she married. The wedding took place less than a month later, on September 16. Mariano and Leonor Martí did not attend.[15]

Amid the household uproar surrounding Chata's engagement, Pepe Martí was quietly carrying out his own mutiny. To all outward appearances, he continued to play the obedient son, leaving for work every morning, returning in the evening, dutifully handing over the week's earnings to his father. Pepe evidently did not complain about the long hours or meager pay and expressed no resentment even when Mariano, in the midst of his troubles with Chata, forgot to register Pepe at his new school by the deadline. On September 30, Mariano petitioned school authorities to belatedly admit his son and held out hope that they would.[16] For now, however, Pepe's scholarly life seemed a distant memory, his present reality consisting of little more than work.

ALL OF THAT CHANGED ON THE FIRST MONDAY OF OCTO-ber. A corps of Voluntarios spent their siesta hours that afternoon marching in formation down Avenida Isabel II, one of Old Havana's major thoroughfares, and adjacent streets, in honor of Queen Isabella's birthday. Accounts vary regarding what exactly happened when the parade passed the Domínguez home at Industria no. 22, where Pepe was spending his afternoon as usual. Pepe found himself in the company of Fermín's brother, Eusebio, and several of his friends; Fermín himself was not present. All were drawn to the front window by the spectacle of the marching Spaniards, which provoked a burst of laughter from one or more of the assembled Cubans. Accounts differ over whether the young Cubans at the window deliberately mocked the passing Voluntarios or were merely overheard or indeed whether the laughter was directed at them at all. One version alleges that the young men were playing a game that involved tossing orange peels from the window, one of which accidentally landed on a Voluntario's head and provoked laughter from within the house. Whatever the real or imagined slight, the Voluntarios drew their own conclusions and acted accordingly: they returned to the house at Industria no. 22 that evening with the local inspector in tow and had several young men arrested.[17]

Fermín, Eusebio, and three of their friends were arrested that evening on charges of insulting the Voluntarios and sent off to prison. Pepe was not at the Domínguez home that evening, but that alone did not spare him the Voluntarios' wrath. The others present that afternoon were promptly rounded up and jailed by the authorities, likely because the Domínguez brothers divulged their names.[18] That they did not name Pepe suggests an attempt to protect him not only from arrest but also from his father's anger. We do not know for certain that Pepe was visiting the Domínguezes without his parents' knowledge, but given the great lengths to which they had gone to bar him from revolutionary activities, they would likely not have wanted him associating with a fellow student of Mendive. The Domínguez brothers' attempt to shield Pepe, and Mariano's reaction once he learned the truth, indicate that the Martís neither knew of nor welcomed their son's continued friendship with Fermín.

Mariano's response to his son's newest brush with disaster was predictably harsh. The ensuing row that night in the Martí household was by all accounts an ugly one, with emotions still raw over Chata's recent estrangement and Pepe's revolutionary publications. Given the family's continued financial struggles and the ongoing war, all of these factors no doubt contributed to Mariano's violent reaction to his son's foolish behavior, which could have endangered the entire family.

But this was not the same Pepe of nine months before, who, shaken by the sudden loss of his mentor and school, finally bowed to the pressure from his parents and Mendive himself to stand down. There was no withdrawing or apologizing on this night, as the slender but suddenly iron-willed teen withstood his father's withering barrage of insults to the Cuban cause and reproaches to his own behavior. The experience, and his resentment at having to bear his father's insults, remained with the adult Martí. In an 1878 letter he would cite his parents' inability to "forgive my savage independence, my brusque inflexibility, or my opinions regarding Cuba."[19] For now, however, there was nothing for the young man but to endure the circumstances.

Pepe's newfound stoicism did not necessarily replace the quiet, sensitive, acutely emotional nature of the child his parents knew. He had simply grown a thicker skin. In the months after he fled Mendive's bullet-riddled house under his mother's cloak, Pepe came to understand that resisting Spanish rule commanded a high price. The colonial government's increasingly repressive tactics demonstrated Madrid's desperation as well as its resolve. Rather than dissuading Pepe, however, Mendive's imprisonment and later deportation actually cemented the young man's dedication to the cause and his sense of eventual doom. If Mendive, a highly respected educator and poet, was not safe from Spanish retribution, no one was safe. No act of resistance, however small or ambiguous, would escape punishment.

The emergence of these conflicting emotions in Pepe, this simultaneous sense of resolve and fatalism, made his continued existence as an office clerk unbearable. Pepe's visits to the Domínguez home were his only outlet not only for political activism but for intellectual stimulation of any kind. The afternoons with Fermín and Eusebio could not compare to his empowering, intoxicating experience under Mendive's tutelage, but he had been grateful for them. And now they too were gone, his friends imprisoned and soon to be deported or worse. Pepe found himself suffering an internal exile of his own, his life a dreary combination of indentured servitude by day and house arrest by night. In his anguish the young man turned to the only person he knew would understand his pain.

> Mr. Mendive:
>
> I have been awakened from a stupid apathy and an almost English sadness, by the news that your letter of yesterday has brought to Micaela [Mendive's wife] like a light from heaven. . . .
>
> The Domínguezes and [Manuel] Sellén are still in prison. They released the Frenchman [Atanasio] Fortier upon the first reclamation from the consul. These people, as sanguine as they are cowardly, believe a Frenchman to be innocent and a Creole guilty, when, if there be something of which to be guilty, both would be. . . .
>
> I work now from six in the morning to eight at night and earn 4½ ounces [of gold] that I give to my father. He makes me suffer more each day and has come to hurt me so that I confess to you with all the rude frankness of which you know me capable that only the hope of seeing you again has kept me from killing myself. Your letter of yesterday has saved me. Someday you shall read my diary and in it, that this has not been a child's tantrum but a weighed and measured resolution . . .
>
> Until tomorrow, farewell from your disciple and son who asks your blessing—
>
> JOSÉ MARTÍ[20]

Although Pepe did not date his letter to Mendive, its references to the prisoners and to Mariano's harshness toward him suggests that Martí wrote it during the first week of October 1869. At this point Pepe Martí was fairly certain, as his letter to Mendive makes clear, that the worst that would come of this incident for him would be the loss of his friends and estrangement from his family. Perhaps that is why he makes no reference to another unsent but deeply incriminating letter he had written to a former classmate. Pepe left it in an unsealed envelope in the drawer of a desk he shared with Fermín in the Domínguez home. It perhaps did not occur to him that after arresting the Domínguez brothers, the authorities might search the house for evidence of conspiracy and find the letter. Perhaps he had simply forgotten about it.

The local inspector who found Pepe's unsent letter on the evening of October 4 thought little enough of it that he did not even think to detain its author. The only reason he had the letter at all is that it had been collected as part of a general but very careful search of the Domínguez home that turned up a large number of pro-independence publications and other suspicious writings. Given the volume of material collected that evening, it is possible that the inspector did not read the letter at all. The indictments handed down on October 7, three days after the initial arrests, did not mention the name José Martí. Of those arrested only Atanasio Fortier, a French national, was released from prison at the request of the French consul. The rest remained in prison awaiting trial.[21]

On October 9 a staff member in the *secretaría* (Secretary of State's office) was scouring the Domínguezes' confiscated documents for evidence when he discovered this:

> Comrade:
> Have you ever dreamed of the glory of apostates? Do you know the ancient penalty for apostasy? We expect that a disciple of Mr. Rafael María de Mendive will not let this letter go unanswered.[22]

Pepe signed the letter "José Martí." After Martí's death in 1895 Fermín Valdés Domínguez claimed to have co-signed the letter, and he produced two versions of it at different times. Although his handwriting was very similar to Martí's, both letters have since been dismissed as forgeries.[23] Unfortunately, Valdés Domínguez's lie has become crucial to the Martí myth, as it sets the stage for one of the most celebrated moments of the Martí legend: his fiery public denunciation of Spanish rule at his trial.

The trial was set in motion by an inspector's complaint to his superior:

> Please direct your attention to the [letter] in folio 24, and you will be convinced that it is written by a declared enemy of Spain and that it attempts to separate a soldier from his duty in a time of war, among the gravest offenses known to military law; in that regard, by not having comprehended this, the Inspector will perhaps render impossible the discovery of what happened between Mr. José Martí and the cadet Mr. Carlos de Castro y de Castro [*sic*] because he should have proceeded immediately to imprison Martí to his registered dwelling and to ascertain how those documents came to be in Domínguez's house.[24]

A second report in the same dossier corroborates the letter's contents and confirms Martí's sole authorship:

> The undersigned can only say that he has seen a letter in the government's file signed by Martí, advising a friend, a cadet fighting against the insurgents, to desert. In it he is called *apostate* and is asked whether he knew how the Romans punished that class of men in Republican times.[25]

It is perhaps a product of the colonial government's inefficient bureaucracy that it took another twelve days before sixteen-year-old Pepe was finally arrested. On October 21 he was charged with conspiracy and sent to the national prison to await trial. On the following day Mariano received a formal response to his request to allow Pepe to register for classes after the deadline. His appeal was denied.[26]

IT IS NOT CLEAR HOW MUCH TIME PASSED BEFORE THE Martís received any word from their only son or information about him. No conclusive record exists of either Leonor or Mariano visiting him before his trial, although he requests in a November 10 letter that Leonor bring his sisters to see him. Pepe complains in the same letter of having struggled to get mail out, although it is not clear why the authorities would withhold mail privileges but allow visitations; perhaps he was wary of having his mail read by the prison staff. The most striking thing about Pepe's November 10 letter to Leonor, however, is its curiously sanguine portrayal of his situation. He writes optimistically of being found innocent or at least of the possibility of somehow "undoing" his offense:

> The Domínguezes and [Manuel] Sellén will in the end be freed, and I will remain incarcerated. The consequences of prison do not frighten me; but I do not suffer being imprisoned for long. And this is all I ask. That things move quickly, that to whom has done nothing, nothing is to be done. At least, they will not be able to find me guilty of anything that I cannot undo.[27]

Later in the letter Pepe offers Leonor an early glimpse of the romantic, somewhat morbid persona that would fully emerge in adulthood:

> I deeply lament being behind bars; but my experience in prison will serve me well. It has given me many lessons for my life, which I augur will be short, and I will not fail to make the most of them. I am 16 years old, and many old men have told me that I resemble an old man myself. And they have a point; because if I have in full force the bewilderment and effervescence of my few years, I have on the other hand a heart as small as it is wounded. It is true that you suffer a great deal; but it is also true that I suffer more. May God grant that someday, in the midst of my happiness, I may tell you of my life's troubles![28]

The letter's curious mix of optimism, gloom, and resentment perfectly captures the young man's conflicted state. Pepe strives to comfort his mother with hopes of acquittal or leniency even as he reproaches her for underestimating his "life's troubles." For their part, Leonor and Mariano anxiously followed all developments in Pepe's case through frequent contact with the office of Captain Francisco Lanzas y Torres, the prosecutor assigned to the case.[29] They shared to some degree their son's optimism and held out hope that his youth and perhaps his father's long record of service and loyalty would sway the court in his favor.

However necessary it may have been at the time, the family's optimism was misplaced. Martí would go on to produce many prescient writings, but his November 10 letter was not one of them. Among the letter's many predictions, only the release of Manuel Sellén proved correct.[30] About the rest—acquittal, undoing his offense, and especially achieving a final future happiness after life's troubles—he was completely and tragically wrong.

PEPE MARTÍ'S TRIAL BEFORE A MILITARY TRIBUNAL ON March 4, 1870, has long passed into legend. The one written record of the trial that remains is a summary statement containing the names of those present, the charges, and the court's verdict and sentences. The only known eyewitness accounts of the hearing itself are those of Fermín Valdés Domínguez, according to which he was tried along with Pepe in order to determine the authorship of the letter to the cadet Carlos de Castro. Valdés Domínguez has proven less than reliable as a historical source; aside from his later forgeries of the letter to support his story, his account of the trial contains several demonstrable falsehoods.[31] Yet Valdés Domínguez's remains the only extant account of Martí's conspiracy trial beyond the court summary. Thus despite the untrustworthiness of its source and its variance from the historical record, the story of Pepe Martí's heroic courtroom stand has become an inextricable part of the Martí myth.

The centerpiece of Valdés Domínguez's apocryphal account is a dramatic scene in which he and Pepe vie to prove sole authorship of the co-signed letter that the prosecutor could not determine due to the defendants' very similar handwriting. According to an account Valdés Domínguez published in 1908, Pepe moved quickly and unambiguously to resolve the matter:

> The two thus confronted, Martí silenced the one he called his soul brother and energetically demonstrated that the guilt was all his and, formulating harsh attacks against Spain and proclaiming, in correct and eloquent paragraphs, the right of Cubans to independence, astonished by his audacity and dominated by the magic of his words that tribunal of military men bloodthirsty and little acquainted with the application of the law. That was his first speech and the most beautiful demonstration of his loyalty as a grateful and noble friend. Such acts are proper to exemplary souls such as his. Martí was then 16 years old. The prosecutor

requested the ultimate penalty for him, and for Valdés Domínguez 10 years of hard labor. The sentence was six years of hard labor for each.[32]

In a different version, Fermín has Pepe actually kiss him on the forehead before stepping before the tribunal and, cheekily lifting a pen from the judge's desk, signing his name for all to confirm his authorship of the letter. In this alternate version of the legend, Pepe goes as far as to berate the court as cowardly for daring to prosecute adolescents.[33] All of this, unconfirmed beyond Valdés Domínguez's account, has become part of the accepted biography.

At least one facet of Valdés Domínguez's story—the sentencing—is immediately and verifiably false, as the official court record unambiguously confirms:

> [The court] has condemned and does condemn Mr. José Martí y Pérez to the sentence of six years' hard labor, in accordance with the spirit of Article 142, Rule 5 of the cited Code, and Mr. Fermín Valdés Domínguez to six months imprisonment subject to the same Article. Havana, March 4, 1870.[34]

The discrepancy between Valdés Domínguez's recollection and the actual sentence is a relatively minor one that does not in itself disqualify the entire account. The much bigger lie is that of the co-signed letter upon which his entire account depends. If, as the evidence demonstrates, Martí was the sole signatory of the letter to Castro, there would simply have been no reason for the court to have the two defendants confront each other. This technique, known in the Spanish legal system as *careo*, literally "confrontation," was typically used only in cases when two or more witnesses presented contradictory testimony.[35] No such contradiction would have existed in this case, as the inspector who originally found the letter and his superior explicitly named Martí as its sole author and signatory.

Beyond this contradiction, Martí's sentence of six years' hard labor is actually less severe than others handed down for conspiracy during this period. In another civilian case of the time, a Cuban man named José Valdez Nodarse received the identical sentence for "having uttered seditious words"—and Cuba's captain-general had the judges imprisoned for two months for being too lenient, finding their sentences "not in accord with the regulations, codes, and existing laws."[36] Given the severity of the Voluntarios' response to a group of young men for allegedly mocking their parade, as well as a historical context in which teenage males were being shot just for being away from home without cause, the idea that a Spanish tribunal would reward such open, vocal defiance as Valdés Domínguez describes with a less severe sentence simply stretches credulity. Valdés Domínguez's account of the trial is thus simply false: the discrepancy between Martí's sentence and his own confirms not the court's wrath at a young man's speech but its finding of guilt in his authorship of a treasonous letter.

THE MARTÍS DID NOT LEARN THE COURT'S VERDICT FOR several weeks, during which time Pepe languished in the national prison.[37] His cell's single window offered a view of the prison's front gates, through which he watched the so-called work brigades — essentially chain gangs — depart before dawn en route to their various workplaces throughout Havana and return well after sunset.

The colonial penal system into which Pepe was entering was a relic of the eighteenth century, antiquated and barbaric by the standards of the time.[38] The pace of modernization in Spain lagged well behind that of its European and North American counterparts, a problem partly due to ongoing political instability dating back to the Napoleonic wars earlier in the century. The consequences for the Spanish economy were a nearly century-long downward spiral of debt, disease, poverty, and backwardness. The timing of the war's onset in Cuba was especially bad for Spain, as in 1868 Spain was still struggling through the aftermath of the 1865 cholera epidemic as well as the latest in a series of subsistence crises. The resulting rise in migrations to Latin America and especially to Spain's remaining colonies put further pressure on Cuba's already tenuous economic situation.[39]

Spain's penal system was no exception to the general malaise. In contrast to the modern penitentiaries and evolving approaches to incarceration in North America and elsewhere in Europe, Spain's penal system at home and in the colonies remained a thinly veiled system of indenture. Prisoners were put to work on public works projects and often hired out to private plantations and even homes.[40] In the colonies as well as in the mother country, inmates were housed in converted military forts or convents and slept in former military barracks. Inmates were exposed to crowding, poor hygienic conditions, inadequate food and water, corporal punishments, and grinding work routines that even healthier, better-fed laborers would have found daunting. Reports of sexual abuse and violence among prisoners were frequent; those who did not die at the hands of guards or fellow prisoners risked more drawn-out deaths from cholera or tuberculosis, which circulated easily through the prison population due to inadequate sanitation and poor ventilation in the barracks.[41] From its administration to rank-and-file officers, the prison system was run by the military, which explains much of its brutality.[42]

Luckily for the Martís, the Spanish penal system was as profoundly inefficient as it was cruel. Beneath its apparently implacable bureaucracy lay an informal network of patronage and other contingencies that favored certain sectors of the population—namely, whites, members of the military and their families, and people with connections in the hierarchy. Racial classifications played a marked if informal role throughout the system, manifesting in everything from the length of prisoners' sentences to their quality of life as inmates. Prisoners classified as nonwhite drew harsher work assignments and more frequent and severe corporal punishments when they committed infractions. They received fewer privileges and even inferior accommodations within a prison itself. Political prisoners—a classification by which the system distinguished civilians convicted of conspiracy from those who actively joined the revolution—were also disproportionately white and middle- or even upper-class, and their treatment in captivity was less severe. Such prisoners were generally housed separately from other kinds of inmates and rarely mixed with the general prison population.[43]

Most importantly for the Martís, wealthy or military families with connections in the prison administration could work the system to win favors for their own. Concessions could range from easier work assignments and days off to permission to visit family members or even reduced or commuted sentences. Connected families could expect longer and more frequent visits and were allowed to supplement food rations and other necessities for their imprisoned kin.[44]

As bleak as Pepe's outlook seemed, Mariano Martí could draw on two significant contacts in the hope of reducing his son's stay in prison and protecting him as much as possible from its hazards. The most important of these was José María Sardá y Ginorella, who ran the San Lázaro quarries (*canteras*) and leased the site as a concession from the colonial government. Sardá was a friend from Mariano Martí's days as chief inspector of Batabanó, and the former officer appealed to his friend to spare Pepe the hardships of work in the *canteras* and assign him some less onerous task. He similarly appealed to Ramón Miguel, a distinguished former officer and a friend Mariano had known since they first journeyed together to the island nearly twenty years before.[45] Although now retired, Miguel remained influential among the colonial leadership, and Mariano hoped Miguel's intercession on Pepe's behalf might hasten his release. Given the tense situation on the island due to the ongoing war, the Martís knew that their efforts would not prevent Pepe from serving at least some of his sentence and that he would suffer, but they strove to do as much as they could for their only son.

ON THE MORNING OF APRIL 4, 1870, PEPE DID FINALLY JOIN the work brigade and took his first predawn walk through the empty Havana streets to the *cantera*. The official record shows that newly registered Prisoner

#113 was assigned to a whites-only work unit, in keeping with the colonial penal system's racial policy. His hair was cut, and he was issued the gray, loose-fitting uniform that rendered him indistinguishable from his fellow prisoners. Finally, an iron shackle was bound to his right ankle and linked to a heavy chain around his waist; he wore the shackle and chain throughout his prison term.[46]

Once processed, Pepe settled into the grueling routine of the work brigade. He later wrote about the daily walks through Havana from the prison to the *canteras*:

> And what is it?
> Nothing.
> To be beaten, trampled, dragged, in the same street, by the same house, by the very window, from which a month before we received our mother's blessing, what is that?
> Nothing.
> To spend there, in water to our waists, with picks in our hands, shackles on our feet, the hours that in bygone days we had spent sheltered in our homes because the sun hurt our eyes and the heat damaged our health, what is that?
> Nothing.
> To return blind, lame, worn, bruised, lacerated, to the sound of clubbings and profanities, of blows and jeers, through the same streets where months before they had seen me stroll serenely, at ease, with my beloved sister in my arms and the peace of contentment in my heart, what is this?
> Also nothing.
> A horrible, terrible, heartbreaking nothing![47]

The "nothing" of Pepe's daily march to and from the *canteras*, physically trying as it was, actually did pale in comparison to the mental anguish, the existential horrors that came with the realization of actually being imprisoned and enslaved, the grinding labors and abuses of life in the quarries, and the squalid, disease-riddled conditions in which the prisoners lived.

Pepe's first months of incarceration followed the decades-old routine established for prison laborers. He rose at 5 a.m. to a breakfast of coffee and bread and departed for the *canteras* by 6. The prisoners worked a five-hour shift before breaking after 11 a.m. for the midday meal of beans and rice accompanied by a daily shot of rum. After the customary siesta, prisoners began a four-hour shift at 1 p.m. At 5 p.m. the work brigades returned to the prison, where they would take an evening meal of beans and rice with the occasional bit of meat, usually pork. Prisoners participated in compulsory prayers just before lockdown and lights out at 9 p.m. The only variations in this routine were Sunday mass and visits from relatives for those allowed to receive them.[48]

Prisoners' files from the nineteenth century reveal very little about their contacts with the outside, suggesting that visits were neither regular nor often granted. Before the late nineteenth century, it was not even customary for prison administrators to keep relatives apprised of changes in a prisoner's health or general condition; as late as 1880, documented cases exist of deceased prisoners being buried before next of kin were notified.[49] In the case of political prisoners, relatives may have avoided their imprisoned kin for fear of being suspected themselves. Permission to visit prisoners was not automatically granted to those who wished it, and it took Mariano Martí significant time and trouble to achieve this privilege.

Mariano's efforts were part of a larger campaign by the entire Martí family to help Pepe in any way possible, with the ultimate goal of having him released early from prison. These efforts were not entirely altruistic; with aging Mariano's job prospects dwindling and five of the couple's six surviving daughters not yet married, their imprisoned son represented the family's only real hope of economic survival. Mariano limited his lobbying efforts to his own contacts within the government, while his wife took a more direct approach. According to later statements by Pepe's sister Amelia, Leonor and the Martí daughters made daily visits to the offices of Antonio Caballero de Rodas, Cuba's new captain-general, in hopes of gaining an audience with him. When after multiple visits they finally gained admission to his office, Leonor was prepared. The Martí women kneeled collectively at Caballero's feet and pleaded with him to transfer Pepe from the *canteras* to a less arduous work assignment. Leonor also delivered to the captain-general the following letter:

> Esteemed Sir:
>   You see here before you the sisters and saddened mother of the disgraced José Martí, a youth who has just turned 17 and has been sentenced to six years' hard labor for three words written when he was barely 15 years old, in a letter he addressed to a schoolmate, which never reached its intended recipient but was discovered during a search of another schoolmate's house 10 months ago. Because of this, Esteemed Sir, I see my son today in shackles alongside the worst of criminals, and not having in all the world any more support than that of my only son, that by working he may help support his six younger sisters, and with his father being old and sick and unable to bear such hardship, and trusting in Your Excellency's merciful heart, it is because of all this that I venture to appeal to Your Excellency to spare my poor son from such a harsh

sentence and [replace it] with any other that Your Excellency finds it appropriate to impose that will not deprive him of working to alleviate our shameful condition, I pledge Esteemed Sir that we will not abandon him, that with my counsel and your indulgence he will be a man useful to his country and that otherwise he may become a villain if he is treated too harshly.

This is, Sir, what this unhappy mother hopes to gain by your goodness.[50]

Curiously, Leonor's letter to the captain-general does not mention her husband's history of service to Spain, and her reasons for this omission are not clear. Perhaps she believed that he would already know of Mariano's successful military career and subsequent civilian service; perhaps she mentioned it in the personal appeal that accompanied the letter. Or perhaps she feared that her husband's spotty postmilitary record had somehow tarnished his reputation and lessened its potential to sway the captain-general. Whether because of Leonor's ardent appeal or her husband's efforts, Mariano did eventually gain permission to visit Pepe in prison.[51]

From the sequence of events that followed quickly upon Mariano's visit—and his having witnessed firsthand the physical hardships that Pepe was suffering—we can surmise that the visit occurred no later than July 1870. Mariano took with him some small pads or pillows that Leonor had fashioned to protect Pepe's skin from the constant irritation of the shackles he wore around the clock. This kind of direct physical contact with prisoners was expressly prohibited by Spanish regulations, which stipulated that visitors had to remain behind a fence at a distance of two *varas* (about six feet) from the prisoner. This rule was often flouted or ignored altogether at privately owned work sites, where despite the guards' presence the proprietor's workplace rules held sway.[52] It is not surprising, then, that as a personal friend of the owner Mariano did not spend his visit behind a barrier.

When Mariano went to place the pads on his son's body, he discovered that the shackles around Pepe's waist and ankle had already caused considerable damage. Martí would later describe

> that bitter day on which he managed to see me, and I tried to hide from him the fissures of my body, and he to place some small pillows from my mother to prevent the rubbing of the shackles, and he saw at last, the day after he had seen me walking the prison halls, those purulent sores, those limbs bled white, that mingling of blood and dust, of matter and mud, on which they forced me to support myself, and run, and run! Bitterest of days! Clinging to that unformed matter, he looked at me

in horror, as he stealthily dressed [the wounds], again looked up at me, and, at last, feverishly embracing the mangled leg, broke into sobs. His tears fell upon my open sores; I struggled to dry his tears as heartbreaking sobs choked in his throat. Then the work bell rang, and an arm tore me roughly away, and he remained kneeling where my blood had wet the ground, and I was prodded by the stick toward the pile of quarries that awaited us for the next six hours.[53]

Distraught by his son's deteriorating physical state, Mariano quickly prevailed upon his friend Sardá to visit Pepe at the prison and see for himself how urgently the young man needed a transfer to a less onerous work assignment. Sardá's visit to Pepe confirmed Mariano's assertions and more; he discovered that Pepe's eyes were being seriously damaged by exposure to the harsh sunlight and ubiquitous limestone dust raised by the workers' picks and shovels. More critical still was an inguinal injury, likely a hernia, which Pepe claimed to have suffered due to a self-inflicted blow with a heavy chain. The constant pain in his lower abdomen severely hampered his ability even to walk. Alarmed by Pepe's condition, which proved even worse than Mariano could glimpse during his brief visit, Sardá appealed to the prison authorities to transfer Pepe from the *canteras* to less taxing work in the prison itself. Leonor's anguished appeal in her August 5 letter to the captain-general emphasizes both Pepe's tender age and her own hardships without "the salary [Pepe] earned as a clerk, a salary that, combined with the recourse to her own needlework, subvented however limitedly the expenses of a numerous family of the weaker sex."[54]

A reply to Leonor dated August 8 indicated that Sardá's request would not be immediately granted but had been relayed to Captain-General Caballero with the stipulation that "His Excellency will deign to resolve [the case] in the manner he deems most expedient."[55] An internal communication dated August 16 orders that Leonor be notified to present proof of her son's age, in the form of a certificate of baptism. She received this request on August 20 and presented Pepe's birth certificate to the authorities two days later.[56] Another week passed before the captain-general's office received confirmation of Leonor's compliance; by month's end Pepe was finally reassigned to the cigar factory inside the prison, a move that likely saved his life. During those final days before Pepe's transfer, Leonor received a letter from her son, dated August 28, along with a photograph of himself in his shackles and prison uniform (figure 3.1). On the back of the picture she found this brief poem:

> See me, mother, and for love's sake don't cry:
> If, enslaved by my age and my doctrines,

FIGURE 3.1. *The famous 1870 photograph of Martí in his prison uniform and shackles, copies of which he sent to his mother and Fermín Valdés Domínguez. On the back of Valdés Domínguez's photo, Martí wrote: "Brother in pain, never see / In me the slave that cowardly cries; / See the robust image of my soul / And the beautiful page of my history."* JMOC 17:30. *Photo: Archivo de* BOHEMIA, *Havana.*

I have filled your heart with thorns,
Remember that among the thorns grow flowers.[57]

As she read her son's words, Leonor suffered the pain of a very different, unexpected thorn: on August 29 the Martís' youngest child, Dolores "Lolita" Eustaquia, died after a brief illness. She was not yet five years old.[58]

Mariano's networking efforts soon yielded benefits beyond rescuing Pepe from hard labor. After barely six weeks of work in the prison cigar factory, on October 13 Pepe was delivered from his Havana prison into exile on Isla de

Pinos (Isle of Pines), an island roughly fifty miles south of Cuba's western province of Pinar del Rio. More importantly, the young Martí's destination on the
island was El Abra timber plantation owned and operated by José María Sardá,
Mariano's longtime friend. It was likely through Sardá's efforts that Mariano
was able to visit Pepe in prison, and Sardá's intercession with Spanish authorities may have contributed to the young man's transfer to the less arduous labor
of the prison cigar factory. Pepe's two-month stay at El Abra amounted to little
more than house arrest; Sardá removed his shackles immediately upon the
teen's arrival at the port of Júcaro and placed the debilitated young man under
the care of his own wife in the family home.[59]

Under the care of Trinidad Valdés, whom Pepe affectionately called doña
Trina, he began to revive physically and intellectually. He returned to reading,
discovering among other works Victor Hugo's *Les Misérables*; he gained weight
and recovered from various physical ailments, including the chronic conjunctivitis that had threatened to destroy his eyesight.[60] Pepe's experience at El Abra
did not erase the bitterness of his prison days, but it gave him much-needed
respite at a crucial moment of his physical and intellectual development. Pepe
was sufficiently grateful to later send several gifts from Spain, among them a
crucifix dedicated to doña Trina, "who placed upon my life maternal care and
hands," and a photograph on the back of which he wrote, "Trina, my only regret
in having known you is the sadness of having to leave you so soon."[61]

Martí's unexpectedly brief stay at El Abra was a direct result of Leonor's
efforts. In a letter dated December 6, Leonor petitioned Spanish authorities for
permission to have Pepe continue his studies in Spain:

> Da. [doña] Leonor Pérez, native of the [Canary] Islands, and resident
> of this city, with all due respect to Your Excellency asks: that her son,
> presently deported to the Isla de Pinos, and that being an inappropri-
> ate place to advance his career and provide some relief to his impover-
> ished family [illegible writing]. I come to Your Excellency to plead for
> his transfer to the Peninsula [mainland Spain] where he may overcome
> earlier difficulties. This she hopes [to be granted] from the elevated sen-
> sibilities of Your Excellency. Havana, December 6, 1870.[62]

This permission was granted less than a week later, and by December 18
authorities on the Isla de Pinos sent word to Havana that Pepe was headed
back to prison, where he would await permission to board a steamer bound for
Spain. In the weeks that followed, Mariano and Leonor continued to work on
their son's behalf, expediting his passport, forwarding school transcripts to the
peninsular authorities, and securing permission to see him one last time before
his departure. Although Mariano's networking efforts undoubtedly saved his

son from much hardship, it was Leonor's formal appeal through official channels that ultimately got his sentence commuted entirely, though at a high price. Pepe would now be exiled to Spain, where he would live, work, and study far from the protection of his family and friends.

ON THE MORNING OF JANUARY 15, 1871, LEONOR AND MARIano Martí, their daughters, and some fifty friends and well-wishers joined Pepe in Havana harbor to see him off. It was a scene of much anguish, his parents especially still torn over their choice of exile rather than continued house arrest at El Abra. Mariano delivered to his son all the money he was able to raise in the brief period since learning of Pepe's impending departure, enough for the journey and for Pepe to establish himself upon arrival in Madrid.[63] Neither Leonor, nor Mariano, nor Pepe, nor his sisters succeeded in comforting each other with the idea that Pepe was finally free or that they might all be together again someday. In truth, none of them knew whether they would ever see each other again.

HAVANA FAREWELL

*F*OR ALL THE FRIENDS AND LOVED ONES WHO AS-
sembled to see him off, the single most important person in
Pepe's life to that point could not be there. Rafael María de Mendive
had himself been exiled since May 1869 and was now living in New
York City. It is thus indicative of Pepe's lasting devotion to his erstwhile mentor that he wrote this impassioned letter in the waning
hours of his life in Cuba:

> January 15, 1871
> Mr. Mendive:
>   In 2 hours I depart, exiled to Spain. I have suffered much, but
> have the conviction that I have known how to suffer. And if I have
> had sufficient strength to do so, and if I believe I now have the
> strength to truly be a man, I owe it only to you, and from you and
> only from you have I gained what goodness and virtue I possess.
>   Tell Micaela [Mendive's wife] that if I have committed many
> imprudent acts, the grace with which she forgives them makes me
> love her all the more.
>   And to Paulina and to Pepe and to Alfredo [their children] and
> to everyone, all my love.
>   Many hugs to Mario, and for you all of the heart and soul of
> your son and disciple
>   MARTÍ[1]

Twenty months before writing this letter, sixteen-year-old Pepe had
suffered profoundly the departure of his mentor into exile. Now,
having been forged in the furnace of his own experience of impris-

onment and exile, the author of this brief note reveals much about his own transformation. Much of the groundwork for that transformation, as the letter happily acknowledges, was the intellectual and political foundation that Pepe acquired under Mendive's tutelage. The experiential engine that completed the boy's psychical growth to adulthood—from Pepe to José—was undoubtedly his nearly fifteen-month ordeal in Spanish custody.

Pepe's bond with Mendive was not diminished by the teacher's forced absence or the disciple's imprisonment, and Pepe's enduring devotion is evident in his letter. Just as clear is the relegation to secondary status of his biological father, Mariano, despite his efforts to free Pepe and obvious anguish at having seen him so broken by his ordeal. That Mariano merits not a mention in the letter is less significant than Pepe's implicit dismissal of his father's having any influence in his life and development; if Pepe had the strength to survive his prison experience and the "goodness and virtue" to not become embittered by it, he credits this singly to Mendive's influence and example.

Amid Pepe's declarations of gratitude and enduring devotion, however, lies an implicit farewell to his beloved mentor. For all the hardships visited upon the young man's body and mind, the definition of suffering that emerges in this letter is far from a passive one. To successfully bear such punishment for one's convictions was already for Pepe an achievement and a point of pride: "I have learned," he asserts, "how to suffer." That he says as much in his last known letter to Mendive is as much a declaration of gratitude as of graduation. For if Pepe had suffered much, he had to learn to do so without the supporting and structuring presence of his family and his teacher; whatever Leonor and Mariano did for their son during his ordeal and however well Mendive's guidance and example prepared him for it, the hardships of prison and hard labor—and now exile—were his alone.

Nine years would pass before Pepe would see Mendive again, a disillusioning encounter that would serve as their real farewell. In the interim, Pepe's newfound awareness of how to suffer would become a staple of his private correspondence and inner make-up, though he would take care not to let it inhabit his public persona or writings in a debilitating way. From the very beginning of Pepe's exile, a palpable and increasingly well-guarded split between the man's public life and inner demons will begin to emerge in his writings. His first major publication in exile, "El presidio político en Cuba" (Political Prison in Cuba), focuses not on his own suffering but on that of others—a series of portraits of fellow prisoners who, like himself, learned under the worst possible circumstances how to suffer with grace, dignity, and a quiet defiance that would come to characterize Martí's finest works as a writer and thinker.[2]

For now, however, for a young man at the threshold of a lifetime of hardship and uncertainty, having learned how to suffer was already the most valuable lesson of all.

Part Two

EXILE (1871–1880)

CHAPTER FOUR

Spain

Glory and triumph are no more than a stimulus for
the fulfillment of duty.

"THE SPANISH REPUBLIC BEFORE THE
CUBAN REVOLUTION," 1873

THANKS TO HIS FAMILY'S RELENTLESS EFFORTS, MARTÍ
served only a fraction of his original sentence of six years' hard
labor—four months in the labor camp and a little over a year in custody overall.[1]
The Martís succeeded in freeing their son but at a high cost: the young Martí
would be exiled to Spain.

Martí's prison experience left physical and emotional marks that remained
for the rest of his life. The young man already displayed a martyr's leanings early
in his prison term: "To die for the fatherland / Is to live all the more."[2] The
brief but acute hardship of the labor camp fueled the young Martí's burgeoning
conviction that suffering for his country was not only necessary but desirable.

On the morning of January 15, 1871, a somewhat recovered Martí stood on
the dock in Havana harbor with his parents and several of his sisters as he was
shortly to embark for Spain on the steamer *Guipúzcoa*.[3] Although he would
briefly reunite with his family later in Mexico City, the occasion marked the
last time the teenager would see his assembled family and friends in one place.
The tearful farewell in Havana also marked the start of an adult life filled with
many such scenes, with sudden, hurried departures and fitful, restless travels.
As much as his adolescent experience in prison forged and pained him, adulthood for the young Martí coincided with the onset of this journey—the onset,
that is, of his life as a more or less permanent exile.

MARTÍ SPENT HIS EIGHTEENTH BIRTHDAY ALONE ON THE *Guipúzcoa*, his solitude reinforced by the vast ocean that surrounded the steamer on its eastbound journey. His health deteriorated significantly during the crossing. Beyond the lingering aches and pains stemming from his recent incarceration, he suffered from ongoing fevers and a persistent pain in his right testicle. He spent most of his waking hours alone in his cabin, chatting occasionally with the ship's majordomo and with fellow passengers at mealtimes.

There was one passenger on the *Guipúzcoa*, however, whom Martí did know: Lieutenant Colonel Mariano Gil de Palacios, the commanding officer of the Havana prison during Martí's incarceration, now apparently reassigned to the mother country. Gil managed to board without being recognized, but Martí spotted him among the passengers lunching in the ship's dining room on the second day of the voyage. According to eyewitness accounts, the young exile then proceeded to share with his fellow diners tales of his experiences in prison and of the abuses and hardships of the labor camp. Having won their sympathy and outrage, Martí then identified Gil as the prison warden responsible for the evils he described. Infuriated by the young man's audacity but helpless to do anything about it, a humiliated Gil retired to his cabin.[4]

THE *GUIPÚZCOA*'S TWO-WEEK JOURNEY ENDED WITH ITS arrival on February 1 at the port of Cádiz, where Martí rested a few days while arranging onward travel to Madrid. By the sixteenth the newly exiled Martí reached the capital city, presenting himself to the provincial government upon arrival as required by the terms of his exile.[5] His health had deteriorated significantly since leaving Cuba; aside from the fevers and the pain in his testicle, Martí continued to suffer from an unhealed sore on his right ankle caused by the constant friction of his prison shackle. He had the additional misfortune of arriving in the midst of the Spanish winter, which although mild by northern European standards would still have had a significant impact on a new, unacclimated arrival, particularly one in an already weakened state.[6]

However much Spain lagged behind its European neighbors economically, the Madrid that young Martí discovered in February 1871 was a significantly more modern and sophisticated place than the Havana he had left behind. It was Europe's sixth-largest city, its population of more than 360,000 dwarfing Havana's, which at some 200,000 was easily the island's largest city.[7] Most of Madrid's streets were gaslit, and the city's many tree-lined roads and public squares and gardens were beautiful and well kept. It was in the midst of a growth spurt, with many new buildings and several palaces — even an entirely new neighborhood, Salamanca — under construction. The year 1869 also saw the establishment of Madrid's first public library, the first in the city to allow its patrons to check out books.[8] Most attractive to Martí was the capital's thriving arts scene, which boasted no less than eleven active theaters presenting a wide array of musical and dramatic works. The Museo del Prado, established in 1819, was even then a world-class museum of European art with an unrivaled collection of Spanish masterpieces.[9] Martí's deep and far-ranging interests in music and art found their origins during his first years in exile.

But Madrid was also the capital of an empire in decline and its acutely unstable government. Isabella II, the monarch responsible for the tentative steps Spain had taken toward modernity in the forms of a railroad system and some industrialization in the northern regions, was driven into exile in 1868; a very shaky coalition of liberals, moderates, and conservative republicans managed the country—badly—for the next three years while searching for a suitable successor for the deposed Isabella. By the time of Martí's arrival in Madrid, the Italian-born Amadeo I had sat on the Spanish throne for all of ninety-two days. Amadeo's precarious position as an outsider was further compromised, perhaps fatally, by the murder of his most powerful supporter, General Juan Prim y Prats. Prim led the 1868 revolt against Isabella and played a major role in Amadeo's selection; he was assassinated in Madrid just two days before the new king's coronation.[10]

Realizing the urgency of establishing himself in the mother country, the newly arrived Martí moved quickly to contact fellow Cuban exiles in the city. Chief among these was Carlos Sauvalle, a fervent early supporter of the Ten Years' War who preceded Martí in exile by a year. Sauvalle had also been one of the chief organizers of the 1869 theater program that prompted the Voluntario-led riot outside Havana's Villanueva theater. Sauvalle was a regular contributor to pro-independence newspapers including his own publication, *El Laborante*, which he ran until his deportation to Spain in October 1870.[11]

By providing emotional and material support during a difficult time, Sauvalle filled the paternal void left by Martí's separation from Rafael María de Mendive, the first of several older men to temporarily replace Mariano Martí in the young man's heart and mind. Martí and Sauvalle had been casual acquaintances in Havana, possibly through their mutual friend Mendive. But in Madrid the thirty-two-year-old Sauvalle's friendship became invaluable to the young Martí, partly because his home was an unofficial center for Cuban exiles all over Madrid. Sauvalle actively supported Martí's anticolonial writings, going as far as financing his first major post-exile publications. He also may have played a major role in Martí's initiation into Freemasonry by introducing him to prominent members of a Cuban exile community that included leaders of local Masonic lodges.

A July 1, 1871, document from *Caballeros Cruzados* (Gentlemen of the Cross) no. 62 identifies the Madrid lodge's grand secretary as "Anáhuac," which Martí used as a pen name and later as a pseudonym in his revolutionary activities. In keeping with the Masonic tradition of concealing members' identities behind pseudonyms, Martí chose "Anáhuac," an indigenous term for Mexico's *mesa central* that today encompasses Mexico City, as his Masonic name. Martí signed other Masonic documents from this period with his real name, which confirms his identity as Anáhuac. These and other documents suggest that Martí was initiated into Freemasonry shortly after his arrival in Spain in January 1871.[12] Although later statements by Fermín Valdés Domínguez and others attest to the new arrival's quickly established reputation among fellow Cubans as a young man of ability and character, Martí's rapid rise through the Masonic ranks is most easily explained by Sauvalle's early efforts to integrate him into the exile community's civic and professional elites.

It was thanks to Sauvalle as well that Martí found employment as a private tutor, with pay that covered his living expenses but not his various medical needs. His first two such engagements were in the homes of Cuban Leandro Álvarez Torrijos and Barbarita Echevarría, the Cuban-born widow of Spanish General Joaquín Ravenet y Marentes.[13] Beyond her strong sympathy for his political views, Echevarría quickly grew personally fond of the frail young man and heartily recommended him to others as a tutor. Martí's relationship with Echevarría may have blossomed into something beyond friendship and political affinity; their subsequent correspondence suggests that the two became lovers, a liaison that lasted throughout Martí's time in Spain but that neither ever publicly acknowledged.[14]

Most importantly, however, Sauvalle shepherded Martí through his first major illness after leaving the island and eventually paid for the operation that may have saved the younger man's life. As his closest friend in Madrid, Sauvalle was the first to recognize in Martí's symptoms and general poor health the possibility of a more serious illness. He urged Martí to seek medical help, but even as the pain and fatigue became chronic the younger man did not relent, largely out of a refusal to allow Sauvalle to pay for his treatment. But by April his condition had further deteriorated, with the pained testicle now alarmingly swollen and the hernia and ankle lesion showing no signs of improving. It likely was the cumulative effect of all these maladies that compelled Martí to finally seek medical help.[15]

Sauvalle took him to see Dr. José Ramón Gómez Pamo, who immediately recognized the seriousness of the young man's condition. Gómez Pamo determined that Martí's recurrent fevers were due to an infection of the lymph nodes, adenopathy, in the groin, where the swelling made even walking painful. In the years before the discovery of antibiotics, the only viable treatment for infections such as Martí's was to drain the afflicted area as many times as necessary until the swelling and pain subsided on their own. With no other option available, Gómez Pamo recommended just such a surgical procedure to try to ease the painful swelling in the testicle.[16]

Martí was eventually diagnosed with sarcoidosis, a disease in which groups of inflammatory cells form nodes or nodules that can become extremely painful. Symptoms related to sarcoidosis include many that Martí exhibited during this period, such as chronic fatigue, weight loss, aches and pains throughout the body, dry eyes, and blurred vision. This diagnosis is consistent with Martí's various symptoms, including swelling and infection of the lymph nodes. Although the cause of sarcoidosis remains unknown, it can often be triggered by an unrelated infection or external injury. This perhaps explains the acute pain in Martí's right testicle that was due to a growth called a sarcocele likely caused by the constant friction of the prison chains on his right groin. Dr. Hilario Candela performed the surgery sometime during late April or May, and Martí relented and allowed Sauvalle to pay for the procedure.[17]

With his symptoms reduced but not eliminated, Martí immersed himself in his writing, the lingering pain perhaps inspiring his first major works. During 1871 Martí published several essays in Spanish and U.S. newspapers, including "Castillo," an early version of what would become his first major publication: the account of his prison experiences tersely titled "El presidio político en Cuba" (Political Prison in Cuba).[18] Although Martí resisted Sauvalle's offer to pay his medical expenses, he agreed to have his friend fund the production of "El presidio político en Cuba," which was published in Madrid in the summer of 1871. The long essay was a scathing exposé of daily life in the colonial labor camps, revealing in excruciating detail the physical and mental abuses of political convicts.

Martí strategically chose to make "El presidio político en Cuba" less a memoir of his own suffering in prison than a Dantean gallery of the suffering of others. The essay presents a series of portraits of fellow prisoners bearing hardships far beyond Martí's own, among them the senile centenarian Juan de Dios Socarrás and twelve-year-old Lino Figueredo, who was not excused from work even after contracting smallpox. The essay is also likely somewhat fictionalized for dramatic effect; although subsequent research has affirmed the identity of Nicolás del Castillo, a wealthy Cuban landowner sentenced to hard labor, no such evidence has emerged for Socarrás or Figueredo, who were probably composites of actual persons Martí saw and stories he heard in prison. Castillo was not the septuagenarian of Martí's essay, according to others who knew him, and was only sixty when he left prison.[19] The discrepancies do not detract from the undeniable power of the essay, which presents the suffering prisoners less as individuals than as examples of Spanish cruelty.

In "El presidio político en Cuba," an indignant Martí not only indicts the

Spanish officers and administrators who inflicted this suffering but apportions the greatest blame on a passive, willfully ignorant civilian population that did nothing to stop them even as citizens "clamored unthinkingly" for their own rights:

> When nations err, when out of cowardice or indifference they commit or excuse misconduct, if their last vestige of energy disappears, if the final, or perhaps the first, expression of their will keeps an awkward silence, such nations weep, they atone for their faults, they perish, mocked and humiliated and shattered, as they mocked and destroyed and humiliated in their turn.
> The idea never succeeds in covering the intoxication in the blood.
> The idea never excuses the crime or the barbarous refinement of the crime.[20]

With the publication of "El presidio político en Cuba," Martí gained his first significant recognition among Cuban exiles in Spain and the United States. Aside from its importance as the first mature articulation of Martí's anticolonial philosophy, the early essay established several traits that would become familiar features of Martí's later work. Most prominent among these is the eighteen-year-old Martí's already developed penchant for the idea of martyrdom. Although the term appears only four times in the essay, it always comes precisely in the context of divine justice, in keeping with the larger Old Testament-flavored theme of prophesy and godly intervention. "God exists," Martí announces on the opening page, "and I come in his name to shatter in Spanish souls that cold vessel that encloses their tears."[21] After describing the Spanish guards beating the exhausted Nicolás del Castillo, he declares that martyrdom

> for one's country is God himself, as the good, as ideas of spontaneous universal generosity. Beat him, wound him, bruise him. You are too vile for him to respond blow for blow, wound for wound. I feel within me this God, I have within me this God; this God in me feels pity for you, more pity than horror or disdain.[22]

Later, Martí describes the boy Lino as leading a "martyr's life." But the links connecting martyrdom, political will, and divine retribution appear most clearly at the essay's close as Martí urges Spaniards to stop their government's abuses lest the martyr's tears "evaporate and rise to the skies and condense; and if you do not stop them, the sky will collapse upon you."[23]

If for the young Martí martyrdom was God's vehicle, the author himself was the prophet who would deliver God's people from suffering. His description of Cuban Creoles as "the longest-suffering race" ready to trade "a comfortable and secure life for one nomadic and persecuted" reinforces the essay's focus on martyrdom and divine retribution.[24] The essay's most explicitly Old Testament admonition has Martí casting himself not as Moses but as Daniel, who was called before decadent King Balthazar to interpret three mysterious words that appeared on his wall during a drunken feast with his wives and concubines. In the eponymous Old Testament book, Daniel, a learned spiritual exile, reads in the words God's judgment against the king and his undoing:

> [Thou] hast lifted up thyself against the Lord of heaven . . . and thou hast praised the gods of silver, and gold, of brass, iron, wood, and stone . . . and the God in whose hand thy breath is, and whose are all thy ways, hast thou not glorified:
> Then was the part of the hand sent from him, and this writing was written.
> And this is the writing that was written: MENE, MENE, TEKEL, UPHARSIN.
> This is the interpretation of the thing: MENE, God hath numbered thy kingdom and finished it.
> TEKEL, thou art weighed in the balances, and art found wanting.
> PERES, thy kingdom is divided, and given to the Medes and Persians.[25]

The Spanish empire would not fall as quickly or decisively as King Balthazar, who was murdered on the very night of Daniel's prophecy.[26] Yet behind Martí's portrayal of Cuba as the insignificant insect that would "surprise Balthazar at his banquet and be for the unguarded Government the *Mane, Thecel, Phares* of modern prophesies" lies his own self-characterization as Daniel, reading the writing on the colonial wall and foreseeing death and disgrace for the empire.[27]

THE PUBLICATION OF "EL PRESIDIO POLÍTICO EN CUBA" called Cuban exiles' attention to Martí as a pro-independence leader at precisely the moment that a political breakthrough seemed possible, if not imminent, for the island colony. The recent establishment of King Amadeo I, a liberal who promised to reign as a modern constitutional monarch, also raised hopes among the exiles for Cuban autonomy or even independence. During this same period Martí was admitted to the law school at the Universidad Central de Madrid and enrolled in courses in Roman law, political and administrative law, and European political science.[28]

Pro-empire Spaniards likewise began to take notice of the new Cuban voice for independence; an anti-Cuban article published in the pro-empire newspaper *La Prensa* in early September triggered an exchange of letters published in Madrid newspapers, with the Cubans' contributions appearing anonymously as "Various Cubans." The public debate culminated with Martí's and Sauvalle's names being identified as the letters' authors in *La Prensa*, and they co-signed a September 22 letter rebuking *La Prensa* and the unnamed person at the liberal paper *Jurado Federal* who divulged their identities.[29] The debate led to the establishment in November of the League of Spanish Anti-Filibustering Newspapers, an alliance of Madrid's most conservative papers to oppose any change in Spain's relationship with its remaining colonies.[30]

For the rest of the spring and summer of 1871, Martí maintained his busy life as a law student, tutor, and political activist despite his precarious health. Outside of work and his classes, he spent many hours in the research library at Madrid's Ateneo, a private literary and cultural center and gathering place for the city's intellectuals. There he studied and kept up with the latest news from Cuba and the rest of the world. In contrast to his stellar academic record as a child, Martí struggled in his first year of law school. Due to the combination of failing health, the distractions of his political activities, and the stresses and struggles of an exile's life, the brilliant young man failed two of his first four courses at the Universidad Central de Madrid.[31]

With the onset of winter Martí's health again began to decline, his relentless work ethic and the colder weather taking a toll on him. The mental stress of his public quarrel with anti-independence pundits, culminating with his outing as a Cuban activist in the pages of in Madrid's newspapers, may have contributed to the decline in his health. The most severe blow to Martí during this time, however, was not physical but an unexpected emotional shock that, along with other factors, triggered his second major illness in seven months.

The medical students enrolled at the Universidad de Havana were almost uniformly pro-independence, and many of them openly supported the war against Spanish rule. In November 1871 a group of forty-five first-year medical students were accused of vandalizing the grave of the journalist and Spanish patriot Gonzalo de Castañón Escarazo, who was killed the previous year in a duel in Key West. Among those students was Martí's best friend, Fermín Valdés Domínguez, with whom he had been arrested in Havana and whom he had not seen since their sentencing the year before. Although the government had little if any evidence against the students, an intense public campaign by Cuban Voluntarios compelled the authorities to press charges.[32]

On November 25 the accused students were arrested while attending class. An initial tribunal that exonerated most of the defendants, finding only a handful guilty of minor offenses, led to a redoubled outcry by Voluntarios and their political allies. Thanks to their pervasive influence on the colonial government, heightened by the ongoing war against Cuban rebels, the authorities again relented and held a second trial, at which eight of the students were sentenced to death. Of the other defendants, eleven were sentenced to six years in prison, twenty to four years, and four to six months. Two of the original forty-five were released through the intervention of their professor, the Spaniard Dr. Juan Manuel Sánchez de Bustamante. None of the condemned was more than twenty-one years old; the youngest was sixteen. The political nature of the entire process is perhaps best exemplified by the sentencing to death of seventeen-year-old Carlos Verdugo Martínez, who according to testimony, was not even in Havana when the alleged vandalism occurred.[33]

At 4:30 on the morning of November 27, the eight condemned students were executed by firing squad. They were blindfolded and made to kneel, hands bound behind their backs, then shot two at a time. At least two Spanish officers, including Captain Federico Capdevila Miñano, who represented the students at trial, resigned upon hearing of the executions and the manner in which they were performed.[34]

Valdés Domínguez was among those students sentenced to six years in prison, but Martí did not know that. Rumors of the students' arrests and executions circulated in the exile community for days before the first reports appeared in the papers, and at first no one knew for certain the number of students arrested or which ones had been shot. That uncertainty—along with the conviction that his friend was among the detained and perhaps dead by an executioner's hand—exacerbated the already frail Martí's condition. Although news of Valdés Domínguez's incarceration assuaged the worst of his fears, the initial shock had taken its toll. By early December the pain in Martí's right testicle necessitated additional surgery to drain fluid from it; the procedure succeeded in lessening but not fully relieving the pain. Martí did not return home for some time after the operation, convalescing instead in the home of Sauvalle, further suggesting that the procedure did not achieve its desired effect of restoring his health.[35]

By year's end Martí was well enough to return home, somewhat restored physically but still plagued by thoughts of the imprisoned Valdés Domínguez. His December 30 poem "¡Mi madre!" (My Mother!) captures the loneliness and despair of a sleepless night:

> I did not think of you: I had forgotten
> That only you were my life. . . .
>
> Sleep escapes me. How strange
> These hours that I steal from my rest.
> Oh! If I regret dying, it is because,
> Once dead, I will no longer see you![36]

Martí's first year in exile ended very much as it began, with the young man sick, isolated, and impoverished. For the first time in his life, he grasped what it meant to be profoundly alone, an ocean away from those dearest to him.

BY THE SPRING OF 1872 THE SCANDAL SURROUNDING THE wrongful execution of the eight Cuban students had grown to such a pitch and the international outcry so relentless that on May 9 the Spanish government decided to free the remaining imprisoned students in an effort to defuse the anger.[37] By such a stroke of luck was Fermín Valdés Domínguez exiled to Spain on May 30, his six-year sentence commuted after only five months in prison. Temporarily buoyed by the news, a visibly diminished Martí welcomed his dearest friend to Madrid in June 1872. Despite his own weakened condition after prison and the long sea voyage, Valdés Domínguez was appalled to find Martí in such an alarming state:

> Oh, how sorry I was to find him in Spain sick and impoverished, living in someone's attic and surviving thanks to a few lessons he gave at the home of Don Leandro Alvarez Torrijos. . . . Our first meeting was a very sad one. He saw that I was ill, and I believed him incurable.[38]

Although Valdés Domínguez's published accounts regarding his own life and Martí's contain numerous errors and misrepresentations, his description here confirms what others have observed of Martí's precarious condition during this period.

Not surprisingly for a medical student, Valdés Domínguez rendered an informal assessment of his friend's health that proved prescient. Martí fell ill once again in July and underwent a third surgical attempt to relieve the pain and swelling in his right testicle. This time the operation achieved the desired result, and as the pain and swelling subsided Martí returned to a modicum of health.[39] He felt well enough by August to enroll in at least one course at the university.[40] More importantly, the return of his fellow conspirator restored Martí's fire for Cuba and gave him the will to soldier on.

His health mostly restored, Martí resolved with Valdés Domínguez to renew their efforts on behalf of Cuban independence. Martí continued to agonize over the fate of his fellow students, and Valdés Domínguez's firsthand account of the students' unjust treatment in the courts and the hardships they endured in prison only heightened Martí's self-loathing at not having stood among them in their hour of crisis. These conflicting emotions generated in Martí an intense political and emotional commitment, but one fueled by a gnawing, near-masochistic sense of guilt. So the young would-be revolutionary found himself in Madrid, an ocean away from the war being fought for Cuba's independence,

FIGURE 4.1. *Martí (left) with Fermín Valdés Domínguez and his brother, Eusebio (standing). The photo was taken in Madrid on September 19, 1872.* From Iconografía del apóstol José Martí (*Secretaría de Instrucción Pública y Bellas Artes. Havana: El siglo XX, 1925*).

agonizing over the suffering and death of his fellow Cubans and despairing of his inability to help.

After many lengthy conversations about their respective experiences in prison and their martyred classmates, the exiled friends finally found a suitable project for their revolutionary energies. They decided to organize a public commemoration on the anniversary of the November 27 executions as a way of raising consciousness in the exile community. Encouraged by Martí, Valdés Domínguez decided to publish his own experiences as a memoir, to which Martí contributed the poem "A mis hermanos muertos el 27 de noviembre" (For My Brothers Fallen on November 27).[41]

On the morning of the anniversary, however, it was a slender pamphlet authored by Martí and undersigned by Valdés Domínguez and fellow medical student Pedro de la Torre that roused the exile community to action. Although Martí continued to publish frequently on the cause of Cuban independence, his essay "¡27 de noviembre!"—first circulated in Madrid on the anniversary of the medical students' execution—gave the independence movement its first popular momentum. The pamphlet encouraged Cubans to gather that day in the students' memory, and the community responded by holding memorial services at Madrid's Caballero de Gracia church and other locations around the city.[42]

The day's final commemorative event took place in the home of Carlos Sauvalle, where Martí used the occasion to deliver an impassioned speech (now lost) for Cuban independence.[43] In all, Martí's and Valdés Domínguez's first organizing effort was a success and played a key role in establishing November 27 in Cuban minds as a date inseparable from the idea of independence. By January 1873, when Martí published "A mis hermanos muertos el 27 de noviembre," the executed students had effectively become the burgeoning revolution's first martyrs, a development for which Martí's writings and organizing efforts were largely responsible.

WITHIN A MONTH OF MARTÍ'S SUCCESSFUL ACTIVISM, THE circumstances that would compel him to leave the city began to converge. Martí's ongoing commitment to the Cuban cause intensified after Valdés Domínguez's arrival in June and became a real distraction from his studies. Martí's less-than-stellar performance during his first year of law school and the possibility that his now public identity as an activist had begun to generate ill will among the university faculty may have compelled the young organizer to consider a change of scenery.

The opportunity for just such a change came in mid-December, when Martí accompanied Valdés Domínguez to Zaragoza, a provincial capital some two hundred miles northeast of Madrid, on the occasion of the graduation of Fermín's brother, Eusebio, from medical school.[44] Like his brother, Eusebio Valdés Domínguez was an old friend of Martí's, having been among those arrested following the October 1869 incident that led to Martí's imprisonment and exile. Eusebio did not receive a prison sentence as had his brother and Martí and had been attending medical school in Zaragoza since his expulsion from the island in March 1870. For Martí the opportunity to visit the Universidad de

Zaragoza, which coincided roughly with Fermín's decision to follow his brother into medical school there, figured significantly in his decision to move there himself.[45]

One additional factor may have proved decisive for the young Cuban. It is not clear when or where Martí met Blanca de Montalvo, the young Zaragozan woman with whom he had his first serious love affair. The two may have met during Martí's initial trip to Zaragoza in December 1872 or in Madrid sometime earlier. What is clear is that Martí and Montalvo had already established a relationship before his departure for Zaragoza, as evidenced by his passionate dedication to her of his short story "The Hour of Rain," published on April 29. By the time Martí left Madrid, his relationship with Montalvo well eclipsed any lingering emotional attachment to the widow Barbarita Echevarría, although correspondence suggests that he continued to see Echevarría at least up until his departure for Zaragoza in May 1873.[46]

THE REIGN OF KING AMADEO I PROVED EVEN MORE SHORT-lived than Martí's stay in the Spanish capital. His reign was marked by a series of political crises, military uprisings, and assassination attempts; when the Progressive Party, his last remaining source of support, split into monarchist and constitutionalist factions, the young king decided that he had had enough. On February 11, 1873, barely into his third year as king, Amadeo abdicated the Spanish throne, famously declared the country to be "ungovernable," and announced his intention to return to his native Italy. At 10 p.m. on the same day, the Spanish Cortes (Parliament) proclaimed the establishment of a republic and installed Republican Party leader Estanislao Figueras as its first president.[47]

The establishment of what is now known as the First Republic heightened hopes among Cuban exiles that with the new parliamentary government in Madrid would come an end to the ongoing insurrection on the island and a political settlement — at the least autonomy and perhaps even outright independence. This air of enthusiasm was not lost on Martí, who around this time famously draped a Cuban flag over the balcony of his room overlooking Calle Concepción Jerónima as a sign of hope that change was in the offing.[48] His belief in the possibility of change went well beyond symbolism, however, as evidenced by his February 15 essay "La República Española ante la revolución cubana" (The Spanish Republic before the Cuban Revolution), which he published as a pamphlet later that month.[49]

Not all in the exile community shared in the hope that the arrival of new government heralded change. Many feared that Amadeo's abdication would simply sink the country back into the disorder that followed the overthrow of Isabella in 1868 and that the new government would lack the leadership and direction to significantly alter its relationship with its remaining colonies. Martí did not necessarily share that view, but he was also not as sanguine as those who believed that Spain would voluntarily grant Cuba its freedom. "La República Española" captures both the hopes and the ambivalence that many Cubans felt at the time by presenting the new government's arrival as a moment of historical and moral choice. The essay's thesis is as forceful as it is straightforward: Now that Spain has successfully fought to become a republic and free itself from an oppressive monarchy, how can it morally deny Cuba that which it deems essential for itself? Now that Spain is a republic, Martí asks, how can it in good faith suppress other people's desire to govern themselves?

> The insurgents do not yield.... Four years gone by without respite, without sign of yielding in their determination, demanding, even unto death, as Spanish republicans have so often demanded their liberty, their freedom from oppression, their liberty and honor. What honorable republican would dare to deny a people the rights he claims for himself? ... Does it not appall the Spanish Republic to think that Spaniards are dying in battle against other republicans?[50]

Its moral force and rhetorical virtuosity aside, "La República Española" is remarkable for Martí's articulation of Cubans as a distinct and unique people who have grown away from the mother country and can no longer live in its shadow. For Martí, Spain could no longer morally hold Cuba against the will of a people whose "community of interests, unity of traditions, unity of ends, sweetest and consoling fusion of loves and hopes" no longer had anything in common with the mother country except "the right to possession by force."[51] In many ways "La República Española" serves as a template for Martí's work as the first substantive articulation of a position that he would continue to refine and develop for the rest of his life.

MARTÍ CONTINUED TO WRITE AND PUBLISH INTO THE SPRING of 1873, even as he prepared to move to Zaragoza. The Sevillian newspaper *La Cuestión Cubana* proved especially receptive to his work during this period, reprinting "La República Española" and publishing the Martí essays "The Solution" and "The Reforms."[52] In May Martí successfully petitioned the registrar at the Universidad Central de Madrid to grant his transfer to its counterpart in Zaragoza, and later that month he and Valdés Domínguez departed Madrid in time for the start of classes at their new school.[53] Before them lay the promise of a new start academically and — for Martí — romantically. Martí's physical separation from Madrid initiated a period of relative normalcy during which he was able to focus on his studies and enjoy the everyday pleasures of friendship and love even as the troubles that had so deeply marked his life raged on somewhere else.

> For Aragón, in Spain,
> I have in my heart
> A place all Aragón,
> Frank, fierce, faithful, without anger.
>
> If some fool wants to know
> Why this is so, I tell him
> That there I had a good friend,
> That there I loved a woman.[54]

The "good friend" in this, Poema VII of Martí's 1891 collection *Versos sencillos*, is not Fermín Valdés Domínguez, with whom Martí moved to Aragón's capital city in May 1873, but the artist Pablo Gonzalvo Pérez, whose renowned paintings of the interiors of famous Spanish churches Martí would have discovered in Madrid.[55] Despite Gonzalvo's being twenty-five years his senior, he and Martí formed a strong bond that the younger man would treasure the rest of his life. The poem's suggestion that Martí made Gonzalvo's acquaintance in Zaragoza is, however, misleading; although the painter was a Zaragoza native, he had lived in Madrid for more than a decade and kept his studio there. In fact, Gonzalvo's Madrid studio is likely where Martí watched the artist work on his famous *Vista del interior de La Seo de Zaragoza* (View of the Interior of La Seo of Zaragoza, 1876), an experience he mentions in his later essay on the painter. Nevertheless, Martí's dearest memories of Zaragoza as expressed in Poema VII of his *Versos sencillos* revolve around his friendship with the older Spaniard and his passionate affair with Blanca de Montalvo.[56]

Despite Madrid's undeniable role in facilitating Martí's most important relationships during his time in Zaragoza — not only Gonzalvo and Montalvo but his reunion with Valdés Domínguez — his new home offered a second chance that would have been impossible in the capital. Martí successfully petitioned the registrar at the Universidad de Zaragoza to retake exams for the subjects he failed at Madrid, and he regained the form that had made him a childhood prodigy in Havana. Although it was not nearly the cosmopolitan mecca that was Madrid, Zaragoza had a flourishing arts scene and especially enabled Martí to develop the knowledge of theater and painting that would serve him well throughout his writing career. Zaragoza was also a significantly cheaper place to live than Madrid, no small consideration for a young man of very limited means.[57] Most importantly, Zaragoza's physical distance from the capital removed Martí from the sustained political activities that so consumed him during his time there — and which, along with his failing health, caused him to struggle during his first year of law school. With a steady girlfriend, good friends, and a relative return to health, Martí quickly settled into the normal life of a college student. The almost wistful fondness in his recollection of Zaragoza in his later *Versos sencillos* is in hindsight no surprise; after the trouble and turmoil of the previous two years, the eighteen months he spent there offered a welcome and much-needed respite. It would also prove to be the last relatively peaceful period of his turbulent life.

IN MAY 1873 ZARAGOZA NUMBERED SOME 70,000 INHABI-tants, less than a fifth of Madrid's population at the time. Although the smaller city could not match Madrid's artistic and intellectual resources and lacked the capital's sense of bustle and energy, the new arrival found much to like about it. Zaragoza was a city of significant architectural beauty whose two landmarks, the Cathedral of La Seo and Basilica of El Pilar, overlooked the natural setting of the Ebro River along the city's northern edge. Its interior streets did not feature the more modern amenities such as gas lighting that were common throughout Madrid, but Zaragoza was better served by rail and telegraph than many Spanish cities of its size, and in the spring of 1873 it was in the midst of a significant infrastructural project to upgrade its older residential areas.[58]

Zaragoza enjoyed a thriving theater scene to which Martí found himself increasingly attracted. Although some politically oriented works and events were staged, unsurprisingly given the country's ongoing political turmoil, the larger theaters — including the 1,500-seat Teatro Principal, which Martí frequented — favored more mainstream fare such as the *zarzuela*, Spain's unique hybrid genre incorporating opera, popular song, and dance. Martí's friendship with two of the city's most prominent theatrical figures, the playwright Eusebio Blasco y Marcos Zapata and especially the celebrated actor Leopoldo Burón, enabled him to frequent the theater more often than he otherwise would have been able to afford. Burón was quite fond of the young Cuban and often welcomed him and Valdés Domínguez as his guests to performances at the Teatro Principal.[59] Martí reciprocated Burón's generosity by contributing a poem to a December 22 event at the theater honoring the Spanish actor that Burón read onstage.[60] It was perhaps that taste of public approval that inspired Martí to write *Adúltera* (Adultress), the lead male part which he wrote specifically for Burón. Although Martí never managed to stage the play as originally intended, *Adúltera* marks his first serious theatrical endeavor.[61]

It is difficult to assess whether Martí's budding interest in the theater started to replace his revolutionary fervor or whether it was merely his physical distance from Madrid and its politics that drew his energies in a new direction. It is clear that neither his theatrical ambitions nor his courtship of Blanca de Montalvo affected his studies as his activism had done in Madrid. This was perhaps partly because of the previous year's widespread commemoration among exiles of the November 27 anniversary and subsequent upsurge of interest among Cubans and progressive Spaniards, which had raised Martí's hope for change in Spain's relations with the island colony. The enactment of the new republican government on February 9, 1873, and its formal establishment as a democratic federal republic on June 1, heightened hopes for a political solution to the ongoing war between Spain and the Cuban insurgency despite the new government's initial affirmation of Cuba as inseparable from the mother country. Whatever the contributing factors, on June 4 Martí received passing grades in five subjects, including the three he had not successfully completed in Madrid, and on August 29 he enrolled in eight more courses.[62]

Given that Martí did not attempt so many simultaneous subjects during his first year of law school, the August term's heavier course load suggests a young man in a hurry to graduate. Additional steps confirm this judgment; on August 30 he enrolled in a second college at Zaragoza, the university's Faculty of Philosophy and Letters, and requested permission from the registrar to proceed directly to final examinations without attending classes for all required subjects toward a bachelor's degree. Nor was Martí alone in his desire to complete his studies; on November 24 Mariano Martí requested and obtained certification from the Havana school where his son was enrolled before his arrest for coursework completed in order for his son to receive credit at Zaragoza for a bachelor's degree in philosophy and letters.[63]

Mariano's intervention was part of the family's larger plan to escape what had become an untenable situation in Havana. Although Leonor later destroyed almost all of her son's early letters to her, we know from references to them elsewhere that Martí corresponded intermittently with his mother from Madrid. Her own letters, in which she scolded her son for not writing more often, made no effort to conceal her alarm at his failing health and especially his return to activism, warning him repeatedly that "the redeemers always end up crucified."[64]

But in Zaragoza letters arrived from Havana more frequently and with greater urgency. In what appears to have been a coordinated effort, sisters Amelia and María del Carmen wrote letters to express their concerns over a litany of troubles: the family's increasingly dire financial straits, the failing health of their sister Ana, and the general hardship and desperation into which the ongoing war had plunged the island colony.[65] Leonor and her daughters were keeping the family afloat through their work producing garments for the Spanish army, work they obtained thanks to Mariano's remaining military contacts. But the aging Mariano could not himself find work either as a policeman or in the private sector.[66] A letter from Leonor from the same period confirmed her daughters' assessments, adding news of Mariano's debilitating asthma, the younger children's sickly and malnourished state, and the widespread poverty that nearly six years of war had wreaked upon the island's civilian population.[67] The rebels' scorched-earth tactic of burning down captured sugar mills, which damaged Spain's economy and therefore its ability to continue funding the war, was compounding the island's hardships, as it directly affected the already struggling civilian population. The combination of domestic and external pressures—and the impossibility of their son's return to the island to help support them—led Mariano to decide, with Leonor's and Ana's enthusiastic support, that leaving Cuba was their only hope. But rather than return to their native Spain, the Martís chose to immigrate to Mexico and urged their son to join them there. In an independent nation, they reasoned, freed from the nightmare of colonial life, the family could reunite and build a new, more prosperous life together.[68]

Martí eventually replied to accept their proposal and to ask that they contact him again once the family made more definite plans. Although most of the surviving correspondence from this period is undated, Martí's sudden haste beginning in late August to complete his studies suggests that the flurry of letters, culminating in his decision to join his family in Mexico, transpired between May and August 1873.

Although his family's dire situation in Cuba was Martí's primary motive for joining them, the growing unrest in Spain also influenced his decision to emigrate. The Cubans' early hopes for the new government quickly faded as Spain soon proved no more competent as a republic than it had been under King Amadeo. The new republic's precariousness was amply demonstrated by the four presidents who served in 1873 alone, successive administrations that proved unable not only to reach a settlement with the Cubans but even of suppressing insurgencies within its own borders. Divided and deeply unpopular throughout the country, the new government had little time or energy to expend on Cuba because by July 1873 it was fighting no fewer than three insurgencies at home: the Third Carlist War in the interior, launched in February and now spreading north to Catalonia and the Basque region; the Cantonal Revolution in the southern provinces; and the so-called Petroleum Revolution, a workers' revolt in southeastern Alicante Province.[69]

In addition to its domestic troubles, Spain's standing abroad was irremediably crippled by the international uproar that followed the October 30 capture of the *Virginius*, a U.S. ship carrying guns, munitions, and 103 Cuban, British, and American men en route to join Cuban rebels on the island. The vessel's capture in international waters and the summary execution of 53 of the *Virginius*'s crew members and passengers the following month proved the final straw for a troubled republic. Heated diplomatic exchanges with the British and U.S. governments led the young Spanish government to the brink of what would have been a disastrous war, and although in the end negotiations managed to halt further executions—including those of three thirteen-year-old recruits—the incident irretrievably damaged Spain's relations with the world's two most powerful nations.[70] Worse, the incident and its aftermath made the new government appear weak and rudderless internationally and at home; the Cuban governor's reflexively brutal and excessive response to the failed filibustering expedition reflected especially badly on the new republic, as it exposed the degree to which Madrid had lost control over its remaining colonies.

On December 29, Manuel Pavía, the captain-general of Madrid, renounced his allegiance to the republic and called on the warring parties to form a new national government under General Francisco Serrano, who had briefly served as prime minister under Amadeo before going into exile. Besieged at home and embattled abroad, the crippled First Spanish Republic fell in a military coup on January 3, 1874. Although Pavía's declaration and more directly his dissolution of the Spanish Cortes effectively ended the republic, the actions did not end the fighting. The Carlists, who disputed the line of succession to the throne and had been fighting since the 1830s, continued their rebellion.[71] Remnants of the republican government, including those in Zaragoza, also resisted, a development that brought the capital's once distant turmoil to Martí's doorstep.

In the hours following Pavía's successful coup, military and civilian forces loyal to the erstwhile First Republic formed a counterrebellion of their own, barricading streets and clashing with monarchist forces. The uprising was short-lived, as monarchists soon overwhelmed the disorganized and outnumbered republicans. For Martí the experience was a formative one, not least because of the memory of an Afro-Cuban man who stood with the republicans. Over time the episode became for Martí an uplifting image of solidarity against oppression; nearly twenty years after the ill-fated revolt Martí wrote admiringly of Simón, a laborer employed at a boarding house who fought against the monarchists: "In Zaragoza when Pavía trampled the congress in Madrid and the Aragonese rose up against him, there was no rifle in the plaza . . . more valiant than that of the black Cuban Simón."[72] In their immediate aftermath, the events of January 3–4, 1874, combined with his family's desperate situation in Cuba, fueled Martí's resolve to complete his studies and quit the country as soon as possible.

In the aftermath of the January coup, Martí returned to the activities and interests that had earlier engaged him as he awaited word from his family regarding their departure for Mexico. He continued to speak out for the cause of Cuban independence, most notably at a January event organized to raise funds for the families of those who died in the Zaragoza uprising. By February he finished a first draft of *Adúltera*, although Martí would leave Spain before it could be staged.[73] He continued to see Blanca de Montalvo, though it is not clear when she became aware of his plans to leave the country.

The anticipated news from home arrived in the early spring, and on April 22 Mariano, Leonor, and their four youngest surviving daughters boarded the steamship *Eider*, bound for Veracruz. Their eldest daughter, Chata, did not immediately join them; in the seven weeks before their departure she had given birth to one child, Oscar Eusebio, on March 5, and lost another, three-year-old Maria Andrea, three weeks later. The Martís brought with them Chata's second-born, two-year-old Alfredo, to help her and her husband during this difficult time. The extended family's final destination was Mexico City, where they anxiously awaited their son's arrival.[74]

Martí spent the end of May and early June in Madrid, perhaps due to ill health, as stated in his June 11 application to undergo final examinations for the law degree. It is not clear whether health was the only reason for his extended absence from Zaragoza, as correspondence from the woman identified only as "M," presumably Barbarita Echevarría, suggests that he visited her during this time. Martí's physical state notwithstanding, perhaps Blanca de Montalvo was not the only focus of Martí's romantic energies, regardless of his health.[75]

Whatever Martí's extracurricular activities, his primary focus in summer 1874 was the completion of requirements for his law and bachelor's degrees. He attacked this objective with a fervor not seen since his Havana childhood, and by the end of the 1873–1874 academic year he had completed no less than ten courses. On June 30 his thesis, on the theme "Opening Paragraph of Book One, Title Two of the *Institutiones of Justinian*: Natural, Common, and Civil Law," was approved, thus completing the requirements for the degree of *licenciado* in civil and canonical law. The university did not issue him a diploma, however, because he could not pay the required fee.[76]

On August 31 the newly minted attorney enrolled for his final courses for the bachelor's degree in philosophy and letters as an external, or independent, student, a status that allowed him to continue his visits to the capital.[77] However much those visits to the capital may have involved the woman known as "M," he was at this point very much focused on getting on with the next stage of his life. In a draft of an unsent letter, Martí writes, "[Now], on October 19, I have left Madrid and will very soon commence, away from Spain, the practice of my career."[78] The very next day he submitted his request to the registrar for final examination at Zaragoza, and on October 24 he took the exam on the topic of "Political and Forensic Oratory among the Romans. Cicero as Their Highest Expression: Discourses Examined in Accordance with His Rhetorical Works." Martí's lifelong fascination with Cicero, whose writings deeply influenced his development as a public speaker, can be traced to his years in Spain and studies at Zaragoza. That fascination spurred him to do his best work as a student, and his efforts earned him a mark of Outstanding from the Zaragoza examiners. As with the law degree, however, Martí did not receive his bachelor's diploma due to his inability to pay the necessary fees to have it issued. This later proved a significant but not insurmountable obstacle, as Martí was able to produce official transcripts of his academic work to Mexican authorities to prove his qualifications.[79]

Having thus completed the requirements for his law degree and now the bachelor's in philosophy and letters, nothing remained to hold Martí in Spain. Not even Blanca de Montalvo.

MARTÍ LEFT ZARAGOZA FOR GOOD IN NOVEMBER, TRAVEL-ing to Madrid to finalize the necessary paperwork for his departure. During this period Martí made several visits to Lorenzo Jiménez, a young Cuban doctor imprisoned in Madrid for providing material support to rebel forces on the island.[80] During eleven visits to Cuba, Jiménez tended to the rebel wounded and transported mail, clothing, medicine, and other goods to and from the island. According to an 1875 essay by Martí, Jiménez was captured at sea as he attempted to reach Cuba a twelfth time and was spared his life only due to the colonial government's relatively conciliatory stance toward the insurgency at the time.[81] Although we do not know the specifics of Martí's conversations with Jiménez, he would certainly have been interested in the young doctor's first-hand knowledge of the rebel forces' progress and conditions on the ground. More generally, the visits confirm that during those hectic final weeks in Spain, he had not forgotten the Cuban cause.

Martí also never forgot the two women who loved him. He bid Montalvo (his "Blanencha," as he came to call her) a painful farewell in Zaragoza, and although he apparently stopped writing to her sometime in early 1875, she continued to appear in his poems and unpublished writings for another fifteen years. For her part, Montalvo long mourned the loss of her beloved "Pepe of my soul" and continued to write him for more than two years after he left Zaragoza. She later married Dr. Manuel S. Pastor y Pellicer, a Spaniard and professor at the University of Zaragoza's medical school. The marriage produced a son whom, perhaps as a mother's secret tribute to a long-lost love, she named José.[82]

No such resolution, however bittersweet, came for the woman known as "La Madrileña," likely the widow Barbarita Echevarría. Her parting with Martí sometime in December was apparently as difficult for her as had been Montalvo's but with no reciprocal anguish on his part. Martí stopped writing to her a few months after his departure, as he did with Montalvo; but unlike his letters to the younger woman, in which he implored her to "never forget" him, his final letter to "M" (now lost) downplayed their four-year affair, asserting that she had never really loved him. The abandoned lover's declarations of love and anguish at the loss of her "idol" soon grew, over the course of several letters, into angry recriminations and accusations of duplicity:

> You are a cold-hearted monster. In you there is no heart but only reason. You do not love me, and I am not satisfied. . . . You are cruel, you have killed me after destroying my heart and my life, and you said that I, that I alone would be your soul mate, that you would love none but me, and you made me awake from the lethargy into which my prostrate heart had fallen. And not one hope, or comfort, or mercy.[83]

Over the next eighteen months "M" would write to Martí at least twice more and sent additional letters to his friends and family requesting news of him. But Martí never responded to her increasingly desperate missives and aside from a possible reference in his March 1874 poem "Without Love" never mentioned her in print again.

SOMETIME IN DECEMBER 1874 MARTÍ FINALLY DEPARTED Spain. The Martís' situation in Mexico City was dire; the expenses of transporting themselves and all their possessions and of securing a place to live left them on the verge of destitution. Compounding their misery was their daughter Ana's disintegrating health; the city's higher altitude aggravated an existing heart condition, and by the time of Martí's departure from Spain she was bedridden and near death. With no money for doctors or treatments, the Martís' fate fell into the hands of strangers; neighbors wrote to the editors of the newspaper *La Iberia* to ask for help in soliciting funds for the destitute family. The paper's December 30 issue published an appeal for donations under the title "Disgraced Family."[84]

Yet it would be another two months before Martí would join his family. Rather than traveling directly to Mexico, Martí and Valdés Domínguez went to Paris, where they stayed until traveling to England later that month. On January 2, 1875, Martí finally left Europe, traveling alone from Liverpool in a third-class cabin on the transatlantic steamer *Celtic*. But his destination was New York City, where he remained for twelve days awaiting a Mexico-bound vessel.[85] By the morning of January 6, his fourth day on the *Celtic*, Ana was dead.[86]

CHAPTER FIVE

A Young Man's Travels

There in Paris, the land where the mire
Mingles with the flowers and the mystery,
There stands a tomb that says it all
In the cemetery's solemn voice.

"LETTERS FROM SPAIN," OCTOBER 17, 1875

THE TOMB IN QUESTION IS THAT OF PETER ABELARD and Héloïse d'Argenteuil, renowned intellectuals and perhaps more importantly, legendary star-crossed lovers in twelfth-century France.[1] Martí visited the well-known tomb at the Pére Lachaise Cemetery during his Paris holiday in December 1874. His primary interest and emotional identification lay with Abelard; beyond the numerous references to the legendary lovers, his only mention in an 1882 essay of d'Argenteuil is a fleeting nod to "the loyal Héloïse."[2] Martí's scattered references to Abelard, most notably in his unpublished notebooks, reveal a more than passing familiarity with the medieval philosopher's concept of scholasticism and his formal, rational approach to questions of religion and metaphysics. This affinity for Abelard's scholasticism is understandable, given its appeal to Martí as a well-educated young man and recent convert to Freemasonry. Martí's emotional attraction to Abelard centered on the scholar's life as a martyr standing against intellectual and religious orthodoxy—and as a passionate lover denied by narrow morality and cruel circumstance. As someone well versed in French letters and literature, Martí almost certainly would have read *The Letters of Héloïse and Abelard*, the collection of anonymous letters that forms the foundation of the lovers' legend.[3]

The "Letters from Spain" of the poem's title are those sent by Blanca de

Montalvo, the woman Martí left behind in Zaragoza. Her letter of December 26 would have reached him in Paris; beyond its professions of love and a promise to see him again, it brought distressing news of her family's attempts to match her with a new suitor.[4] If Montalvo's letter was not the sole reason for Martí's visit to the tomb of Abelard and Héloïse, it was clearly the inspiration for the poem's deeply pained language of lost love:

> Kisses you send: you ask for embraces
> Enough to drown your ills:
> Oh, perpetual flower, loving ties
> Of a good and loyal love!
>
> Poor me! You weep, and I am here — silent
> In a way that reveals the dead man in me —
> I hold always within me some waiting kiss
> That I cannot give and send to you to the sky! . . .
>
> Listen: I am anguished; in pain I sleep
> By a miserable light in a hard bed,
> And I am — Oh, my soul! — a poor wretch
> Ailed by strange ills that have no cure.[5]

The poem's melding of the young poet's intellectual interests with his emotional struggles opens a window into Martí's state of mind as he wrote the poem in Mexico nine months after receiving the letter. Martí continued to receive letters from Blanca de Montalvo after his arrival in Mexico.[6] But by the time the poem appeared in print in October 1875, Martí was deep into a secret, doomed affair with an "Héloïse" of his own: Cuban-born, married actress Eloísa Agüero de Ossorio. "Letters from Spain" thus reveals as much about his time in Paris as it does about how that visit informed not only his specific relationship with Agüero but also his evolving views on love, beauty, and personal suffering that would find their fuller expression in later years. In its dual focus on a past visit to the lovers' tomb and his enduring sense of isolation and loneliness, "Letters from Spain" reveals Martí's own reflections on a period of his life about which little is otherwise known.

SURPRISINGLY LITTLE IN THE WAY OF LETTERS OR OTHER documents survives from the period between Martí's departure from Spain and his reunion with his family in Mexico. What seems clear is that during the first leg of his travels, the time spent in Paris, he was not spending his own money; surely the young man who could not afford to pay the fees required to receive his college diplomas did not have the funds for an extended European vacation. It is thus more than likely that Valdés Domínguez at least partly bankrolled the trip, a curious exception to Martí's general resistance to receiving financial help even for urgent medical needs.

Whatever the case, Martí and Valdés Domínguez departed Zaragoza for Paris in December 1874. The "icy hand" with which he touches Abelard and Héloïse's tomb in "Letters from Spain" was likely more than a metaphoric device, but literally true, as Paris was suffering through an unusually foggy and frigid winter. The December 23 edition of the Paris newspaper *Le Rappel* notes that the previous days had brought heavy snows and icy streets to the city, transforming it "into a veritable London by a yellow fog quite comparable to those of the English capital. The fog joined its color to an icy dampness that penetrated passers-by to the bone."[7] Paris at this time was also, if not as mired in mayhem and intrigue as the troubled Spanish state, experiencing its own period of political turbulence. The recently established Third Republic was still struggling with the aftermath of 1871 Paris Commune uprising of workers and anarchists that ended with a bloody reprisal in which around thirty thousand people were killed; another fifty thousand later were executed, imprisoned, or exiled.[8] President Adolphe Thiers was forced to resign under pressure from conservative groups; his successor, Patrice MacMahon, was left, along with the French National Assembly, with the task of producing a new constitution amid continued political bickering and rumors of rightist coups.[9]

What redeemed this grim moment in French history for Martí was the sense of national pride and political commitment implicit—and in the case of Victor Hugo, explicit—in the nation's writers and artists. Among contemporary French writers Hugo was the one Martí most revered, and meeting him became his single fondest memory from the Paris trip. Martí had made the acquaintance of noted French poet Auguste Vacquerie, who in turn offered to introduce the young Cuban to his lifelong literary idol. Martí had been reading Hugo since his teens, and his work was the young Cuban's inspiration for learning the French language. The renowned French novelist was known to be sympathetic to the cause of Cuban independence and progressive causes generally. For example, Hugo advocated for amnesty for the participants in the Paris Commune uprising; so it was Hugo's politics as much as his literary work that made the prospect of meeting him even more exciting for the young writer and activist. Very much pleased with Martí's translation of one of his poems into Spanish, Vacquerie persuaded Hugo to have the young Cuban translate a new short piece, "Mes fils" (My Sons), which Martí published in Mexico's *Revista Universal* the following March.

Martí later wrote glowingly of his encounter with the seventy-two-year-old dean of French letters:

I have seen that head, I have touched that hand, I have felt at his side
that plethora of life within which the heart seems to swell, and from
the eyes come the sweetest tears, and the words are stammering and
foolish, and in the end one lives a few moments far from the oppres-
sions of living. The universe is the analogy. So is Victor Hugo a snow-
crowned mountain from whom escape rays of light that warm Father
Sun himself.[10]

Nor was Martí's sense of wonder merely a passing thrill or a case of youthful
enthusiasm upon meeting a boyhood idol. Although Martí would later write
reverently of a number of prominent writers, most notably Walt Whitman and
Ralph Waldo Emerson, Hugo was for Martí the first really compelling model
of a writer whose significance within his national culture transcended the literary to encompass the nation's very identity and sense of self. In the October
26, 1875, issue of *Revista Universal*, Martí invokes Hugo in precisely this way, as
a living example of the kind of intellectual ideal to which a young Mexican republic should aspire:

And what powers might we not discover in ourselves, by casting the
light of Victor Hugo upon our six million inhabitants? And as with
us, so throughout South America. We are not yet sufficiently American; every continent ought to have its own expression; ours is a legated
life and a stammering literature. We have in America men who have
perfected European literature; but we lack a writer who is exclusively
American. There should be a poet who blossoms on the summit of the
Alps, of our sierra, of our proud Rocky Mountains; a potent historian,
more deserving of Bolívar than Washington, because America is the re-
buff, the bursting forth, the revelations, the vehemence, and Washington
is the hero of calm; formidable, but peaceful; sublime, but tranquil.[11]

What the young Martí calls for in this essay is not the adoption in Latin
American culture of the great Frenchman's style or language but the pursuit of
what Hugo represents for his own people: a writer who through his work exer-
cises a powerful formative influence upon a nation's culture and identity. This
lofty standard, to which he would consistently hold national literatures and
their writers—and especially his own work—throughout his life has its origins
in the young man's fortuitous encounter with Victor Hugo.

THEIR PARIS HOLIDAY CONCLUDED, MARTÍ AND VALDÉS
Domínguez now turned their attention to the return voyage and the respective futures that they imagined awaited them. For Martí, that meant a long,

wearying transatlantic journey and a reunion with his long-struggling family in Mexico City. He had not corresponded with them since departing Zaragoza nearly a month before and was understandably wary of the troubles and challenges that might lie in store.

The first leg of the friends' journey was uneventful enough but for the increasingly amorous Martí not without its transient pleasures. Martí and Valdés Domínguez traveled by train together from Paris to the port of Le Havre, where on December 28 they took the ferry to Southampton in England. Years later Martí wrote of his fleeting encounter there with a young Englishwoman: "[In] Southampton, during a luminous half hour, I saw a sweet young girl, we loved each other, and we said goodbye forever."[12] Whether Martí's idyllic reminiscence from an 1880 newspaper article describes a mere platonic flirtation or a literal sexual experience we will never know; Martí's fond recollection of the interlude suggests that his various romantic attachments in Spain were no fluke but rather early indicators of a young man's robust sexual appetite.

Two days later the friends' train arrived in Liverpool, where they went their separate ways: Valdés Domínguez to his well-to-do family in Havana and the life of a practicing physician and Martí to a considerably less certain future in Mexico City. He bought a third-class ticket on the New York-bound steamer *Celtic* and departed with ninety-seven fellow passengers on the morning of January 2, 1875, quite alone.

Curiously, the *Celtic*'s passenger list identifies Martí not as a Cuban en route to Mexico but as an Italian musician planning to reside in America. He appears on the ship's list along with four Italian travelers under whose names appears the following information: "Occupation, *Musician*; The Country to which they severally belong, *Italy*; The Country of which they intend to become inhabitants, *U. S. A.*; Part of the vessel occupied by each passenger during the voyage, *Steerage*."[13] Martí would have had no reason to conceal his identity or occupation, since he was traveling with the knowledge and permission of the Spanish government; had it been otherwise he would have at least withheld his real name. The incorrect listing is more likely the result of a misunderstanding with the processing officer, perhaps due to Martí's spoken English. Or perhaps the officer in question, not having encountered many Cubans, simply assumed by his appearance and language that he was Italian and grouped him with the four musicians — an early, albeit in this case benign, case of racial profiling.

Martí's Atlantic crossing was an unusually arduous one even by the standards of the North Atlantic's typically stormy winter months. An article in the January 9, 1875, *New York Times* confirms that the stormy conditions faced by the *Celtic* were quite widespread, with incoming ships bringing accounts "of perilous adventure" and "long records of encounters with stiff westerly winds, gales, rain, hail, and snow-storms and heavy seas." The storms wreaked havoc with shipping schedules, as almost "all the great ocean steamers [were] more or less delayed."[14]

On this last point Martí could count himself fortunate; while other New York-bound vessels departing Liverpool took up to seventeen days to arrive, the *Celtic* experienced no significant delays, completing its twelve-day crossing on January 14. The *Celtic* did not manage to avoid the rough winter weather, however, and its struggles with at least one dangerous storm left a lasting impression on Martí, as he recalls in an unpublished 1877 essay:

> Sea and vessel were like masses of immense spirits; they took pleasure in the combat and stood back from their blows like generous enemies. There comes the black mountain, its mouth crooked, its edges rising, windblown and horrible; and it crests, it grows, it rises, now it roars and crashes over the ship. And the great *Celtic* swells, it twists, it slants, its deep, powerful, steely edge side by side with the wave, it spreads its iron arms as if the better to drown the mountain, and it straightens and shakes it off, the conquering giant; it shakes the horrible wave and casts it out.[15]

Having survived its trial at sea, the *Celtic* arrived in New York, where a weary Martí found that the dangerous weather during his crossing also delayed the arrival of many other ships — including any southbound vessels that would carry him on to Mexico and his family. After the withering sea crossing, Martí found himself marooned in New York with very limited funds for an indefinite period as he awaited an available southbound ship.

That period turned out to be twelve days, as Martí found no booking on a Mexico-bound ship until January 26. What little information we have from Martí's own writings suggests that he spent much of his unplanned layover as a *flâneur*, walking the city's various neighborhoods and visiting its landmarks. His few references to New York City during this time suggest that he came away less than favorably impressed; in an 1878 essay he recalls his acute disappointment upon seeing "in Union Square the puny statue of Lincoln."[16] Nor did the Manhattan he first encountered in 1875 fare well alongside the booming city he later came to know; in an unpublished fragment from 1889 Martí declares that anyone "who saw New York fifteen years ago would not recognize it today," and he goes on to describe its "somber rows of brownstones" and a Wall Street whose tallest and most luxurious buildings had since been "dwarfed" by "new babylons of cream brick and terracotta."[17] The opulence of 1880s New York only heightened Martí's recollection of the relatively impoverished place he first knew.

Martí departed New York with no better impression of its politics and culture than he did of its architecture. Having no easy access to the city's libraries, whatever Martí learned about the state of the American union during his visit would have come from the New York papers. There he would have read accounts of a nation in acute distress, the headlines a veritable litany of government corruption, rising crime, and growing public unrest. In 1875 the U.S. culture of unrest and corruption reached the nation's highest offices. The Whiskey Ring scandal, which was not exposed until later in the year, involved officials including Grant's private secretary in the embezzlement of alcohol taxes from the federal government, and Congress's investigation of bribery and other improprieties in the Pacific Mail Company implicated several of its own members.[18] Grant's troubles were exacerbated by Reconstruction's ongoing implosion; on the morning of January 18, 1875, the fifth day of Martí's stay, the president had to send a company of troops to Vicksburg, Mississippi, to quell a political uprising in which the city's black sheriff was ousted—the third such political insurrection U.S. troops had crushed since 1871, after those in South Carolina and Arkansas.[19] Earlier in the month, General Philip Sheridan sent a telegram urging Grant to declare so-called White Leaguers in Louisiana as "banditti" to enable military intervention against them.[20]

Public unrest grew over aggressive rhetoric and tactics of the Grant administration and culminated in a massive demonstration at Boston's Faneuil Hall to protest federal actions in Louisiana; other such protests sprang up in St. Louis and New York over similar grievances.[21] New York City newspapers, led by Whitelaw Reid at the *New York Tribune*, followed and abetted the growing drumbeat of discontent; papers like the *New York Sun*, with its regular front-page feature "Curiosities of Crime," provided a counterpart to the *Times* and *Tribune* political headlines, with tawdry accounts of nightly rapes and murders. The disconcerting tenor of the times would have been unmistakable for any but the most casual reader.

The effect on Martí became clear as soon as he started writing regularly on the United States and its politics, arts, and culture. In the 1877 article that documents his ocean crossing Martí bemoans the nation's outsize material ambitions and impoverished morality, and he despairs for its future: "Oh! The North American nation will perish soon, like all avarice, like all extravagances, like all immoral riches. It will die as horrifically as it has lived blindly. Only the morality of individuals preserves the splendor of nations."[22] If he found much of the same greed, corruption, and immorality in Paris, France might yet be saved, he reasoned, by its superior culture and love of beauty—qualities he found singularly lacking during his brief layover in America:

> The rhythm of poetry, the echo of music, the beatific ecstasy that produces in the soul the contemplation of a beautiful painting, is a soft

melancholy that masters the spirit after these superhuman encounters, they are mystical vestments, gentle omens of a time when all will become clear. Oh, that this light of centuries has been denied the people of North America! This nation's only greatness is its size . . .

North America does not know that artistic pleasure that is a kind of celestial aristocracy. Only elevated souls appreciate the intimate beauty of that extramundane world.[23]

Martí ends the unpublished essay with a brief meditation on ancient Greece, whose cultural, political, and artistic contributions to humanity far outlived its physical existence as a nation. The implicit judgment of a corrupt, culturally impoverished United States doomed to history's dustbin is unmistakable. It is a judgment that Martí would refine and qualify in later years; he never renounced his admiration for American principles of democracy and individual freedom or his reverence for Washington and Lincoln. But the template for Martí as a trenchantly critical observer of U.S. politics and culture in the late nineteenth century—arguably the greatest single such critic of his time—was formed during a young man's first, anxious days in January 1875 walking the streets of New York City.

DURING HIS JANUARY 1875 STAY IN NEW YORK CITY MARTÍ may have visited Néstor Ponce de León, an exiled Cuban activist to whom he had written from Madrid in the spring of 1873 with an offer of support for the cause. Curiously, no record exists of his having seen erstwhile mentor Rafael María de Mendive despite the latter's having lived in New York since he was exiled five years earlier. Martí sent no advance notice of his arrival to Ponce de León, Mendive, or anyone else in New York, clearly because he did not expect to be there very long. His twelve-day stay in New York was an unwelcome delay because of his family's desperate situation and the declining health of his sister Ana, who he believed was still alive.

On January 19, as Martí waited in New York for a ship that would not come for another seven days, Mexico City newspaper *La Iberia* reported that its December 30 plea for help on behalf of the destitute Martí family succeeded in raising $72.50 in Mexican pesos—the equivalent today of roughly $1,400.[24]

The money came too late to save Ana, for whom the impoverished Martís had no money for a proper funeral. Only the generosity of neighbor Manuel Mercado, who gave the Martís a plot belonging to his family, spared her the indignity of a pauper's grave.

CHAPTER SIX

Discovering America (1)

MEXICO

*Farewell to Mexico, to which I came with a terrified spirit and from which
I depart with hope and with love, as if were spread over all the land the
affection of those in it who have loved me.*

LETTER TO MANUEL MERCADO, JANUARY 1, 1877

MARTÍ HAD GOOD REASON TO BE WARY OF THE FUTURE when he finally arrived in Mexico in February 1875.[1] His monthlong journey from Europe was a difficult and at times disturbing experience; he endured a horrifically tempestuous ocean crossing, an anxious twelve days in New York awaiting a Mexico-bound vessel, and the indignities of Cuban authorities during a brief stop in Havana. He left behind the loves and friendships nurtured over his four years in Spain, including those of Blanca de Montalvo and Fermín Valdés Domínguez. Although the young Mexican republic held much promise for Martí professionally and artistically, his future as an attorney, as an aspiring writer, and as a man seeking to work for the liberation of his country was less than certain. Martí harbored deep apprehensions about his relationship with his father: Would the long separation enable a new warmth and affinity with Mariano, or had the years apart merely hardened the loyal Spaniard against his son's political convictions? All of this, and he still did not know that his beloved sister Ana had died.

ON THE MORNING OF JANUARY 26, 1875, MARTÍ FINALLY LEFT New York, one of sixty-one passengers on the steamer *City of Merida* bound for Veracruz. He spent his twenty-second birthday on the ship, the second time in his brief life that he celebrated a birthday on an oceangoing vessel alone. The *City of Merida*'s itinerary included three intermediate stops, one of them being

Havana, where on January 31 Cuban authorities prohibited Martí from disembarking. He spent the next two days aboard the vessel until it set off again on February 2 bound for its Mexican ports of call. On the afternoon of February 8 the *City of Merida* docked at Veracruz. Given his delay in New York and diminishing funds, it is perhaps understandable that Martí spent only a few hours in Veracruz before boarding the first available train to Mexico City and sending word of his imminent arrival.

After a two-day train journey, a no doubt exhausted Martí finally arrived at Mexico City's Buenavista station on the evening of February 10. Awaiting him were Mariano Martí and Manuel Antonio Mercado, a neighbor who had befriended the Martís since their arrival in the Mexican capital. The meeting was an auspicious one not only for Martí's reunion with his father, whom he had not seen for more than four years, but for his first encounter with a man who would become an important confidant and lifelong correspondent.

Although others enjoyed more intimate friendships or substantial relationships with Martí at various stages of his life, these were invariably defined by initial attraction that waned after some months or, less often, a year or two. Even Fermín Valdés Domínguez, generally regarded as Martí's closest lifelong friend, had very little contact with him between 1875 and 1892, a period spanning nearly half of Martí's life. Neither Rafael María de Mendive nor Carlos Sauvalle, father figures who formed intense emotional bonds with and exercised significant formative influence over the young Martí, maintained any kind of relationship with him after their respective physical separations in 1869 and 1873. Yet despite the relative brevity of Martí's time in Mexico, Manuel Mercado managed to surpass previous surrogate fathers in forming with the young Cuban a lasting intellectual and emotional bond.

Mercado was, like Martí, a lawyer, having completed his law degree and passed the Mexican bar in 1861. And significantly for the young Martí, Mercado hailed from a liberal family that fought bravely for Mexico's independence from French rule; he lost his father and four brothers as well as the family fortune during the struggle to rid Mexico of Maximilian I's occupation of the country.[2] Mercado seems to have enjoyed a more illustrious law school career than his protégé and was invited while still a student to deliver the January 19, 1860, commencement address at the law school's Academy of Jurisprudence.[3] After graduation, he went on to enjoy a successful career as an attorney and politician, and during Martí's time in Mexico Mercado served as secretary of state for the Distrito Federal (Mexico City) under President Sebastián Lerdo de Tejada.[4]

As with Mendive and Sauvalle before him, Mercado's appearance in Martí's life was both serendipitous and timely; Mercado's liberal intellectual bona fides and history of anticolonial struggle as well as his successful legal and political career made him an ideal mentor and advocate for the younger man during a difficult transitional period. Beyond all of this, Mercado endeared himself to the Martís—and particularly to Mariano—as a friend and benefactor during the family's early hardships in Mexico City. Mercado's ties to the Martís were enhanced by Ana's courtship with his college friend Miguel Ocaranza, the Mexican painter to whom she was engaged at the time of her death. Ana and their mother, Leonor, wrote glowingly of Mercado in their letters to Spain, which would certainly have made a strong impression on the young Cuban in advance of the two men's first meeting. And as with Mendive, Mariano's ongoing decline, both physically and in the eyes of his family, created the necessary paternal vacuum for Mercado's emergence as a surrogate. Martí's first glimpse of the two standing on the platform at the Buenavista station, the wizened patriarch alongside the younger, more successful man, must have made the contrast exceedingly clear.

MARTÍ LEARNED OF ANA'S DEATH ON THAT FIRST EVENING in Mexico City when his father delivered the tragic news before their carriage reached the Martí household. The initial shock of losing his sister so unexpectedly was a profound one for Martí, and his acute grief had the unfortunate effect of prolonging the family's misery at a point when they might otherwise have begun to recover from the loss. For Martí, however, grief was compounded by guilt; although his arriving sooner might not have saved Ana or even prolonged her life, he understood that his travels in Paris meant that he was absent at a moment of urgent need for his family, an epiphany that Mercado's timely intervention only partly assuaged. Her absence cast a pall over what might have been a joyous homecoming and instilled in the family, but especially in José Martí himself, a sense of loss and regret that did not soon subside.

Martí's profound sense of guilt over his sister's death emerges most clearly in the long valedictory poem he wrote shortly after his arrival in Mexico and published the following month in the capital's *Revista Universal*. As Martí's erstwhile mentor Sauvalle had done in Madrid, Mercado took pains to introduce the new arrival to prominent civic and professional leaders in Mexico City and brought his writing to the attention of the editors of the *Revista Universal*, an important liberal magazine of the period. Martí's intellectual precocity and obvious writing talents immediately impressed the *Revista*'s veteran editorial staff, and the young Cuban soon became a regular contributor. Martí's poem for his dead sister, titled "Mis padres duermen" (My Parents Sleep), appeared in the *Revista*'s March 7 issue, baring its author's wounded psyche for all to see:

> It is now also night—
> And she wets the ground that covers her
> With tears of love shed for me!

You are not here! Not here! The pages that in tears
I inscribed with my pain, — for their loveliness —
I have open before me, as if to say
That the angel who saw them has departed . . .

Oh, ray of light, that to that pearl
Of divine pain, your sky opened! —
Oh, sparkle of Sun, that within you held
In your final farewell, the finest glimmer!

Tell me how she died,
Tell how she came to die without me,
And — since she truly now sleeps far from me —
Tell me how it is that I remain here alive![5]

The acute sense of torment that pervades "Mis padres duermen" emerges even more clearly in contrast to the much more lighthearted poem Martí improvised in a letter to Ana before his departure for Mexico. The poem alludes to Martí's infrequent correspondence and playfully begs her forgiveness:

MY LOVELY LITTLE SISTER

Happy is the moment when I receive
Your letter; happy is this day,
Because of you I think and to you I send my love . . .
Upon the turgid sea of my papers
Peaceful serenity cannot settle,
And, as I am a bachelor [*doncel*], I act shamelessly
As did young noblemen of old:
I write, save, lose,
I love you dearly, and later you forgive me,
And if my mad judgment thought it sane
For a sad one to adorn himself with crowns,
The most beautiful would be
Those that came from your lovely hands,
Your laurels the most consoling.
To forgive me for losing
That which, being yours, would have been
The most beautiful of all my papers.
Impatient and stupid mail,
Battles and conquers my love and my desire.[6]

Despite not offering a straightforward narrative, this earlier poem-letter reveals much regarding the depth of affection and level of comfort Martí felt for his sister Ana. It is especially remarkable for being one of the very few of his writings to adopt such a light, playful tone, particularly given the grim news from Cuba that necessitated the family's flight to Mexico. The lighthearted tone of this early letter suggests that Martí may have underestimated the severity of his family's struggles; since Leonor destroyed all of his letters to her sometime in 1880, we will never know whether he signaled to his mother any growing awareness of the family's desperate situation in Mexico. Such an awareness would seem at odds with the decision to spend a month in Paris after graduation rather than join the family in Mexico sooner. It is possible that Martí received news from the family during his travels that hastened his departure for Mexico, as a passage from another 1875 poem suggests: "There in the cold and miserable land / My poor heart would lament: / Oh! When will I return, could I have lost / The candorous girl who once / Found in my arms a warm nest, / And scented my dreams with love?"[7] Whatever the case, it is clear from Martí's poetry of this period that Ana's death left a deep and lasting mark, more so for being the first death of someone close to him. In terms of its emotional impact, it was a blow as devastating as his untimely separation from his childhood mentor Mendive.

THE MEXICO THAT MARTÍ ENCOUNTERED IN FEBRUARY 1875 was a young, liberal republic that had recently restored itself after several years of French rule under Maximilian I (1864–1867). Mexico established its independence in 1821 after a protracted and chaotic struggle against Spanish colonialism only to fall to Napoleon III's invading army forty years later. Maximilian attempted to rule the country as a limited monarchy governed by the rule of law and human rights for all subjects. But his rule was beset from the start as the liberal forces he sought to appease opposed the idea of a monarchy, while conservatives rejected his liberal policies and soon abandoned him. His rule was also beset by military resistance from forces loyal to the liberal Benito Juárez, Mexico's president at the time of the French invasion, who continued to claim the title under Maximilian's rule. Once Napoleon III withdrew French forces from the country, Maximilian's defeat and execution at the hands of Mexican republicans soon followed.[8] Once renewed, the Mexican republic under Benito Juárez's presidency (1867–1872) brought a new sense of normalcy and stability that seemed to continue under Sebastián Lerdo de Tejada (1872–1876). The Catholic Church, which had enjoyed broad powers under Maximilian, found its influence waning in the restored republic; under Juárez it was banned from owning property beyond actual churches and monasteries and turned over education and marriage, among other institutions, to state control.[9] By the time of

Martí's arrival in February 1875, Mexico was enjoying an unprecedented period of peace and prosperity.

Mexico's recent history, and specifically its defeat of colonizing forces and rebirth as a liberal republic, no doubt appealed to Martí as a young attorney and anticolonial activist. He was hardly the first to find Mexico's past struggles and promising future attractive, as the country had been a haven for exiled Cubans since declaring its independence from Spain in 1821. Mexico granted asylum to Cuban poet and attorney José María Heredia after his exile for treason in 1824 and again in 1836; a secret society of Cuban exiles known as the Gran Legión del Águila Negra (Grand Legion of the Black Eagle), which tried unsuccessfully to liberate Cuba in 1826, was also based in Mexico.[10] After the onset of the Ten Years' War in 1868, Cuban insurgent leaders like José Miguel Macías, Rodolfo Menéndez de la Peña, and Nicolás Domínguez Cowan, all of whom Martí would praise in later writings, migrated to Mexico and founded chapters of the Partido Revolucionario Cubano (Cuban Revolutionary Party) in exile in Veracruz and elsewhere.[11] Mexico remained officially neutral during the Ten Years' War in Cuba, but President Juárez privately supported the insurgency; his own daughter was married to a Cuban insurgent, Pedro Santacilia.[12] In these and many other cases, Cuban exiles and liberal Mexicans found common cause in the shared ideas of republicanism and democracy despite the opposition of Mexico's Spanish immigrants and other conservative constituencies such as the Catholic Church.

Martí proved no exception to Mexico's history of welcoming Cuban exiles, and Manuel Mercado embraced the younger attorney as a friend and colleague. But beyond his material and moral support of the struggling Martí family and his efforts at introducing this new charge to Mexican politics and society, Mercado's greatest contribution to Martí's burgeoning career may be the role he played in landing him his first professional employment as a writer. *Revista Universal* was Mexico's preeminent liberal magazine, founded in 1868 by Spanish émigré Enrique de Olavarría y Ferrari, and boasted a staff of veteran writers and artists including the Cubans Alfredo Torroella and Antenor Lezcano.[13] Impressed by the young Cuban's precocious erudition and mastery of a range of languages and subjects as well as his infectious intellectual energy, editor and proprietor José Vicente Villada agreed to hire him as a staff writer.

Martí's first article in the *Revista* appeared on March 2, 1875, and launched one of the most prolific periods of his writing career. Some ambiguity remains regarding unsigned works attributed to him; nevertheless, during his twenty-one-month tenure at the *Revista* he is credited with 104 pieces published under his own name and the pseudonyms Anáhuac and Orestes; these ranged from poetry to art criticism, from news to editorials and political commentary, to his translation of Victor Hugo's "Mes fils."[14] Fellow writer Juan de Dios Peza later testified to the young Cuban's prodigious output: "We have seen him at one go write the editorial, variety, and gazette sections of a paper in a single day."[15] Martí's prolific output may be partly attributed to financial need; his newfound work was simply crucial to restoring his struggling family to some semblance of solvency. But his position at the *Revista* also offered the talented young writer and thinker his first real opportunity to regularly reach a receptive audience for his rich and varied writings.

With his employment at the *Revista Universal*, Martí became the de facto head of the household, a subtle yet momentous shift against which Mariano could offer little resistance. Martí insisted that his mother and sisters cease the work they had been doing as seamstresses for the Mexican army that until then had been essential to the family's survival; after some discussion, he agreed to let his siblings accept a few small jobs to cover their personal expenses but no more. Although he often worked well into the night at the *Revista*'s offices, Leonor insisted on waiting up for him, and his sister Amelia would stay up with her mother, reading to her until he arrived. As they lived on a second floor, it was necessary for Martí to announce his arrival by tossing a small stone at their upstairs window; this was Amelia's signal to descend the stairs with the enormous front-door key and let him in.

Martí's intense work schedule kept him away from home much of the time; his now steady income allowed him to indulge in pleasures previously denied him. Chief among these was Mexican coffee, which he later praised as "America's haschisch, which makes one dream without dulling the senses; tea's conqueror; the hot nectar, [whose] perfume grows like a dream of love, as the winds that waft a cloud across the sky."[16] During this period Martí apparently indulged in hashish of the literal kind as well, as his June 1875 ode to the narcotic makes exceedingly clear:

> The crazy troubadour takes up his lyre:
> The indolent Arab to haschisch aspires.
> And the Arab does well, because that plant
> Inhaled, the scent intoxicates, enchants . . .
>
> Oh woman's kiss, call at my door!
> Haschisch of my pain, come to my mouth![17]

Within the context of the late nineteenth century, Martí's affection for stimulants of the metabolic (coffee) and creative (hashish) kind is hardly unusual; many of the French writers whom Martí admired, including Baudelaire and Balzac and the critic Théophile Gautier, embraced both to varying degrees as part of the creative process.[18] The appearance of Martí's poem "Haschisch," among his longest from this period, in the pages of the mainstream liberal *Revista Universal* suggests that if its use was considered bohemian, it was hardly controversial or stigmatizing. Nevertheless, Martí's enthusiastic references to these substances during the period indicate that along with his new professional life — and lifestyle — also came some adult habits.[19]

DESPITE THE MARTÍS' IMPROVED FINANCIAL SITUATION and now relatively serene existence, they were still living in the house in which their beloved Ana had died. Ana's physical absence belied a lingering sense of sadness and regret that no amount of money or good news could assuage. After a time Martí resolved to move his family to a new location in a different part of town, where the sorrowful memory of Ana's final days might be laid to rest. The move to a new home was not without its ironies, chief among them its proximity to the Panteón de Dolores, the city's new and lovely cemetery. Yet their new surroundings, a spacious, airy home fronted by a lovely garden and bordered by pleasant, tree-lined streets, brought the family no small comfort, especially compared to the cramped quarters in which they had lived in the heart of the city. The house was large enough for Martí to have his own spacious room in the back that doubled as a study.[20] They moved only a few miles across town, but their new surroundings brought them a renewed sense of peace and the promise of better days.

The Martís soon came to regret their choice for a new house, if not the move itself. The spring rains revealed the house's, indeed the entire neighborhood's, greatest shortcoming. Flooding had been a problem for Mexico's capital ever since its conquest and rechristening as Mexico City in the early sixteenth century; the Great Flood of 1629 killed several thousand people, and the city spent the next hundred years filling in Lake Texcoco and surrounding lakes to resolve the problem and allow the city to grow.[21] Despite being only a few miles from the firmer ground of the city center, the area surrounding the Martís' new home was prone to flooding at times so badly that an outside breezeway leading to the bedrooms could only be navigated by a small boat the family acquired for the purpose. The ongoing problems with flooding overrode their fondness for the house, and the Martís soon moved again, this time to a smaller but more secure house north of the city center in Huacalco.[22]

Soon after this move, perhaps from the humidity and dampness of the former house or the stress of moving again, Mariano fell ill with a cough, high fever, and chest pains, symptoms that suggest a bout of pneumonia. The recurrence of his asthma, from which he had suffered periodically for years, complicated the patriarch's condition and confined him to bed. Martí became alarmed at the suddenness and severity of his father's illness, the more so for having lost his sister so recently. During this time he was a constant presence at Mariano's bedside, personally administering medications and taking charge of feeding and otherwise caring for him, with a tenderness that until now had been utterly lacking in their relationship. Mariano eventually recovered, but the ordeal weakened him considerably; Martí dutifully acquired a rocking chair that would allow the old man to sit in comfort when away from his bed.[23] The experience of caring for his sick father significantly affected Martí's view of Mariano, the initial sympathy and tenderness he felt toward the old man growing into a belated admiration and respect for his father's steadfastness and sense of duty in the face of much suffering. These feelings emerged most notably in the son's contribution to the *Revista*'s August 12 issue of a glowing tribute to his father in all but name:

> An example to novices, a staff for the beginner, pride of the nation, and cause for worship and veneration: Our gray-haired elders are all this, and more . . .
>
> Oh, gray head, life so true for embodying the beginning and end of this life, image of the perpetual and of the eternal moving toward what is called death bestowing gifts that strengthen those who do not yet carry the heavy and necessary burden of living! Oh, ancient men, delight for the spirit, joy for the eyes, pride of the young, and the rich shine and luster of the nation's abundant remembrances![24]

Martí's early writings for the *Revista Universal* revealed that his family, especially Mariano and Leonor, were much on his mind during the first months of their reunion in Mexico; it was then that he published the poem "Mis padres duermen" and a reminiscence titled "El reporte de ayer" (Yesterday's Report), of his mother's courageous rescue of him during the attack on Havana's Villanueva theater and subsequent massacre on the night of January 24, 1869.[25] But the appearance of "La ley de veneración" (The Law of Veneration) in the *Revista*'s August 12 issue affirmed what everyone in the Martí household already knew: that Martí's relationship with Mariano had deepened and grown through their shared trial of the father's illness, from resentment and mistrust to a wary respect, to a tenderness born from sympathy, to admiration and, yes, finally, to love.[26]

WHATEVER DOMESTIC CHALLENGES MARTÍ FACED DURING his early months in Mexico, professionally he was thriving. His regular contributions to the *Revista Universal* marked him as a new and exciting voice in Mexican letters, an up-and-coming talent to watch, and soon the capital's literary and political elites began to reach out to him. Within three weeks of his debut at the *Revista* Martí was accepted by unanimous vote into the Liceo

Hidalgo, Mexico's foremost literary association. On the evening of April 5 he participated in his first panel discussion at the Liceo and quickly thereafter became one of the city's most popular and sought-after presenters. By May 7 he was listed on the *Revista*'s masthead as one of its editors. As his reputation as a writer and public speaker grew, the invitations became more prestigious and frequent. The capital's Subcommittee for the School of Law invited Martí to the May 14 inaugural session for the new term; on August 8 he was present at a ribbon-cutting ceremony for a new elementary school by invitation of the Office of the President.[27] Although his work at the *Revista* played a major role in Martí's newfound esteem, he also benefited significantly from his continued association with Mercado and his new alignment with the city's Freemasons, a community known for its support of liberal politics that counted the late president Juárez among its members.[28]

Along with his ascendant status as a writer and public figure, Martí's notoriety grew as an anticolonial activist and passionate supporter of Cuban independence — a reputation that soon led to heated exchanges with conservatives in the pages of Mexico City's newspapers. Martí's position at the *Revista* enabled him to closely monitor political developments in Spain and Cuba; as he had in Madrid, he soon found himself at odds with pro-Spanish sympathizers in Mexico City. In the May 12 issue of the *Revista* he reproached the conservative, pro-Spanish paper *La Iberia* for an editorial criticizing Guatemala for recognizing Cuba's revolutionary government. Two weeks later he took on *La Colonia Española* of Mexico City in defense of the Cuban insurgency, lamenting that he could not be there to fight alongside them: "Since I cannot, due to illness, go fight alongside those who defend my country's independence, it would be dishonest to allow, when I am in a position to respond, such gratuitous and vulgar statements to stand without an appropriate response."[29] As he had done in Spain, Martí took every opportunity to expose and counter anti-Cuban and pro-imperial polemics wherever he found them. With the *Revista*, however, he had found a bully pulpit from which to advocate for his cause and punish its enemies. His strident advocacy of Cuban independence was earning him more numerous — and eventually more powerful — enemies; in Mexico these were far outnumbered by his friends and supporters. After years of being treated by the Spanish as an undesirable, as a criminal, imprisoned, beaten, exiled, marginalized, the young man found himself welcomed, even celebrated, by a community he barely knew.

THE SPRING OF 1875 MARKED A RETURN TO THE ROMANTIC entanglements that characterized Martí's time in Spain. Here it was not Mercado who served as gatekeeper but fellow *Revista Universal* correspondent Juan de Dios Peza who accompanied Martí to many social gatherings and introduced him to the capital's literati.[30] It was at one such event in March 1875 that Peza introduced Martí to poet Rosario de la Peña, with whom the young Cuban fell swiftly in love. He was hardly the first to do so, as the twenty-six-year-old de la Peña had by then been queen bee and muse for a long line of smitten poets and writers. Despite her beauty, intellect, and considerable charm, she suffered an undeserved reputation as a sort of black widow with a dark romantic history; her fiancé, a Captain Juan Espinoza, died in a duel when she was only nineteen, and she was later wrongly blamed for the suicide of poet Manuel Acuña, whose poem "Nocturne for Rosario" portrayed her as the object of his obsessive and unrequited love.[31] Martí's first meeting with de la Peña likely occurred at one of the regular literary gatherings she hosted in her home at which she played a fluent piano and recited from memory her favorite poems of the time. His attraction to her was both immediate and intense; his first written declaration of love appears in an album that de la Peña kept as a memento of her gatherings in which guests were invited to write dedications, bits of poetry, or whatever else they wished to contribute. On March 27, 1875, Martí added a lengthy untitled poem to de la Peña's album that leaves no doubt of his feelings for her:

> I do not woo her for this life: —
> For but a few hours along the path we walk,
> And between kisses and tears, speak
> Of the shared instant of our parting! . . .
>
> What a pleasure to think! And what good fortune
> To dream of a woman as pure shadow!
> And how many, how many the hours
> Whose shadowy ills I hold within,
> How many dawns have found me, surprised,
> As I dreamed of lips and awaited kisses!
>
> Oh, let me remember! Go and leave me
> To love more than your love, your memory,
> As a likely good reflects truly,
> And a delight but of air is still delightful![32]

A mere two days later, on March 29, Martí dedicated to his new muse a second, shorter poem with a more pointed declaration:

> Rosario, I thought of you, of your hair
> That the world of shadows would envy,

And focused my mind upon it
And wished to dream that you were mine.[33]

During the weeks that followed, Martí continued to be a regular guest at de la Peña's social gatherings but made no headway in his attempts to win her affection. Three undated letters to her survive, the first of which he sent while covering sessions of the Mexican Congress in April 1875. Martí's frustration at his beloved's continued resistance is outdone only by his bewilderment at his inability to work; this was a first for Martí, who had until now managed to maintain his prolific writing output and political passions amid personal and romantic turmoil:

> I am at the Congress; I should be writing my chronicle for this session, and I sit down to write, not of thoughts that I now do not have, but of my need for these hours to pass that yet separate me from you.
>
> Perhaps tomorrow I will not feel such haste; but I feel it today, and I write it down.
>
> . . . I lived an instant yesterday by your side. Such sweet joys I had then, such intimate and unforgettable gratitude that my lips would have wanted to come to rest at your hands — but Ramírez is doing me great harm today.
>
> And they speak now of budgets and furniture — there are here many of life's troubles.[34]

The "Ramírez" of the penultimate sentence is Ignacio Ramírez, fellow contributor at the *Revista Universal*. It is not clear from the letter why Martí intimates that Ramírez has done him "great harm." He might have been involved in assigning Martí to cover the sessions, thus indirectly compelling his distance from de la Peña; or perhaps he merely interrupted the "instant" Martí describes, which in his mind might have lasted longer or provided some further opportunity for intimacy with his beloved. Whatever the case, it is clear from this and other letters to de la Peña that Martí was, for the first time in his life, deep in the throes of unrequited love.

Although no written responses from de la Peña to Martí survive, we know from his references to them that she sent him several brief — and for him, unsatisfying — letters. Having been scarred by her experiences with Acuña's suicide and the earlier death of her fiancé, de la Peña kept her distance from the many suitors who followed. Her polite yet firm rejection of Martí's advances thus suggests as much her lack of interest in him personally as a wish to withdraw more generally from romantic entanglements. Whichever the case, Martí's final known letter to her comes in response to her apparent attempts to dissuade him from his fruitless pursuit. Despite his still ardent declarations of love, the letter hints at a recognition of defeat and more specifically of having reached certain limits that he would not breach:

> It seems that I should respond now to your letters. So wrapped am I now in shame that although I believe it to be true, whatever I told you of it would be lies. Once again you have attempted to contain your heart before me; you could have told me more than what your letters say; but I do love them as they are and love them the more each time I see them, and however brief and few, I still forgive you in spite of my demanding will, and in these modest or calculatingly cold letters, I rejoice and read and love in the end.[35]

Along with his lasting devotion, however, Martí also declares his resolution not to be destroyed by love as he believes de la Peña's previous lover was:

> It is distressing to feel oneself so alive and full of tenderness and of undying kindness and to sob for hours on end, — without my soul allowing me the right to release moans, in this tepid atmosphere, in this unbearable smallness, in this monotonous sameness, in this measured life, in this emptiness of love that weighs upon my body, that overwhelms it, and that perennially suffocates and oppresses me within it. Sickness of living: the sickness that killed Acuña.
>
> Rosario, awaken me, not as you did him, pardonable for his highness of soul, yet in the end weak and unworthy of me. Because to live is a burden, so I live; because to live is to suffer, so I live: — I live, because I would be stronger than every obstacle and every force.[36]

And so a heartbroken yet unbowed Martí lived on, matching Manuel Acuña in the written expression of his despair but choosing not to emulate the Mexican poet's tragic end. As the futility of his love for Rosario de la Peña became clear, Martí again immersed himself in his work. Aside from an April 18 poem, "Without Love," which served simultaneously as a farewell to de la Peña and an apology to his abandoned Spanish loves, he returned to the polemics against pro-Spanish publications that had characterized his time in Spain.[37] In addition to his aforementioned May editorials denouncing anti-Cuban remarks in *La Iberia* and *La Colonia Española*, he published on June 9 a response to the former paper's view that his continued advocacy of Cuban independence from exile constituted an abuse of Mexico's hospitality toward its immigrant population. Martí's rebuttal was preceded by a statement of support from the *Revista*'s editorial staff affirming "that on matters regarding the Island, we share his views," emphasizing his right "to express his views as he pleases," and praising the young Cuban for the restraint and responsibility of his Cuba editorials.[38]

In the months that followed, Martí's renown as a writer and public figure continued to grow, and he would also fulfill a dream from his days in Zaragoza: the production of his very own play, *Amor com amor se paga* (Love with Love Repaid). Yet he continued for a time to mourn de la Peña; letters from his erstwhile Spanish lovers, especially Blanca de Montalvo, whose marriage to another man he still deeply regretted, went unanswered.[39] With the fall of 1875, though, came new love in liaisons that would try his relationship with his family and strain his bond with Manuel Mercado. Even as he nursed the wounds from his break with Montalvo and his failure to woo de la Peña, the amorous Cuban found himself entangled, as he did in Spain, with at least two women at the same time.

IN LATE MAY OR EARLY JUNE, MARTÍ MADE THE ACQUAINtance of a new arrival to the Mexican theater, twenty-five-year-old Cuban-born Eloísa Agüero de Ossorio. He had not seen her perform but was sufficiently impressed by her reputation as a talented young actress to write a cordially enthusiastic profile of her in the June 6 issue of the *Revista*. Two days later he again praised Agüero's debut at the Teatro Principal in a column otherwise dedicated to the event itself, a fund-raiser for striking workers in which she had performed.[40] It was at this event that Martí learned of the young actress's support for the ongoing Cuban insurgency, a political position that would have endeared her to him.[41] In August Agüero participated in another Teatro Principal fund-raising effort, this time for the victims of the flooding of France's Garonne River that killed five hundred to a thousand people and leveled Toulouse and its environs.[42] Martí wrote about the event in the *Revista*'s August 7 issue, and although he did not mention her directly, he had by then taken notice of Agüero as someone who embodied so many of the qualities and virtues he valued.[43]

Over the course of their relationship between August and November 1875, Martí wrote an unknown number of letters to Agüero; these are now lost, perhaps destroyed by the actress, who was married at the time. Twelve of Agüero's letters—likely the whole of her correspondence to him—survive, and these neatly define the arc and depth of their affair.

The first of Agüero's letters to Martí, dated August 31, is cordial and focuses mostly on theater business; Agüero is lobbying for something, perhaps a role, and has been promised a response by the following week. This first letter concludes in an almost courtly manner: "I send my sincere affection, extending my hand, your true friend, Eloísa."[44]

The distance implied by the letter's "hand" of friendship has quickly diminished by Agüero's second letter, sent during the week of September 6, in which she announces that she will be home in the evening and pointedly asks, "Will you come? What time?" Martí did not visit Agüero that evening, a circumstance she takes for a misunderstanding in her letter of the next day: "Yesterday you misunderstood a paragraph of mine; I said 'Will you come see me?' You thought I meant at the theater."[45]

The shift from the professional to the personal in Agüero's next letter—and the unmistakable jealous streak that emerges in it—strongly suggests that the two started an affair sometime in September. As a married woman—even one whose estranged husband remained in Cuba—Agüero could not risk any public display of affection that might raise the suspicion of colleagues or the theater-going public. She thus complains bitterly to Martí, sharing her frustration at having to conceal their relationship even as others flirted openly with him:

> How embittering it is to have to speak in enigmas, all the more so when so many are listening! I cannot take this, Martí; I can't, I won't. . . . How many of those did you see last night who would have you believe that *they* are your ideal beloved, created by Nature for your happiness? But the worst of it all is that you so frequently delude yourself.[46]

The letter's pointed declarations suggest that the affair's secretive nature was not necessarily Agüero's choice or if it was, that she found the prospect of maintaining the façade unbearable. Martí seems not to have responded, at least in writing, to his lover's complaints, as Agüero's next letter several weeks later makes no mention of a reply.

Compounding the social and strategic complexities of Martí's affair with Agüero was his return to the life of the theater. Martí met the Spanish actor Enrique Guasp de Peris back in February 1875 as a fellow passenger on the *City of Merida* en route to Veracruz. The two appear to have fallen out of touch until a mutual friend, Cuban writer Nicolás Azcárate, reintroduced them at a gathering some months later.[47] When in late September Guasp assumed the directorship of a new government-sponsored theater company, the Conservatory of Music and Drama, he quickly commissioned Martí to write a play for him and the company's leading lady, Concepción (Conchita) Padilla, to be staged at the prestigious Teatro Nacional.[48] Padilla entreated the Cuban writer to produce "a light entertainment, a modest work, a plaything, a proverb"—language that appears almost verbatim in the finished play.[49]

Martí in fact quoted—in a sense, transcribed—much of what was happening in his life at the time into the play. *Amor com amor se paga* is, as Guasp and Padilla requested, a relatively slight albeit inventive and beautifully written bit of entertainment, a romantic comedy in verse staged in a single act with just two characters. The play provides a valuable snapshot of a moment in time, a portrait of Martí's life and state of mind in late 1875. Amazingly, he wrote the play in a single day, as a metafiction that portrayed not only the process of its own production but its author's frustrated passion and desire to love anew.[50] The play unfolds as a dialogue between its two characters, Julián and Leonor, who collaborate on the writing of a romantic comedy and in the process fall in love. Beyond directly referencing his own real-life circumstances as he wrote the play, Martí includes at least one nod—or perhaps a smirk—to Agüero's incomplete quote in a letter of the old proverb "He who waits . . ."; in the play Leonor begins to speak the line, but Julián finishes it: "—Despairs, as they say."[51] In turning the mirror on the realities of his life and the production of the play, Martí effectively replaced his real-life lost loves with the character Leonor, putting the actress in the beloveds' place; the result is a fictional reenactment of loves won and lost, a fantasy staging of a second chance to find true and enduring love. Its closing speech, delivered by protagonist Julián, declares this very intention: "Nothing better can I give, / Who without homeland in which to live / Nor woman for whom to die, / Nor arrogance to try, / Suffer, and waver, and flatter myself / Thinking that here tonight, if nowhere else / Is Love is with Love Repaid."[52]

Given that Julián and Leonor have just exchanged passionate mutual declarations of undying love, his closing assertion that he lacks a "woman for whom to die" makes no sense unless one grasps it, and really the entire closing speech, as unmediated self-portraiture. It is as if, caught up in the play's mounting romantic tension and its characters' climactic, rhapsodic declarations of mutual love, its author no longer even bothers to conceal himself behind his protagonist and speaks directly to the audience. Thus read as autobiography, the statement "Nor woman for whom to die" strongly suggests that Martí was no longer seeing Agüero, or, if he was, thought little of the relationship when he wrote the play in late September.

Although we cannot know for certain the state of Martí's relationship with Eloísa Agüero as he wrote *Amor com amor se paga*, we can construct a timeline based on the play as well as Agüero's letters and Martí's poem "Letters from Spain," which he wrote in late September and published in the *Revista Universal* three weeks later.[53] The poem's explicit longing for Montalvo amply confirms that his affair with Agüero had not dimmed the torch he still carried for her. The poem's portrayal of a man visiting the tomb of famous star-crossed lovers Abelard and Héloïse and bemoaning the absence of his own beloved deeply disturbed the already jealous Agüero. The revelation that her lover had all along been pining for someone else, even if that person was thousands of miles away, unnerved her enough that she contacted Martí for the first time in weeks.

Agüero's letter is undated, but her reference to the poem's publication "yesterday, Sunday" means that she wrote it on the morning of October 18, the day after it appeared in the *Revista*. The letter reveals that Martí had written the poem "three weeks ago," which would mean the last week of September. That three-week gap suggests a corresponding one in Agüero's and Martí's relationship; how else to plausibly explain her awareness of the poem's creation three weeks before yet her utter surprise at its contents now? Given Martí's penchant for self-portraiture in his poems and his awareness that Agüero might read this particular one in the *Revista*, it seems unlikely that he would so publicly reveal his lingering attachment to Montalvo while still seeing Agüero. This becomes a more likely scenario in the context of Agüero's admonition from the previous letter that she "cannot take this, Martí; I can't, I won't."[54]

In retrospect Agüero's declaration, followed by the weeks of silence separating it from the poem's publication, suggests her first unsuccessful attempt to end an affair that was causing her considerable pain. Her insistence in the later, October 17 letter that she is "resolved not to write [to him] again" seems directed more to herself than Martí, a reminder to herself not to reengage him after the emotional shock of the poem compelled her to write. For Martí's part, his inclusion of her in "Letters from Spain" via the historical Héloïse d'Argenteuil is only the most obvious hint that suggests a response to the earlier kiss-off letter: he also paraphrases Agüero's description of her suffering as "an ill that has no remedy" in the poem as "strange ills that have no cure" — except that he suffers not for her but for the absent Montalvo.

Compounding Agüero's anguish was her belief that the direct beneficiary of Martí's fading ardor for Rosario de la Peña would not be her but the actress Conchita Padilla. This unwelcome transference happened partly due to the secretive nature of the affair, as Agüero had little opportunity for public contact with him and thus little knowledge of his interactions with other women; it was thus inevitable that some other attractive, clever, and less socially hampered young woman would eventually catch his eye. The main catalyst for Martí's specific attachment to Padilla, however, became his regular presence at rehearsals for *Amor con amor se paga* where he worked closely with the actors, especially her. The play's ardently romantic dialogue undoubtedly fueled the pair's mutual attraction, as its author often stood in for leading man Guasp to help Padilla practice her lines. These included exchanges such as this one, when the lovers reach the passionate crescendo toward which the entire play has been building:

> SHE: Julián! . . .
> HE: Leonor! . . .
> SHE: *(Disturbed.)* I don't know . . .
> HE: The words so difficult to say,
>   If an honest soul they're born from,
>   Quickly, quickly to your lips come!

SHE: I love you! I love you!
HE: [. . .] Now that I have heard
　　"I love you" from your lovely lips,
　　There is more blue in the sky,
　　More warmth on this earth there is,
　　And the air a kiss, another,
　　Wave upon wave carries away.[55]

We will never know for certain whether Martí and Padilla acted on their mutual attraction and consummated their relationship. Padilla denied that it ever happened, insisting in a 1925 interview that the friendship remained a platonic one "that never transgressed the limits of polite courtliness."[56] Padilla recalled that she rarely saw Martí outside of work, that her father, an actor, always accompanied her to rehearsals, though he remained in the dressing room, and that he too considered Martí the perfect gentleman.[57] Martí's sister Amelia, who was twelve years old at the time of the events, asserted in a 1924 interview that her family believed otherwise; she said Leonor Martí vehemently disapproved of the relationship and recruited family friend Manuel Mercado to find a more suitable match to derail her son's interest in Padilla.[58]

Whether or not Martí and Padilla entered into an affair, it seems that neither the Martí family nor Mercado had any idea of the affair that he was carrying on with Agüero. It was perhaps Agüero's awareness of Martí's growing attraction to Padilla and the knowledge that she could lose him for good that led her to renege on her pledge to stay away and to send him this terse note: "I wish to see you: I will wait for you until 6. I am somewhat unwell. Goodbye. If you think [of me]. I have been thinking [of you] a long time and have suffered for it. Your friend. Eloísa."[59] Their affair thus resumed, even as rehearsals for *Amor con amor se paga* continued and Martí's and Conchita Padilla's mutual affection grew apace.

IN THE WEEKS THAT FOLLOWED, MARTÍ'S PHYSICAL STRUGgles continued and became more pronounced as he neared the biggest night of his artistic life: the December 19, 1875, premiere of *Amor con amor se paga*. Since his arrival in Mexico in February and through all that subsequently transpired—Martí's increasingly tangled web of relations with Agüero, Padilla, the absent Rosario de la Peña, and the ghost of Blanca de Montalvo; his long hours at the *Revista Universal*; and now rehearsals for his play and the pressure of supporting his family and especially his ailing father—his health, though at times precarious, did not fail him. Yet as far back as May 27, in a *Revista Universal* editorial he lamented that only his ill health prevented him from joining his fellow Cubans in their ongoing insurgency on the island.[60] By year's end the combined stress of work, women, and the theater were beginning to wear Martí down. On November 2, a Tuesday, he felt unwell enough to stay home, and a concerned Manuel Mercado paid him a visit. November may have brought Cuban politics, with the attendant stresses and complexities, back into his life as the insurgent leader Manuel de Quesada y Loynaz was in Mexico with President Lerdo's blessing organizing an invasion that never materialized. No evidence has ever linked Martí directly to the planned invasion, but given Quesada's connections to high Mexican officials and others in Martí's circle, he is likely to have at least known about it.[61]

Compounding Martí's worries at this time was the unraveling of his affair with Eloisa Agüero and the emotional breakdown she was suffering because of it. Her last four letters to him, sent between mid-October and November 22, strongly suggest that the lovers' renewed affair was doing her significant harm. The shift in these letters from addressing him in the formal pronoun *Usted* to the more intimate *tú* suggests a resurgent sense of closeness and affection that Martí seems to have somewhat reciprocated;[62] he was by now comfortable enough with Agüero to show her love letters from another woman, on one of which she wrote playful, patronizing remarks about the sender. Agüero evidently believed she had nothing to fear from the letter's author, twenty-two-year-old Carmen Zayas Bazán, and was seemingly more concerned about the prospect of losing Martí to fellow actress Padilla.[63] Thus although Agüero's experience of reading "Letters from Spain" on October 17 may have inspired her change of heart, it was the more immediate perceived threat posed by Padilla that compelled her to abandon former restraints even as she recognized that the affair was doomed.

Agüero's last four letters to Martí portray a woman aware of the impossibility of ever living openly with her beloved yet struggling mightily with the dawning realization that their affair must end. In her first letter from this phase — the seventh overall — she asks her secret lover, "Tell, why cherish what cannot, should not be realized? . . . I do not want to see you. At the sight of you I forget even myself, I want to fly into your arms and repeat a thousand and one times: I love you, my sweet, I love you madly, as I am capable of loving!"[64] The next letter suggests a growing intimacy between the two, as Agüero playfully writes of a sweet she will use to attract Martí to her bed: "I have prepared a dessert, which I myself have cooked. Do not laugh [at my simpleness], my love. . . . I am simply explaining, to let you know that in an hour's time you will find it in the bedroom, where I dream of joining you."[65]

By November Agüero had become aware of yet another rival for Martí's affections. Zayas Bazán emigrated from Cuba with her family in 1871, three years before the Martís left. Attorney Francisco Zayas Bazán, a widower, moved to Mexico City with his three daughters, Isabel, Rosa, and Carmen. The Zayas Bazáns traced their lineage back to Spain's earliest incursions into the New World; Francisco was a descendant of don Ignacio Zayas Bazán, who in the 1620s had served as president of the Audiencia Real de Santo Domingo, the first court the Spanish crown established in the Americas, and later became governor of Santo Domingo. Other prominent ancestors included Cristóbal Zayas Bazán, who served in Cuba's colonial government in the mid-eighteenth century.[66]

According to several widely accepted but apocryphal accounts, Martí did not meet his future wife until December 1875; one such version, later circulated by Martí's nephew Raúl García Martí, has him seeing Carmen for the first time at a performance of *Amor con amor se paga* and asking Mercado for an introduction.[67] But this is false, as letters confirm that the two already had met by early November. Martí met Carmen's father through Ramón Guzmán, Martí's landlord and the husband of Carmen's sister Rosa.[68] The Zayas Bazán home on Calle San Francisco stood right next door to the *Revista Universal*'s offices, and by the time the play premiered Martí was a frequent guest there, often coming to play chess with Francisco. It was during one such visit that he met Carmen.

Agüero's written remarks on an early letter of Carmen's to Martí confirm that the younger woman was pursuing him in November 1875 and that Agüero knew it. Carmen's third, undated letter to Martí, a brief note in which she explains that she cannot see him and therefore can only contact him via letter, contains this comment later added by Agüero: "What lovely little love notes. Truly you were wasting your time despite believing you could *love her faithfully some day*. It is a waste of time to reply to such [illegible]." The italicized words paraphrase Martí's own to Carmen in a previous letter and that Carmen quoted back to him in her reply, making it clear that Martí shared with Agüero all of his correspondences with Carmen to that point.[69] But the exchange demonstrates that Carmen's first love letters to Martí well predated not only the premiere of *Amor con amor se paga* but also Agüero's departure for Havana in mid-November. In fact, they were likely written even earlier in November, as Agüero already had stopped seeing Martí when she left Mexico.

Carmen's first, undated letter to Martí from November 1875 confirms that she knew him before she started writing to him: "I have long loved you," she writes, "but in silence, long has my heart belonged to you."[70] This and other early letters from Carmen reveal that she was, if not the pursuer, then at least frankly desirous of being pursued, as she declares in her first letter: "I loved you ever since I first saw you, [and] from that moment I felt being born in my heart the inextinguishable flame of first love."[71] In his reply, now lost, Martí expressed some doubts, if not of Carmen herself then perhaps about the wisdom of entering a relationship with her. But the ambivalence of his response, far from discouraging Carmen, only heightened her desire to win him:

I adore you with the delirium of a pure heart!!! Love me as I love you.
I swear to adore you unto death.

Tell me, what do you not believe from my letter? Do you think I
would lie to you? I, who love you so much? Not for a moment, for I believe that matters as sacred as love should be treated with the utmost
frankness.

Despite my little experience and age I have the misfortune of doubt-
ing everything, for I have seen so many hearts withered before their
time by disillusion. I have seen enough to be afraid, especially when you
tell me that perhaps, maybe, you could love me faithfully, this is terrible.
Where I enthusiastically expected to read in your letter words of love
I find only doubt and coldness. I beg you to be more loving in another
[illegible].[72]

Beyond the possibility that he was simply not interested in her at the time,
Martí's ambivalent response to Carmen could suggest a reluctance to begin
what would be a very visible courtship between a well-known public figure and
the daughter of a prominent family while continuing to secretly see Agüero.
Martí knew that Carmen's father opposed the potential union, believing that
however impressive the young Cuban's talents and advanced degrees, he was
not a suitable match for a family of the Zayas Bazáns' wealth and lineage.

By early November, Agüero resolved to end the affair and return to Cuba,
where she would formally separate from her estranged husband: "It is necessary
that we stop seeing each other, to stop this affection that grows by the day."[73]
Her final letter before leaving Mexico reveals both her deep devotion to Martí
and her resolution to leave him:

For pity's sake I ask that you flee from me. Do not ask whether this is
my desire, no, it is not, I want but to live by your side sharing the breath
that intoxicates and maddens me, but I can no longer stand seeing you'
with this seemingly calm and amicable coolness. . . . Do not question
me, I beg of you, and I ask compassion. Receive my final kiss and my
eternal Goodbye.[74]

On November 22 Agüero, now back in Havana, wrote to Martí one last time.
This final letter confirms that she received a formal separation from her husband—whom she calls "this infernal shadow"—and implores Martí to both remember her and "[let] the secret die with you."[75]

They never saw each other again. But the lovers' secret did not die with Martí
and did not remain secret for long. A poem by Agüero found years later among

Leonor Martí's papers confirms that the young woman wrote to Martí at least once more in hopes of reviving the relationship but that her correspondence never reached him.[76]

Whatever relief or simplification Agüero's departure provided for Martí at a crucial moment, the end of the affair removed but a single thread from the complex web of relations and circumstances that defined this stage of his life. Now all of the remaining threads of a life held together by seeming force of will were converging toward a single point: the night of December 19, when *Amor con amor se paga* would debut on the stage of Mexico City's Teatro Principal.

IF MARTÍ HAD ANY CONCERNS OR RESERVATIONS ABOUT *Amor con amor se paga*, he need not have worried. The play opened on December 19 to a packed house and glowing reviews, launching what promised to be a long and successful career in the theater. Word of mouth attracted the cream of the city's literary and artistic communities as well as Martí's friends and acquaintances, among them his colleagues from the *Revista Universal*. In one box sat the family of the late president Benito Juárez, including his son-in-law and Cuban insurgent Pedro Santacilia. In another, near the stage and adjacent to the Juárezes' box, sat Martí's own family: Mariano, Leonor, and sisters Antonia, María del Carmen, Amelia, and the recently arrived Chata.[77] Also present was Carmen, taking advantage of a rare opportunity to see Martí if only from a distance; as her brief third letter to him reveals, their interactions at this time were limited to writing due to her father's opposition: "I think we should communicate in writing because any other way is impossible."[78] On December 19, Carmen caught much more than a glimpse of her beloved; she witnessed a triumphant moment after the play's conclusion that raised his stature in her eyes even more.

Martí's name did not appear either on the marquee or advertisements for the play, so when the final curtain fell the approving crowd called out for the author. After some resistance from the young playwright, Conchita Padilla managed to retrieve him from the wings and bring him on stage to boisterous applause. As Martí stood scanning the house full of friendly faces — Juan de Dios Peza and other friends from work; fellow poets such as José Peón y Contreras and Justo Sierra; his parents, crying tears of happiness — Padilla attempted to place on his head a laurel crown that the company had made to honor him. Refusing the coronating gesture, Martí instead held the laurel to his chest in a symbolic gesture of gratitude, to even louder cheers from the adoring crowd.[79]

Drinking in the footlights and the applause, basking in the adulation of friends and supporters, the frail young man on the stage of the Teatro Principal finally realized a long-cherished dream. Martí and his family could, for at least one night, forget their past sufferings and the struggles yet to come.

Reviews the next day were generally enthusiastic. *El Eco de Ambos Mundos* and *El Ciglo* hailed *Amor con amor se paga* as a fine work by an important new artist. *La Iberia*'s reviewer hailed Martí as "a young man with an immense future" and praised the "enchanting novelty of [the play's] simple plot, its graceful verses that seem as if sprung from our own Golden Age, the delicacy of its sentiment so elegantly expressed, and [which] so naturally unfolds."[80] *El Socialista* was even more effusive in its praise, embracing Martí as "a brother" who earned "with his talent and sentiment a place in our society, in our journalism, in our literature, and in our theater." This expression of welcome was apparently widespread, as the very next day Martí was informally accepted into the prestigious Sociedad Gorostiza, an organization of Mexico's most prominent artists and writers, at one of its regular Tuesday-night gatherings.[81]

The press's only negative remarks, in *El Monitor*, in fact targeted not the play but its author's own extemporaneous gestures on the stage:

> Mr. Martí was called to the stage and warmly applauded, but the audience was supremely displeased by the manner of struggle he carried on with Miss Padilla and with Mr. Guasp. Such fits of modesty are fine behind the scenes but not in front of the public, before whom one should act more respectfully.[82]

Such minor quibbles little blunted the play's popularity among Mexican audiences. For several months *Amor con amor se paga* played regularly on Thursdays and Sundays to generally packed houses and enthusiastic applause. But despite his obvious enjoyment of that moment on the stage of the Teatro Principal, Martí did not seek to relive it. Stung perhaps by *El Monitor*'s criticism or perhaps trying to avoid problems with Carmen, who had divulged her jealousy of other women, he opted thereafter for the anonymity of the wings or the theater box and did not again appear before the audience.

Another possible reason for Martí's reluctance to reprise his triumphant appearance on the stage of the Teatro Principal was his family's regular presence in the theater. Given Leonor's reaction once she learned of the mutual attraction between her son and Conchita Padilla, we may reasonably surmise that Martí anticipated that disapproval and wished to avoid any further displays of affection in his mother's presence. Such a pre-emptive measure, if in fact it was calculated, nevertheless failed to avert Leonor's suspicion.

The Martís became a fixture at the Teatro Principal's Thursday and Sunday performances of *Amor con amor se paga*, sitting always in the same box by the stage. For Martí's sister Chata, the play was her only diversion outside the home, as her brother refused to let his married sister accompany him to social gatherings and events as he did her single siblings.[83] Despite the absence of any explicit signs — or even perhaps of any acknowledgment between Martí and Padilla themselves — of a budding romance, Leonor Martí either finally heard the rumors that had begun to swirl around them or simply intuited that something was afoot. She disapproved strongly of the real or imagined union, not only because at thirty-two the actress was nine years older than Martí but because she wished for her son to marry someone more firmly positioned within the country's affluent classes. Rumors about Padilla — some of which confused her with Martí's erstwhile lover Eloisa Agüero — may have exacerbated Leonor's opposition, as she mistakenly believed the actress to have an estranged husband in Havana.[84]

Wishing to avoid the kind of ugly confrontations that she witnessed years before between him and Mariano, Leonor opted for stealth, enlisting the help of her daughters and family friend Mercado in an effort to dissuade or otherwise redirect her son's affections elsewhere. Fortunately for the would-be matchmakers but unbeknown to them, their desired diversion was well under way thanks to Carmen Zayas Bazán.

In the wake of Martí's triumphant theatrical debut, Francisco Zayas Bazán's opposition to his courtship of Carmen seems to have waned, and the young lovers now began to appear together as a couple at various dances and social events. By year's end Martí introduced Carmen to his sisters, who brought the happy news home to their mother. The match was more than Leonor dared hope for: beyond her son's affections being directed away from an undesirable potential union, he now held the prospect of marrying into a wealthy and prestigious family.

At the end of 1875 José Martí was a young man with a bright future, one that he had built against seemingly impossible odds. By age twenty-two he had overcome an impoverished childhood and the intransigence of an uneducated father and survived imprisonment, exile, and serious illness; yet he managed to earn a law degree, launch a promising career as a journalist, poet, and playwright, and win the hand of a beautiful young woman from a wealthy family. The new year, however, would bring a stunning reversal of fortune for the Martís, one that would plunge them back into the darkness they had so recently escaped.

ALMOST FROM THE START OF MARTÍ'S TIME IN MEXICO he enjoyed the support and friendship of the country's most powerful liberal politicians, including President Lerdo de Tejada. His friendship with Manuel Mercado opened many doors for the Cuban neophyte, most crucially those of the *Revista Universal*, which brought his talents and work to the attention of the country's educated classes. By the end of 1875 Martí's connections among

Mexico's elite included not only Lerdo and Mercado but the family of the late president Benito Juárez, whose private box at the Teatro Principal sat alongside that of Martí's own family. The new year, however, brought massive changes to the Mexican political landscape that threatened to bring down the network of friends and contacts that Martí had so carefully cultivated—and Martí himself.

Much of what happened in 1876 was set in place well before Martí's arrival the previous year. In many ways it was the settling of old scores: General Porfirio Díaz, who eventually toppled Lerdo's government, had run unsuccessfully against Juárez in the 1871 elections even as he led an unsuccessful revolt against him.[85] Upon Juárez's death on July 18, 1872, Lerdo, his vice president at the time, succeeded him as interim president, and the Mexican Congress made him president shortly afterward. Lerdo ensured his popularity largely by continuing Juárez's policies and keeping the late president's cabinet essentially unchanged. He offered amnesty to the Porfirian rebels, a move calculated to unify the country and preempt further unrest.[86] Díaz initially accepted amnesty but returned to politics in 1874 as a congressman from Veracruz.[87]

Lerdo managed to largely pacify a rebellion-prone country and actually enjoyed a successful first term. Lerdo presided over a period of prosperity, foreign investment, and modernization that included the completion of a railway between Veracruz and Mexico City—the very one Martí later used to reach the capital.[88] His presidency's greatest achievements were the Laws of Reform, a series of Juárez-era policies that Lerdo enshrined into the Mexican Constitution on September 25, 1873. Among the reforms were the separation of church and state, freedom of the press, abolition of special religious and military tribunals, establishment of marriage as a civil institution, and a ban against church-owned property for nonreligious ends. Subsequent changes, such as the reestablishment of a national Senate as a balance for the established Congress, the banishment of church institutions such as the Sisters of Mercy, and the creation of presidential authority to appoint judges and limit judicial power, were intended to limit opponents' ability to rescind reforms by consolidating power in the executive branch.[89]

Díaz, however, had other ideas. In December 1875 he traveled to New Orleans and Brownsville, Texas, to organize and raise funds for a new rebellion. In January 1876 Díaz returned to launch his Plan de Tuxtepec, named after the Oaxaca district from which he launched it. The plan was announced on January 10, 1876, with the aim of toppling the Lerdo government and installing Díaz as president while also upholding the new constitution and reform laws that Lerdo had established.[90]

Lerdo's reforms, especially the consolidation of executive power, angered many opponents such as conservative landowners and the church, which despite Lerdo's efforts retained much of its influence among the people. His attempt to circumvent a long-standing constitutional ban against reelection, which Juárez succeeded in doing more than once, became his undoing. In January 1876 Lerdo maneuvered to have the Mexican Congress approve his bid for reelection in direct contradiction to the country's Supreme Court. Hopes ran high among Lerdo's supporters that his reelection would extend the advances of the previous four years, particularly the continuation of technical and economic progress and the centralization of executive power. But the gambit proved an enormous political miscalculation because it gave his opponents, especially Díaz, the perfect pretext to rise up against him. Indeed, Díaz's December trip abroad coincided with Lerdo's first intimations in the press that he intended to run for reelection, and the general timed the January 10 launch of the Plan de Tuxtepec under the slogan "Sufragio efectivo no reelección" (Effective Suffrage, Not Re-election) in direct response to Lerdo's official candidacy.[91]

None of these developments particularly alarmed Martí or his fellow Lerdo supporters, partly because no immediate military action followed Díaz's declaration at Tuxtepec. A handful of Mexican generals declared their allegiance to the new movement in February, but Díaz had not yet accumulated the necessary men and resources to launch his insurgency. In March he moved his base of operations across the U.S. border to Brownsville. He reintroduced his plan from Brownsville on March 22, adding the so-called Palo Blanco reforms that called for the presidency to be assumed on an interim basis by Supreme Court Chief Justice José María Iglesias, thus lending the insurgency the appearance of legal and constitutional cover. Díaz continued to build a broad coalition of support that ranged from rural and religious conservatives to wealthy landowners and U.S. business interests, but he did not win over many supporters in the capital, even with the growing uneasiness surrounding Lerdo's rule and reelection plans.

Despite the capital city's distance from the brewing unrest and its relative safety, the mood among its political and journalistic classes was beginning to sour. News started coming from Oaxaca and Yucatán and even nearby Puebla of generals preparing forces and declaring allegiance to Díaz and of skirmishes with government troops. Martí's fellow writer Ignacio Altamirano described Mexico City in February 1876 as "uneasy and sad. People are shut up in their homes for fear of being recruited, and this carnival fills me with dread."[92] The atmosphere of quiet paranoia soon proved toxic for the city's papers and journalists, whose published attacks on each other intensified to a level Martí had not seen since his arrival the year before. More disturbingly for Martí, sniping began among his fellow writers at the *Revista* as disaffected former Lerdo supporters became frustrated by the magazine's continued support of him.

Martí published his own concerns regarding Díaz's insurgency, noting a growing rift between the capital and provinces that threatened to destroy the nation's hard-won stability:

> The ideal politics is being consummated; but in order to realize it we need social unity. . . . [There is] among us a criminal indifference toward a race for which there is yet hope but which may come to overwhelm us with its enormous weight. Instructed, it could achieve greatness; and dull-witted it is a hindrance. Although we would not be obligated by generosity to educate them, self-interest should compel us to become their apostles and their teachers.[93]

This assessment in mid-January seemed to have little impact on his colleagues in the capital whose uneasiness was partly assuaged by their sense of distance and insulation. Behind the scenes, however, Lerdo's government protested furiously, but to no avail, the appearance of U.S. complicity with Díaz by allowing him asylum in Brownsville.[94]

WHATEVER ANXIETY MARTÍ FELT REGARDING DEVELOP-ments in the provinces, during the first months of 1876 his life continued to revolve around the theater, Mexico's burgeoning arts scene, and his courtship of Carmen Zayas Bazán. His last "Parliamentary Bulletin" under the pen name Orestes appeared in November 1875, and in the new year his contributions to the *Revista Universal*, published under his own name, covered mostly developments in the art world.[95] Concerns about his health may have played a role in Martí's reduced activity in the political realm, although his frequent public appearances seem to contradict this. In the early months of 1876 he kept up a busy schedule of speeches at award ceremonies and literary panels as well as a January 26 fête in honor of his friend and theatrical collaborator Enrique Guasp de Peris.[96]

When Martí did start turning his attention to politics in February 1876, his efforts focused not on Cuba but on Mexico. He began writing for *El Socialista*, an official publication of Mexico's Gran Círculo de Obreros (Great Workers Circle), which fervently supported the Lerdo government. He assumed a leadership position in the organization with his selection on March 5 as a delegate to its first National Workers Congress.[97] Martí continued to monitor developments on the political front, as his April 1876 publication "Mexico and the United States" amply attests. The essay is notable for its recognition of the U.S. role in the ongoing unrest and the danger this covetous neighbor posed not just for Mexico but for all of Latin America.[98]

Martí's political writings were overall relatively scarce in early 1876. Social and literary concerns continued to occupy his energies, and he burnished his artistic resumé with the publication in March and May, respectively, of *Amor con amor se paga* and the love poem "Carmen."[99] The poem, an ode to his new love, abandons the dark romanticism of earlier works for the placid bliss of domesticity: "I miss, work, in her arms I dream / Of a home raised by my hand."[100]

By summer Martí's dream of domestic bliss was imperiled not by revolution but by his own failing health. His condition had been less than robust for some months; in a January 31, 1876, letter he excused himself from a speaking engagement due to illness, and an undated letter from this period to Mercado indicates that he was forced to cancel another one: "I was going to speak tonight so that you could come hear me. — And since I have been denied the pleasure of so gratifying you, it saddens me to be unable to speak."[101] But in May his sarcoidosis returned in force; he began to again suffer from acute pains in his groin caused by inflammation of the lymph nodes, as well as from a high fever and general weakness. By May 9 Martí was unable to work, and the editors of the *Revista Universal* were sufficiently alarmed to publish this brief statement of concern and support:

> José Martí. — This beloved companion of ours finds himself prostrated in his bed from pain, due to a serious illness acquired while imprisoned for defending his country. We have confidence in the doctors who are attending to him and that soon the *Revista* will once again be graced by his work.[102]

Martí's condition worsened over the coming days, and surgery became inevitable. An alarmed Mercado quickly placed his protégé under the care of Dr. Francisco Montes de Oca, who after a preliminary procedure similar to those Martí had undergone in Spain found it necessary to remove his right testicle. The operation was successfully performed on or about May 13, as newspaper reports the next few days of a recovering Martí confirm. His delicate condition following the operation required a period of convalescence, and his employers at the *Revista* had to appoint fellow writer José Negrete to fulfill Martí's duties in his absence.[103]

Although Montes de Oca's intervention relieved Martí of the pains he had endured intermittently for years, the convalescing young man now had a new problem: his bed quickly became a point of convergence for people and problems he had until then endeavored to keep apart. With Carmen a fixture by his side during this recovery, Martí had to endure no doubt awkward visits by Conchita Padilla and a third woman, Edelmira Borrel, the daughter of a Mexican captain who earlier had contracted with the Martís to sew for the military.[104] During the Martís' first months in Mexico Borrel often sent his daughter to their home on errands, which is likely how she met Martí. Now, despite the apparent lack of any amorous relationship, she nevertheless felt compelled to bring chocolates to his bedside and fuss over his health.[105] Such visits caused no small consternation for Leonor, who had believed her son free of such ongoing entanglements, and for Carmen, who found her jealousy and fears regarding her beau amply confirmed.

But the incident that most acutely endangered Martí's engagement with Carmen involved the discovery of other women's letters. According to a family anecdote, after Carmen's departure one day a bedridden Martí noted the absence of a packet of love letters he kept on a dresser. Alarmed by the prospect of Carmen reading them, he leapt up to pursue her, only to be barred by Leonor and locked in his bedroom. A desperate Martí somehow climbed out an open window and intercepted Carmen, whom he somehow managed to persuade to return the letters unread.[106] This story, although possibly apocryphal, gains a degree of plausibility in the context of the since-discovered November 1875 letter from Carmen to which Eloisa Agüero added snide remarks. Carmen is unlikely to have known of Martí's secret affair with Agüero at the time; if the letter on which Agüero commented was among those in the packet, Carmen would have discovered that Martí once had a secret, married lover and that he betrayed Carmen's trust by sharing private correspondence with this lover. Such a revelation could very well have spelled the end of their courtship. Luck was on Martí's side that day, but other, more inexorable forces were already in motion that would change his life in ways he could never have imagined.

THE JUNE 1876 ELECTIONS WERE IN MANY WAYS A FOREgone conclusion; with Díaz and his followers boycotting it as a protest for what they saw as Lerdo's illegal candidacy, the president's only opposition came from Chief Justice Iglesias, who garnered less than 5 percent of the vote. There remained only the formality of congressional certification, which was sure to come in October. For his part, Martí published a brief editorial before the election titled "The Time Approaches" in which he urged the nation's workers to show their support for Lerdo's reelection.[107] It was also in June that Martí and several other prominent exiles enthusiastically added their names to the Cuban insurgency's new registry of Cubans abroad who supported the cause.[108] But the shadow of certification in the fall hung palpably over the exiles, indeed over all who had reason to wonder how Díaz and his forces would respond to the news of Lerdo's reelection.

In the months between the vote and the certification of results, life for Martí continued much as it had before the election: dates with Carmen, visits to the Zayas Bazán home and now also to that of fellow exile Nicolás Domínguez

Cowan to play chess, a return to writing for the *Revista* and for *El Socialista* as well, and most notably a reprise at the Teatro Principal of *Amor con amor se paga* by popular demand.[109] The nation's growing anxiety over the coming announcement of Lerdo's reelection, however, was lost on no one.

THE END, WHEN IT CAME, FELT MORE SUDDEN TO THOSE IN the capital than it actually was. The Mexican Congress convened on October 26 and, as expected, certified the election and declared Lerdo the winner. And as many had feared, this proved to be the beginning of the end. Lerdo's opponent Iglesias, in his capacity as Supreme Court chief justice, declared the election unconstitutional due to the reelection ban; he subsequently resigned his post and left for nearby Salamanca, Mexico, where he declared himself interim president and began organizing his own rebellion against Lerdo.

Meanwhile, Díaz, who had been stockpiling money and men for months, was no longer organizing. He was ready and had in fact been awaiting just this moment to denounce the election as fraudulent and start the war. Three weeks later at Tecoac Díaz's forces won a crucial victory over the Mexican army under General Ignacio Alatorre. Having defeated Lerdo's army, Díaz proceeded to occupy nearby Tlaxcala and the city of Puebla and found himself within a day's march of the capital.[110]

A favorite of the president and darling of the Mexican left just a few weeks earlier, Martí soon found himself fearing for his life. He was not alone in this; because of the spreading rumors that Díaz planned to execute all of Lerdo's remaining followers including journalists upon his arrival, many of Martí's erstwhile colleagues switched allegiances or left town upon learning the news. Due to the acute lack of writers but also out of fear of reprisals, almost all of Mexico City's newspapers and magazines, the *Revista* among them, shut down within days.[111] Lerdo fled within a week without even bothering to officially resign before taking a train to Veracruz on his way to exile in the United States.[112] By the time a triumphant Díaz entered the capital to ringing church bells and the cheers of adoring throngs on November 23, Martí was hiding with his family in a mezzanine apartment above the *Revista Universal*'s former offices.[113]

Martí's worst fears did not immediately materialize. Díaz did not move to punish opposition voices right away, opting instead to quell the remaining opposition. He tried to consolidate his power by negotiating a settlement with former chief justice Iglesias in a bid to simultaneously create the appearance of legality and remove his last significant obstacle to power. When Iglesias refused Díaz's terms, specifically the Plan de Tuxtepec, Díaz unilaterally declared himself interim president on November 28 and moved against Iglesias's forces.[114]

The rivals' unfinished business gave former Lerdo supporters like Martí a respite and bought them some time, though it was impossible to know how much. His income having disappeared along with the *Revista Universal*, Martí's first priority now was to find work until he could determine his next move. He knew that he would depart Mexico within weeks, if not days, and that with him gone, his family would again be left without an income. Complicating this scenario was the illness of his sister Antonia, who around this time started showing the same symptoms that had felled Ana Martí the previous year. Given Mariano's advanced age and precarious health and now Antonia's illness, the family was in no condition to follow him into an uncertain future.

The best move for the Martís would be a return to Havana, where Leonor and Mariano had connections that might allow them to find work and Antonia could escape the high altitude and thin Mexican air that seemed to be killing her. Ana Martí's 1875 death certificate lists the cause of death as heart failure, and forensic scholars have since concluded that this happened due to a congenital defect aggravated by the higher altitude, and thus thinner air, of the Mexican capital. Antonia's similar symptoms and worsening condition convinced the family that she too would die if she did not leave the country soon.[115] The Martís could not afford to relocate the whole family, but the situation was urgent enough that Leonor returned to Havana with Antonia in early December.[116] Martí was confident that his ever-resourceful mother would find work and a place to live, but he worried that the additional burden of caring for Antonia alone would be too much for her. Thus before Martí could determine his own next move, he had to figure out how to get the rest of his family back to Havana.

Martí's reputation as a talented and prolific writer, combined with the exodus of journalists from the capital, enabled him to find work relatively quickly. By December 7 he was writing for *El Federalista*, one of Mexico City's few remaining papers. Knowing that he would soon leave the country and perhaps believing himself already doomed to a bad end at Díaz's hands, the few essays he wrote during his brief tenure there focused squarely and trenchantly on the ongoing crisis. In these articles Martí openly rebuked Mexico's leaders, especially Díaz, for unnecessarily plunging the country back into chaos. His first piece for *El Federalista*, "Alea jacta est" (The Die Is Cast), is seething in its contempt for Díaz and outrage at what he was doing to the country:

> So then it is true? That Mexicans are once again killing each other? That a tradition has been violated, a government overthrown, a nation bloodstained for an entire year, only to shed more blood, to further discredit ourselves, to drown in seed the advances we were making and make the self-respect we were starting to earn even more impossible?
>
> And who moves these armies? Who carries those weapons? Who

sends to their death those robust men who go into the field on the arms of their women, indifferent and serene, with their babies slapping and rocking on their packs? . . .

It is a faction that wants at all costs to raise its leader to the republic's definitive presidency; it is a phalanx of partisans who egg their chiefs on and mislead them; it is a group of disordered wills that have laid waste the nation's broken heart.

Thirty thousand men, perhaps more, will fight in the next campaign; they will encircle a mountain, they will spread out over a field, battle cries will cross with bullets, the thoughts of men will die beneath the horses' hooves, men will fall upon each other like waves and will later spread out in foam and in circles of blood; and after the clamor of the infernal cries, of the barbarous slaughter, of the bloodied waves, will there float upon that dark purple sea a single man, smiling and triumphant, a happy statue on that pedestal of Mexicans?[117]

By December 10 Díaz finally began to move against journalists and other political enemies, and Martí's response, while brief, makes little effort to conceal his disgust:

Without legal cause, without a court order, without time to arrange their affairs, without even an explanation, Messrs. Delfín Sánchez, Manuel Sánchez Marmol, Pedro Santacilia, and Felipe Sánchez Solís have been imprisoned and sent to Queretaro . . .

Here are our restored liberties. There is our guarantee of individual rights. There is our Constitution reestablished.[118]

Such public denouncements of the new regime were certain to eventually earn Martí a place alongside his imprisoned colleagues. But by now he had found a way out of the country. Among Martí's many admirers in the capital was Ramón Uriarte, Guatemala's ambassador to Mexico. Recognizing in the young Cuban a potential asset and valuable ally for Guatemala's liberal government, Uriarte persuaded Martí to immigrate there, promising him letters of introduction from prominent Guatemalans and the security of a government or university position. No letters from Uriarte to Martí survive, having perhaps been destroyed by Martí himself to protect his friend from possible diplomatic trouble with the Díaz government. Martí does specifically describe his arrangement with Uriarte in a January 1, 1877, letter to Mercado: "[Uriarte] assures me, promises me that I will have from the first moment in Guatemala the comfortable situation that I seek. Professorships are easy [to obtain], and private [schools] abound."[119] With a university appointment and the help of powerful government allies, Martí would have time to establish himself in Guatemala City before marrying and bringing his new bride to live with him. Carmen had no objections to this plan, and in the absence of other viable options, Martí agreed to the move.

Having found a way forward for himself, the question remained of how Martí would resolve the problem of reuniting his family in Cuba. In Guatemala he could raise the necessary money to fund their move, but that would take time, during which Mariano and his three other daughters would be left alone and without an income. And while at nearly fifty years old Leonor remained a vigorous and capable woman, it was unreasonable to burden her with arranging such a major move and finding employment for her husband herself while tending to the needs of the ailing Antonia. He decided instead to go to Cuba himself, in clear violation of the terms of his exile; in Havana, he reasoned, he could raise the necessary funds, find a suitable home for the family, find work for Mariano, and arrange for the move. Since he had made no public appearances on the island before his arrest, he could move about the city in relative anonymity so long as he did not encounter Spanish officials or acquaintances who might remember him.

As a known enemy of the state, Martí could not travel under his real name. Nor was landing on the island covertly, even under cover of night, a real possibility; with the war that had started in 1868 now stumbling into its ninth year, the colonial authorities were ever on the lookout for expeditions or even individuals coming to aid the rebels. Capture in either case would certainly land him back in prison.

The only remaining option was to travel under an assumed name with a fake passport. Although the regulation of travel by individuals using official documents had existed for centuries, in the nineteenth century passport systems were in their infancy, and opportunities for subterfuge abounded even in Europe's most developed countries.[120] In mid-1870s Mexico a fake passport would have been easily acquired either by bribing officials or through outright forgery. Martí was unlikely to have had direct knowledge of such matters himself, but it would have been easy enough for a government-connected friend to acquire a perfectly legal-looking Mexican passport. Mercado is unlikely to have been the source for the fake passport; Martí's January 1, 1877, letter to him, in which he reveals his possession of the passport and the name on it, indicates that Mercado had no previous knowledge of it.[121] Partly as a tribute to his mother and partly to assuage his own sense of hypocrisy for engaging in such subterfuge, Martí chose as his new identity the name Julián Pérez, a combination of his own middle and Leonor's maiden names.[122]

Mariano and Leonor expressed their opposition to the trip in the most vigorous terms. Martí did not listen. Carmen became so distraught that her father offered to pay for his family's move. She begged Martí to accept the money rather than risk his life needlessly. He refused. María del Carmen and Amelia also pleaded with their big brother not to go. He ignored them. He ignored them all.

His mind was made up.

WITH EXIT PLANS IN PLACE, ON DECEMBER 16 MARTÍ'S FINAL essay for *El Federalista* appeared. "Extranjero" (Foreigner) was a final response to his political enemies:

> And you, foreigner, why do you write? — One might as well ask me why I think . . .
>
> What does this foreigner bring to the table whose food he never tasted? He brings indignation, with its great power; brings an inner force, which neither pursues its own way, nor seeks comforts, nor ferrets out conveniences, nor reasons. Beggars compare it to themselves: the honest embrace it with affection; — to the beggar, an idiocy to be scorned; — to the honest, the shelter of love.[123]

And it was a heartfelt farewell to a country he had come to love:

> I did not seek citizenship when it would have served me to better flatter the powerful; I did not speak of my love for Mexico when gratitude would have seemed servile flattery and humiliating supplication; now that I depart from it; now that I expect nothing from it . . . now, I reclaim my part, I ingest this suffering, naturalize my spirit, bring the will of a wounded man, the dignity of a proud conscience. Conscience is the universal citizenship.
>
> [It is] to Mexico that I owe all this. Here I was loved and lifted.[124]

It is fitting that Martí's final sentence in this parting essay promises allegiance not to country, not even to citizenship itself, but to the peril of defending country and citizenship: "[To] flattery, always a foreigner; to danger, always a citizen."[125] We do not know whether Ramón Uriarte ever read "Extranjero," but if he did he may have wondered whether the foreigner who pledged himself to the danger of defending his country was not himself intuitively following where danger leads. Certainly neither he nor Martí foresaw any such dangers in the Cuban exile's coming to the ambitious young republic of Guatemala.

BEFORE THE NEW YEAR MARTÍ WAS GONE. HE LEFT MEXICO City in the early morning hours of December 30, 1876, bound for Veracruz with a fake Mexican passport and fifty pesos he borrowed from Mercado.[126] New Year's Day found Martí in Veracruz awaiting the steamer that would carry him to Havana. During his last hours on Mexican soil his mind was filled not with recriminations or regret or bitterness but with the lightness of a man who has cast off an enormous burden and the utter confidence of one ready for whatever comes next. "It seems that Guatemala is opening its arms to me," he wrote to Mercado, "the soul is loyal, and mine heralds good luck."[127]

But Martí was not yet bound to return Guatemala's embrace. He was headed instead for a place where, if he was lucky, he would be utterly invisible.

A SECRET MISSION

O N THE MORNING OF JANUARY 2, 1877, MARTÍ DE-
parted Veracruz on the Havana-bound steamer *Ebro*. By the
time he arrived in the Cuban capital on January 6, Porfirio Díaz's rise
to power in Mexico was complete when he defeated the remaining
forces loyal to José María Iglesias and forced their leader into exile.[1]

But by then Martí, traveling under the name Julián Pérez, had
more pressing concerns: finding work for his father in Cuba, raising
money for his father's and sisters' return to Havana, and securing a
suitable home for the reunited family. Leonor and his sister Antonia,
who had preceded Martí to Havana, were staying in the home of his
sister Chata and her husband, Manuel García. Chata had stayed behind in Mexico to care for Mariano and her youngest child and her
sisters until Martí could send the necessary money for their relocation. It was Leonor, Antonia, and García who met Martí at Havana
harbor and took him back to the García home, where he too would
be staying.[2]

Martí's mission in Havana would likely not have succeeded without at least five individuals who risked prison or worse to help him.
The first of these was García, thanks to whom Martí had a safe
place to stay; as Martí well knew from his father's days as a lawman,
Havana's *celadores* routinely inspected the registers at hotels and
boarding houses for suspicious newcomers and had informants who
would alert them to the presence of wanted or suspicious persons in
their areas. It is not clear whether García notified the local *celador*
regarding his guest Julián Pérez, as the law required, or simply hid
Martí at his house. Either choice would have entailed considerable

risk, as the discovery of a state enemy at his home would have meant not only prison but the likely loss of his house and property as well.[3]

Having found safe haven with García, Martí now had to figure out how to raise money. Because he had come to Havana under a false name, he could not use his university credentials to seek employment. His Mexican passport would also likely have made it more difficult for him to find even a menial clerical position, and in any case such work would not have paid enough to raise the amount he needed in the time he had. The very fact of presenting himself as a Mexican seeking work in Havana might also have been unusual enough to arouse suspicion. Martí could thus only find work through the help of a trusted contact who would either hire him or provide an introduction to a suitable employer. Seeking such a contact is precisely what he did, as he explains in his January 22 letter to Manuel Mercado: "One of my old and paternal friends from Spain is well positioned here, and his affection has saved me from what would otherwise have been a grave danger."[4]

That old and paternal friend could only have been José Mariano Domínguez, father of Fermín and Eusebio Valdés Domínguez. We know that Martí was in contact with the Domínguezes during this stay in Havana because his signature as a witness appears on José's will dated February 8, and he gave a reading at their home of his Zaragoza-era play *Adúltera* at a February 18 gathering that Fermín organized. José Domínguez's was among the letters of introduction that Martí later carried with him to Guatemala.[5] Besides, the Domínguezes were the only well-positioned family in Havana whom Martí trusted enough to involve in such a perilous matter — and the only ones likely to have risked prison to help him. The length of Martí's Havana stay, nearly two months, suggests that the Domínguezes did not lend or give him money but rather helped him find work, probably in a law office. We know few specifics regarding their role in assisting Martí, but the circumstantial evidence strongly suggests that their help was indispensable.

It is not clear whether Martí's Havana employer knew his true identity. But at least one other person who helped him did: ophthalmologist Juan Santos Fernández Hernández. Martí's vision had not fully recovered from his time in prison; by the time he arrived in Havana what was a chronic but bearable discomfort had developed into full-blown conjunctivitis, an acute infection of the eyes. This recurring malady put Martí in a bind; he had to seek treatment in order to work but risked discovery if he went to a doctor. Serendipitously, Fernández Hernández had been an acquaintance and fellow student of Martí's in Madrid before completing his training in Paris.[6] He also may have known the Domínguez family, or at least brothers Fermín and Eusebio, from his medical training in Spain, and that connection would have made it easier for Martí to trust him. Regardless, Martí's need for treatment and lack of any better options made the Spanish-trained doctor the only viable choice.

Martí first visited Fernández Hernández's office on January 22, more than two weeks after his arrival in Havana. Possibly his condition had not worsened enough for him to seek treatment until then, or perhaps he did not have the money to pay; it is also possible that due to his fear of being discovered, he had hesitated to see a doctor at all before learning of his old classmate's practice. Whatever the case, Martí came to Fernández Hernández complaining of a dryness and irritation in his eyes for the previous three months that worsened after his arrival. Martí shared with the doctor his belief that the long hours spent editing and proofreading as part of his job might have aggravated the condition. After an initial examination, Fernández Hernández diagnosed the condition as chronic catarrhal conjunctivitis in both eyes. He found a nodular inflammation on Martí's right eye that he recognized as a conjunctival phlyctenule. In his report the doctor concurred with Martí's correlation of the condition to his earlier work as an editor.[7] This suggests that Martí failed to inform Fernández Hernández of his history of sarcoidosis, 25 percent to 30 percent of whose sufferers also experience this condition; both are also auto-immune disorders of unknown origin. This would suggest that Martí's eyes suffered not from overwork but from an allergic hypersensitivity stemming from sarcoidosis.[8]

Whatever the shortcomings of Fernández Hernández's diagnosis, it is clear that he took a significant risk in treating Martí. As a well-regarded ophthalmologist, he had a great deal to lose; the discovery that he knowingly treated Martí without reporting him to the authorities would have cost him prison time, his practice, and possibly his license. Fernández Hernández thus played a small but crucial role in the success of Martí's secret Havana mission.

The sense of freedom and possibility that buoyed Martí during his journey to Havana quickly evaporated upon arrival as the combination of physical malady and unrelenting mental stress left him troubled and exhausted. Despite having accomplished much of what he set out to do, Martí in his letter to Mercado of January 22, the day of his first visit to Fernández Hernández, portrays a man besieged by worries:

> I punish and slap my forehead whenever I think of the likely sor-
> rows my poor little ones are suffering in Mexico: I shake off these
> thoughts as I would a bad deed:—and you know I have not com-
> mitted one.—By the American packet I will send you $200,[9] suf-
> ficient for them to make, albeit in painful austerity, their trip to
> Havana via the French packet, the cheapest, quickest, and most
> comfortable of the ones departing from there. They may well
> collect by the 10th or 12th what I will send from here on the 3rd
> and book their passage on the packet for the 18th. . . . [These]
> matters have been resolved so that, upon recovering my liberty
> and necessary way of life, they will live here peacefully, my sister
> [Chata] with her husband and children, where my mother and
> my Antonia now live, the modest Amelia probably at a school, my
> father at peace, and [sister] Carmen with a loving cousin of mine
> who strongly wishes it so. . . . I take special pleasure in speak-
> ing to you at length . . . of these intimate things that are a relief
> to my soul and justification of my conduct, for which I still re-
> proach myself, for I think that my duty has not been well done
> but is rather dying in your eyes of impotence, of exhaustion, and
> of pain.[10]

Exacerbating Martí's worries was the state of the Cuban insurgency, worn down and divided by nine years of war. The Spanish had
largely succeeded in penning the rebels behind a *trocha*, a series of
defensive trenches designed to keep them in the island's two far-
eastern provinces and away from major cities and civilian populations.[11] General Máximo Gómez succeeded in breaching the *trocha*
in January 1875 and did extensive damage to Spanish interests to the
west, destroying eighty-three sugar plantations and freeing hundreds
of slaves. But the rebels squandered their momentum amid internal
politics and squabbling among their leaders, and two years later the
wealthy exiles in New York and elsewhere who had been funding the
war were withdrawing their support. Sensing victory, Madrid sent
seventy thousand reinforcements in the winter of 1876 while offering amnesty to all except leaders who surrendered before the end of
the war. By the time of Martí's arrival in Havana, Gómez's troops had
been forced back behind the *trocha*, and desertions even among officers were increasingly frequent.[12]

Martí nephew and family historian Raúl García Martí later claimed that Martí met with rebel separatists at the Louvre café and elsewhere.[13] But this seems unlikely, given the risk of being seen in a public place with suspected sympathizers and the high level of caution Martí exercised in every other aspect of this trip. Judging by Martí's assessment of the situation in his January 22 letter to Mercado, what little he had gleaned, whether from the papers, hearsay, or rebel sympathizers, made him optimistic, if cautiously so, for the insurgency's "ultimate victory in open battle" over "a discouraged and divided Spain."[14] But neither here nor in any other correspondence from this stay in Havana does Martí display any inclination to remain in Cuba to aid the rebel cause; on the contrary, his portrayal of the war's situation ends with his stated desire to escape both the island and its war as soon as possible: "Meanwhile, the brazen stupidity and debasement of character such as I have never seen— villainous Byzantine characters—appall and upset me, and I will take to the sea in search of open air and the greatness of nature."[15]

True to his word, Martí concluded his business in Havana within a month, although even this was longer than he wished. In his February 3 letter to Mercado, he despairs at being able to send only $30 of the promised $200 for the Martís' return trip: "I am going finally to the post [office], being unable to await any longer the payment I have been expecting. Well shall I suffer until the 10th."[16] The latter date was likely a payday, which finally yielded—barely—the desired amount for the voyage:

> I am sending for my family the necessary funds for their journey,
> $220, . . . so that they can come on the English packet. Emphasize
> to them that they must neither pay debts nor buy anything [with
> this money],—as what is sent is the exact amount, and there is no
> need for them to suffer unnecessarily.[17]

Having thus completed the last of his objectives, Martí remained in Havana just long enough to earn the necessary funds for his own departure. Although work occupied most of his final two weeks on the island, he made occasional visits to the Domínguezes' home; for example, on February 18 he attended a literary gathering there and read his play *Adúltera*. It was during one of these final visits that José Mariano Domínguez added his own letter of introduction to those of Manuel Uriarte and other prominent Guatemalans. On February 20 Martí made a last visit to the ophthalmologist, who prescribed eyeglasses to correct farsightedness. Martí never wore and likely never purchased the glasses.[18]

On the morning of February 24, 1877, Julián Pérez boarded the Mexico-bound steamer *City of Havana*. Leaving behind him the relentless stresses and perils of the previous two months, he was in no hurry to reach Guatemala. In a few days he would meet his father, sisters, and two nephews at the seaside town of Progreso on the Yucatán Peninsula during a layover on their own journey back to Havana.[19] After that, he would take the time to discover an America that until now he had known only through the refined, insular lens of Mexico City. A new set of challenges awaited him in Guatemala, and a new life. But not yet, not now.

Now, having done his duty and survived in the process some of the most dangerous days of his life so far, the once and future José Martí looked forward only to "open air and the greatness of nature."

CHAPTER SEVEN

Discovering America (2)

GUATEMALA

*José Martí. — Our beloved friend, true and heartfelt poet, our fellow
writer these past few days, quits the Mexican land that has shown him
such affection, and heads for Guatemala. Upon departing, Pepe has
asked us to bid farewell to his friends. We fulfill this errand, feeling still
the warmth of his parting embrace.*

EL FEDERALISTA, DECEMBER 30, 1876

O N FEBRUARY 28, 1877, MARTÍ DISEMBARKED FROM THE
City of Havana at Progreso, a port town on Mexico's Yucatán
Peninsula. Having discharged his familial duties in Havana, he now lingered for
a few days in Mexico before moving on to the next stage of his life. Martí was
less than sanguine about the future that awaited him, as he confessed in a February letter to Manuel Mercado:

> I foresee in my journey to Guatemala, now that I see it up close, a use-
> less sacrifice; but I rejoice in the pleasure of sacrifice. . . . I do not doubt
> that I will find work in Guatemala; but I know that I will not meet with
> the miraculous sum necessary so that once my family is settled, I could
> accumulate what is needed for my union with Carmen.[1]

With no other feasible prospects and the burden of his chosen obligations
weighing upon him, he saw no choice but to soldier on.

Martí's travels through Mexico and Central America during the next six
weeks were more a product of necessity than the willful digression of his trip
to Paris; much of it was due to the difficulty of traveling in lands that lacked
steamship service or railways. However unavoidable these hardships, they af-

forded Martí time and space to clear his mind and restore energies depleted by the trials of previous months. He remained mindful of promises made and the challenges to come, as his letter of the same day to Francisco Zayas Bazán affirms: "You give me my greatest treasure and highest glory; you give me my Carmen . . . earned her I have with my soul, and I will earn her even more by my labors."[2] Martí assures his future father-in-law that he was departing for Guatemala having fulfilled all duties to his family and with the conviction that he could now devote himself fully to this new stage of his life with Carmen:

> I do not struggle for a single moment with the considerations to which I now must give preference: and I have determined maturely and deci-sively what I must do. I have helped my family with more than human efforts, amidst incredible and silent sacrifices of an incomprehensible horror. . . . I, who owe to Carmen the resurrection of my powers and the shaking off of such wrongful ties and such lethal agonies, to Carmen I now consecrate myself completely. . . . If my parents could not live with-out me, I would return to my parents; —but this is not the case now, for-tunately. My own family should be grateful for this liberty at which they leave me; because through it I enrich my experience, educate my ways with new tasks, and with Carmen's exemplary affection I rejuvenate and beautify my heart.[3]

For their part, Martí's parents understood that the time had come for their son to start a new life with a career and family, although Leonor was never fully persuaded that Carmen, a young woman unaccustomed to uncertainty and hardship, was the ideal mate for her Pepe.[4] Nevertheless, her son had made his choices and set off to find his future.

Upon arriving in Progreso, Martí immediately wrote to Manuel Mercado to share his planned itinerary. The February 28 letter also expresses its author's sense of relief at having escaped the perils and pressures of his recent stay in Havana:

> This is a land strewn with thistles but adorned with good hearts. I came from Havana, wounded by fever and by exhaustion; here I gain new lungs, I think virile thoughts and stride firmly. From here by canoe to Isla Mujeres; later, by cayuco [Indian-style canoe], to Belize; by boat to Izabal; on horseback, to Guatemala [City]. I do what I must, and love a woman; —thus I am strong.[5]

Martí closes with the news that he would depart the next day for nearby Mérida and begin the long journey south within five days.[6] The following day he arrived on muleback in Mérida, where a small community of Cuban expatriates had sprung up since the onset of the war in 1868.

Little is known regarding Martí's specific activities during these first days of March 1877. This is likely out of an abundance of caution on Martí's part, since Díaz had by then solidified his control of the Yucatán; on January 8 he installed Colonel Protasio Guerra as governor, with orders to begin rounding up Lerdo's former supporters in the area. It is understandable in such an environment that Martí's hosts would have wanted to keep his presence among them as quiet as possible.[7]

Martí made the acquaintance of many in Mérida's Cuban community, particularly writers and intellectuals. One of these, Yucatán museum director Juan Peón y Contreras, brother of the poet José Peón y Contreras, took Martí to see the Chac-Mool, a pre-Columbian stone statue recently discovered by archaeologist Augustus Le Plongeon. Martí was especially taken by the Chac-Mool, so much so that he spontaneously drew in pencil a curious, whimsical portrait of himself with the body and posture of the ancient indigenous figure. He later made the Chac-Mool the centerpiece of an unfinished play in which he introduces it as the "spirit of the nation, apparently asleep, but capable, by its own power, of rising up to act at a critical moment."[8] These otherwise minor gestures suggest that the image of the Chac-Mool impressed Martí deeply as an iconic symbol of indigenous American power and cultural resonance. This is an idea that he would continue to develop over the next several years, beginning with his Guatemalan writings on Latin America's burgeoning cultural and political identity.

Martí did have one remaining bit of family business to resolve before departing for Guatemala. By March 4 he was back in Progreso, where his father, three of his sisters, and his nephews Alfredo and Oscar were stopping briefly en route to Havana. When they arrived on the steamer *Ebro*—the same ship that had carried Martí to Mexico two years earlier—he was waiting on the dock. Their joy at seeing each other again, if only for a few hours, was even more gratifying to Martí for the letters Mariano brought to him from Mexico: one from Carmen and the other from her father granting his permission for the couple to marry.[9] The brief reunion deeply moved Martí, who later counted as one of the "supreme moments" of his life "my father's kiss, before I left for Guatemala, on the steamer."[10] Having seen his family off to a better and more secure future, Martí now set off to seek his own.

AFTER SPENDING SEVERAL DAYS VISITING VARIOUS LOCA-tions in Mexico, Martí undertook the monthlong journey of more than seven hundred miles to Guatemala City. During that journey—most of it by canoe, much of it on horseback—Martí discovered a rural, indigenous America that was the polar opposite of cosmopolitan Mexico City. This Central America of fishing villages and jungle trails, of Indian guides and pack mules was a revelation for Martí, deeply transforming what he thought of as America's relationship to Spain, to Europe. This journey through the heart of a different America ringingly confirmed what Martí had intuited in his last writings from Mexico: that by abandoning the capital and launching his revolution from the provinces—thus appealing to the country's indigenous populations—Porfirio Díaz tapped into a formidable cultural, political, and economic force that Lerdo and his fellow urban liberals had unwisely ignored. This, thought the young Cuban, as he rode on horseback and sailed on canoes, this is the real America.

In 1877 there was no easy way to reach land-locked Guatemala City from the Yucatán; Guatemala would not begin construction on its first railway line until later in the year, and no passenger ships served the coastlines.[11] The only means of travel available for the journey were *cayucos* and horses or mules for inland travel. Roads even between larger towns were rare and paved ones nonexistent. Much of Guatemala's population, with the exception of its capital city, was concentrated in coastal towns and villages; the country's rugged and mostly untamed landscape with steep climbs through mountainous terrain made inland travel daunting for all but the heartiest travelers, which Martí decidedly was not.

In the 1870s travel to such remote outposts of civilization was still relatively uncommon, and there was no tourism of the type we know today. Martí's travels through Mexico's coastal islands thus brought him into contact with an America that would otherwise have been unimaginable for him and certainly beyond the purview of even his most well-traveled and knowledgeable friends. The experience enabled him to develop a vision of Latin America that would begin to blossom during his time in Guatemala and reach its highest expression in his celebrated 1891 essay "Nuestra América" (Our America). We can see it beginning to emerge in Martí's journal entries chronicling his journey to Guatemala in the early spring of 1877.

The sea portion of Martí's voyage followed the Yucatán Peninsula's northern and eastern shores as well as the shoreline of Belize before arriving at the mouth of the Río Dulce in Guatemala, for a total of more than five hundred miles. The *cayucos* moved along shallower routes close to the shore, passing the occasional marsh or swamp, long stretches of limestone flats, and pockets of men fishing in the brackish waters of the bogs. Martí traveled alongside men of all stripes and occupations, laborers, fishermen, merchants carrying their wares from one island or seaside market to the next. Given the journey's difficulty and the *cayucos'* very limited space, he likely brought with him only the most essential things—clothes, his letters, and perhaps a few books. As the *cayucos* were primarily used to ferry passengers over short distances, they provided few comforts for the long-distance voyager. Martí spent the days exposed to the wind and sun and ocean spray; at night the nonsmoker had to endure the smoke of his fellow passengers' hand-rolled cigarettes before drifting off to sleep beneath the stars. Yet not all was suffering and hardship for the ever-amorous young Cuban; years later he would write fondly of "a flexible, svelte, but voluptuous Indian woman who revealed to the thirsty traveler all the majestic charm of a new kind of amazing and suggestive beauty," confessing that he "loved, and was loved."[12]

Martí kept an informal journal of his travels, thanks to which we can trace the trajectory of his journey and his thoughts and observations along the way. Some days after departing Progreso he stopped about 180 miles east of his starting point on the island of Jolbós (Holbox), where he saw "a tiny fishing village, much less important than the island, frequented only by *cayucos* and smaller canoes, which trade in turtles and *cazones* [dogfish]." Aside from the fishing trade he found little to distinguish the village beyond "*milpas* [cornfields], meager haciendas [small farms or ranches]," and villagers who traveled as far as Progreso to sell their wares.[13]

Martí wrote much more extensively, and generously, some days later at his next stop, Isla Mujeres, praising the island's beautiful beaches and pleasant climate and observing at the sight of its well-kept cemetery that "death would be impossible here, among so many kind women."[14] Despite the chasm of race, culture, and class that set him apart from the people he was observing, Martí's "discovery" of this other America bears little resemblance to that of his conquistador forebears; we find no hint in his writings of the Columbus who once rhapsodized about the Caribbean's potential for colonization and profit, or of Francisco Hernández de Córdoba, who discovered the Yucatán accidentally on an expedition to capture and enslave Indians.[15] The benefit of nearly four hundred years of hindsight allowed Martí to see not only the same kind people and natural beauty as the long-ago conquerors but the lingering effects of their reign:

> The *criados*, who are basically slaves, subjected to their *amos* [masters], which they call them still, who [depend on] the capricious advances these pay them, for which they demand much account in the way of personal services, go down to the sea in March and April, carrying corn for their food; by some small hut in a mangrove, their nets framed with great chunks of wood, they fish patiently for three or four months.[16]

This and other such experiences harken back to Martí's childhood memory of the slave ship he saw with his father at Batabanó and the slave hanged nearby. But it was this later experience of traveling through Mexico and Central America and seeing the lingering effects of colonization and slavery on the continent's indigenous and black populations that allowed Martí to give the child's sense of outrage and injustice a mature political and cultural voice. If he had personally experienced the injustices of colonization in relatively modern Havana, here he saw how liberal Mexico's promises of modernity and nationhood had also failed its most vulnerable populations: "It is, nevertheless, an impoverished place. Its children have not learned to make use of such rare advantages, such productive land, such an amenable climate, and, without commerce, without traffic even, lacking stimulus, lacking basic needs, lacking employment, the scraggly population diminishes, and the natives, who have here reached old age, emigrate."[17]

On Isla Mujeres Martí was able to observe race and class relations from the master's perspective. There he met Augustus Le Plongeon, the English-born explorer who had found the Chac-Mool and attempted to send it abroad before agreeing to leave it in Mexico. Martí marveled upon learning that Le Plongeon and his wife, Alice Dixon, paid only six pesos — roughly $120 today — for a small house on the island. But his larger portrait of Le Plongeon casts him as a product of his colonial times, a more refined version of America's original *conquistadores*: "erudite American, part hierologist, part archaeologist, loquacious and avaricious, industrious in science, which he has studied in order to profit from it, six pesos he has paid for this chintzy *bohío* [hut] in the shape of an oval."[18] Martí saw the fallen adventurer and would-be archaeologist as less a modern conquistador than a man defeated:

> I was walking this morning with this rare man who has memorized Genti — Bernard, and Voltaire, and Boileau, and Rousard, and Molière; who plays deliciously the very tender music of Flotow; who travels with a single cloak and two hammocks, with his Bouchirt's Dictionary and two doctoral degrees; with his wrinkled face and pleasant conversation, practically barefoot, with pockets totally relieved of money. . . . [When] I read in the poverty and neglect of this life, and in this old age without glory and without support, a guilty and painful secret, I believe that, since this man is not a political exile, he must be an exile from himself.[19]

It is easy to read Martí's vignette of the fallen adventurer as a broader portrait of colonization's depravity and ultimate decadence. Martí had begun to realize that the future of this other America, whatever it turned out to be, did not lie with the erudite but hopelessly European Le Plongeon any more than it did with his own urbanized colleagues in Mexico City. Clearly another kind of man was needed.

THAT NIGHT MARTÍ COULD NOT SLEEP AND LAY AWAKE IN his hammock listening to the sea. Half-suffocated by the lamps' "smell of turtle oil, light here for the affluent and the poor," he heard his fellow passengers tell stories of the Indians in Cozumel and how they continued to defend against the whites their fortified city of Tulima, whose ruins were "no less important than those of Chichén Itzá and Uxmal."[20]

In the morning Martí boarded another *cayuco* and continued his journey southward along the Yucatán coast. Over the coming days he passed Cozumel, catching a distant glimpse of the ruins of Tulima; after enduring "a scorching northeaster, in a speeding *cayuco*," he crossed into calmer waters in Belize: "We have, then, reached English territory."[21] The sea odyssey ended several days and some 250 miles later, when Martí at last reached the port town of Livingston in Guatemala around March 18, some two weeks after he set off from Progreso. In that time he had traveled approximately 500 miles and found himself a little more than 200 miles from Guatemala City. But those last 200 miles proved the most difficult of all. It would be another two weeks before a bone-weary Martí glimpsed the capital.

What he found in Livingston, on Lake Izabal at the mouth of the Río Dulce, was "an enchanting little village" where "not a white face could be seen, but the eyes of the pure-race Negroes danced with happiness." The downtrodden, languorous natives of the islands were here replaced by black people who were "lucid, clear, clean, without a single gray hair, the women rounded like Venus, the men naked like Hercules."[22] And if Martí admired the natural beauty of the islands he had visited on the way, he was now positively enchanted by the landscape of his new country:

> [The] tall forest at their back, the wide sea before them, and that mass of coconuts strewn along the shore [beckons], as if opening America's generous arms to the traveler ...
> ... [Here] the land offers itself, it does not shrink. — The gentle rain that falls year-round. The flowers upon the rocks. The penetrating song of the *ramatutu* [trogon, a native bird]. Flock of white birds. Solemn entrance. Majestic march.[23]

Despite the week of arduous inland travel that lay ahead, Martí's arrival in Livingston energized him. Distant as it was from his beloved Cuba and alien from the life of Havana or Mexico City, Guatemala had already given Martí a glimpse, and more than a glimpse, of an America he professed to love but hardly knew before now. However mindful of the challenges ahead, for now he could rejoice in the welcoming embrace of "the lands of my Mother America."[24]

From Livingston Martí began a weeklong trek down the Río Dulce that ended at Izabal, a small port town that he found considerably less charming than Livingston.[25] There he spent a peso on a coarse hammock and a straw hat for the inland journey and found a meal and a place for the night before setting off the next day: "I paid twelve reales [a little more than a peso] for two eggs that I ate and a night that I did not sleep."[26] Part of the trouble seems to have been "a very loquacious daughter of the innkeeper who would bite the dust for an hour's conversation with some gentleman from the city."[27] Martí eventually escaped his enthusiastic conversation partner and settled in for a cold, windy night in what "was supposed to be a bed, but if it was it did not seem so.... My pillow was straw; I lifted the blanket, clean and worn, and saw that the mattress was made of sack."[28]

On the morning of March 26, a bleary-eyed Martí began the final inland leg of his journey to Guatemala City. He hired a muleteer and his wife as guides for the trip, and "revolver at the waist and with machete at my thigh, I set my legs across the smallest, most stubborn and malevolent mule to ever see the mountain of Izabal."[29] Martí did not think much of the company during his journey, describing his party in a rare moment of levity as "one person and five mules, unless, out of an abundance of pity, we do not count among their number the muleteer and his wife. Oh, the muleteer's wife!"[30] Yet neither his unpleasant stay in Izabal nor the mule nor the contrariness of a muleteer who "disagreed completely with my way of being and speaking" could diminish Martí's sense of rapture at the Guatemalan wilderness, with

> soul invigorated by the magnificent spectacle that adorned the majestic shores of a great river; those great green curtains attached to my soul like wings, hung from the sky, ill-fastened on the waves of the Rio Dulce, its moving folds splashed by white fowl and smaller, more colorful birds.
>
> And this roaring lion, this Arabian steed, and this soaring eagle that I feel within my soul! Imagine all this, astride a lowly mule.[31]

Martí was hardly the only traveler in his day to delight in the beauty of the Guatemalan forest. Other travelogues of the time agree that it was among the wonders of the Western Hemisphere, among them one written by ethnologist Augustus Henry Keane:

> By day the eye feasts on the sparkling emerald of the mountain stream flowing between some rocky cleft, overgrown above by a tropic vegetation, and richly adorned with all manner of trailing and twining plants. Lovely birds of the most gorgeous plumage light up wood and mead, while beautiful butterflies hover from blossom to blossom.[32]

As Martí no doubt also knew, judging by his purchase of the straw hat in Izabal, Keane warned that "the wayfarer must guard against the scorching rays of the sun" and would find scarce comfort at the end of a hard day's travel: "At night he will have to seek repose in some Indian rancho, for the dusky children of the land are still hospitable, although themselves doomed to a weary life of hardships."[33] The evening meal, as Martí discovered in Izabal, often consisted of little more than iguana eggs, which the Cuban traveler complained were "not sufficiently nourishing for such a hard day."[34] The cuisine at even the best-stocked *rancho* left much to be desired; despite the unexpected good fortune of finding meat and milk and coffee, Martí found himself choking down a plate of smoked beans with a tortilla "more green than white."[35]

Compounding the forest's challenges was the difficulty of the terrain itself. Roads were scarce when they existed at all, and even the better ones made for slow progress. Keane describes the road to Gualan, the only viable path "through a rocky and wooded country," as "an almost invisible track" and the road connecting the larger town of Zacapa to the capital as "an extremely rough highway."[36] Another travelogue of the time describes the typical Central American road as "merely a track cleared in the woods by cutting down the trees and bushes, but without any attempt being made at levelling or draining, or even removing the stones and other natural impediments."[37] A day's travel along such roads might cover less than twenty miles, assuming that landslides or heavy rains did not slow progress even further.[38] Martí fared no better in this regard than other travelers, covering the forty miles between Izabal and Zacapa in just over three days.[39]

A little after midday on March 29, the last Thursday before Easter, Martí's party rode into Zacapa, a relatively large town less than a hundred miles from Guatemala City.[40] Zacapa's relative proximity to the capital made it a less desolate, more accommodating place than the villages they encountered to that point, and an enthusiastic Martí happily anticipated the change of scenery:

> To Zacapa! To Zacapa! To the town of the agave and the mangoes! To the city of shops and cheeses! The one with barracks, courthouse, plaza, violin, bass, church: of silk shawls, of Chambray shirts or of the broad [illegible word]; of the high hills; of the great river . . .
>
> What is this childlike joy that I feel? . . . It is the scent of a town, which arouses the traveler's curiosity. It is the way station, the most populated town, the only true city since Izabal. . . . The oasis in the sand. The nearness to the beloved object. Perhaps they will be waiting with open arms to welcome me to this town!

We do not know whether Martí's welcome at Zacapa met his expectations or for that matter much else about the final ninety-five-mile trek to Guatemala City because his travel diary ends here with the words "This is Zacapa!"[41] Ten months later he would describe what the approaching traveler might see upon first glimpsing Guatemala's capital city:

> Coming from Izabal by the broad cart path, which will soon carry [one] to the North—great perspective!—the sugars and coffee of the West can be seen in the distance, beyond the river, tall churches rising over pleasant valley, vast expanse, open air, kind lady, great and beautiful city.[42]

Unlike his anticipated Zacapa welcome, Martí's rendering of the traveler's first glimpse of Guatemala City—which, it is fair to assume, was also his own—reveals how deeply that experience moved him. His description is especially poignant for appearing in a glowing book-length portrait of Guatemala he published in February 1878, just before the life he hoped to build there began to unravel. At the time, however, they were the words of a man who dared believe that, after so many disappointments, he had finally found a home.

ON APRIL 2 AN EXHAUSTED, ROAD-WEARY MARTÍ FINALLY arrived in Guatemala City, hoping that his letters of introduction would help make his way in the country. Among these were recommendations from longtime friend Eusebio Valdés Domínguez, former teacher of Guatemalan President Justo Rufino Barrios; Antonio Carrillo, childhood friend and Spanish émigré; prominent attorney Pablo Macedo;[43] and most importantly Ramón Uriarte, Guatemala's ambassador to Mexico and trusted advisor to both Barrios and former president Miguel García Granados.[44] The letters were addressed to Barrios, García Granados, Minister of Foreign Relations Joaquín Macal, and prominent Cubans who had established themselves in Guatemala. Chief among these were José María Izaguirre, director of the Escuela Normal, a private school, and José Joaquín Palma, professor of literature at the university. Thanks to Izaguirre and Palma, Martí was able to land teaching positions at both institutions, pending confirmation of his credentials from the university in Zaragoza.[45] These first acquaintances helped introduce Martí to Guatemala's small but influential Cuban exile community.[46]

As a new arrival Martí needed every bit of influence in those letters and every contact they brought him. Despite his prolific output and literary triumphs in Mexico, his work was unknown beyond a small but growing band of admirers. In April 1877 Martí was far removed from the celebrated young writer and man about town he had been only a few months before; here he was just a twenty-four-year-old exile looking for a place to establish himself and raise a family. But Martí's reputation and at least one of his early writings preceded him; Izaguirre later recounted how he recognized Martí's name as soon as he introduced himself:

[O]ne day there came to see me a young man come from [Mexico] seeking a faculty position. His demeanor was very proper, his appearance pleasant, and his manner of expression easy and agreeable. I liked him. I asked him to tell me who he was and what skills he had for the classroom, to which he responded:

"I am Cuban, I've come from Mexico, and my name is José Martí. My teaching skills . . .

"José Martí!" I interrupted. "That name is not unknown to me: I've seen it as that of the author of a pamphlet that speaks of the torments that the Spanish government inflicts upon the poor Cubans it sends to the work camps in Africa. Perhaps . . ."

"Yes sir, I am the author of that pamphlet and the martyr to which it refers."

"Well then, Mr. Martí, your twofold worthiness as a Cuban and martyr make you completely worthy of my sympathies: You may count on the position you seek."[47]

According to Izaguirre, Martí informed him at this first meeting of his plans to wed later that year and that he would require a month's leave to travel to Mexico City for the nuptials and return trip to Guatemala with his bride. Izaguirre readily agreed to this arrangement and scheduled Martí to teach courses in literature and composition.[48]

Martí initially hoped to find in Guatemala little more than employment and the chance to build a new life. What he found, however, sparked his imagination much more than any job: a promising young nation barely a half century removed from independence and just establishing its own national civil code. Guatemala declared independence from Spain on September 5, 1821, and briefly joined the Mexican Empire under Augustín I. Guatemala later formed part of the ill-fated Central American Federation (Federación de Estados Centroamericanos) until its breakup around 1840.[49] After nearly three hundred years of Spanish rule and another half century of turmoil, the liberal revolution under General Barrios ended two decades of conservative rule and the hegemony of large landowners and the Catholic Church. Barrios won election to the presidency in May 1873 and began a series of reforms similar to the Leyes de Reforma that Lerdo was enacting in Mexico around the same time. Barrios's reforms, which included freedom of the press and limitations on church power and property, found their first full expression in the Códigos Nuevos (New Codes) of 1877 and signaled a shift toward the rule of law and liberal democracy. As Mexico had done under Lerdo, Barrios made the *códigos* permanent by their inclusion in the Guatemalan Constitution of 1879.[50] And thanks to a robust economy driven by the production and exportation of coffee, Guatemala was not only a progressive young republic but a very prosperous one.[51]

Martí's decision to immigrate to Guatemala was initially the result of a pragmatic calculation; when his situation in Mexico became untenable, he simply turned to the only place that offered the promise of employment and financial stability. He set out for Guatemala with a plan to find suitable employment and establish himself professionally. Once he accomplished these objectives, he planned to marry Carmen and settle down with her in his adopted country. But Martí's first days in the capital crystallized a larger vision that he began to glimpse in his travels through the Guatemalan rain forest. What Martí saw in Guatemala was the promise of redemption for himself but also for the very idea of liberal democracy in Latin America. Here was a young, developing country that shared much in common with the Mexican republic for which he had held such high hopes. Guatemala lagged behind its northern neighbor economically and in terms of infrastructure and technological advances, yet Martí saw in it a second chance, the opportunity to follow in Mexico's footsteps while avoiding the mistakes that caused that nation's descent into chaos and repression.

Chief among the dangers Martí saw was simply the seductiveness of power that might lure the country's leaders to subjugate the rule of law to their own personal ends and ambitions. Martí worried that the neglect of the country's rural and indigenous populations, which in Mexico had grown from cultural ignorance and lack of awareness of these groups' potential for both beneficial and destructive change, would alienate the capital from its people, thus reproducing the conditions that allowed Porfirio Díaz to overthrow the liberal government. In Barrios Guatemala had a leader who came to power, like Díaz, precisely by overthrowing an established government, only in this case a conservative one, and who was committed to modernizing the country at the cost of conscripting its indigenous populations into working on the new coffee plantations. Like Lerdo in Mexico, Barrios moved to disenfranchise the church and redistribute the country's wealth among his supporters, further alienating the country's more conservative factions.[52] Martí nevertheless embraced Barrios's modernizing vision for the country despite his acquaintance with Guatemalan exiles in Mexico who described the Guatemalan leader as "a cannibal, a panther, a satrap, [an] opprobrium of humanity."[53]

Martí's affinity with his vision was partly due to Barrios's support of the Cuban rebels after 1868 and his government's acceptance of Cuban immigrants fleeing Spanish colonialism. It was also, however, because Martí believed that Barrios could succeed where Lerdo had failed and that he could do so without becoming a Díaz-style dictator. Martí recognized the missteps of the Lerdo government and the similar threat they posed for Guatemala; he was aware of

Barrios's autocratic style of rule, which one observer at the time called "omnipo-tent and unlimited."[54] Aware of Barrios's quickness to embrace friends and to punish enemies and cognizant of how his own outspokenness in Mexico had contributed to his necessarily hasty departure from that country, Martí resolved to take a more tempered approach to the politics of his new home; a suddenly circumspect Martí reflects, in his April 19 letter to Mercado, that his sometimes acerbic statements must in Guatemala "be very prudent so as not to appear as presumptions."[55] But if Barrios and Guatemala could avoid Mexico's pitfalls, Martí reasoned—and if he could overcome his own propensity to rhetorical and political exuberance—perhaps both would thrive.

THE NEW ARRIVAL WASTED NO TIME IN PUTTING HIS PLAN into motion. In mid-April 1877 Martí had been in Guatemala City a little over a week, but thanks to his letters of introduction he secured an interview with Joaquín Macal, President Barrios's minister of foreign relations.[56] And so quickly did the two countrymen bond in friendship that Izaguirre invited Martí to stay at his home until he could find a permanent residence.[57] Martí achieved a major objective with his employment at the Escuela Normal, and his upcoming inter-view with Macal represented an important opportunity for the young émigré to establish himself as an ally and potential asset for the Barrios government. His new, expansive idea of Guatemala as a leading Latin American nation made it critical for him to present it to the Barrios government and to articulate his own envisioned role in helping to achieve that bright future.

That first week in Guatemala gave Martí sufficient time to prepare for his meeting with Macal, to study the country's history and current political situa-tion, and to discuss with his new confidant, Izaguirre, how best to present his ideas. A good part of Martí's preparation would have included careful study of Barrios's New Codes; Macal asked his opinion about the codes during their April 10 interview. Knowing Martí's reputation as a writer, the minister also asked the young Cuban for some examples of recent work.[58]

Martí's interview with Macal went well enough that the two continued their conversation in writing. In a letter to Macal written on April 11, the day after their interview, Martí restated his devotion to the cause of Guatemala's future and articulated more precisely how he saw himself contributing to it. Martí fairly gushed over Guatemala's present moment and marveled at the auspi-ciousness of its political fortunes and prospects. He offered the minister an already well-defined portrait of his envisioned new American man and his role in helping build a new society:

> You have asked what I think of the new Code and to see something of
> what they say I have written. — Why do you ask about the past? Life

should be lived daily, fluidly, usefully; and the first duty for a man these days is to be a man of his time. Not to apply foreign theories but to discover his own. Not to disturb his country with abstractions but to ask how to render practical those that are useful. If I have been good for something before now, I no longer remember: What I want is to be more useful now.[59]

This passage, and in fact Martí's entire letter, as well as his subsequent essay on the New Codes illustrate how almost from the moment of his arrival in Guatemala he recognized the crucial importance of a new and uniquely Latin American politics—and beyond that, a philosophy—that would distinguish the region from Europe and the United States. We see in the letter one of the first appearances of a term that would figure prominently in his future writings. Martí defines his radical new vision for Guatemala and by extension for Latin America as action—being "useful" by serving a project that rejects the "foreign" in the name of a new national and hemispheric identity: Guatemala as an American nation, derived yet distinct from Europe.

Lest his appeal to usefulness or utility be seen as simply metaphorical, another theoretical "abstraction," Martí suggests that even his own writing be judged by how it might best serve Guatemala's practical political needs. Seen in this way, his claim in the letter's conclusion that he is not a writer and does not wish to be known as one is more than mere (false) modesty; it is part of a lifelong conviction, expressed fully here for perhaps the first time, that for Martí writing is a vehicle, a tool for the advancement and dissemination of ideas. This is why Martí wants Macal to see him and his potential value to the people and nation of Guatemala less as a writer than as a political agent:

> Please do not announce me to anyone as a writer, as I will have to say I am not. I love journalism as a mission, and I hate it . . . no, for hate is not good, I resent it as a disturbance. As a rule I forbid myself to interfere in the partisan politics of the countries in which I live. There is but one great universal politics, and that I do embrace and will engage: the politics of the new doctrines.[60]

Thus, for Martí the only politics worth pursuing was a politics of the new, one that expressed its newness—its unique identity—by the writing of new doctrines (*nuevas doctrinas*). In the months to come, he would set his own writing and teaching to precisely that task.

Having secured a teaching position and found favor within the Barrios government, Martí now immersed himself in the artistic and political life of his new country as he had in Mexico. His first commission from the Barrios government, requested by minister Antonio Batres Jáuregui, was to deliver a new dramatic work celebrating Guatemala's history and liberation in time for the country's Independence Day celebrations on September 15.[61] He attacked this assignment vigorously, boasting in a letter years later that he completed work on the play "in some five days."[62] On April 21 Martí made his first formal appearance at the Escuela Normal and delivered a short but well-received lecture at the school. On the following day his essay "The New Codes" appeared in the Guatemalan newspaper *El Progreso* along with a brief rebuttal from the paper's editor expressing a different view of the state's relations with its indigenous populations. On April 28 he participated in the school's regular Saturday-evening literary salon and spoke glowingly of a new work by Guatemalan poet Francisco Lainfiesta, who served as secretary to President Barrios.[63] The next day he wrote a brief note to the editor of *El Progreso* likewise praising Lainfiesta's poetry and submitted some samples of the poet's work. Beyond his marked interest in Lainfiesta's work, Martí in his April 29 letter cites several other Guatemalan poets; this, along with his string of public appearances, suggests that within a month of his arrival Martí was well and knowledgably immersed in the letters and cultural life of his new country.

He again found, as in Mexico, quick initial success in Guatemala and made inroads with its professional and political elites; there remained for Martí only to gain an audience with Barrios himself. Barrios, wishing to endear himself to Martí and ensure his loyalty, sent him an unknown but considerable amount of money through an intermediary. Surprised by the president's overture but mindful not to anger him, Martí did not reject the money out of hand but requested an interview with the president. His petition was granted, and in late April Martí and fellow Cuban Izaguirre visited the presidential palace for an audience with Barrios.[64] That Martí would seek such an interview illustrates his enthusiasm and the scope of his ambitions; that he achieved it within weeks of his arrival, when long-established immigrants like Izaguirre had yet to secure such an audience, attests to the newcomer's impressive political and diplomatic skills.[65]

According to the later accounts of those present at Martí's interview with Barrios, the meeting was a cordial one, though not without its tensions and political maneuverings.[66] After some initial small talk, the young Cuban expressed his gratitude for the president's gift but inquired whether the funds came from public sources. Despite Barrios's assurance that the money was his own personal gift, Martí refused it, insisting that only by working for the country that had so generously granted him asylum could he truly repay his debt to it. Impressed with the young man's poise and diplomacy, the president quickly assented, granted Martí a professorship at the university, and, according to one account, made a mental note to use Martí wisely and carefully.[67] Martí likewise came away from the meeting impressed and convinced that Barrios's government was the "new apostolate" that was "necessary" for the young republic's ascendance to prosperity and continental leadership.[68]

Martí thrived under Barrios's patronage, and the favorable impression he made on the president paid immediate dividends. On May 29 he was named professor of languages and history at the Universidad de Guatemala, and in May he was welcomed as a new member of the literary society El Porvenir (The Future), which consisted of the nation's leading intellectuals. Martí was a keynote speaker for a banquet at the Escuela Normal in honor of Barrios's cabinet and wrote an extensive review of the individual ministers' reports to the annual convention in the capital. In June he was praised in the press for offering free composition courses at the private Academía de Niñas de Centroamérica (Girls Academy of Central America).[69]

It was not only government ministers and university students who in the spring of 1877 came to admire the Escuela Normal's newest faculty member. María García Granados, the seventeen-year-old daughter of former president Miguel García Granados, became smitten with the very engaging—and engaged—Cuban professor.

THE STORY OF MARÍA GARCÍA GRANADOS, "LA NIÑA DE Guatemala" (The Girl from Guatemala) who fell hopelessly for Martí and "died of love" shortly after his marriage to Carmen, occupies an outsized place in the Martí legend largely due to his memorializing her in a much-celebrated poem in the 1891 collection *Versos sencillos*.[70] Subsequent attention paid by Martí scholars and others to Martí's relationship with María Granados has focused on its romantic, even melodramatic aspects, but the evidence suggests a much more mundane, if still unfortunate, sequence of events. The portrayal of Martí's relationship with María Granados as a romantic tragedy is overblown in many respects; the cause of her untimely death in May 1878, though arguably hastened by emotional stress and anguish over Martí's marriage, was not heartbreak but tuberculosis.[71] True to the disease's etiology of spreading through close contact and among family members, tuberculosis ran in the Granados family; María's eldest sister, Mercedes, died from the disease in 1868 at the age of twelve, and her father, Miguel, succumbed to it only four months after María's death. Another relative, the poet Pepe Batres, died from tuberculosis in 1844.[72]

At least one scholar has dismissed the attention paid to this episode of Martí's life as "diversionism," protesting that "[if] Martí had not written the verses of 'La niña de Guatemala,' we would not even have known that there once existed in Guatemala a girl named María García Granados."[73] That may be so, but these conflicting positions—the obsession with María Granados as a victim of unrequited love on the one hand and the dismissal of her story as irrelevant to Martí's life on the other—both overlook the insights the episode offers into Martí's life at the time as well as its emotional impact on Martí himself, who came to view his "sacrificing" of María for Carmen as one of the greatest mistakes of his life.[74]

Photographs of María Granados survive, but the fullest portrait of her comes from Martí's friend and colleague José María Izaguirre:

> She was tall, slender, and graceful: her black hair like ebony, abundant, soft and curly like silk; her face, though not supremely beautiful, was sweet and pleasant; her eyes deeply black and melancholy, veiled by long, curly lashes, revealed an exquisite sensibility. Her voice was gentle and pleasing to the ear, her manners so affable, that it was impossible to know her and not love her. She played the piano admirably, and when her hand glided across the keyboard with a certain abandon she brought from it notes that seemed sprung from her soul to move that of her listeners.[75]

When she met Martí, the teenage María had never been engaged or had a serious romantic relationship of any kind; according to Izaguirre and other observers, this was not due to a lack of suitors.[76] Several conflicting accounts exist of María Granados's first encounter with Martí, although the fullest and most credible appears in a 1909 letter to Gonzalo de Quesada y Aróstegui, a young Martí lieutenant and protégé, from Manuel José Izaguirre, José María's brother and a cousin by marriage to Martí's wife, Carmen. According to Manuel José's eyewitness account, that first meeting was "electric":

> I had brought Martí to a costume ball held at the home of García Granados only two days after his arrival in Guatemala;[77] we were standing in one of the [home's] beautiful ballrooms, watching the couples go by [when we saw] two young ladies walking arm in arm. Martí asked, "Who is that in the Egyptian costume?"—"That is María, daughter of the house." I stopped her and introduced my friend and countryman Martí, and the electric spark was lit.[78]

Neither of the Izaguirre brothers suggests that the attraction, or at least its intensity, was mutual; Manuel José recounts in the same 1909 letter that María, tired of dropping hints and frustrated by Martí's unresponsiveness, finally declared her feelings for him only to be rejected: "[She] declared herself, and he would respond with a rude frankness: 'I can't, I am engaged to Carmen.'"[79]

Part of what made María's growing attachment to Martí a problem was his own friendship with her father. Martí had quickly become a favorite of Miguel

García Granados, and for a time he was a fixture at the García Granados home. Martí and the ex-president were avid chess players, and as with his future father-in-law, Francisco Zayas Bazán, chess provided the initial impetus for their friendship. As happened with the Zayas Bazáns, García Granados's daughter became a regular presence during Martí's visits and for the same reason. Unfortunately for María, however, the otherwise romantically inclined Martí apparently balked at the prospect of starting an affair with such a socially visible young woman from a prominent family so soon before marrying Carmen.

We do not know for certain whether Martí surrendered to María's advances and consummated their relationship, but on balance the evidence suggests that he did not. Aside from Manuel José Izaguirre's account of Martí rebuffing her, we have his brother José María's assertion that Martí continued to resist even as her attraction became a near-obsession:

> [Ever since] Martí began frequenting the house, a certain sadness became noticeable in her that no one could explain, as well the silence that would envelop her in his presence. Evidently something was happening inside her; but it was a something no one could explain and perhaps she herself did not understand what was happening to her . . .
>
> This feeling, previously unknown to her, grew day by day until it took on the characteristics of true passion, and although she concealed it behind the modesty proper to a young woman raised to value her honor, Martí well understood what was happening. A gentleman above all, and bound by an equal sentiment to another woman he had vowed to marry, he abstained from fomenting with his gallantry or with displays of affection that passion which seemed close to becoming a veritable fire. He limited himself from then on to treating her simply as a friend and began little by little to distance himself from that creel so that María would comprehend that she should not give herself to the feelings that were overwhelming her, for as much as he recognized her worthiness, as he did, and as well as they got on together, he could not reciprocate her passion.[80]

The Izaguirres' assertion that Martí successfully resisted María's advances finds support in Martí's letters from this period, which never fail to proclaim his love for Carmen and impatience at being away from her. In one such letter sent shortly after his arrival in Guatemala, Martí's declarations of love and commitment seem almost defensive:

> You would laugh if I wrote to you mere pleasantries: as if I could part my desire, adoration, and thoughts from my Carmen! I carry her with

me and before me; to everyone I declare myself committed [*obligado*] to her; and when they speak of me, they speak of her. — Everyone knows it.[81]

At the same time, we can read in these letters traces of a man fighting his own doubts, feeling the need to reassert at every turn his resolve and commitment to the woman he has promised to marry. How else, for instance, to explain in the April 19 letter Martí's use of the word *obligado* ("obligated," or at least "obliged") to describe his engagement instead of the *comprometido* or *prometido* ("committed" or "engaged" or "promised") of common parlance? Given Martí's great skill as a writer and the otherwise carefully structured nature of his longer letters — he did not simply dash them off — such slips suggest the momentary, almost imperceptible emergence of doubt, made visible only by its author's otherwise florid expressions of devotion. Why else assure Mercado, not only his confidant but a friend to the Zayas Bazáns, that he has been so keen to inform everyone of his commitment to Carmen? In hindsight, reading such wording in the context of his 1891 paean to "La niña de Guatemala" and his farewell kiss upon "the brow / That most I have loved in my life!" it is fair to wonder whether María's fevered devotion to Martí and his attraction to her led him to second-guess his commitment to Carmen even as he outwardly declared it.[82]

Whatever his doubts about marrying Carmen and the constant temptation of the attractive and willing María, the evidence suggests that Martí did not succumb. If he was entertaining doubts about his engagement to Carmen, that Martí did not surrender to María's advances is all the more remarkable given his romantic nature and demonstrably healthy sexual appetite as well as his established history of aversion to being without female company. Yet resist he did; the Izaguirres' assertions that Martí told María of his engagement is confirmed by her only known letter to him, written after Martí married Carmen and brought her back to Guatemala. In the January 1878 letter, María reproaches Martí for not visiting her and assures him that she bears him no ill will: "I harbor no resentment toward you, because you always spoke to me with sincerity regarding the moral situation of your commitment to marriage with Miss Zayas Bazán." But Martí's "sincerity" had done little, even at this late date, to diminish María's ardent devotion to him — she signs the letter "your girl."[83]

For María García Granados, the die had been cast long before Martí's marriage, when he became a favorite of her father shortly after his arrival in Guatemala. By the end of April 1877 Martí was thriving socially as well as professionally, thanks in great part to his highly visible friendship with the ex-president; he soon became a fixture in the García Granados household, regularly playing chess with Miguel García Granados and often staying for dinner at María's insistence. Rumors soon circulated that he had begun an affair with María. Yet

while we do not know when specifically Martí informed Miguel García Granados of his engagement to another woman, García Granados could easily have
ascertained as much from any number of their mutual acquaintances such as
the Izaguirre brothers. There is thus no reason to believe that Martí concealed
his engagement to Carmen in order to gain García Granados's friendship or patronage or that he would have allowed the ex-president to entertain any notions
of him as a suitor for María. If anything, María's growing attachment to Martí
would have strained his bond with Miguel García Granados, as Martí found
himself forced to gradually withdraw from the family as a consequence of it.
Yet he could think of nothing else to do. Faced with the implacability of María's
passion and perhaps sensing his own weakness, Martí withdrew and immersed
himself once again in his work.

IF IN MEXICO MARTÍ BECAME A JOURNALIST, IN GUATE-
mala he embraced his calling as a teacher. Beyond his regular course load at the
Escuela Normal and at the university, he began to offer extra courses in language and literature for no additional pay. These included a course in European
literature at the university and, at the Girls Academy of Central America, free
composition classes, which María García Granados dutifully attended.[84]

In the spring and summer of 1877 Martí established a reputation as a passionate, even dramatic speaker and lecturer. An early letter presented to him by
his students is almost embarrassingly lavish in its praise:

> You transport us, Sir, to the ancient times when [poets] weaved garlands
> of letters for their patrons . . .
> The letters must have lulled you to sleep in your crib, perfumed the
> very air in which you were raised, nourished your soul, and imprinted
> their character upon your moral personality . . .
> We listen to you, fearful of breaking even with our breath the fine
> golden thread with which you weave the delicate chain of your reason
> and when you spread your condor's wings and scale the heights of phi-
> losophy and literature and bathe our words in heavenly light, we feel
> electrified and explode in uncontainable excitement out of admira-
> tion for your eloquence, before whose power the soul falls prostrate,
> the will surrenders, and the heart counts itself fortunate in its utter
> enslavement.[85]

Nor was it only his students whom Martí held in thrall with his charisma
and compelling speeches. José María Izaguirre recounts one of Martí's first con-
quests of a Guatemalan audience, during a literary gathering at the Escuela
Normal:

The speakers were the eloquent Guatemalan speakers Martín Barrundia and Lorenzo Montúfar, both Cabinet Secretaries in Barrios's government, and the latter a distinguished historian. Their speeches were well received . . .

Martí was present, and, after hearing the speeches, asked my permission to say a few words. I confess that I granted it fearfully, since although I knew him to be an illustrious, discreet, and articulate young man, I was ignorant of his rhetorical skills. But my fear was short-lived, as his first words were received with pleasure by the distinguished crowd, and, upon finishing his speech, received an exceptional ovation.[86]

Izaguirre was especially impressed with Martí's skill at addressing the relationship of literature and politics, a "thorny" (*escabroso*) and risky topic to address before representatives of the "suspicious" (*suspicaz*), distrustful Barrios government. According to Izaguirre, Martí "cloaked" the difficult topic "in such ways, and knew how to skirt difficulties in such a manner, that the most enthusiastic applause was that of the aforementioned Secretaries."[87] Martí went on from this early success to a string of well-received and high-profile public appearances, including a July 25 speech commemorating the founding of Guatemala City and participation in a September 16 event celebrating Central American independence.[88]

But not all who saw and heard Martí fell under his sway; a small but vocal group of critics and detractors, most of them conservatives who disdained Barrios's policies and reforms, derided him for the very qualities that enthralled his admirers. It was this group that coined the nickname "Doctor Torrent" as a way of mocking Martí for his florid, expansive speaking style.[89] Martí's political enemies correctly portrayed him as a Barrios partisan whose charisma as a public figure could sway public opinion against them. If Martí was by now fully committed, as he asserts in a September 21 letter to Mercado, to a political project that would "give life to America, resuscitate the ancient, fortify and reveal the new,"[90] there were also those in Guatemala, as there had been in Mexico, who felt threatened by that work and were now beginning to act against it. In the same September 21 letter in which Martí would work to reveal the new America of his dreams, he complains bitterly to Mercado of "the absolute lack of greatness, of energy and of liberties, which, in vilifying the characters of others, upsets and injures my own."[91] In the next sentence he bemoans "this foundation of foam on which luck, far from men, has forced me to build my house."[92]

Whatever Martí's growing frustrations in Guatemala, he took solace in having finally raised the necessary funds for his wedding and a new home for himself and his bride. Although the letter provides important insights into

Martí's ambitions and frustrations in Guatemala, its primary purpose was to alert Mercado to his anticipated arrival and ask him to make the necessary arrangements for the wedding in Mexico City. Despite the anxieties and irritations that occupy much of the letter, Martí positively rejoices at being so close to achieving long-sought goals:

> I have now ordered my humble home [to be built]; now they construct my poor furniture; now my heart beats with joy and fear—but at last it beats!—Now I finally see my way to arranging in Mexico what is strictly necessary to make good my wedding venture.[93]

Martí assured Mercado that he would undertake the two-week journey for Mexico City "either on November 10 or the 29th"; it is not clear whether the uncertainty is due to financial reasons or professional obligations. It was neither work nor money, however, that kept Martí in Guatemala until late November, but rather an unforeseen, perhaps unforeseeable, event, one larger than himself that momentarily imperiled the republic—and whose aftermath threatened to unravel, once again, all that he had built.

BY NOVEMBER 1877 MARTÍ'S ENEMIES HAD GROWN BOLDER if not more numerous. On November 3 leaflets bearing the title "Doctor Torrent" satirizing his by-now well-known public persona appeared around the capital, circulated by conservative critics in an effort to turn students and others against him. The missive had little immediate effect on Martí's reputation or standing but served notice that his enemies—and by extension the regime's— were gathering up their courage. The leaflet's authors must have found them an effective tool against Martí, as two new "Doctor Torrent" leaflets circulated the capital on November 17.[94]

By the time the new "Doctor Torrent" flyers appeared, Martí, Barrios, and Guatemala had more pressing concerns. Rumors of a conservative coup had been spreading since at least October, but with no visible signs of an uprising Barrios and his cabinet dismissed them as speculation.[95] The rumors soon proved to be true, although the conspirators managed to keep their plot a secret until nearly the very moment of its deployment. Accounts differ regarding the specifics of the plot, when it was to be carried out, and even how it was discovered; this is due to Barrios's swiftness in responding to the failed attempt and controlling the flow of information to a terrified public.

True to Barrios's ruthless and dictatorial reputation, he dealt harshly and rapidly with the conspirators. Seventeen conspirators were executed within a week of their capture, and many others were jailed or forced to flee the country. None received a trial of any kind. Those first captured were beaten and tortured until they revealed the names and whereabouts of their fellows.[96] After further interrogation and beatings — some administered by Barrios himself — all seventeen defendants were condemned to death by firing squad in the capital city's Plaza de Armas. Barrios selected the site because it offered a clear view from the president's balcony, where, rifle in hand, he watched the executions while surrounded by friends and associates.[97] The conspirators' remains were then put on public display at the general hospital, although the gesture was hardly necessary, as bits of bone and brain and the flocks of buzzards fighting over them were visible at the execution site for days afterward.[98]

Barrios's ferocious response to the failed coup, while clearly intended to make an example of the conspirators, inadvertently made martyrs of them; Guatemala's right wing seized on the incident as the act of a power-mad and out-of-control ruler, hailing the fallen men as heroes and holding annual memorials for them.[99] Barrios's disregard for the legal process in condemning the conspirators did little to assuage the sense among even his supporters that his government had truly become a dictatorship and that mere suspicion was now enough to provoke arrest, imprisonment, or worse.[100]

Martí learned of the failed plot in the papers along with nearly everyone else. Despite his relative closeness with several government ministers, the public executions and Barrios's terse statements to the press on November 5 and 7 were his first inkling that something precipitous and severe had occurred. No public denunciations of Barrios's actions were forthcoming, from Martí or anyone else, in the days following the executions, and Martí only privately expressed alarm at the swiftness and violence of the government's response.

Although Martí had signed a November 6 open letter to the president from the Escuela Normal faculty condemning the plot, the bloodthirstiness of Barrios's retribution troubled him, reminding him of any number of similar atrocities committed by the Spanish but perhaps most pointedly the wrongful execution of eight Cuban medical students on November 27, 1871.[101] Porfirio Díaz's persecution of Lerdo supporters in Mexico might also have weighed on Martí's mind as he wrote to Mercado of the failed Guatemalan plot:

> A terrible event, drowned in blood, gave the people pause and arrested the traffic of business. A somber conspiracy, of clergymen and soldiers, has animated the high offices and top people. It could only be made sympathetic by the rigor with which it has been punished. . . . Certain attacks are not plotted except against they who somehow deserve them.[102]

In this November 10 letter Martí recognizes that the abortive rebellion failed due to "its lack of intelligence and the cowardice of the nation." But he avers that Mercado and he "long ago decided that in a Republic power should only lie in the hands of civilians. Sabers cut. — Dress coats can hardly make whips out of their tails. — So it shall be."[103] Martí's doubts about Guatemala and the future of "the American mind" continued to nag at him over the coming weeks, as he confessed in a November 27 letter: "I fear that it does not want to arrive."[104]

This gnawing sense of latent trouble was no doubt unwelcome for Martí, coming at the very moment he planned to marry Carmen and bring her to live in Guatemala. He had never been sanguine about his prospects for a long, happy life: "Fortunately, I will not live long and will have but few children," he confided to Mercado as an assurance that he would not "make [Carmen] suffer."[105] As the wedding date approached, Martí wondered that no catastrophe had yet derailed his plans: "It astonishes me that luck has allowed itself to be thus surprised. Oh — and at times I fear it will take revenge!"[106] Even as the tone of these letters grew agitated, Martí expressed confidence that with Carmen at his side he would "conquer" fortune, "shake though it will its angry wings."[107] The foiled November plot and Barrios's violent response to it nevertheless seems, perhaps because of its unforeseen nature, to have shaken Martí in a way other obstacles and pressures up until then had not. Above all, their timing, coming right before Martí's wedding, did little to reassure the young Cuban that his confidence in his adopted country had been well placed.

MARTÍ'S WEDDING SOJOURN TO MEXICO CITY DID NOT ENtail nearly the hardships he endured when he traveled to Guatemala. Having received a thirty-day leave of absence from work, on November 28 he departed the capital by Escuintla to the Pacific Ocean, a distance of a little over fifty miles. The next day he boarded a vessel from the Línea del Pacífico steamship line at the port of San José bound for Acapulco. Upon his arrival on December 5 or 6, Martí was unable to alert Mercado due to the absence of telegraph lines and so continued on to Mexico City. Unlike in Guatemala, where one could simply hire a muleteer and travel the roads without fear of assault, in Mexico it was necessary either to hire a private coach with an armed escort or, for those of lesser means, to join up with one of the informal caravans traveling the roads together for their mutual security.[108] Whether out of necessity or an abundance of financial caution or simply because no coaches were then available, Martí joined one such caravan and headed inland toward the capital.[109]

That inland journey ended on December 11 when Martí arrived at the front door of Mercado's Mexico City home carrying a draft of a projected book on Guatemala.[110] His former colleagues at *El Federalista* still thought fondly of him and in the December 14 issue happily reported his arrival.[111] Martí spent much of his time the next few days visiting friends in the city as Mercado made final arrangements for the wedding, which was now less than a week away.

JOSÉ MARTÍ AND CARMEN ZAYAS BAZÁN WERE MARRIED on December 20, 1877, in civil legalities at 6 p.m. and the religious ceremony less than a half hour later at the nearby Sagrado Metropolitano church. The witnesses at the civil ceremony were Carmen's father, Francisco Zayas Bazán; Manuel Mercado; the late Ana Martí's fiancé, Miguel Ocaranza; and Ramón Guzmán, husband of Carmen's sister Rosa. After the religious ceremony at the church, the wedding party moved to an intimate, somewhat reserved reception at Mercado's home. Also present at this gathering were those who had befriended Martí during his tenure in Mexico, among these Guatemalan Ambassador Ramón Uriarte, Cuban-born attorney Nicolás Azcárate, and poet-dramatist José Peón y Contreras.

They and other guests wrote their dedications and verses and well wishes, in the custom of the time, in the Martís' wedding album.[112] Among the many entries appears this note from Mercado, which, curiously, is his only known piece of correspondence to Martí:[113]

> Carmen:
>
> Your dreams of good fortune are now certain. Today has been accomplished as you deserve, the union forever of your fortunes to those of your chosen soul mate, that privileged being in whom admirably converge the most beautiful and brilliant gifts of intelligence and of sentiment. He too will very happy, he who in your eyes will always find ample compensation for the terrible sufferings of times past and the sorrows that may yet come . . .
>
> Goodbye, Carmen, goodbye, Pepé: May you always keep the memory of those here who delight in your good fortune, and do not be disturbed by the loving tears of the dear friends you leave behind.
>
> Mexico City, December 1877

El Federalista and *El Siglo XIX* newspapers ran announcements of the Martí–Zayas Bazán wedding the next day. *El Federalista* added to its congratulations the wish that the couple might "one day return to the land of their fathers, and their *patria*'s own breezes of liberty rock the cradle of their first child."[114] *El Federalista* editors' wish for the newlyweds did in fact come to pass, but not in the manner or for the reasons that they or the couple might have imagined that day.

CARMEN ZAYAS BAZÁN'S FIRST DAYS AS MRS. MARTÍ WERE pleasant, even joyful ones. Despite Martí's concern to not abuse his monthlong leave from the Escuela Normal, the newlyweds stayed another six days after the ceremonies, perhaps to celebrate the holidays among friends. Well-wishers continued to shower the couple with warmth and attention. Mercado organized a lunch for Martí in the garden café at the Tivoli de San Cosme, the capital's poshest eatery; on December 21 the Martís were guests at a school awards ceremony, where he gave a brief speech;[115] and on December 25 they attended *El Federalista*'s Christmas dinner. That evening, their last in Mexico, Uriarte visited the couple at Mercado's house to bid them farewell and deliver a bill of exchange (equivalent to today's checks) in case of any unforeseen expenses.[116] We do not know whether the Martís ever used the money or whether it came from state funds, President Barrios, or Uriarte himself.

On the morning of December 26, the happy couple finally set out on the nearly 1,100-mile journey to Guatemala City. Both would soon look back on these first days together as some of the happiest in an otherwise beset, often painful marriage.

The Martís set off from Mercado's home at daybreak in a mule-drawn coach under armed guard. Carmen's trunks and other accouterments would have required the additional cargo capacity of a carriage, and there was no question of taking Carmen, who was unused to such travel, to Guatemala on horseback. The armed escort was also a necessity, given the frequency with which bandits attacked travelers on the Tlalpan Road connecting Mexico City with Cuernavaca.[117] A full day's travel covered slightly more than fifty miles, and it was nightfall before the exhausted Martís finally reached Cuernavaca, too tired and pressed for time to see anyone or do any sightseeing. The newlyweds sought only to rest and make arrangements for the next leg of the journey.

December 27 was a rest day for the Martís, but the following morning found them back on the road toward Iguala some sixty miles southeast of Cuernavaca. This leg of the journey was more desolate and rugged than the previous one; they carried their own food, having been advised that rest stops along the way would have little to eat. Their coach converged along the route with other small groups traveling in the same direction, and before long the Martís were part of an impromptu caravan moving together to ward off bandits.[118]

On December 28 the Martís crossed through Xochiltepec and stopped to visit the pre-Columbian ruins of Xochicalco; Martí later wrote of "the temple of chiseled granite, with its enormous blocks set so close together that one cannot see the join, and of a stone so hard that it is not known what instrument they might have used to cut it, nor what machinery they employed to lift it [to the summit]."[119] It was encounters such as this, immersed within the larger experience of again traveling through the outbacks of "Mother America," that animated the pages of Martí's book on Guatemala, on which he continued to work throughout the trip. In the early morning hours of December 29 Martí found time to write to Mercado and send revisions for the book that he had completed since departing Mexico City. He seems pleasantly surprised by his wife's good spirits and resilience: "Carmen is doing beautifully and speaks constantly of you all," he tells Mercado. "By tonight she intends to bravely reach as far as Iguala."[120]

For Martí much depended upon the completion—and favorable reception by the Barrios government—of his book. Martí's *Guatemala* was more than a historical study, more than a travelogue of the type often published at the time by American and European explorers; it was the first full articulation of an entire philosophy and vision of an alternative America, one liberated from the shackles of overt colonialism and of dependence, economic as well as political and cultural, on Europe and the United States. More pragmatically, Martí conceived *Guatemala* as a love song to a country he loved deeply and in which he had invested a great deal in the hopes of winning its enduring love in return. So he worked tirelessly on his "very quick pages, written almost entirely in the hills and on horseback," with a bride astonished by her husband's powers of endurance and concentration.[121]

The evening of December 29 did, as Carmen predicted, find them in Iguala. Martí's leave having nearly expired, the couple had no time to rest and set out again in the early morning of December 30. They traveled the entire day and into the night without reaching even the semblance of a town that might shelter them; so the young couple and their escort spent the night in the open air by the banks of the Río Mezcala. On the morning of December 31 they crossed the river by boat, hoping that day to reach accommodations in the town of Chilpancingo that Mercado had arranged for them. This they did, after a day spent negotiating the difficult, mountainous terrain and broken roads that led to the state of Guerrero's capital city.[122] Upon reaching Chilpancingo, the road-weary Martís found a measure of comfort, courtesy of Mercado; they were welcomed at the spacious hacienda of José Manuel Emparan, a Guerrero government official, who promptly delivered to Martí a letter from their mutual friend. There the Martís stayed to ring in the New Year as Emparan's guests, in a welcome respite from the road.[123]

But Martí was unwell when he awoke on January 1, possibly due to a flare-up from his chronic sarcoidosis.[124] In his letter to Mercado that evening he notes, "I suffered all this afternoon—my sorrows are slow to leave me—a small attack—sufficient to rob me of my time and my sense."[125] Martí did not explicitly identify the illness as sarcoidosis-related but did describe it as being "of the same type" for which he had received treatment in Mexico. The episode apparently subsided by the time he wrote the letter, and the next morning Martí was well enough to start covering the remaining nine hundred miles between them and Guatemala City.

On the morning of January 2 the Martís and their escort of federal officers provided by Emparan proceeded southward toward the Mexican Pacific coast, which they would follow southwest toward their destination. The last third of the trip was the most arduous, as the couple no longer had the luxury of coaches and had to revert to mule- or horseback.[126] Carmen found herself for the first time traveling as her husband had the previous winter, on a horseback trail under a straw hat, in the heat and the ubiquitous dust. We know relatively little about their experiences in this last segment of their route, as he did not keep a regular journal due to his work on *Guatemala* and wrote only twice to Mercado before reaching Guatemala; what little information we have comes from the book itself.

It is clear that accommodations for the traveler were fewer and farther between than they had been to this point; aside from Acapulco, those villages and outposts they encountered offered little beyond the bare essentials. But as Martí reveals in *Guatemala*, what he saw in these remote communities, populated almost entirely by the indigenous peoples that Lerdo had neglected and Barrios was now bending to the task of building Guatemala's burgeoning coffee industry, was a force with the potential to transform the American continent: "Ah! They are—oh, the terrible punishment that those who provoked them should suffer—they are today the obstacle, tomorrow the great mass that will propel the young nation."[127]

It took the Martís three more days to reach the ocean and Acapulco. The town of three thousand, a relative metropolis after the trek from the capital, offered them the chance to rest and recharge before tackling the last 850-plus miles to the Guatemalan capital. The time in Acapulco was a productive one for Martí, as he included with his January 7 letter to Mercado seventy-seven more pages from the projected book for his colleague to edit.[128] That he had managed to produce so much of the manuscript in little more than a week—he had sent an earlier section of the book before departing Cuernavaca on December 29—speaks to the single-mindedness that Martí could bring to his work as well as his powers of concentration in the most adverse conditions, as he describes them in the January 7 letter:

> Regarding the journey, what shall I say that you cannot imagine? When
> I left, the wings I carried covered my eyes; now that with my wings I
> had to protect her, I have seen all the cruelest vicissitudes, rough nights,
> high hills, mighty rivers which, for good reason, travelers avoid.... [We
> have traveled] over the long stretch of the 26th to the 5th in a daze, with
> three days' rest along the way, [and] gangs of bandits, fortunately scared
> off by the escorts.[129]

Yet through it all Martí continued to write his "opus majus," and not merely out of compulsion or an outsize work ethic or devotion to Guatemala, although these contributed to the book's rapid development. For as he confesses to Mercado in the January 7 letter, Martí saw the publication of *Guatemala* as a means of escaping apparently difficult financial straits: "For my immediate prospects, [its publication] seems to me essential."[130] On January 9, just before boarding a Guatemala-bound steamer—only two days since he had sent the previous pages to Mercado—Martí wrote his friend a brief farewell note along with the rest of the manuscript: "correct it with care, and guess at what you do not understand, for you know of these matters."[131]

Martí had well exceeded his thirty-day leave from the Escuela Normal when he returned to teaching on January 15. Overstaying his leave soon proved to be the least of his worries, however, as personal and political developments in his absence had converged to make the couple's homecoming far from welcome. A change for the worse in the country's political climate following the failed plot accelerated the unraveling of Martí's dreams of professional advancement and of domesticity in Guatemala more than he could have imagined.

DESPITE ITS OUTWARD SHOW OF STABILITY, MUCH HAD changed in Guatemala in Martí's absence. The failed coup attempt of November 1 dealt a sobering blow to President Barrios, whose paranoia in the plot's aftermath now engulfed even his closest allies. Once trusted ministers and aides labored in an atmosphere of unrelenting suspicion, knowing that even the appearance of disloyalty was enough to trigger arrest, imprisonment, or in some cases exile.[132] Exacerbating matters for Martí was Barrios's about-face regarding immigrants; because Major Antonio Kopesky, a foreigner, headed the failed plot, Barrios's once welcoming stance toward exiles and other immigrants hardened considerably. Martí's compatriots in the capital and soon he as well would feel this shift in the president's attitude.

The other major event that hastened the Martís' departure from Guatemala was the end of the Ten Years' War in Cuba. The war had remained at an impasse for several years until the winter of 1877–1878, when Spain finally began to wear down the rebels through a dual policy of massive reinforcements—twenty-five thousand new troops, for a total of seventy thousand on the island—and negotiation with those rebel contingents open to a settlement. Spain's clever manipulation of the lingering racism among the rebels also played a key role; the question of abolition had long divided the rebel leaders and stalled their progress, and suspicions about the political ambitions of General Antonio Maceo, a charismatic Afro-Cuban, allowed Spain to drive a wedge between wavering Cuban contingents.

The signing of the Treaty of Zanjón on February 11, 1878, marked the end of official hostilities and initiated a general amnesty for the rebels and others who had run afoul of the colonial government since 1868. Not all rebel forces accepted the treaty; Antonio Maceo and others vowed to fight on, and almost all of the leaders chose to remain in exile rather than bow to its terms. But neither the recalcitrance of the rebel leaders nor the deep reservations expressed by the exile leaders in New York persuaded a thoroughly demoralized Cuban populace to derail the treaty's enactment.[133]

So lumbered to an ignominious end the war of independence that Martí had embraced in his adolescence—and for which he had suffered imprisonment and exile. The hundreds of thousands who had devoted a decade to the cause and the fifty thousand who had given their lives had little to show for it in the end;[134] beyond the amnesty, Spain agreed to allow the election of forty Cuban deputies to the Spanish Cortes as well as local and municipal representatives on the island.[135] Yet after ten years of struggle, Cuba remained a Spanish colony.

Worse, Spain calculated the cost of the decadelong war at $300 million— more than Cuba's entire gross domestic product over that span—and added that amount to the Cuban debt. The island thus found itself in a markedly worse economic position than before the war. Much of its infrastructure was destroyed due to the widespread razing of sugar mills upon which its economy heavily depended; this, combined with the massive war debt it now shouldered, left Cuba and its people not just militarily defeated but financially devastated and spiritually crushed.[136]

Although Martí was among those who harbored deep suspicions about the Treaty of Zanjón and its promised reforms, he had more pressing concerns. In February the Mexican newspaper *El Siglo XIX* published Martí's book *Guatemala* as a paperback, and he awaited the book's appearance as a hardback volume the following month.[137] But his hopes for the new book had changed considerably, in accordance with the drastically altered political climate in Guatemala. In his March 8 letter to Mercado, *Guatemala*'s publication was no longer the final piece of his plan to establish himself in the country but merely a way to keep enemies at bay long enough to pay off his debts and move on:

> I understand that the book will be truly useful to me here: It will serve as a weapon for those who are fond of me against others for whom I am, despite my obscure silence, a threat or a nuisance. — I have decided, after I pay my debts, to leave this place.[138]

Toward this end of raising money for the projected move, Martí informs Mercado of several articles he plans to write for *El Federalista* and asks Mercado to send word from him that "with pleasure I would produce from here whatever they ask."[139]

Events in the spring of 1878 soon validated Martí's decision to leave Guatemala. He was removed from his faculty position at the university but was permitted to continue teaching, without pay, his History of Philosophy course.[140] Martí complains at length in the March 30 letter to Mercado of his mistreatment and misrepresentation at the hands of "self-proclaimed liberals" who have "exploited my passions, and ignored my prudence . . . depicted my silence as hostility; my reserve as aloofness; my modest science as fatuous arrogance."[141] Yet in the same letter he curiously ascribes his demotion to the "inexplicable jealousy of the Rector of the University"[142]—apparently not grasping the likely causal link between his political troubles and his dismissal from the university. Or perhaps Martí simply chose not to engage in what he saw as an unseemly political game he describes as "a war of nerves [*guerra de zapa*]" in which he was "defeated from the start."[143] He still held, for now, his position at the Escuela Normal, where he could count on Izaguirre's protection. Yet Martí's references in his March letters for alternative occupations—from a well-conceived but ultimately doomed proposal for a Guatemalan magazine to a daydream of building a small coffee plantation—reveal a man who knew that he could no longer rely on the state's goodwill for his livelihood.[144]

It is reasonable to dismiss Martí's imagined idyll of retiring with his friends to "a little coffee farm" as a passing fancy,[145] the musings of a man wearied by long and fruitless struggle. As a reader of Voltaire, Martí surely knew that he was no Candide, that he lacked both the naïvete and resignation, even in his present state, to withdraw into a life of quiet domesticity.[146] In hindsight, however, Martí's projected *Revista Guatemalteca* reads as more than merely a rough draft of the literary journal he would later establish in Venezuela or more abstractly of the political newspaper *Patria*, which would become the voice of the Cuban independence movement in New York. As Martí describes it in his March 1878 prospectus, his proposed *Revista Guatemalteca* emerges as nothing less than an alternative manifesto for the field, then in its infancy, of comparative literature. His vision of the magazine as a vehicle for chronicling and celebrating Guatemala's little-known writers, artists, and scholars and bringing these to greater public awareness in Latin America and beyond is in a sense a culmination of his concept of Guatemala as the lynchpin for his larger American vision.[147]

Martí published his call for a new and vital American literature and culture even as another visionary, Hugo Meltzl de Lomnitz, was conceiving the discipline of comparative literature as a European project that pointedly excluded the Americas.[148] Although Meltzl's model undoubtedly found more acceptance at the time, forming the basis for an enduring academic discipline, Martí's vision was easily the more radical in both its inclusiveness and its claim to parity with European letters. The power of Martí's "Revista Guatemalteca" essay lies in his recognition of the invisibility of Latin American culture, even to itself, and its implicit boast that it is he who is ideally positioned to bring its greatness to light: "Who among us knows, apart from a few select insiders, better than I that we have men whose erudition runs parallel to that of the advanced nations? . . . Do they know in Europe what beauties, what riches, what natural industries this nation holds?"[149] Martí's prospectus and his larger vision of American literature and culture posit precisely such self-knowledge as a necessary precondition to the region asserting its own intellectual, cultural, and economic parity with Europe; he presents the *Revista Guatemalteca* as an important vehicle for that task: "To such necessities does the *Revista*, in part, respond."[150]

Martí's proposed magazine did find a taker in the literary society El Porvenir, which went as far as setting an April 15 publication date for its first issue.[151] But the Martís' decision to quit Guatemala brought the project to an end, and that first issue never appeared.

Taken in the context of Martí's evolving vision for the Americas and Guatemala's potential role within it, his recognition in his essay's closing paragraph of the enormity of his project refers as much to the magazine itself as to a larger life's work he had already begun to intuit: "The program is vast; for this reason I accept it; because of this, and because it is useful."[152] Although as an unrealized project the *Revista Guatemalteca* remains little more than a footnote in Martí's vast canon, it is important as a marker of his maturing vision for a post-Spanish, post-European America. The essay's focus and clarity of argument are especially remarkable given the many pressures and tribulations assailing its author, a man whose dreams of security and advancement were crumbling around him as he wrote it. The ability to maintain his focus as a thinker and writer—to produce in fact some of his finest work—in an environment of immense complexity and adversity would serve Martí well in later years. And he brought this skill to its first full fruition during this period of his life, in his travels with and without Carmen and the couple's final, trying months in Guatemala.

NEITHER THE PUBLICATION OF *GUATEMALA* NOR MARTÍ'S plans for the unrealized literary magazine were enough to deflect the larger political forces that converged against him in the spring of 1878. As bitterly as he complained about losing his university teaching position, worse things were on the way that would very much hasten the Martís' departure from Guatemala.

Like Martí, José María Izaguirre had long been targeted by right-wing elements and the jealous directors of lesser institutions, as had the Escuela Normal, which with President Barrios's support he had built into the nation's preeminent secondary school. With the political sea change that followed the failed Kopesky plot, Izaguirre's enemies no doubt recognized his sudden vulnerability as a foreigner and were emboldened to move against him. On March 19, Izaguirre's birthday, his students and colleagues organized a musical celebration for him in the Escuela Normal's main hall. His enemies seized on the event, complaining both publicly and through official channels that it demonstrated the director's narcissism and lack of seriousness in carrying out his duties. Such protests would have carried little weight in the days before the Kopesky plot and might even have backfired on the complainants for presuming to attack a Barrios ally. Barrios's sudden change of heart toward Guatemala's immigrants, however, gave him a willing ear for the burgeoning criticisms that soon reached his desk. Barrios reacted to the unsubstantiated rumors just as their instigators had hoped, promptly summoning Izaguirre to his office and demanding—and receiving—his immediate resignation.[153]

Izaguirre later recounted how Martí, enraged by the news of his friend's forced resignation, renounced his own teaching post at the Escuela Normal over Izaguirre's strenuous objections:

> "What they have done to you is an indignity. I am going to tender my resignation immediately."
>
> "Do no such thing—it would be madness," I replied. "If the salary you have here is your only means of maintaining yourself and your wife, to what [consequences] will you be subjected if you resign?"
>
> "I will resign," he responded firmly, "though my wife and I starve. I prefer this to being complicit with an injustice."
>
> My counsel was not enough to dissuade him from his intention, and he did as he said he would.[154]

And so he did. The office of the secretary of public education notified Martí on April 6 that it had received and accepted his resignation, effective immediately. Barrios made no effort to contact him directly or dissuade him in any way.[155]

Given the sudden expulsion of the more established and highly positioned Izaguirre, Martí may have reasonably surmised that he had little hope of retaining his own job for long. Read this way, his ardent declarations of solidarity with Izaguirre may have been largely symbolic; if Martí assumed that his own dismissal from the Escuela Normal was imminent, it would have made sense to at least use the opportunity to express solidarity with his countryman. "Before they abandon me," he explained in a letter to Mercado, "I have abandoned them."[156]

Regardless of whether we see Martí's decision to resign as calculating, admirable, or rash, it is clear that the choice put him and his wife in very difficult financial straits. Undone by what Martí called the government's "hypocritical animosity . . . against foreigners," he and Carmen found themselves in an urgent but for him familiar dilemma: they needed to quickly find a more hospitable place to live and work, and they would use up their already limited resources to get there. Through it all, Martí marveled at his wife's serenity and steadfastness, confessing to Mercado in an April 30 letter, "My love and my sadness grow with Carmen's every act of devotion and tenderness."[157] He reveals to Mercado his first choices for new employment, in Honduras and Peru—locations he selected to lessen the burden on Carmen of another lengthy journey.[158] Having halted work on both the literary magazine and a book on law he was drafting, Martí set his one priority to find a new home for himself and his wife before money—and time—ran out.

THROUGH ALL OF THIS, MARÍA GARCÍA GRANADOS WAS THE last thing on Martí's mind. He never mentions his earlier interactions with her or the García Granados family in his letters, and he had not seen her since leaving the capital in November 1877 to be married. Although apocryphal or otherwise uncorroborated accounts of accidental meetings on the street or at mutual friends' homes have circulated over the years, no supporting evidence has surfaced for these. One such account would have García Granados, alerted to Martí's imminent arrival but unaware that he was returning with Carmen, waiting at his house; according to the story, the mutually unexpected encounter ended with Martí introducing García Granados to his new bride.[159] We know the story to be apocryphal because of García Granados's January 1878 note to Martí that she signed "your girl," in which she reproached him for avoiding her, declared no resentment as he was honest about his engagement and ended with "I beg you to come soon."[160] García Granados's complaints notwithstanding, Martí's reluctance to see her is consistent with assertions of the Izaguirre brothers, among others, that he all but withdrew from her life before marrying Carmen.

Given the penchant for jealousy that Carmen displayed from early in their courtship, his desire to avoid even the appearance of impropriety is also understandable. Doing so may have spared Martí a lengthy and debilitating illness or, given his less than robust health, even saved his life. For sometime in early 1878 the tuberculosis that had lain dormant in María García Granados's body came roaring to life, and she fell ill. Uncharacteristically for the usually slowly progressing disease, her decline was relatively rapid, suggesting either that she was already ill around the time Martí left to marry Carmen or that, conversely, her emotional anguish and depression at his wedded return accelerated the disease's progress.[161]

As she was the celebrated daughter of a former president, María García Granados's death on May 10 shook the nation. Throngs turned out for her funeral the following day. Martí attended the funeral but without Carmen. According to José María Izaguirre, he was among the last to leave: "at the last there remained but three friends: José Martí, José Joaquín Palma, and myself, who wished to remain by the young woman's side until her final moment above ground."[162] The funeral was front-page news in the national press, and several of Guatemala's finest writers, including Joaquín Palma and Izaguirre, published memorials dedicated to the beloved María. Poet Guillermo F. Halla brought his ode to "the celestial and beautiful nymph" to the funeral and placed it on her tomb.[163] Notably absent from this outpouring of loving tributes was Martí; not a word of praise or regret or sorrow from him appeared to mark her passing. Only thirteen years later did Martí write his ode to García Granados and of his enduring regret and longing for "The girl from Guatemala / Who died of love."[164]

Although peripheral to the core material causes of his undoing, María García Granados's death loudly if symbolically closed the book on Martí's time in Guatemala. Now jobless, with a wife to support, a child on the way, and his closest allies either turned against him or themselves besieged, the only question was where to build the life he had sought in Guatemala.

BY JUNE THE MARTÍS' PROSPECTS WERE GROWING DIMMER as the hoped-for offer of a teaching position in Honduras did not come. Then, on June 11 Martí received word that the Peruvian consulate in Guatemala had certified the authenticity of his academic credentials, thus clearing him to seek employment in Peru.[165] With the cessation of hostilities and general amnesty in Cuba, however, both Carmen and his family on the island argued that there was no longer any reason for him not to go home. As much as Martí previously bemoaned his fate to "wander like this from land to land, with so much anguish in my soul, and so much misunderstood love in my heart," he preferred an exile's life to that of a colonial subject in an impoverished, still subjugated homeland. Yet against his own wishes and better judgment, Martí finally succumbed to their entreaties, as he explains to Mercado in his letter of July 6:

> Even yesterday, over the supplications of Carmen, who cried, over
> my mother's own tears of which she does not speak, despite my own
> word of promise to the generous Zayas, I resisted all attempts to go to
> Cuba and had firmly decided to go to Peru. — They were expecting me
> and preparing for my arrival. — Now, my friend, the foundations of all
> my hopes have run aground. I drown my impulses; I listen to my pru-
> dence, — and I bend once again to the needs of others.[166]

Carmen was thrilled with the new plan, as is evident from her letter to Mercado's wife, Lola:

> From Mercado you will know that we are going to Cuba. . . . Pepe is
> suffering a great deal now, [but] I believe that by and by he will have

a better and happier life: helping his parents, and with my love to help him, he will forget a little this sorrow for his country that is so grave in souls such as his. I am frankly glad of the peace in Cuba, which brings peace to many and that for us is also a great good, as it means no more trips to strange countries where my Pepe was feared and not helped, and where he would be consumed in a veritable solitude.[167]

Together the two letters, sent in a single envelope to the Mercados, reveal their authors' radically different feelings about their return: Martí wary but resigned and his wife hopeful that the homecoming would bring not only a change of fortune for them but, more misguidedly, a change of heart for her man. It is not clear why Carmen Martí believed that a return to Cuba would cure him of the "sorrow for his country" that she even then intuited as a threat to their happiness as a couple; it was arguably only his physical distance from the island and his involvement in the culture and politics of other lands that distracted Martí from what had once been his overriding obsession with Cuba. Yet Carmen and Martí's entire family pinned their hopes on Cuba as the site of their Pepe's redemption and their collective happiness.

But those hopes were profoundly misplaced, as Martí's July 6 letter to Mercado makes abundantly clear. It is a dispirited but determined Martí who will return to Cuba, renewed in his resolve to help liberate his country: "Need I tell you what lofty propositions, what potent flights of the imagination boil in my soul? That I carry my poor wretched people in my head, and that it seems to me that their liberty will one day depend upon a blow of mine?"[168] It would be, he declares, "not as a boyish martyr, but to work for my own, and to strengthen myself for the fight [that I] go to Cuba."[169] More ominously, Martí emerges in this letter as a man who already regrets having married, with the burdens of family keeping him from a larger mission: "Free and childless, I would now have them talking about me.... And, instead of this, I will return now as a docile sheep to its flock!"[170]

By the end of July Carmen Martí was six months pregnant, but that did not stop them. On the morning of July 27 the Martís and their intermingled but very different hopes and fears departed Guatemala and set off on the long journey home.[171]

CHAPTER EIGHT

Homecoming, Interrupted

What a night, Carmen, and what horrible days! Now I will learn what it is to die.

LETTER TO CARMEN ZAYAS BAZÁN, SEPTEMBER 18, 1879

THE MARTÍS' 450-SOME-MILE OVERLAND TREK FROM Guatemala City to the Honduran port town of Trujillo took them nearly thirty days to complete by mule or horseback.[1] Due largely to the difficult terrain and inadequate roads but also out of an abundance of caution for the six-months-pregnant Carmen, the couple covered roughly 15 miles per day, a pace significantly slower than the roughly 20-mile days they had managed coming from Mexico seven months earlier.[2] The first half of the journey retraced in reverse Martí's itinerary of March 1877; after 150 or so miles on horseback, the Martís reached Lake Izabal, at which point they traveled by canoe as far as the seaport of Livingston.[3] From Livingston they followed the coast eastbound in the same kind of *cayucos* that had carried Martí to Guatemala sixteen months earlier. The exhausted couple finally boarded the Havana-bound steamer *Nuevo Barcelona* on August 28 and arrived in Havana harbor three days later. It was an enraptured Leonor Martí who stood at the dock to welcome her son and his young wife.

After so many struggles, life seemed to have granted the extended Martí–Zayas Bazán clan one more chance to build a life together as a family. The new arrivals settled into a house at Calle Tulipán no. 32 that stood not far from Industria no. 122, the address of the Domínguezes, whom the couple began to visit frequently, as had Martí in his younger years.[4] Martí's visits during this time would have had little of the enthusiastic fervor of his Havana youth or the nervous energy and determination of his Madrid collaborations with Fermín. It was an embittered, angrily resigned Martí who sat in the Domínguezes' parlor and who wrote to Mercado shortly after his arrival on the island. In that first letter from Havana, Martí bemoans both his country's continued subjugation and his own helplessness to change its fortunes:

> Finally I send a letter from Havana—would that I could come myself instead! . . .
>
> I am, however, being ungrateful.—Affectionate gestures surround me; I have all I need; and I will want for nothing, as soon as the authorities here receive my credentials from Spain:—but these for me, if debts of the heart, bitter comforts.—I would like to free my family from the arduous—if not miserable—situation in which I find it today;—and quickly build myself a small fortune so that my wife and my son—for in December I will have him—may weather the natural consequences for my rebellious and unyielding character. But it is a terrible torment, this, to see the necessity of a great work, feel within oneself the strength to carry it out, and be unable to do it! . . .
>
> . . . I will say no more, as it means little to say what one feels, when one cannot do what must be done.[5]

As a firm believer in a nationalist cause that most considered definitively lost, Martí acutely grasped both "what must be done" and the overwhelming difficulty that any new movement would face in accomplishing it. After a decade of war, most Cubans who thought at all about the island's future were willing to believe that the Treaty of Zanjón's concessions and promises were enough and that they would occur as promised. Few beyond a handful of holdouts among the old leadership had the stomach for renewed hostilities, and none had the money. Martí had no way of contacting the war's erstwhile leaders and knew no one beyond the Domínguezes who sympathized with his nationalist beliefs. He found himself utterly estranged from the majority of his countrymen, who either believed in the new treaty or were sufficiently war-weary to at least give it a chance to work. Rendered politically irrelevant and alienated from his own people—even his own wife supported the treaty—Martí now well and truly grasped the paradox that has always defined the lived experience of the colonized: he was now essentially an exile in his own country.

THE UNADDRESSED TENSIONS THAT SIMMERED BENEATH the surface of the Martís' marriage did not have an immediate impact on their transition to a quiet life in Havana. The three months that passed between the

Martís' return to Havana and the birth of their son on November 22 were relatively uneventful ones during which Martí nevertheless cultivated connections
with anticolonial elements on the island and established contact with the New
York–based Comité Revolucionario Cubano (Cuban Revolutionary Committee).[6] His only significant setback at the time was his inability to secure permission from the government to practice law on the island; Martí had not paid
the required fees to receive the actual diploma for his law degree, and the colonial authorities did not accept transcripts as a substitute.[7] Thanks to his contacts in the legal community, he found work as a clerk in the practices of fellow
Cubans.[8]

In the summer and fall of 1878 the couple gave every appearance of settling
into the routines of domestic life; Martí established a daily work routine while
Carmen busied herself in the home and with preparations for the arrival of their
child. Martí's parents rejoiced in the new domestic idyll, Leonor especially ap-
preciating the presence of her son and anticipating the joys of helping to raise
the new baby. The couple visited Mariano and Leonor often. But happiness in
Cuba proved as elusive for the Martís as the formal peace supposedly established by the Treaty of Zanjón. The anxieties Martí expressed in his letters to
Mercado soon became impossible to contain.

Martí found little encouragement in these early overtures; his reunion with
childhood mentor Rafael María Mendive, who also had returned to the island
under the Zanjón amnesty, was especially disillusioning for him. He paid a visit
to his former teacher in nearby Matanzas, where Mendive had assumed the
editorship of the local liberal paper; Martí perhaps hoped to rekindle the bond
that had first inspired his love of country. Instead he found a tired old man who
was resigned to the realities of Zanjón, a once fiery advocate of independence
grown, at best, ambivalent: "And think you," Martí later quoted him as saying,
"that if, for ten years at least, there were some hope, I would be here?"[9] The
two never met or corresponded again after that November 1878 visit, and when
Mendive died in 1886 Martí was not among the many who wrote memorials for
him. Only in 1891 did he produce his tribute to Mendive, doing so then only
upon the request of a fellow newspaper editor.[10]

With the birth of their son, José Francisco (known as Pepito), on November 22, 1878, Carmen redoubled the pressure on her husband to abandon his
political ambitions and embrace family and professional life. Her labor was difficult; she underwent an episiotomy, a surgical cutting of the vaginal opening
to facilitate the baby's birth.[11] The young family bonded for a time (figure 8.1),
and if the childbirth and new fatherhood did not definitively cure Martí of his
revolutionary anxieties, then at least they subdued them. Martí revealed the
profound impression that Carmen's ordeal made on him in his January 17, 1879,
letter to Mercado:

FIGURE 8.1. *The earliest known photograph of Martí with his son, taken in Havana in late 1879. From Gonzalo de Quesada y Miranda,* Iconografía martiana *(Havana: Oficina de Publicaciones del Consejo de Estado, 1985).*

> You will have read in my previous letter of the pains which, to give life to my son, my Carmen suffered.—With great care they operated on her, but I fear that she will be convalescing for some time.—The three of us live now in a most intimate union. Only we three, and the homes of a few noble friends, seem the only real things on this earth.[12]

Yet it was perhaps Martí's visits to the home of one such friend, the dying poet Alfredo Torroella y Romaguera, that set in motion the undoing of the Martís' fragile domestic bubble. Like Martí, Torroella had found asylum in Mexico during the Ten Years' War, and the two had bonded over their shared belief in the Cuban cause. The thirty-three-year-old Torroella's health was declining when he returned to his native Cuba under the Zanjón amnesty, and by December 1878 he found himself near death. Martí went to see him frequently and began to fear the worst; he confided to Mercado in the January 17 letter that Torroella had "been dying in my arms these past three days." Four days later, Torroella was dead.

TORROELLA'S DEATH MOVED MARTÍ DEEPLY, WELL BEYOND the bounds of mourning the loss of a friend and colleague. The young poet's passing in fact proved the catalyst for Martí's return to activism, which in turn set in motion the events that brought his life in Cuba to an abrupt and traumatic end. By January 1879 Martí had not received permission from the authorities to practice law and was clerking for the law office of Nicolás Azcárate, whom he had befriended in Mexico and who likewise returned to Cuba under the Zanjón amnesty. It was through Azcárate that Martí began making inroads with the island's literary and cultural communities; Martí was elected to serve as secretary of the literature division of the Liceo de Guanabacoa, of which Azcárate was president.[13] And it was along with Azcárate that Martí delivered his first public speech in Cuba, at a January 22 memorial service for Torroella held at the Liceo.

Standing at his fallen comrade's coffin before the crowd of mourners, what was ostensibly a eulogy for Torroella became instead the beginning of Martí's rise to renown as a new and powerful voice of independence. Although he did not explicitly denounce the Cuban colonial government or the exile of dissidents, Martí lavishly praised Mexico for its embrace of Cuban exiles during the Ten Years' War, reminding the mourners of that nation's support for the rebel cause: "Cuba loves you! . . . Your bread did not taste bitter to us, your gaze gave us no offense! Beneath your cloak I found shelter from the cold!"[14] Martí's impassioned discourse was not pointedly political, but his references to Cuba and Mexico as "brother peoples" and his gratitude in terms of "the love of a people" were surely not lost on those in attendance.[15]

Martí became a sought-after lecturer and public speaker after Torroella's funeral, much as his initial public speeches in Mexico and Guatemala had brought him recognition among audiences in each place. On February 28 he again spoke of his late friend Torroella, this time at a literary function honoring the poet's work, and read a brief biography of Torroella that he composed for the occasion.[16] If Martí had needed to restrain his more fiery sentiments under the watchful eye of Guatemala's Barrios regime, in Cuba such circumspection was a life-and-death matter; Zanjón's putative reforms notwithstanding, the Cuban colonial government had little patience for radicalism of any kind, and no one had yet dared test the limits of the authorities' forbearance. Martí also had a more personal, pragmatic reason for moderation in his public utterances, as he was in the process of securing permission from the government to work as a teacher in the capital's secondary school system.[17]

Unprepared to choose or perhaps even to acknowledge the imperative of the choice itself, Martí seemed content for a time to juggle the competing demands on his time and energies of professional and family life, suppressing the urge to enter the political fray. But his reputation as one of Cuba's leading young orators grew apace, especially in nationalist circles, where his enthusiasm and energy stood in stark contrast to a Cuban opposition left exhausted and worn by a decade of war. It was only a matter of time and circumstance before Martí would give vent to the sense of outrage at Spain's continued subjugation of the island — as well as his latent resentments toward the wife and family that he saw as tying his hands. This period of stalemate in the Martís' home neatly paralleled the island's larger political scene, as the colonial government ignored tensions left unresolved by Zanjón and tolerated nominal opposition that did not seriously threaten Spanish rule.

The start of March 1879 found Martí in a sort of holding pattern. He continued his employment as a law clerk, now for fellow Cuban Miguel Viondi; he taught classes on the side and made regular appearances at the Liceo to speak on literary and cultural topics. He remained frustrated by the bureaucratic obstacles that kept him from practicing law on the island. On March 12 he again petitioned the governor's office for permission to do so while awaiting the arrival of his diploma from Zaragoza, which he had requested five months earlier. By now, however, Martí's law career had already taken a back seat to his renewed political commitment.

Martí's first known clandestine activity in Cuba came on March 18, when he attended a gathering of conspirators forming a Club Central Revolucionario (Central Revolutionary Club) that would then establish branches throughout the island. Those in attendance elected him vice president of the Havana branch. Curiously, Martí alone among the officers signed onto the organization's charter with a pseudonym, his Masonic alias Anáhuac. As the others signed their real names to the document, anonymity may not have been Martí's motivation for the gesture; he perhaps signed as Anáhuac to signal his displeasure with the club's expressed aim of establishing a central revolutionary movement on the island independently of exile groups in New York. If so, his reservations soon proved correct, as an April 13 meeting in New York City between the Cuban group's representative and its northern counterparts ended with the New Yorkers' disapproval of the proposed change.[18] Although we know little of Martí's specific activities as part of the Havana group, at least one of his travels, his late-March trip to the town of Las Pozas in neighboring Pinar del Río Province, seems to have been intended to establish a branch of the organization; the trip's timing and the fact that Martí had no other compelling reason to visit Las Pozas support this hypothesis.[19]

It is not clear whether Carmen knew the purpose of her husband's trip to Las Pozas or in fact that he went at all; the lack of any references to politics in her few writings to friends and relatives then suggest that she did not, and it is reasonable to surmise that she would have strongly disapproved if she did. For his part, Martí's visible activities betrayed no sign of his rededication to the Cuban cause; his regular appearances at the Liceo were strictly literary and academic, and his two publications in March and April—a March 23 fluff piece in *El Progreso* on a party held over the weekend and his earlier tribute to Torroella—equally eschewed politics. The baptism of José Francisco took place on April 6, with Carmen's father and Martí's mother serving as godparents.[20] Perhaps the only clue of Martí's renewed radicalism was his rejection of the Partido Autonomista (Autonomist Party) invitation to stand for election in April; he vigorously declined the party's nomination for a seat in the Spanish Cortes as the representative from Santiago, declaring that he could only do so to advocate "the only thing that in my judgment a sensible Cuban could defend there, for the good of the island and Spain's: —Cuba's independence." Martí's letter of response found its way to the Havana police, and it is not clear whether its recipient, party head Urbano Sánchez Hechevarría, himself turned it in.[21] Although Carmen, if she knew of the overture and his rejection of it, might have interpreted it as a sign of her husband's withdrawal from politics, Martí's stated reason for doing so strongly suggests otherwise. Whatever Carmen's level of awareness regarding her husband's political activities until now, events in the spring and summer of 1879 would bring them up to the surface for all—including the Spanish authorities—to see.

IT IS MORE THAN LIKELY, GIVEN MARTÍ'S TEMPERAMENT and his strong feelings about Cuba, that he would sooner or later have rejoined the struggle for independence no matter the circumstance. As he joined the island's small circle of conspirators, there remained for Martí only the moment of opportunity and the emotional trigger or catalyst that would move him to act—or make further inaction unbearable.

That tipping point came on April 21 at a banquet in honor of Cuban journalist Adolfo Márquez Sterling at Havana's Louvre café, a longtime home of dissident thinkers. Although the banquet itself was not a political event, Sterling, founder of liberal papers such as *La Libertad* and *La Discusión*, was an outspoken supporter of Cuban independence. Martí had made no explicitly political statements at the funeral of Alfredo Torroella, whose separatist beliefs were as well known as Sterling's. It was perhaps the combination of Cuba's tense political climate and Martí's growing frustration at an unrelated event that enabled Martí to cross the psychological Rubicon that previously bound him: the government's rejection once again of his petition to practice law in Cuba.[22] Although he never stated as much, we may well wonder whether the rejection of his petition compelled the temperamental Martí to finally abandon discretion and transform what began as a toast to honor a distinguished colleague into a scalding indictment of Spanish colonialism and a call for independence as Cuba's only viable future path.

It would be hard to overstate the recklessness of Martí's April 21 speech in light of Cuba's political climate of the time. It was hardly just police and government officials who were on guard against dissident activity; Spanish loyalists remained on the lookout for any statements in print or in public venues that even hinted at a return to arms. Cuban autonomists also sought to suppress the separatists, but for a different reason; they hoped for an eventual softening of Spanish rule and a more equitable relationship with the mother country, feared a return to martial rule, and saw continued calls for independence as a threat to future reforms. Liberal voices struggled to be heard at all in this environment, as Sterling himself, the island's leading separatist, saw two successive post-Zanjón newspapers shut down within a year of their debuts.[23]

Martí's outright denunciation of Spanish colonial rule in his letter declining the Autonomist Party's nomination only hinted at the lack of circumspection that would emerge full-blown in his April 21 toast to Márquez Sterling. He opened the speech by praising the Cuban journalist as "a symbol" who had spoken out honestly "in these days of our incomplete and conquered liberty, by no one granted" and saluted "the justice and righteousness embodied in his work."[24] According to eyewitnesses, Martí raised his glass to toast, then averred that he could only drink to a "more ample and complete" Cuban politics, one that reflected "the defined and legitimate aspirations of the country" beyond "the compensation of the mercantile interests, the satisfaction of a threatened social group, and the latent and incomplete redemption of a race that has demonstrated its right to redemption." Only if, Martí declared with raised glass, "in our thoughts, in our words, in our reclamations, we do not repent our only glory and conceal it in shame; —for pride, for dignity, for energy, I drink to Cuban politics."[25]

What came next, however, would have astonished even the audience's most fervent or disgruntled dissidents:

> But if by following a narrow and tortuous path we do not set forth the problem in all its elements, not arriving, therefore, at immediate, defined, and concrete solutions; if we forget, as lost or undone, potent and ardent elements; if we harden the heart so that it will not divulge the truth that escapes our lips; if we would be no more than voices of our country, costumes of ourselves; if with gentle strokes on its mane, as from an untrusting tamer, they would soothe and deceive the noble and impatient lion, then I throw down my glass: I do not drink to Cuban politics.[26]

With those words, Martí threw his glass down, and it shattered on the floor of the banquet hall. And although he once more acknowledged "the brilliant writer who has gathered us here," Martí's final salute was not for Márquez Sterling, but for "the stern and vigilant *patria*, the proud and weakened *patria*, the infirm and agitated *patria* that fuels his courage."[27]

Martí's speech reverberated throughout Cuban political circles and brought him to the attention of the island's colonial leadership. Word of his performance soon reached Captain-General Ramón Blanco y Erenas, who had been alerted to the presence of elements in New York organizing a new uprising. Surprised and perhaps intrigued by the sudden emergence of such a strident new voice, Blanco resolved to hear Martí at the earliest opportunity and judge for himself whether he represented a true threat to the island's tense and fragile peace.[28]

The captain-general did not have to wait long, as Martí was to speak at an April 27 event at the Liceo honoring Cuban violinist Rafael Díaz Albertini. As he had the previous week, Martí used the social event to advocate for the cause of Cuban independence, railing against the abuses of Spanish rule and the half measures of the Treaty of Zanjón. According to family biographer Raúl García Martí, Blanco was stunned by the directness of Martí's speech and resolved to think of him as "a fool, but yet a dangerous fool."[29]

Curiously, after the barn-burners of April 21 and 27, Martí made no further public statements on the matter. Perhaps he became alarmed at the possibility of being arrested and deported again or worse. Fellow conspirators may have advised Martí that continued outbursts would endanger more important clandestine work. Whatever the reason, the rest of the spring and summer of 1879 found Martí in a state of anxious calm, the appearance of domestic routine only just veiling a burgeoning revolutionary labor.

Martí all but abandoned his work in Viondi's offices as his activities on behalf of the Havana Club Revolucionario and the New York–based Comité Revolucionario Cubano consumed more and more of his time. Martí continued to teach his classes and to attend the Liceo's regular Saturday-night gatherings, in particular a recurring roundtable discussion on "the origins of man."[30] More significant, however, were his regular trips to a Pinar del Río ranch owned by longtime confidant Carlos Sauvalle, who had befriended the teenage Martí in Madrid and now offered his support to the new revolutionary effort.[31] Even Martí's supposed working hours for Viondi became a revolutionary activity, as Martí started holding secret meetings in a back room that Viondi set aside for the purpose; worried that he might compromise his friend, Martí moved the gatherings into his own home. If Carmen had until now remained ignorant of the nature and object of her husband's clandestine activities, she could do so no longer, as the men who were frequenting Martí's gatherings at Viondi's offices became fixtures at his own nightly gatherings.

The most important of Martí's new collaborators was the Afro-Cuban Juan Gualberto Gómez. Having correctly identified Spain's exploitation of Cuban racism as a major factor in the war's failure, Martí and Gómez were keen to articulate a revolutionary ideology of actively promoting abolition and guaranteeing the rights of black Cubans. Gómez's contributions proved essential to Martí's later success in recruitment and fund-raising among black Cubans in exile, who formed a crucial component of the coalition that eventually ended Spanish rule. For now, the two found themselves at odds with many separatists who remained ambivalent about abolition and the status of freed slaves in a liberated Cuba.

So swept up in such matters and in the coming revolution generally was Martí that when the government revoked his teaching certification on July 24, he hardly noticed; the director of the Instituto Provincial de La Habana had earlier notified the authorities that Martí's May 5 deadline for producing his diploma had long passed with no sign of the document.[32] Undaunted, Martí sought work as a writer; but unlike his experiences in Mexico and Guatemala, the island's various magazines and newspapers, even the left-leaning ones, mostly stayed away from him. By the first week of August, the only writing work Martí could find was for the Havana children's magazine *La Niñez*. Despite all, Martí kept up the appearance—at least to the outside world—of a routine domestic life with the tacit cooperation, if not the approval, of his wife.

THE UNEASY TRUCES THAT UNTIL NOW DEFINED MARTÍ'S life in Cuba—his domestic détente with Carmen and the colonial government's seeming forbearance toward dissenters—ended abruptly with the onset of the Guerra Chiquita (Little War) on August 24, 1879. In many ways the Little War was an extension of the Ten Years' War that had so recently ended, as its major players and ultimate aims were the same. Because the previous war's surviving leaders universally rejected the terms of the Treaty of Zanjón, they were pointedly excluded from its otherwise general amnesty; unsurprisingly, given that a return to Cuba meant arrest and almost certain execution, they chose to remain in exile.[33] Although Spain's reluctance to welcome the recalcitrant rebels was understandable, the decision to deny them amnesty allowed exiled leaders to reorganize beyond the reach of direct surveillance.

In the absence of Spanish influence or coercion—and especially of the outgoing Captain-General Arsenio Martínez Campos, who had engineered the fragile peace established in the Treaty of Zanjón—rebel leaders abroad and a small group of dissidents on the island proceeded to plan a new uprising. In coordination with the exiled New York leadership, funds were raised and men recruited; several major figures of the Ten Years' War, including Calixto García and José Maceo, agreed to head the new rebellion.[34] Fueling the separatists' ardor were the twin convictions that the Treaty of Zanjón was an unacceptable half measure that Spain could not be trusted to honor and that given the impossibility of negotiating in good faith, armed insurrection was the only means of achieving a free Cuba.[35]

The new uprising suffered the same fate as the previous one but much more quickly. The effort was doomed from the start by a combination of poor organization, insufficient resources, and timely Spanish intervention; García, the rebels' supreme commander, was not initially successful in recruiting General Antonio Maceo, who did not join the war until well after its launch was stifled. Much-needed local support did not materialize, either, as a weary and dispirited population had little stomach for renewed conflict, preferring a subjugated peace to another decade of struggle. Well-trained and -armed Spanish troops moved quickly to find and neutralize rebel contingents throughout the island and disrupted the remaining leaders' ability to communicate and coordinate with each other. By the time García finally landed in Cuba in May 1880, the war was all but lost; outnumbered and outgunned, García could do little but stay one step ahead of pursuing Spanish forces, and the insurgents surrendered in August 1880.[36]

Martí did not remain in Cuba long enough to see this defeat. On September 17, 1879, less than a month after the onset of the war, he was arrested at his home while lunching with Juan Gualberto Gómez. Perhaps fearing foul play, Martí asked Carmen to have Gómez follow him at a discreet distance to determine where he was being taken and for her to alert attorney Azcárate immediately that he had been arrested. Thanks to Azcárate's efforts, an initial order to keep Martí incommunicado was lifted, allowing him to direct Viondi to destroy incriminating papers that, unbeknown to the lawyer, Martí concealed in his offices.[37] Fermín Valdés Domínguez, among others, later claimed that autonomist informants enabled the arrest of Martí and other conspirators, although this has never been confirmed.[38]

Martí was not the only victim of the Spanish dragnet, which also eventually captured Gómez along with fellow conspirators Antonio Aguilera and Anita Pando.[39] But he was by far the most widely known among those rounded up in the first weeks of the Little War. He received hundreds of visitors in the week he was jailed, a development that no doubt alarmed Captain-General Blanco no less than his experience of hearing Martí speak. Perhaps out of a desire to rid the island of Martí's potential influence on public opinion, the authorities moved to deport Martí without benefit of a trial or even formal charges; within seven days he was sentenced to an unspecified period of labor at Ceuta, a Spanish prison camp in the north of Africa.[40] According to Raúl García Martí, before finalizing Martí's deportation Blanco offered to free Martí if he would publicly renounce the insurgency, but Martí refused. Although no record exists to corroborate the claim, the possibly apocryphal meeting has since become an integral part of the Martí myth.

Within twenty-four hours of his sentencing, Martí found himself again an exile. The separatists sent word to New York of his imminent departure and reported that along with his wife, child, parents, and sisters, more than fifty well-wishers came to bid the prisoner farewell.[41] On September 25, 1879, Martí left his country, family, and friends behind and boarded the steamer *Alfonso XII* bound for Santander, Spain. He left behind the tatters of his wife's and family's dreams of a happy homecoming, of their husband and son settling into a life of peace, security, and domesticity. He was, once again, a man adrift.

The date on which Martí departed Havana on the steamer marked a definitive and irreconcilable break with both Spain and Cuba, or at least the Cuba that remained a Spanish colony. From this point on there would be no negotiations with Spain or with those who would negotiate, no return to Cuba except to win it, to conquer it in the name of the republic waiting to join the ranks of free nations. All considerations of his own happiness or that of his family and loved ones mattered less now than the liberation of his country.

Denied the chance to directly help the cause on the island, Martí knew that the next best place to work for Cuban freedom was in New York, alongside the established exile groups. If he was serious about dedicating himself to the cause, New York was where he needed to be.

BEFORE MARTÍ COULD HELP HIS COUNTRY, HE HAD TO HELP himself. Facing the prospect of an indefinite term at the Ceuta prison camp and cut off from anyone who could help him, he had to figure out how to shorten his time in prison or, if possible, avoid it entirely. Given that Ceuta was where fellow conspirators were being been sent—and that this was Martí's second deportation—he stood little chance of avoiding a lengthy prison term.

On October 11, after sixteen days at sea, the *Alfonso XII* arrived in Santander, a port city on Spain's northern coast. Upon arrival, prisoner Martí was escorted to the city jail in anticipation of his transfer to Ceuta. He would later write of his experience in the Santander prison, living among "Cubans who were wounded, injured, consumptive, fevered, the miserable, the uneducated, who had just been arrested in Cuba, and were being sent on foot to Ceuta, in the very months of the agreement of Zanjón!"[42] On his first day in prison, Martí had an unexpected visitor whom he had met on the *Alfonso XII*: a man identifying himself as Ladislao Setién, member of the Spanish Cortes representing the nearby town of Laredo. According to legend, Setién was a fellow passenger on the *Alfonso XII* and learned of Martí's plight either during the crossing or upon arrival in Santander. Setién took an interest in Martí's case and on October 11 came to the prison to offer his services.

On October 12 the Ministerio de Ultramar, which oversaw the affairs of Spain's remaining overseas possessions, expedited Martí's transfer to Ceuta. But Martí never joined the prisoners' march to Ceuta, nor did he remain in the Santander prison. Instead, inexplicably, he was released by order of the provincial government with the condition that he report daily to the local authorities. Setién seems to have persuaded the authorities to commute Martí's Ceuta sentence and paid an undisclosed amount of bail money to have him released. An apparently astonished Martí wrote to Miguel Viondi: "I owe my liberty, my friend, to a generous man.—Great things I am bound to do, since I have great acts of kindness to repay."[43]

Martí's breathless account notwithstanding, exactly how this reversal of fortune befell him remains a mystery. Martí's sentencing and imprisonment in 1869–1870 began a lengthy family crisis that ended with his deportation only after months of dogged and extensive intervention by Mariano and Leonor.

As he was an active organizer of the current uprising, the adult Martí's offenses were far more serious than the juvenile Pepe's unsent letter to a friend, however treasonous. How is it, then, that the authorities not only spared him from Ceuta but freed a known enemy agent to potentially continue his seditious work? And how is it that a stranger would volunteer to post bail and stand as guarantor for Martí, assuming the not insignificant risk of falling under suspicion himself should the prisoner flee?

At the core of this mystery stands Ladislao Setién, or whatever his real name was. No record exists of anyone by that name ever having served in the Spanish Cortes or indeed of having existed at all.[44] We will likely never know Setién's true identity, but even a cursory consideration of the facts suggests that he was an agent for either the Cubans or Spain who was sent to release Martí. Given that elements in Havana sent immediate word to New York of Martí's arrest, it is plausible that the exile leadership sent Mr. Setién.[45]

Yet none of this explains the surprising speed with which Setién managed to persuade the authorities. What contacts did he have within the provincial government that would have allowed him to circumvent standing orders from Madrid? Given the infiltration within Cuban ranks of Spanish informants and agents, however, it is also quite plausible that Spain expedited Martí's release in order to track his movements and learn of insurgent activity on the peninsula. Whatever the reasons behind Martí's good fortune, it is clear that someone, either among the Cubans or in the Spanish government, had a strong interest in releasing him from prison.

ONCE HE WAS RELEASED FROM CUSTODY, MARTÍ'S SOLE OB-jective was to escape Spain as soon as possible and find his way to New York. Yet he did not immediately flee the country. The promise of daily appearances before the authorities would not have stopped him and in fact did not when the time eventually came; it was, rather, the constant surveillance under which Martí found himself that kept him, for a time, in Spain.

For two months Martí bided his time, first in Santander and then, with permission, in Madrid, where he spent the last six weeks or so before departing.[46] He busied himself with various legal tasks pertaining to cases for Viondi. In his spare time, he visited friends and professional contacts in Madrid, among them the liberal Cortes delegate Cristino Martos.[47] Although Martí corresponded regularly with Viondi to update him on the progress of his work, he did not write at all to Manuel Mercado during his time in Spain. This unusual gap in his correspondence with Mercado suggests Martí's awareness that the Spanish government was monitoring his activities closely. Further evidence, albeit circumstantial, of Spain's interest in Martí is seen in his meetings with Arsenio Martínez Campos, the captain-general of Zanjón now briefly serving as Spain's prime minister, who is believed to have tried to persuade him to abandon the rebel cause.[48]

On November 24 Martí attended a session of the Spanish Cortes, apparently as a guest of Cristino Martos. There he was surprised to hear the delegate employing Martí's arguments in favor of liberalizing Spain's relations with Cuba and the abolition of slavery.[49] Two days later Martí became briefly ill, suffering from an unspecified malady but one apparently triggered or amplified by alcohol: "I took to bed with this poor body," he wrote to Viondi on November 28, "which without the spirit to animate it, — has grown sick and inebriated [*ebrio*]. . . . And in bed I remained until two days ago [*antier*]."[50] It is not clear whether Martí was obligated to continue the daily appearances required by the terms of his release while ill. By the time of his letter to Viondi, his condition seems to have improved and not to have impeded or delayed his impending escape.

Martí's final days in Spain found him pursuing activities unrelated to Cuba or politics. In fact, he spent his final days in Madrid as a tourist; On December 5 he attended a production of *Faust* at Madrid's Teatro Real, and the next day he visited the Museo del Prado, where he took notes on paintings by Francisco Goya and other contemporary artists.[51]

Sometime between December 6 and 18, Martí simply disappeared. We do not know the exact date of Martí's escape from Madrid, which he seems to have timed to coincide with the relaxed vigilance during celebrations surrounding King Alfonso XII's wedding to María Christina of Austria.[52]

His immediate destination was Paris. Martí wrote little about his second visit to the French capital with the exception of his writings on the actress Sarah Bernhardt, whom the starstruck Martí met at a fund-raiser for victims of catastrophic floods in the Spanish city of Murcia.[53] In a letter to Viondi he described shaking Bernhardt's hand: "I felt the marrow run cold in my bones, but also the heat of my heart."[54]

By December 20, two days after his encounter with Bernhardt, Martí had departed Paris for the port city of Le Havre, where he boarded the transatlantic packet ship *Francia* bound for New York City.[55] For the third time in his life, Martí would ring in the new year alone onboard a steamship. This time, he very much looked forward to arriving at his destination.

Part Three

THE GREAT WORK (1881–1895)

CHAPTER NINE

New York (1)

A FALSE START

I am, at last, in a country where every one looks like his own master.

"IMPRESSIONS OF A VERY FRESH SPANIARD," JULY 10, 1880

O N JANUARY 2, 1880, THE *FRANCIA* COMPLETED ITS two-week Atlantic crossing but arrived in New York too late for its passengers to disembark until the following morning.[1] On the morning of January 3 Martí was welcomed to New York by former rebel colonel Miguel Fernández Ledesma, who knew Martí from his Havana prison days.[2] Legend has it that when Martí arrived at the prison work camp, he looked so thin and weak that the robust Ledesma shared his own rations with him out of pity.[3] Ledesma eventually made it to New York, where he aligned himself with the city's separatist exile community; his previous acquaintance with Martí made him an obvious choice to facilitate the young immigrant's transition to life in the city.[4] Martí stayed with the Ledesmas until January 8, when he moved to a boarding house at 51 East 29th Street run by Cuban exiles Manuel and Carmen Mantilla.[5]

Once settled in, Martí wasted no time in establishing himself in New York's exile politics. Within a week of his arrival he was named spokesman for the Comité Revolucionario Cubano, and a week later he attended his first meeting, in the home of leader General Calixto García.[6] During these first weeks in New York Martí landed his first writing job as art and cultural critic for *The Hour* after the magazine's resident artist and fellow boarder Guillermo Collazo invited him to join the staff.[7]

Martí's real New York debut, however, was his January 24 appearance at Steck Hall in Lower Manhattan before an exile audience hoping for the success of the Little War but wary of committing to the uprising so soon after the disappointment of the Ten Years' War. Collazo, who was raising money and recruiting men to join the uprising as soon as possible, was by far the most prominent of the many war veterans in attendance. But it was the relatively unknown Martí who, like so many times before, stole the show, delivering a lengthy and impassioned speech that riveted the crowd and validated the committee's decision to grant him such a high-profile public appearance. Martí's January 24 speech, with its repeated appeals to *pueblo* and *patria*, gave an unexpected and much-needed boost to the war effort and elevated the charismatic Martí to the forefront of the exile political scene in New York. It also, predictably, brought him once again to the attention of the Spanish government.

Even though Martí did not immediately become a particular object of Spanish surveillance upon arrival, as a Cuban immigrant his movements would have been monitored right away as part of Spain's routine surveillance at the time. The Pinkerton and Davies detective agencies regularly scoured ships' registries and other sources for notices of newcomers from Cuba and then systematically followed their movements from the moment they arrived. Having experienced Spanish surveillance and likely having been briefed by his compatriots, Martí certainly would have been aware that these activities did not end with his escape from Madrid. As a regular visitor to the home of exile leader Néstor Ponce de León, Martí may also have read Ponce de León's diary from 1870 and 1871 documenting Spanish surveillance of Cuban exiles.[8] Expense reports and other evidence in fact show that in 1880 the Spanish government, through its embassy in Washington, D.C., employed at least twenty-five men tasked with following Cuban exiles' movements. Spain's spies kept tabs on nearly a dozen of the leading conspirators, and by April 1880 no fewer than six Pinkerton agents were assigned to Martí.[9]

Spanish scrutiny of Martí did not end at the city limits; one Pinkerton agent identified only as "C.D.B." requested reimbursement for expenses from a trip to Cape May in New Jersey, where he had followed Martí on a short vacation.[10] Nor was the surveillance limited to his public movements; an agent identified as "E.S." actually gained admittance to the Mantilla home as a boarder and lived alongside Martí and the Mantillas for nearly four months in the spring and summer of 1880.[11] Martí was well aware of the presence of spies and infiltrators around him, but it is not clear whether he ever discovered the young "student" living under his own roof whom the Spanish government reimbursed for monthly rent ($10), the Spanish lessons he hired Martí to give him ($6), and even the bottle of wine (75 cents) and sweets he bought (20 cents) in an effort to win Martí's and the Mantillas' trust.[12]

THE MANTILLAS' BOARDING HOUSE ALMOST IMMEDIATELY became a surrogate home for Martí. Manuel Mantilla ran a small and not especially profitable cigar business; the boarding house, which was run primarily by his wife, Carmen, supplemented the family's income and helped support the couple's three children.[13] The establishment was distinguished from others of its type in that its boarders were mostly Cubans whom the owners personally knew or who were referred to them by trusted friends; unsurprisingly, their home had long been a center of anticolonial sentiment if not overt revolutionary activity.[14] Carmen Mantilla—or Carmita, as she was known—came from a long line of revolutionaries; her great-great-grandfather Pasquale Paoli led the unsuccessful resistance against the French conquest of Corsica in 1768, and his great-nephew Jorge Juan Paoli was jailed in 1823 after leading a failed expedition to liberate Cuba from Spanish rule.[15] Carmita's family history almost certainly would have intrigued Martí, and this, along with the boarding house's more intimate and familial environment, contributed to the affinity that he and Carmita felt for each other from the beginning. It was a mutual attraction that blossomed into a profound and enduring love.

In the nearly 120 years since Martí's death, scholars' treatment of his relationship with Carmita Mantilla has ranged from grudging acknowledgement to euphemism to outright silence. But the fact remains that except for a few brief periods the two lived together as a couple for the last ten years of his life and may have been lovers up to five years before that. With the exception of his own parents, no one lived at Martí's side longer than Carmita Mantilla. Yet the most intimate details of their daily life together, despite the best efforts of "E.S." and his ilk, remain beyond our grasp; this is partly because of a dearth of such information in Martí's writings but also because not a single letter from Carmita to Martí and very little of her correspondence with others survives.

Much of what remains unknown regarding Martí's relationship with Carmita centers on the period preceding the death of her husband, Manuel, in 1885. And for most scholars, the question that lies at the core of that period—the question within the question—is whether Martí fathered Carmita's youngest child, María, out of wedlock in 1880, five years before Manuel's death. Martí never specifically acknowledged María as his daughter; her birth and baptismal certificates list Manuel Mantilla as her father. The name "Joseph Martí" appears on the same certificate as her godfather.[16]

In a mid-1880s draft of an unsent letter, Martí denies any relationship between himself and Carmita that would be deemed inappropriate for "an intimate friend of the family."[17] But his otherwise elaborate defense of Carmita and indictment of unnamed enemies wishing to impugn her honor stops short of a straightforward denial. The letter also contains at least one claim that, even allowing for the vagueness of its language, we know to be false: that of a life "which I have kept until now above the passions of men and has for this [illegible word] a reputation that I must not lose [*no ha de perder*]."[18] Aside from the statement's obvious falsehood—Martí's multiple romances and more casual

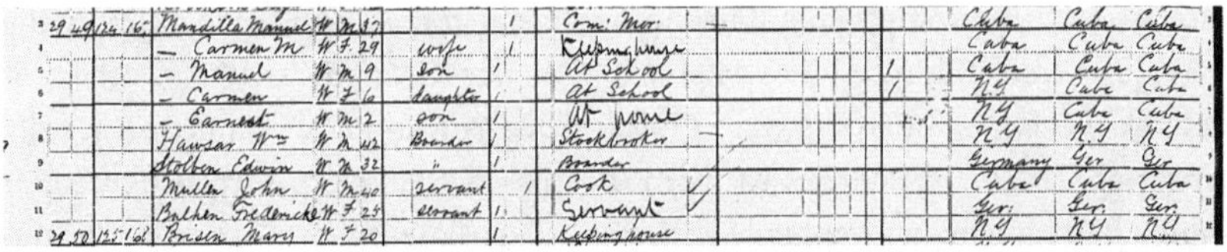

29	49	124	16	Mantilla Manuel	W	M	37		Com: Mer	Cuba	Cuba	Cuba
				— Carmen M	W	F	29	wife	Keeping house	Cuba	Cuba	Cuba
				— Manuel	W	M	9	son	At School	Cuba	Cuba	Cuba
				— Carmen	W	F	6	daughter	At School	NY	Cuba	Cuba
				— Earnest	W	M	2	son	At home	NY	Cuba	Cuba
				Hawsar Wm	W	M	42	Boarder	Stockbroker	NY	NY	NY
				Stolben Edwin	W	M	32	"	Boarder	Germany	Ger	Ger
				Mullen John	W	M	40	servant	Cook	Cuba	Cuba	Cuba
				Balhen Fredericke	W	F	25	servant	Servant	Ger.	Ger.	Ger.
29	50	125	168	Brisen Mary	W	F	20		Keeping house	NY	NY	NY

FIGURE 9.1. *Manuel Mantilla's entry from the 1880 U.S. Census in which he declares himself to be in good health.*

sexual encounters including at least one affair with a married woman, demonstrating the very opposite of a life lived "above the passions"—the ambivalence of the Spanish phrase *no ha de,* which can be translated contextually as "must not," "should not," or even "would not," leaves Martí's meaning indeterminate, perhaps deliberately so. Read in this way, Martí's defensive, somewhat indignant denial of a sexual relationship with Carmita is in hindsight less than convincing.

If Martí was María Mantilla's biological father, Carmita would have had good reason, both private and public, to conceal the fact. It is not clear whether Manuel Mantilla ever knew of or suspected Martí's paternity, but the news would certainly have strained the Mantillas' marriage. Mantilla's death in 1885 coincided with Martí's star rising among the exile revolutionary movement; news of a child out of wedlock would have been politically useful both to Spain and others wishing to discredit or embarrass him. Carmita also never told María that Martí was her father; only much later did María declare herself to be his daughter, explaining that she learned of her true parentage from a family friend in 1935.[19] We have anecdotal observations of María's adult resemblance to Martí's son, Pepe, most strikingly in remarks by his wife, María Teresa Bances.[20] But in the absence of definitive means of determining paternity such as DNA testing, we remain in the realm of speculation and anecdote.

Much of the debate surrounding Martí's paternity of María has hinged on Manuel Mantilla's physical condition—and more specifically, of his virility—at the time. At least one account of Martí's relations with the family in 1881, that of Blanca de Baralt, describes Mantilla as a man "whose health was in decline, to the point of being almost an invalid," and whose physical disabilities necessitated opening the family home to boarders to supplement their income.[21] Scholars have subsequently disputed de Baralt's account, citing evidence that Mantilla remained in good health well into 1884. This evidence includes the 1880 U.S. Census, in which Mantilla declares himself to be in good health (figure 9.1); his death certificate lists the cause of death as "mitral disease of the heart," for which his attending physician began treating him in August 1884 (figure 9.2). On the other hand, recent research into mitral valve disorders shows that patients can suffer symptoms such as chronic exertion-related dyspnea, shortness of breath, well before a diagnosis and that misdiagnoses such as asthma or upper respiratory ailments are not uncommon even today. Even asymptomatic sufferers may voluntarily become less active over time in an effort to avoid symptoms.[22] Attending physician Dr. Annie M. Brown listed Mantilla as María's father on the child's birth certificate, and under "Father's Occupation" she wrote "none," indicating that Mantilla was unemployed before María's birth in November 1880 (figure 9.3); given the Mantillas' difficult financial situation, it seems unlikely that Manuel would have given up his cigar business and stopped working before María's birth unless some extenuating circumstance—perhaps physical disability—compelled it.

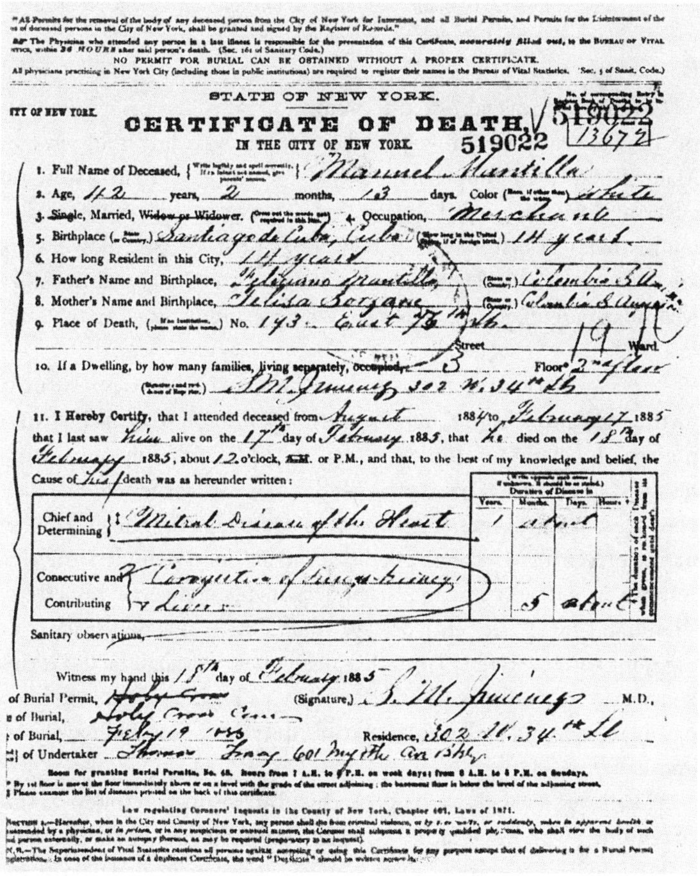
NO PERMIT FOR BURIAL CAN BE OBTAINED WITHOUT A PROPER CERTIFICATE.

All physicians practising in New York City (including those in public institutions) are required to register their names in the Bureau of Vital Statistics. (Sec. 5 of Sanit. Code.)

STATE OF NEW YORK.

CERTIFICATE OF DEATH, 519022

IN THE CITY OF NEW YORK. 519022 13672

1. Full Name of Deceased, Manuel Mantilla

2. Age, 42 years, 2 months, 13 days. Color white

3. Single, Married, Widow or Widower. 4. Occupation, Merchant

5. Birthplace, Santiago de Cuba, Cuba 14 years

6. How long Resident in this City, 14 years

7. Father's Name and Birthplace,

8. Mother's Name and Birthplace,

9. Place of Death, No. 143 East 75th St. Street Ward.

10. If a Dwelling, by how many families, living separately, occupied, 3 Floor 2nd floor

11. I Hereby Certify, that I attended deceased from August 1884 to February 17 1885 that I last saw him alive on the 17th day of February 1885, that he died on the 18th day of February 1885, about 12 o'clock, A.M. or P.M., and that, to the best of my knowledge and belief, the Cause of his death was as hereunder written:

		Years	Months	Days	Hours
Chief and Determining	Mitral Disease of the Heart	1			
Consecutive and Contributing	Congestion of Lungs, Kidney & Liver		5		

Sanitary observations,

Witness my hand this 18th day of February 1885

of Burial Permit, (Signature,) M.D.,

of Burial, Holy Cross Cem.

of Burial, Feby 19 1885 Residence, 302 W. 34th St

of Undertaker

Law regulating Coroners' Inquests in the County of New York, Chapter 401, Laws of 1871.

FIGURE 9.2. *Manuel Mantilla's death certificate, which lists his cause of death as "mitral disease of the heart." Certificate of Death #519022, issued by the City of New York on February 18, 1885.*

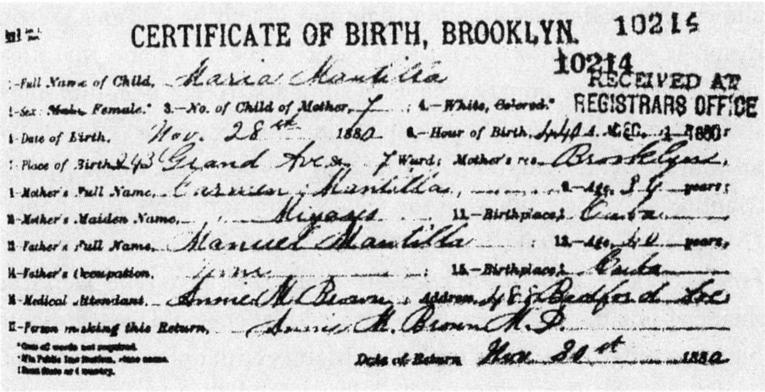

CERTIFICATE OF BIRTH, BROOKLYN. 10214

10214 RECEIVED AT REGISTRARS OFFICE

Full Name of Child, María Mantilla

Sex: Male, Female.* 3.—No. of Child of Mother, 7 ; 4.—White, Colored.*

Date of Birth, Nov. 28th 1880 —Hour of Birth

Place of Birth 243 Grand Ave. 7 Ward; Mother's res. Brooklyn,

Mother's Full Name, Carmen Mantilla, —Age, 39 years;

Mother's Maiden Name, Miyares 11.—Birthplace, Cuba

Father's Full Name, Manuel Mantilla ; 13.—Age, 40 years,

Father's Occupation, ; 15.—Birthplace, Cuba

Medical Attendant, Annie M. Brown ; Address, 48 Bedford Ave

Person making this Return, Annie M. Brown M.D.

Date of Return Nov. 30th 1880

FIGURE 9.3. *María Mantilla's birth certificate, which lists her date of birth as November 28, 1880, and her father as unemployed. Certificate of Birth #10214, issued by the City of Brooklyn on November 30, 1880.*

Given all of this admittedly circumstantial evidence, it is at least possible that by the time Martí moved to the Mantilla boarding house in January 1880, Manuel Mantilla's symptoms—or his wish to avoid them—were sufficient to adversely affect his sexual activity. In the absence of more information regarding his medical history and general health before 1884, however, we cannot know for certain. And without more definitive evidence, the question of María Mantilla's parentage remains open. We may simply never know.

IN THE FIRST FOUR MONTHS AFTER MARTÍ'S SECOND AND final deportation from Cuba, he did not correspond with his wife or family nor with Manuel Mercado, to whom he had written only once during the year he spent in Havana. Leonor and Mariano finally learned that he had settled in New York, whereupon Leonor wrote to complain of his neglect.[23] The secretive nature of Martí's work as an operative and his not unfounded fear of having correspondence intercepted may partly explain his silence, yet his letters to Miguel Viondi, his most frequent correspondent during this period, contain no messages for and few references to his loved ones, although he did express serious concern over Mariano's health: "My father's health, which worsens with every day, is making me crazy.—Ah, terrible duty! Ah, poor old man!—And I even poorer!"[24]

His silence notwithstanding, Martí did arrive in New York with the intention of reuniting with his wife and child and immediately set about raising the necessary funds for their relocation. On February 5 he mailed a package to Viondi in Havana that aside from a brief note contained two tickets to New York and a winter coat for Pepito. Martí's terse letter reveals a man unsure of the future, less driven by love than bound by obligation: "I do my duty: God will protect me. — I do not know what will become of me — what will I not do so that she and my little one will have whatever is necessary! . . . Wish me strength for this laborious struggle."[25]

March 3 saw the arrival in New York of Carmen and Pepito, now sixteen months old. Far from representing a new beginning for the Martís, however, their coming sparked a return to the domestic turmoil the couple had suffered in Havana. Carmen's true purpose for coming to New York soon became apparent: to persuade her husband to repent his revolutionary cause and return with her to Cuba. Within two months of Carmen's arrival, it became clear to Martí, as he acknowledges in his May 6 letter to Mercado, that neither she nor Leonor understood or supported his commitment to the Cuban cause: "Carmen does not share . . . my devotion to my present tasks."[26] It was a man resigned to the consequences of his own promises who wrote to Mercado for the first time in more than fourteen months:

> I scold Carmen because she has ceased to be my wife in order to be [Pepito's] mother. — As for my own, she, like many others, believes that I act impulsively out of blind enthusiasms, or romantic desires; I am re-proached for doing in prose what was considered beautiful when I said it in verse. . . . I do sadly, without joy or hope, what I believe is true to myself and useful for others that I do. I want strength, — which I do not prize, to complete this task. I well know already how rarely the branches of a tree bring shade to the house of he who planted it.[27]

So intertwined is the personal with the political in Martí's May 6 letter that it is difficult to parse the "task" he is struggling to complete, whether the revolution or the added burden of working against the wishes and the at least passive resistance of his own family or perhaps the economic anxiety of having to support a family while continuing to work for Cuba. More likely is that Martí experienced and struggled with all of these difficulties without such parsing, as his personal crises merged with political ones. In mid-May, Calixto García finally landed in Cuba to lead the now nine-month-old uprising. Much had gone wrong in the interim; in contrast to the Ten Years' War, Spanish authorities acted quickly this time to uncover revolutionary cells and arrest their leaders. New York exiles underestimated the civilian population's exhaustion as well. The rebels' unresolved ambivalence toward race also hurt them; the leaders had promised Antonio Maceo command of the island's eastern forces, then reneged for fear that a black general's presence would depress the support of affluent whites in the west. By the time García landed in May 1880, the war was all but

FIGURE 9.4. *This U.S. Census page shows the Martís no longer living with the Mantillas but at 345 Fourth Avenue in Manhattan, a boarding house owned by Henry C. Beers. June 8, 1880, entry from the 1880 U.S. Census.*

lost; he spent the next ten weeks futilely trying to contact fellow commanders and organize the remaining forces but accomplished little beyond evading the Spanish troops that relentlessly pursued him.[28]

As the war effort foundered, Martí's marriage continued to unravel as well. It is not clear how long Carmen remained in New York after Martí's May 6 letter; at some point the Martís left the Mantilla home and relocated to a boarding house at 345 Fourth Avenue in Manhattan (figure 9.4).

If the Martís' move was an effort to save their marriage, it didn't work. The accepted narrative among Martí biographers is that a frustrated Carmen returned to Cuba with her son in October 1880. That much may be true, but evidence suggests that Carmen left Martí well before then. Census records show that the Martís had left the Mantilla boarding house by May 14; but a June 8 census entry for Martí's new address lists him as "Single," and neither Carmen's nor Pepito's names appear at all. Although the June 8 record does contain some inaccuracies that apparently the homeowners reported in his absence—it incorrectly lists Martí's age as thirty and his parents' nationality as Cuban—it is highly unlikely that they would have forgotten or concealed the presence of Martí's wife and child. Census records thus suggest that by June 1880 at the latest, Carmen and Pepito were either living in New York separately from Martí—an unlikely scenario, given the couples' economic straits—or had already returned to Cuba. An October 15 letter from Leonor complaining that neither Martí nor Carmen had written to her for several months would suggest that Carmen was still with him.[29] But relations between the Martís and Zayas Bazáns were by this point quite strained, as evidenced by Francisco Zayas Bazán's shunning of the Martís during a late-September visit to Havana.[30] It is thus quite possible that Carmen returned to Cuba with Leonor's grandson and simply did not inform her, although Martí's failure to inform his mother would be more difficult to explain.

Neither Carmen's nor Pepito's presence in New York could have softened for Martí the disastrous news of August 1. After weeks of fruitless efforts to rally the disintegrating Cuban forces, a beleaguered Calixto García finally surrendered; shortly afterward he and other rebel leaders, including Antonio Maceo's brother José, were on a Spanish warship bound for prison in the mother coun-

try.[31] A handful of men, out of touch with the leadership due to broken communications, carried on for a time. Hopelessly outmaneuvered and outgunned,
these last pockets of resistance were doomed. Once again, the Cuban uprising
into which Martí and the exile community had placed all their hopes and so
much time and money ended in failure.

On October 13 a heavy-hearted Martí wrote to Emilio Núñez, the last remaining commander in the field, in response to a desperate appeal for help:

> My brave and noble friend:
>   You ask for my counsel—and I do not shun the responsibility I
> assume in giving it to you. I believe it is futile—for yourself and for our
> homeland—for you and your comrades to remain in the field of battle.
> You would not have asked, and now, moved to anger by the criminal
> solitude to which the country consigns its defenders, and to love and re-
> spect for your generous sacrifice,—I have been preparing to beg you to
> save your lives, [which you would lose] absolutely in vain for the *patria*,
> in whose honor you offer them. . . .
>   It is hard to say it and all the bile in my soul rises to my lips as I do
> so, but it is necessary, futile as the fight is; unworthy today, because the
> country is unworthy of its last soldiers, *lay down your arms*.

As for himself, Martí confided in Núñez, in the aftermath of the war's—and his
marriage's—unraveling, he faced a familiar choice: whether to "set out for new
lands or remain in this one."[32]

CARMITA MANTILLA GAVE BIRTH TO HER DAUGHTER MARÍA
on November 28. Martí attended the child's January 6, 1881, baptism at Saint
Patrick's Church in Brooklyn as her godfather. By then, Martí had already decided, with Carmita's encouragement, to leave for Caracas, Venezuela, where
she had contacts who could help him find work. Carmita provided him with
letters of introduction from prominent Venezuelans, including her cousin Mercedes Smith de Hamilton, a close ally of Venezuelan President Antonio Leocadio Guzmán Blanco.[33] Although with his wife and child gone and the war lost
Martí had little reason to remain in New York, it is not clear why Carmita encouraged him to leave or whether it was not in fact her idea; given the circumstantial evidence suggesting if not an actual affair then at least a strong mutual
attraction between the two, perhaps they concluded that it would be best for
them to part.

Two days after María's baptism, on January 8, Martí set out for Venezuela.
In the decade since his first deportation from Cuba, he had lived in five coun-

tries on three continents. Now as he headed for Venezuela, freed from the constraints of a broken marriage and an estranged family, he had also lost the one sacred cause that had compelled him to alienate those he loved. For the first time, it seemed that Martí was moving less toward a new life than away from an old one.

IN THE LAND OF BOLÍVAR

ARTÍ'S VOYAGE TO VENEZUELA WAS IN MANY WAYS as ill conceived and mistimed as was the freshly failed Little War. Several Venezuelan friends in New York tried to dissuade him, among them the poet Nicanor Bolet Peraza, who had long been active in the country's politics and was forced into exile after turning against President Antonio Leocadio Guzmán Blanco.[1]

Like Mexico's Porfirio Díaz and Guatemala's Justo Rufino Barrios, Guzmán Blanco was a self-styled liberal who governed as a dictator. At the time of Martí's arrival in January 1881 Blanco was into his second term as president; his first eight-year term had ended in 1877, and he returned to power in the chaotic aftermath of hand-picked successor Francisco Linares Alcántara's death the following year.[2] Although Martí's previous dalliances with this type of leader had ended badly, he was again lured by the promise of secure employment and the president's history of support for the Cuban cause.[3] Martí's abiding respect for Venezuela's founding hero Simón Bolívar (1783–1830), who had liberated much of South America from Spanish rule a half century before, may also have played a role in his ill-fated decision to try his luck once again in the lands of his "Mother America."

Martí arrived at Venezuela's port city of La Guaira on January 20 and reached Caracas by coach a day later. He later wrote of his arrival in Caracas, somewhat romantically, in his celebrated children's magazine *La edad de oro* (*The Golden Age*):

> The story is told of a traveler who arrived in Caracas one night, and without shaking off the dust from the road, did not ask where

to eat or sleep, but where he could find Bolívar's statue. It is said
that the traveler, alone among the tall and fragrant trees that
lined the plaza, wept before the statue, which seemed to be moving, like a father approaching a son. The traveler did well, for all
Americans should love Bolívar as a father—Bolívar, and all those
who, like him, fought so that America would belong to the American man.[4]

As this and Martí's other writings about Bolívar demonstrate, the
great Venezuelan's ideal of a Latin American federation provided
much of the template on which Martí modeled his own vision of a
continental America united against European and U.S. hegemony.
In his adherence to a Bolivarian pan-American ideal, however, Martí
underestimated the power of the continent's *caudillos*—military
leaders not unlike today's warlords and petty tyrants—who eventually undid Bolívar's grand plan and remained the greatest obstacle to
Martí's own vision of a united Latin America.

MARTÍ'S FIRST WEEKS IN CARACAS TRANSPIRED
much as had his earlier experiences in Mexico City and Guatemala,
his arrival at another strange place softened somewhat by his growing notoriety. Newspapers announced and celebrated his arrival,
notably *La Opinión Nacional*, for which he would soon be writing;
within a month he secured a position at Escuela Santa María teaching literature and French grammar.[5] Local intellectuals and writers
soon invited him to speak at various functions, and again Martí
dazzled the crowds with his passionate rhetoric and now well-honed
skills as a public speaker. In keeping with this well-established pattern, however, Martí also soon ran afoul of an autocratic president
disinclined to tolerate dissent from his citizen-subjects.

The spring and early summer of 1881 were a productive and relatively quiet period for Martí. He continued to teach his classes and
publish regularly, and he made several appearances at literary and
social functions in the capital. He briefly brought to realization a
project he left unfinished in Guatemala. His *Revista Venezolana*, of
which only two issues were ever published, grew out of the same
vision of a free, united Latin America that had inspired the stillborn
Revista Guatemalteca and shared that project's advocacy of the continent's intellectual worth and cultural uniqueness.[6] On its pages
Martí made no effort to conceal his liberal democratic political beliefs or disdain for rulers who eschewed the people's will. Thus it was

Martí's success in finally publishing his long-planned *Revista* that led to his expulsion from Venezuela.

When the *Revista Venezolana*'s second issue, published on July 21 after a brief delay, featured an article lavishly praising the recently deceased Cecilio Acosta, an opposition leader whom Guzmán Blanco deeply loathed, the stage was again set for a hasty departure. The enraged president moved quickly against the outspoken foreigner; on July 27 Blanco sent word to Martí that he should leave the country immediately.[7]

On his last night in Caracas, Martí hand-delivered a brief letter of farewell to the *Opinión Nacional* thanking those who had supported him and announcing the suspension of the *Revista Venezolana* and refunds to its subscribers.[8] By the morning, he was gone, a passenger on the steamer *Claudius* bound for what was now the only place on earth he could remotely call home — New York.[9]

CHAPTER TEN

New York (2)

NO COUNTRY, NO MASTER

I want, when I die
With no country, but no master
To have on my tomb a bouquet
Of flowers, — and a flag!

POEMA XXV, *VERSOS SENCILLOS*

WHEN MARTÍ COMPOSED *VERSOS SENCILLOS*, HIS MOST celebrated volume of poetry, he had been an exile for twelve years and had become more New Yorker than Cuban in many ways.[1] Yet the condition he describes in Poema XXV, of living without a country but without a master, had been his experience from the beginning of his second and definitive exile. This was no longer the youthful deportation that everyone understood as a painful but finite punishment; now, alone in the metropolitan North and estranged from his wife and child, Martí faced the more permanent condition of life as an exile.

It was this abiding sense of alienation not just from country but from the life and loves he had cultivated for so many years that inspired Martí's first great work of poetry. During his time in Venezuela Martí was his usual prolific self, although he did not produce anything that stands today among his major political works. Instead, he wrote *Ismaelillo*, a volume of poetry that established his reputation as one of the greatest poets of the nineteenth century and a founder of Latin American *modernismo*. But for all of *Ismaelillo's* stylistic virtuosity, it was for Martí a deeply personal work driven by the pain of being separated from his son, Pepito. The poems that make up *Ismaelillo* circulated to resounding and widespread critical acclaim while he was still in Venezuela, but it was only after returning to New York that Martí could raise the necessary funds to publish the collection. With its richly detailed poetic imagery, complex poetic structure, and poems that articulate the struggles and hopes of its author, it embodies the very aesthetic he championed in the *Revista Venezolana* and its never-produced Guatemalan predecessor: a work of art every bit as accomplished as its European counterparts but uniquely American in perspective and sensibility.

Upon its publication in 1882, *Ismaelillo* was immediately hailed as a major breakthrough in Spanish-language poetry; but the acclaim was small consolation for the suddenly celebrated poet, as the poems were born from his almost bottomless anguish at being separated from his son. Like the child's biblical namesake in Genesis, Ismael, who lived to become a great and mighty freedom fighter, however, Martí wrote out of a conviction that his own Ismaelillo would rise to validate Martí's suffering and assuage his despair.[2] Indeed, from the dedication in the book, Martí sets out the sense of both hope and despair that surrounds its central figure:

SON:
>   Horrified at everything, I take refuge in you.
>   I believe in the betterment of humanity, in the life of the future, in the usefulness of virtue, and in you. . . .
>   . . . These rivulets have passed through my heart.
>   May they reach yours![3]

The poems of *Ismaelillo* read as a virtual gallery of such images, all variations on the theme of the great son redeeming the suffering of a wounded father. The poems also contain more conventional portrayals of the son as comfort, like the "beautiful child / Who rides upon my shoulder" and bestows his "invisible kiss" upon the wearied father in "Amor errante" (Errant Love).[4] But the volume's most striking portraits of Ismael as child hero come in its longest poems, "Musa traviesa" (Restless Muse) and "Tábanos fieros" (Savage Horseflies). The latter portrays a wizened old warrior and the mystical child warrior who saves him from the biting *tábanos*:

>   Like a bee he buzzes,
>   He breaks and moves the air,
>   Hovers, floats, leaves behind
>   The murmur of his bird's wings:
>   Now my hair he grazes;
>   Now upon my shoulder he sits;
>   Now at my side he stands;
>   Now from my lap he springs;
>   Now the enemy troops

Flee, broken and cowardly!
Sons, the strong shields
Of tired fathers!
Come, my knight,
Knight of the air!
Come, my naked warrior
On your bird's wings,
Let us take the path
That leads to that pleasant stream,
And in its clean waters
Wash my rivulets of blood!
My little knight!
Flying warrior![5]

Yet even as Martí poetically placed his hopes upon the "little knight" who would redeem his suffering and sacrifices in the name of a noble fight, the real-life Pepito was in Cuba being raised by a family unsympathetic to his father's revolutionary cause. It is this knowledge that perhaps most crucially informs the emotional maelstrom at the heart of *Ismaelillo*: a father's dreams for his son's future and fears that they may never come to pass.

MARTÍ HAD COMPLETED WORK ON *ISMAELILLO* BY THE TIME of his return to New York on August 10. He took a room in a boarding house at 459 Kent Avenue in Brooklyn, about two miles from the house on Grand Avenue where the Mantillas had moved the year before and where María Mantilla had been born.[6] Martí's goal remained a free Cuba, and it was clear in light of two failed rebellions that he needed to rethink his own approach and the larger political structure of any future movement. Before any of this could happen, however, he needed to find work.

The New York of 1881 was a place utterly transformed from the city he first saw in 1875. That New York was just beginning to rise from the ashes of the crash of 1873 that had wrecked financial markets, fueled massive unemployment, and halted construction projects all over the city.[7] Martí would write in 1889 of the stunning opulence of a city that had in less than six years virtually reinvented itself:

> On Wall Street, for example . . . buildings are today dwarfed that seemed
> gigantic then, those once considered luxurious must now dress them-
> selves up with adornments and new floorings so as to not be unworthy
> of the new babylons of cream brick and terracotta that have sprung up
> next door. Further north, in the residential areas, those somber rows of

brownstones have given way, almost entirely, to the airy and original homes of recent years.[8]

Indeed, Martí returned to New York at a singular moment in its history during which it very much became the economic, technological, and cultural mecca it remains to this day. Much of the city's rise was due to larger economic and political factors; westward expansion had opened up the resource-rich trans-Mississippi territories, U.S. agriculture boomed even as European yields declined, and federal policies like a return to the gold standard and elimination of the income tax enabled a new environment of investment and growth. As a result, the New York Stock Exchange entered a period of unprecedented financial acceleration.[9] The 1880s also saw a massive overhaul of New York's infrastructure, as inventions including the telephone, arc lighting, and the incandescent light bulb radically transformed daily life in the world's first electrified city; many of New York's architectural landmarks, such as the Metropolitan Opera House and Madison Square Garden, were built during this period.[10]

But the "new" New York that Martí was rediscovering was not all marvels and miracles. The return to good times had made the city simultaneously more cosmopolitan and more provincial, richer and poorer, as its established aristocracy sought to insulate itself from a new class of moneyed magnates, and both colluded to protect their interests against an increasingly defiant—and organized—working class. While New York rebounded from its thin years to unprecedented financial prominence—the word "boom" as a descriptor of economic exuberance was coined during this period—the captains of what would come to be called the "Gilded Age" found themselves combating the demands of organized labor even as they battled each other for dominance. The rise of New York–based organizations such as the Cigar Makers International Union and the more radical Knights of Labor, along with rail workers' unions across the country, threatened an end to the relatively uncontested hegemony the monied classes had enjoyed before the boom.[11] The arrival every year of hundreds of thousands of European immigrants, along with thousands of Chinese, further complicated the labor situation and led to conflicts between established ethnic groups and the new arrivals.[12]

Despite his personal commitment to Cuban independence, as a working writer Martí had always been more catholic in his range of topics; his interest and expertise in a wide range of subjects and disciplines had attracted employers in Mexico City, Guatemala City, and Caracas at least as much as did his exuberance and power as a wordsmith. New York's editors soon also discovered the prolific and talented young writer, but they were not alone; leading Latin American papers seeking the latest news from America's greatest city found in Martí a perfect New York correspondent. Everywhere Martí had worked, he had tackled domestic politics, international news, and the arts with equal skill and aplomb. But in 1880s New York he found a tableau unlike any other: the economic and cultural capital of the world's most exciting and ascendant nation, in whose spasms could be seen — and written — all the glories and calamities of a new and rising America.

Martí also found in New York the perfect platform for reaching more readers than ever before. In the months that followed, Martí's international reputation as a journalist and cultural and political critic grew exponentially, due largely to his widely circulated newspaper writings on the United States. Aside from his ongoing contributions to New York magazines *La América* and *The Hour*, Martí served as New York correspondent for some of Latin America's most widely read newspapers; these included *La Opinión Nacional* in Caracas, Mexico's *El Partido Liberal*, and *La Nación* in Buenos Aires.[13] Other national publications, such as Bogotá's *El Pasatiempo*, reprinted his work, exposing him to an even broader readership.[14] Over the next four years Martí wrote and published at a dizzying pace on a broad range of topics. From the assassination of U.S. president James A. Garfield and the trial of deranged killer Charles Guiteau, to the tawdry spectacle of Coney Island and a bare-knuckle boxing match in Mississippi, to the deaths of Jesse James and Karl Marx, to rioting rail workers in Nebraska and the opening of the Brooklyn Bridge, seemingly no topic was too elevated or lowbrow for Martí's omnivorous pen.

Written as a series of letters to the editor, the columns themselves rarely focused on a single subject but segued thematically — and at times, counterintuitively — among several current events or controversies. Martí's October 27, 1881, letter to *La Opinión*, for instance, moved seamlessly from a posthumous ceremony honoring President Garfield to Guiteau's testimony at his trial, then to the opening of the International Cotton Exposition in Atlanta and centennial commemorations of the Siege of Yorktown that helped end the U.S. Revolutionary War.[15] His March 31, 1882, column was even more far-ranging, covering the flooding of the Mississippi River, the bombing of a monument to British spy John André, the killing of a striking rail worker in Omaha by Nebraska state militia, the Chinese Exclusion Act halting Chinese immigration, and festivities in Chicago honoring Philip Sheridan — and his horse, Winchester — on the U.S. general's fifty-first birthday.[16]

Martí's experience as a working journalist buoyed him economically at a crucial moment, but it also made a deep and enduring impact on his political vision. He was now earning a small but steady income from his writing, and by July 1882 he was also working as a translator and editor for Lyon and Company, a Broad Street publisher.[17] It was thanks to his frequent writings for U.S. and Latin American newspapers that Martí raised the funds to publish *Ismaelillo* in the spring of 1882. The book's enthusiastic reception among the Latin American literati heightened his profile and the demand for his work so that by June 1882 he could afford to cut ties with *La Opinión Nacional* when its editorial restrictions on his columns grew too politically confining; he could not, as he later wrote to Manuel Mercado, continue a "labor that would consent to the praise in its pages of the abominations of [Venezuelan president] Guzmán Blanco."[18] Martí's break with *La Opinión* was indicative of how far his present work surpassed the limits he had imposed on even his most strident writings in Latin America; in his omnibus panoramas of new technological wonders, workers' riots, presidential politics, the arts, entertainment and fashion trends, sporting events, opulent society galas, and the squalor of the poor, Martí was giving readers on two continents an erudite, politically astute, unvarnished portrait of life in the United States in real time at its first moment of ascendancy as a world power. As journalism it was and remains a nearly unparalleled achievement, arguably equaled only by Mark Twain's travelogues a decade earlier.

As much as Martí's writings on the United States changed the way many Latin Americans saw their northern neighbor, the experience of producing them also transformed Martí's own understanding of both his adopted country and the potential threat it posed to Cuban independence. From his privileged vantage point as an embedded outsider, Martí observed firsthand the United States' post-Reconstruction rise to hemispheric dominance. He attributed this ascendance to a population uniquely suited to the entrepreneurial and transformational work of nation building, whose innate energy and intelligence were even now outstripping the tired Europe of their ancestry.

But Martí soon became troubled by what he saw as America's creeping spiritual impoverishment, a cultural decadence and shallow materialism that undermined the nation's character even as it grew in wealth and power. His acute observations of U.S. life led him to wonder how a nascent American empire might choose to exercise its newfound powers, and more specifically its influence, over the rest of the hemisphere. Most ominously, Martí began to fear for Cuba's own future in the shadow of an imperial United States; having tried for decades to purchase Cuba, it undoubtedly would move to fill any vacuum left by a waning Spanish Empire. Over time, Martí came to grasp that the greatest threat to Cuban independence may not be Spain, but the United States.

Martí expressed significant reservations about the darker U.S. tendencies even in his early "Impresiones de América." His October 23, 1880, column opens with effusive praise, hailing the United States as the world's greatest hope for a "new era of mankind":

> The splendor of life, the abundance of money, the violent struggles
> for its possession, the golden currents that dazzle and blind the vulgar
> people, the excellencies of instruction, the habit of working, the vision

of that new country arising above the ruins of old nations, excite the attention of thoughtful men, who are anxiously looking for the definitive settlement of all the destructive forces that began during the last century to lay the foundation of a new era of mankind. This could be, and ought to be, the transcendental significance of the United States.[19]

The rest of the essay turns on Martí's implied but never explicit answers to his own question "But have the States the elements that they are supposed to have? Can they do what they are expected to do?"[20] Rather than offer a direct editorial, the remaining paragraphs focus respectively on a precocious, heavily bejeweled seven-year-old girl: "What will this little girl, so fond of jewelry at seven, do for it at sixteen?"; the "electric commotion" of American English; and finally the "many pitiful sights" of the homeless, concluding with that of "a hundred robust men, evidently suffering from the pangs of misery . . . all lying down on the grass or seated on the benches, shoeless, foodless, concealing their anguish under their dilapidated hats."[21] Martí is careful throughout these early essays to not appear too strident or didactic in his criticisms; this essay in fact exemplifies his self-imposed rule, as described to his editor at *La Nación*, of "taking care to never present a hostile judgment without it first being pronounced by native mouths, — lest it appear as my own temeritous voice; — and to advance no suppositions that the dailies, debates in Congress, and word of mouth have not already advanced."[22] His choice of examples in these early essays, however, suggests that Martí's admiration for North American institutions, traditions, and history did not extend to its population of the time or what he saw as a culture of avarice and spiritual vapidity.

MARTÍ PRODUCED SOME OF HIS MOST IMPORTANT POETRY during his first two years in New York, and his prose focused on the United States, while Cuba remained his primary concern. As several of his posthumously published poems from these years such as "Yugo y estrella" (Yoke and Star) and the fiery "Banquete de tiranos" (Banquet of Tyrants) demonstrate, Cuba was never far from his mind.[23] Even as he prepared to welcome his wife and child to New York for the second time and moved to a small house on Brooklyn's Classon Avenue in hopes of rekindling his marriage, he did not abandon the cause that he knew divided them. Editors and critics across two continents hailed Martí's work as a poet and foreign correspondent, and he was working to rebuild a network of collaborators to rise up against Spanish rule in Cuba. The Spanish government knew this well and continued to shadow Martí's every move. And with good reason: a July 6 letter by a certain "P.Y.," intercepted by a Spanish spy and delivered to the colonial authorities in Cuba, named Martí among Cubans involved in a failed fund-raising scheme in Key West.[24]

Martí was at this point reaching out to military heroes of the Ten Years' War, gauging their willingness to join a new insurgency. He did not contact them directly but chose as his messenger fellow conspirator Flor Crombet, who had served in the Ten Years' War alongside Antonio Maceo under the command of Máximo Gómez. Crombet traveled to Honduras in late July carrying letters from Martí to Generals Gómez and Maceo. In his July 20 letter to Gómez, while conceding that the potential for a new uprising lay "at present little in [the realm of] the visible, and more in the invisible and future," he was especially keen to solicit collaboration in "the reapparition, in a form similar to the previous ones, and adequate for our practical needs, of the revolutionary party."[25] Knowing that Maceo was deeply disillusioned by the Cuban leadership's racism in previous wars, Martí tried to convey his high esteem for the Afro-Cuban general and his indispensability for the struggles to come: "I do not know, General Maceo, a braver soldier or a Cuban more tenacious than yourself. . . . I perceive in you a man capable of achieving a glory that is enduring, grand, and substantial."[26] The two men's leadership and heroic standing among Cubans were sorely missed during the failed Little War; Maceo helped Calixto García in its planning but never took to the field, while Gómez declined to participate at all. Their endorsement of any new war effort, Martí knew, would be crucial to its success.

Neither letter fulfilled Martí's objectives in the short term. Crombet wrote on September 25 that he had still not received replies from either Gómez or Maceo, although Cuban exiles in Tegucigalpa, the Honduran capital, generally supported Martí's advocacy for a new insurgency.[27] In his reply on October 8, Gómez stated his belief that any new plans would be premature, but he agreed to continue meeting periodically with Crombet to monitor the exiles' progress. Maceo also declined Martí's overtures, dismissing the exile groups as insufficiently organized.[28]

Having been put off, at least for now, by the two men he considered crucial to the success of any new insurgent venture, Martí saw before him a path that was clear. Before he could count on the participation of Gómez or Maceo, he would have to build a solid and viable movement, one with the resources and political will to support the revolution. And if such a movement was ever to emerge, it was clear that he would have to take charge of it himself.

MARTÍ'S FAMILY WOULD, HE KNEW, WANT NO PART OF ANY such undertaking. His wife and his mother had long opposed Martí's devotion to the Cuban cause, and after the failure of the Little War they became even more adamant in their demands that he withdraw from revolutionary activities and embrace his duties as a husband and father. Martí's continued allegiance to the Cuban cause also led to tension between his family and the Zayas Bazáns; Carmen's decision to leave Martí and return to Cuba with their child the first time had infuriated Leonor, and the resulting animosity between the two women soon compelled Carmen to leave Havana as well and move with Pepito to her sisters' home in the eastern town of Puerto Príncipe. The forced separation from her grandchild further enraged Leonor and greatly upset Martí, who only learned of Carmen's departure after the fact.[29]

During his first years in New York Martí corresponded only sporadically with his family in Cuba. This was partly due to the demands of his writing and revolutionary activities but also because such exchanges were almost invariably unpleasant. Carmen's few letters bemoan her rejection by his family and blame him for her miserable state; even the few pleasant anecdotes about Pepito are darkened by the insinuation that he is growing up without his father. Carmen's rebuke at the close of one such letter is a typical expression of her feelings:

> I, who have sought to avoid obstacles, who have done all that a respectable woman can do and who, young as I am, have borne the weight and suffering of souls most tempered by adversity, have done but one thing, which I will not do: applaud your conduct, because my son is forgotten and your journeys and your inability to live under any government have filled my soul with I know not how much pain and sadness.[30]

Martí did not directly return Carmen's epistolary venom, but his rage toward her did surface in the references to her and to marriage generally scattered throughout his 1881–1882 notebooks. Taken together, these writings reveal a man disillusioned with his marriage and pessimistic about its future, from his oblique statements that unhappy "amorous liaisons" should be ended "with a kiss on the hand" to more direct declarations regarding Carmen ("nothing for my pleasure — everything for my duty") to uglier, if indirect, descriptions of her as immature and shallow ("Those women are like sweets, which once sucked on, come undone").[31] The notebook's most revealing snippets come in its final pages in two statements that tersely sum up their author's fatalistic frame of mind:

> And I will tear out your love that hurts me, as a fox caught in a trap amputates with its own teeth the imprisoned limb.
> And I will walk the earth bleeding; but free . . .
> I feel all the clouds in the world descend upon my heart.[32]

The second example, still more pointed, is the draft of an unfinished and untitled play Martí wrote sometime in 1882 whose synopsis is a barely veiled indictment:

DRAMA. — He, ingenious and grandiose, sees in marriage what a poet
sees. — She, already mundane and frivolous, what a butterfly sees flying
over swamps . . .
    Since we have erred, of our own free will, let us pay for our mistake.
We could well have not erred. But to pay with one's entire life for an
error that comes simply from the honest exercise of our own goodness.
To be unhappy because one is good, or the more so one is the more
miserable.[33]

As if the play's autobiographical content were not sufficiently clear, Martí then
shifts into the first person when describing the fictional couple's unhappy reunion: "The same roof will shelter us as a coffin lid covers two corpses."[34]
    As estranged as Martí was at this point from Carmen, his relationship with
his mother was hardly less troubled. Leonor's frequent letters were no less confrontational than Carmen's, reproaching him for his infrequent replies and for
embracing a thankless cause at the cost of destroying his own happiness and
peace of mind. In Leonor's letter of August 19, 1881, she admonishes her son
most pointedly:

> You will recall what I have been telling you since you were a boy, that
> all who take on the task of redeemer end up crucified and that the worst
> enemies are those of their own race [people], and I tell you again, so
> long as you do not distance yourself from all that is politics and journal-
> ism, you will not have a day's peace . . .
>   What a useless sacrifice, son of my life, is the one you are making of
> your peace of mind and that of all who love you, there is not a soul who
> will truly appreciate it . . . for its true value.[35]

Leonor's letters also described Mariano's declining health and her disappointment at being separated from Pepito. In her letter of October 14, 1881, his
mother even half-jokingly blames Martí for a toothache that she apparently
caused by grinding her teeth while reading his old letters.[36] She was unsparing
in her criticisms of Carmen not only for having abandoned Martí but for her
inability to endure adversity: "she is not one for hardships," writes Leonor in
her August 19 letter, "nor for living with few resources."[37]
    Through it all Martí continued to write and to work toward founding a new
revolutionary party that would finally free Cuba from Spanish rule. He persuaded Carmen to return to New York with Pepito later that year, and by July
1882 he had moved to the small house on Classon Avenue in Brooklyn where
he hoped they would be happy. It is not clear whether or how much Martí saw
Carmita Mantilla when he returned to New York; his December 19 letter to Bar-

tolomé Mitre suggests that he had high hopes for the reunion with Carmen and Pepito: "But after two years of not seeing my wife and child, they have come these past few days, in the midst of harshest December, to make happy my little newly made home."[38]

The month that preceded Carmen's arrival in December was one of intense revolutionary activity for Martí. On November 12 he met with several collaborators to begin the fulfillment of Gómez's directive: the establishment of an organization that would prepare the way for the launch of the definitive war of independence, to be headed by Gómez, Maceo, Crombet, and other veteran leaders. The group agreed to draw up a formal charter and elect officers at its next meeting. More urgently, they decided to reach out to a population that previous organizations had neglected: New York City's predominantly black cigar workers.

In their initial outreach on November 14, the group did not directly request contributions for the independence movement. They instead collected donations to establish a legal fund for the liberation of three black rebel officers who sought asylum in British-held Gibraltar after the Little War but were extradited to Spain in violation of international law. The tactic was a brilliant one not only in its tapping of a long-neglected resource but for demonstrating the group's belief in the value of its black compatriots. The fact that one of the three officers was José Maceo, Antonio Maceo's brother, surely entered into Martí's calculations as well.[39]

The men formalized their union with the founding on November 20 of the Comité Patriótico Organizador de la Emigración Cubana de Nueva York y Sus Suburbios (Patriotic Organizing Committee of the Cuban Emigrants of New York and Its Suburbs), with collaborator Salvador Cisneros Betancourt elected as president. The new group was especially heartened by Antonio Maceo's November 19 reply to Martí's July 20 letter; in the reply Maceo declared himself ready to fight for Cuba and requested that the committee keep him apprised of all developments.[40]

After more than a decade of struggle and disappointment, Martí and his fellow conspirators could begin to hope for a different outcome. With Gómez and Maceo signaling their willingness to lead a new revolution and an organization with a plan to prepare the way, the committee members needed only to put their plans into action.

THE MONTHS THAT FOLLOWED THE COMMITTEE'S ESTAB-lishment were relatively quiet ones for Martí, perhaps because of the arrival in December of Carmen and Pepito. Perhaps he did not wish to upset his wife with his conspiratory activities so soon after her arrival; a more tangible factor was the need to support her and Pepito, which meant more and bigger writing assignments. In December Martí committed to producing more correspondent's columns for *La Nación* and wrote the prologue for a new edition of J. A. Pérez Bonalde's *Poema del Niágara* (Poem of Niagara).[41] A translation into Spanish of *Notions of Logic* by the English philosopher William Stanley Jevons, commissioned by New York's Appleton Press, occupied him during the first two months of 1883.[42] In March he began writing for *La América*, an industry magazine devoted to spreading news of U.S. scientific and technological advances to the Spanish-speaking world; within ten months he would become the magazine's general editor.[43]

The demands that constant deadlines and the sheer volume of writing placed on Martí's time brought their own pressures, as he now had to balance the need to support his family against the desire to devote himself fully to the revolutionary cause. The expectations that came with being a foreign correspondent responsible for covering the United States in all its cultural, economic, and political complexity, combined with his own immense intellectual curiosity, compelled him to delve into areas that strained even his considerable erudition and to portray events that he did not witness firsthand. Martí had written about current events beyond the immediate purview of New York City from his earliest writings on the United States, from the Omaha rail workers' strike and John L. Sullivan–Paddy Ryan prize fight in 1882 to the flooding of the Ohio River the following year, but he presented these far-flung events from a localized perspective. In his piece on the Sullivan-Ryan fight, Martí describes anxious New Yorkers awaiting the next day's newspapers covering the fight, and his segment on the Ohio flood is subtitled "La indiferencia de Nueva York" (New York's Indifference).[44]

Soon, however, Martí began to insert himself into the narratives as a direct observer, an implicit eyewitness to events and statements he could not possibly have seen or heard; these included a heated debate during a March 1884 session of Congress, the January 1885 inauguration of President Grover Cleveland, the 1886 Charleston earthquake, Jefferson Davis's triumphant speaking tour of the U.S. South on the twenty-fifth anniversary of the onset of the Civil War, and even interactions among voters in line at the polls in Kansas, where in 1887 women were allowed to vote for the first time.[45] Martí's writing in each of these examples combines reportage, likely translated and paraphrased from English-language newspapers, with embellishments such as richly descriptive scenes, dialogue, and anecdotes. From the congressmen "whispering" among themselves as they entered the House chamber to a Kansas husband and wife deciding to go home after finding that their opposing votes would only cancel each other out to Martí's declaration that he had "never seen a more beautiful sight" than the Confederates' twenty-fifth anniversary gathering in Montgomery, these and other enhancements can best be described as fictional.[46]

In the decades after Martí published what came to be called his *crónicas*, several writers who later became major U.S. authors first established themselves as reporters, among them Stephen Crane, Willa Cather, and Upton Sinclair. They often worked for the new tabloid papers that emerged in the nineteenth century and that featured salacious stories of "how the other half lives," murders, sensational events, and shocking exposés of urban poverty. Young writers like Theodore Dreiser launched their careers in the tabloids, visiting factories and ethnic ghettos and filing stories of corruption and squalor. In these cases, however, editors and the reading public would expect the reporter to have been present at the scene. The most notable exception to this nineteenth-century standard was Mark Twain, whose travelogues *The Innocents Abroad* (1869) and *Roughing It* (1872) combined journalistic accuracy and wild exaggeration and caricatures and whose protagonist was a fictionalized stand-in for the author. Even Twain, however, often footnoted his sources, and he did not portray himself as a participant in the events he described.[47] Martí's more radical melding of journalism with fiction would thus have flown in the face of U.S. journalism of the time. While cognizant of the need to gain and keep readers, members of the press generally prided themselves on strict adherence to facts and an almost forensic imperative to get "to the bottom of things."[48]

In Latin America, where a typical front page would indiscriminately mix editorials, fiction, and even poetry with straight journalism, the rules were considerably different; the *modernista* update of the medieval chronicle that Martí practiced gleefully crossed genres and brought an unabashedly personal dimension to historical observation that would have been unethical, if not downright dishonest, in the U.S. press.[49] The distinction between journalists and literary writers was similarly blurred, and papers like the ones that employed Martí routinely hired writers with the understanding that they would not produce strictly journalistic pieces.[50] It is significant, then, that Martí did not write anything resembling his *crónicas* for U.S. readers; his essays on life in the United States were strictly for foreign readers who understood the more catholic nature of his enterprise. These writings, which spanned the 1880s, collectively came to be seen as groundbreaking work that captured the shifting nature of life in the kaleidoscopic modern, urban world. And Martí, as the foremost exponent of the new *crónica*, has since been hailed as a pioneer in the genre.

AFTER THE ARRIVAL OF CARMEN AND PEPITO IN DECEMber 1882, Martí juggled the competing demands of work and Cuba with home as well, leading a hectic life that reflected the ongoing and unresolved conflicts among his loyalties and interests. The revolutionary work continued apace as Martí attended regular meetings of the committee. In March 1883 he met in

Philadelphia with Emilio Núñez, the last general to surrender at the end of the Little War, and a group of like-minded revolutionaries. In June he hosted a gathering of conspirators in his own home that included Colonel Carlos Manuel de Céspedes y Quesada, whose father had launched the Ten Years' War in 1868.[51] And on July 24 Martí raised the Cuban cause's international profile with a well-received speech in honor of Simón Bolívar's centennial at Delmonico's steak house in Manhattan that was attended by Honduran President Marcos Aurelio Soto and several Latin American diplomats.[52]

If Mariano Martí's June arrival in New York did not directly impede Martí's revolutionary activities, the presence of his aging and ailing father complicated Martí's life financially and logistically. He welcomed Mariano's visit and strove to make the old man as happy and comfortable as possible, but his presence meant another mouth to feed and another person around which to schedule everything else he did. Another worry for Martí was the distinct possibility that Mariano would not take to the northern climes and that with the arrival of colder weather in the fall his health might suffer.

Yet Martí's writing and especially his revolutionary work continued, as the Spanish operatives who shadowed his every move well knew. Surveillance reports filed in June and July document a spy's presence outside the Martí home during the June 20 meeting with Céspedes "until midnight"; the informant, while later posing as a reporter, also gained important information from a credulous attendee about escapees from Ceuta who pledged to fight in Cuba in a future uprising.[53]

The year Mariano Martí spent in New York was a tumultuous one for his son during which he suffered new setbacks on both the personal and revolutionary fronts. The highlight of this otherwise difficult period was undoubtedly Martí's triumphant speech at Steck Hall on October 10, 1883, commemorating the anniversary of the launch of the Ten Years' War. This event was the subject of a report from a notably alarmed Pinkerton agent, who noted both the size of the gathering and the ardor of its participants:

> In the hall there were very nearly 300 people of various races and ages. The stage was adorned with portraits of Céspedes, Varona, Agramonte, etc. and at the rear were unfurled the flag of the U.S. and on either side of the columns the *rag of Cuba*, along with other various decorations . . .
>
> The speaker Mr. José Martí took the stage and *tragically* noted the loss of their late heroes, the indispensability of *Unity* to the final conquest, the present state of Cuba, of its demoralized Government, of Slavery and the present system, of the authorities' tyranny and oppression and concluded (nearly in tears) with an elegy to Cuban women,

and an enthusiastic entreaty to Cuban men, that they may contribute in all their efforts to bring to Cuba the aforementioned campaign etc. etc. and received an immense ovation from those present — [54]

The Pinkerton report confirms that Martí's gifts as an orator were undiminished, but his public appearances such as the October 10 speech were few that year. This was partly due to the grind of his work and writing schedule, but also because of his desire to accommodate his wife's and father's wish that he lead a more normal life.

Mariano wrote home often during his year in New York, regaling his wife and daughters with tales of the city's many marvels and challenges. Together his letters also offer a window into his son's life during this period and especially into his struggles with Carmen. Mariano's June 30 letter to his daughter Amelia is the most upbeat of these, as he describes the joy of reunion and an old Spaniard's wonder at New York's wide, tree-lined streets and efficient mail service, technological advances such as the subway and the newly christened Brooklyn Bridge, and the dizzying bustle and plenty of its department stores. He marvels at his son's mastery of English and reports that Carmen is making progress in learning the new language.[55] All seemed well for a time.

In the weeks that followed, however, unresolved disagreements between Martí and Carmen began to take their toll on the marriage. Without specifically naming the source of their discord, Martí's references to Carmen darken his otherwise upbeat letter of August 30 to Manuel Mercado:

> Carmen is not now entirely well, although she is not suffering any major illness. Papá brightens my life, to see him in good spirits, and pure, and finally at rest. My son, turbulent and brilliant, is an exemplary creature . . .
>
> In a book of fiery verses, which I do not know whether I will publish, there is this one:
> I die of solitude, of love I die.

Martí's solitude despite the presence of his wife, child, and father would only grow in the coming months as his revolutionary work and her intractable opposition to it became an ever-widening chasm between them.

By October 30, when the couple helped Mariano celebrate his sixty-eighth birthday, the growing tension between them had begun to wear on Mariano. The unpleasantness that permeated the Martís' home, along with Mariano's unfamiliarity with English and the anticipated hardships of a New York winter, led to his decision to return home. Martí persuaded his father to stay a while longer, but Mariano soon came to regret the decision. Mariano's December 21 letter to Amelia's husband, José, opens with congratulations on the December 12 birth of the couple's first child, then turns quickly to his own unhappy state:

> My stomach still ails me and I am quite isolated because if there is something to see I cannot go see it the distances are too great and I cannot walk them nor pay [for transportation] nor dedicate myself to learning English because I no longer have the head for it because of which I am unhappy. The cold is now at its apogee and though I am warmly dressed I feel it quite a bit because I do not any exercise because I cannot. Just today we have a foot and a half of snow in the backyard and in front of the house . . .
>
> Everyone goes around warmly dressed and always in a hurry. I do not go out for fear of slipping on the snow because my legs are extremely weak so my stay here could never be a long one because I am missing my daughters, my wife and my sons-in-law, especially my [daughter] Antonia.[56]

Yet Mariano remained another six months, enduring a difficult winter. He fell ill shortly after the New Year, forcing Martí to cancel at least one engagement in order to care for him.[57] Although Mariano continued to bemoan his reduced state in letters to Havana, he also gained a new appreciation for his son, if not a true understanding. Mariano began to send home clippings from Martí's various writings; the long shut-in days, along with his son's growing estrangement from Carmen, drew father and son together into conversations that may not have otherwise taken place.[58] This belated rapprochement marked a sort of turning point for Martí's relations with his family, as Leonor soon also softened her objections to his cause and began to see him as an exceptionally brilliant and dedicated man, however naïve or misguided. For Martí and Carmen, however, there would be no reconciling.

THE FIRST MONTHS OF 1884 CONTINUED IN A KIND OF STASIS or holding pattern, the tensions of the Martís' marital difficulties and Mariano's souring mood remaining in suspension for a time. Professionally Martí's career was thriving, with his elevation to the directorship of *La América* and the completion of another translation for hire, this time of A. S. Wilkins's *Roman Antiquities*. His only professional setback came from Charles A. Dana, director of *The Hour*, who regretted not being able to publish Martí's writings in English because they lacked the style of his Spanish-language work.[59]

The relative calm ended abruptly on April 1, when Cuban insurgent General Carlos Agüero and forty men departed Key West on the schooner *Adrián* bound for Cuba. On April 4 they landed at Varadero, less than a hundred miles east of Havana, launching a guerrilla campaign aimed at rousing the island population to battle. The expedition was organized and funded by the New York Comité Patriótico under the leadership of Juan Arnao, but it is not clear how involved Martí was in its planning. His relative lack of participation may have stemmed partly from deference to Carmen; Martí also remembered well Gómez's and Maceo's reluctance to join any underfunded or badly organized effort and grasped the importance of the two titans' participation for the success of any new project.

It was perhaps Martí's relatively low profile among the revolutionaries along with his enhanced international reputation as a writer and political pundit that earned him his first diplomatic post. On May 22 Martí was appointed interim general consul for Uruguay to fill in for fellow Cuban Enrique Estrázulas.[60] Although it was a relatively minor post, Martí's diplomatic status could not have pleased Spain, as it implicitly validated his public advocacy for Cuban independence—a position shared by Uruguay—and gave him access to high-level ministers and diplomats from across Latin America, and that could in turn help build support for a new Cuban revolution. Such networking was unlikely to help the current uprising, which after six weeks had failed to make any significant headway on the island.

Proud of his son's accomplishments and at peace with his political commitments, Mariano finally resolved to leave New York in June 1884. In the early morning of June 19 he arrived in Havana on the steamer *Saratoga*, mostly recovered from his New York ills and thrilled to once again see his wife and family.

For his son there could be no such return as long as the Spanish flag flew over Cuba. And even as Agüero's guerrillas struggled fruitlessly to gain a foothold in Cuba, new hope came with the news that Gómez and Maceo had arrived in New Orleans on August 9 with the intention of personally assessing the readiness of exile groups for a final, definitive war of liberation.[61] Martí met with Gómez and Maceo for the first time on October 2, at Madame Griffou's hotel at 21 East Ninth Street in Lower Manhattan.[62] The generals' New York visit electrified the exile community, whose support of recent revolutionary efforts had been at best lukewarm. As Martí had envisioned, the presence of the veteran leaders raised hopes among exiled Cubans that their country's deliverance from Spanish rule was finally at hand.

If this initial meeting went well, it was only because the disagreements that would divide the three revolutionaries had not fully emerged. Martí's dream of a grand coalition was now threatened by the same obstacles that had unraveled previous such efforts; at the meeting the generals voiced their particular displeasure with the apparent lack of a central organization and of coordination between New York and revolutionary groups in New Orleans and elsewhere and with the seeming distrust among key players and factions.

The primary cause of the movement's initial failure, however, was Maceo's and Gómez's unwillingness to share power with a civilian leadership, as Martí insisted, and their general reluctance to take their younger, inexperienced comrade seriously. Although they shared the common goal of Cuban independence, the political differences between Martí and his military counterparts were significant. Martí, and by extension the New York Comité Patriótico, believed unyieldingly in the establishment of civilian rule as the only way for Cuba to become a truly democratic state; the two generals could not abide such an arrangement, insisting that the island nation at least at first had to be guided by a strong military government. In the end the three agreed to table their differences for the moment, perhaps as a show of unity in anticipation of the upcoming October 10 anniversary of the launch of the Ten Years' War. They agreed to meet again after those celebrations to plan the new and, they hoped, final war of liberation.

The atmosphere at Tammany Hall on the night of October 10, 1884, was euphoric, with hundreds of Cubans packing it to see the visiting war heroes and hear Martí speak. Earlier that day Martí resigned his position as Uruguayan consul in order to devote his full energies to the planning and execution of the war he believed would finally liberate Cuba from Spanish rule. His speech that evening again electrified the crowd and deeply impressed the visiting generals, who knew of his reputation as an orator but had never seen him in action.

On the morning of October 18 Martí met again with Gómez and Maceo for the purpose of organizing the new war of liberation. Here the differences that emerged on October 2 could no longer be deferred; neither Martí nor the generals would yield from their respective visions of Cuba's future government. Martí had been wizened by his brushes with military dictatorships in Guatemala and Venezuela; however left-leaning or well-meaning in their reforms, such governments, he knew, could never be true democracies. The two Cuban generals, and especially Gómez, remained steadfast in their belief that a civilian leader should not stand at the forefront of the revolution. Martí thus decided, perhaps even before the end of the lengthy and contentious meeting, that he could not participate in a revolution that so conflicted with his core beliefs. Two days later, in what amounts to a resignation letter, Martí chides Gómez for wanting to found the new nation "as one commands a military camp," even as he regrets the need to chastise the general:

> What a shame to have to say these things to a man whom I believe to be sincere and good, and in whom reside the notable qualities to achieve true greatness! — But there is something above all the personal sympathies that you may inspire in me . . . and it is my determination to not contribute one iota, out of blind love for an idea into which I am ex-

pending my life, to bring to my land a regime of personal despotism, which would be more shameful and disastrous than the political despotism that it now endures . . .

The *patria* belongs to no one: and if it is someone's, it shall be, and that only in spirit, for those who serve it with the greatest disinterestedness and intelligence.[63]

And with that, and a final, categorical word — "no:" — Martí effectively severed his ties to the revolution that he had spent much of the previous three years building and for which he had sacrificed his own happiness and peace of mind.[64] The revolution would go on, but it would do so without him.

CHAPTER ELEVEN

New York (3)

THE GREAT WORK BEGINS

The hour seems to have arrived.

LETTER TO MÁXIMO GÓMEZ, DECEMBER 16, 1887

I T WOULD BE ANOTHER THREE YEARS BEFORE MARTÍ
could write those words and more than a decade before the launch
of the revolution that would eventually end Spanish dominion over Cuba.[1]
With his sudden withdrawal from the movement he so prominently and visibly
championed, his dream of liberating the island seemed as distant as ever.

Martí now found himself in a most precarious public bind. He understood
that some would misinterpret his abdication as a withdrawal from the larger
Cuban cause. He also knew that most of those who learned of his break with
Gómez would side with the renowned war hero and that many others would
simply dismiss him as having only superficially supported independence, perhaps for reasons of personal gain. Martí's vocal support for Cuban independence had earned him the enmity of many fellow exiles; some favored U.S.
annexation over another long and bloody war, while others sympathetic to independence—including prominent veterans of the recent wars—did not believe the inexperienced civilian capable of leading such a movement. To remain silent would only tacitly confirm such impressions—and give his enemies
license to spread them further. Yet Martí understood that any public airing of
his differences with Gómez ran the risk of hurting the larger cause, of creating
a perception of division and disarray that would weaken the movement just as
it was gaining momentum. To avoid the appearance of discord, he would have
to refrain from publishing anything that would criticize Gómez or otherwise
expose their differences.

What Martí perhaps did not immediately grasp was how quickly his enemies and political rivals would use the opportunity to discredit him and how Gómez, no political novice himself, would move to absolve himself of responsibility for their split. In late October 1884 the Asociación Cubana de Socorro (Cuban Aid Society), a front organization created to raise funds for the war, elected Martí their president, unaware of his break with Gómez and withdrawal from the movement mere days earlier. Martí resigned the position almost immediately and with little explanation, leaving a puzzled and in some cases offended membership. Gómez, resolved to soldier on without Martí, avoided any public criticism but both privately and in his diary complained of the "furious" Martí's abandonment, citing his "insulting letter" of October 20 as proof of his poor conduct and dismissing as a "frivolous pretext" Martí's concerns about a potential military dictatorship.[2]

At first Martí continued to attend exile gatherings, hoping to remain apprised of any new developments as an interested observer. That such an approach would not work became clear at a November gathering at Tammany Hall where fellow exile Antonio Zambrana, perhaps aware of Martí's presence, questioned the commitment to the cause—and the manhood—of those who did not support the present plan for insurrection.[3] An enraged Martí, feeling personally taunted, promptly stormed the stage and had to be physically restrained from attacking Zambrana. After this incident, Martí disappeared completely from the Cuban exile scene.

The seven months of silence that followed the Tammany Hall incident in November created an opening for Martí's enemies and rivals, and they moved quickly to discredit him. Beyond their political differences, Martí's enemies found ammunition in his personal foibles and struggles. Disapproving murmurs of Martí's abandonment of his wife and child, insinuations that he led a double life with Carmita Mantilla, and rumors of heavy drinking and general physical decline had long circulated among the exiles and may have contributed to Carmen's decision to leave him again and return with Pepito to Cuba. So successful was this campaign of character assassination that even Spain lost interest in Martí and apparently ceased its surveillance of him after the break with Gómez.[4]

One of the first revolutionaries to understand what Martí's departure was costing the movement was Gómez himself. In January 1885 the old general's fund-raising initiatives in Paris, Mexico, and New York failed miserably, and he found himself with his wife and children in New Orleans "surrounded by Spanish and American enemies [while] the Cubans abandon me in the venture and distance themselves from me as from a leper."[5] So dire did Gómez's situation become that he asked prominent New York exile and mutual friend Juan Arnao to intercede with Martí on his behalf.[6] We have no record of either Arnao's meeting with Martí or Arnao's January 15 letter to Gómez, but the general's January 20 reply indicates that Martí rejected Arnao's attempt at rapprochement:

> As for Martí's negative [response], I am not surprised. From the first day he met me in New York Martí would have separated from me but did not find a suitable means, until chance brought him one. . . . He is not a man who can move in any circle without aspiring to dominate and upon taking my pulse told himself: "With this old soldier it is impossible to do that, and what is worse I can see myself in the end having to follow him into battle in Cuba — because instead of me helping to push this one he can pull [me in]. — This man pays little heed to the orators and the poets and what he wants is gunpowder and bullets and men to come with him to the battlefields of my country to kill its tyrants." Here, my friend, neither more nor less, are the thoughts of that young man whom we must leave in peace, now we will go fight to win a nation for him and his children. We will no longer bother with these trifles.[7]

Gómez ends his January 20 letter declaring that he will "move ahead" on his own, but his attempts to raise money and men went nowhere. Whatever momentum Martí had managed to build before Gómez's arrival in New York was now all but gone. Fund-raising dried up even more with the news on March 5 that General Carlos Agüero, who had landed in Cuba eleven months earlier with a small force, had been assassinated; two days later Cuban authorities executed the last of another group of revolutionaries, including their leader Ramón Leocadio Bonachea.[8] In early June, Maceo attempted reconciliation with the estranged Martí, again through their mutual acquaintance Arnao, but likewise was rebuffed.[9]

THE FIRST MONTHS OF 1885 FOUND MARTÍ AS ISOLATED personally as he was politically, as his withdrawal from Cuban exile politics did not forestall Carmen and Pepito's return to Cuba in mid-March. Alone and adrift in New York, Martí wrote to longtime confidant Manuel Mercado of his alienation and a life lived "in hopes that some heroic task, or one at least difficult, will redeem me."[10] He returned to his writing with a novel (under the pseudonym Adelaida Ral), *Amistad funesta* (Tragic Friendship) and pieces for local New York magazines, but he declined all public speaking requests.[11] Martí's sole comfort during these months was the rekindling of his relationship with Carmita Mantilla, whose husband, Manuel, had died on February 18 of heart disease. Martí moved to the Mantilla boarding house shortly after his wife's departure, ostensibly as a boarder but really forming a de facto household with Carmita and her children; he showed no interest in returning to the revolutionary movement that was foundering without him.

IT WAS NOT ARNAO'S ENTREATIES THAT SET MARTÍ BACK ON the path to revolutionary politics, but a public provocation. It is not clear why it took the Asociación Cubana de Socorro nearly eight months after Martí's resignation to elect new officers, but this was the order of business for the organization's public meeting of June 13. Martí's removal as president was an empty formality, given his long absence. Word reached him that several of those present, not content with upbraiding him for his withdrawal, also attacked him personally, and he decided to confront his enemies directly in a public forum. On June 23 Martí circulated an open letter "To the Cubans of New York" declaring that he would appear at Clarendon Hall "to respond to whatever charges my fellow citizens wish to bring against me."[12] Two days later Martí stood before a packed house at Clarendon Hall to face his accusers, whoever they might be. The Puerto Rican writer Bernardo Vega offers this eyewitness account handed down from his father:

> When Martí took the stage, the crowd rewarded him with a thunderous applause. At that moment Martí's enemies lost their nerve. When the ovation subsided, that small, fragile-looking man asked with a serene expression and deep voice that those who had accusations against him express themselves. And after those first words there came a disquieting silence.
>
> At last someone asked to speak from a far end of the hall. . . . He began to speak, but soon got a lump in his throat. He could not continue and sat back down. Another silent interval followed. Martí again urged those who wished to accuse him to do so without fear. More minutes of silence. None took up the gauntlet.[13]

Having silenced his enemies, Martí proceeded to speak to the assembled exile community. Although no transcript exists of the extemporaneous speech, in Vega's account Martí was magnanimous toward his critics, declaring that the work of liberating Cuba was worth having to suffer the ingratitude of some. Many in the audience undoubtedly came to see a showdown, and many more—including the working-class artisans and cigar workers who filled much of the hall—left with the conviction that Martí was a man who could lead them to freedom.[14]

The success of Martí's gambit at Clarendon Hall restored him in the exile community to the forefront of the revolution, and he began again to receive—and decline—requests to speak at public functions. The most important of these was an invitation to speak at the annual commemoration of the onset of the Ten Years' War at which Maceo had agreed to appear.[15] In his October 9 letter to the organizers Martí emphasized that he had not wavered in his allegiance to the cause or to those who had fought and died for Cuba's independence: "Not for a single instant do I regret having stood with the defeated since the conclusion of our war, and remaining among them."[16] But he also expressed strong misgivings regarding the present war effort, remarking of Gómez's strong-arm leadership that "tyranny is all one in its various forms, even when clothed . . . in beautiful names and great acts" and explaining that he chose neither "to stand in the way of those who think differently" nor to "contribute to works that in my judgment have jeopardized the revolution, and with it the nation."[17]

Even without Martí's participation, Maceo's return to New York was enough to give the flagging revolution a temporary boost. The event raised $12,000 (equivalent to more than $280,000 today), much of it from the Afro-Cuban cigar workers who championed both Maceo and Martí.

The leadership promised that a new uprising was imminent, but when it did not materialize, pessimism returned to the exile community; fund-raising again dried up, and New York's once thriving exile press all but disappeared. And with Martí absent from the scene, the exiles' harshest criticisms and recriminations were now directed at Gómez and Maceo. It had been nearly four months since anyone had seen or heard from Martí, who effectively disappeared after his triumphant Clarendon Hall speech back in late June. The rift with Gómez was now a year old, and wounds on both sides would be slow to heal.

IN THE TWO YEARS THAT FOLLOWED MARTÍ'S JUNE 1885 speech, the independence movement entered a period of relative inactivity. The exiles' disenchantment with revolutionary leaders only increased with the formal abolition of slavery on the island on October 7, 1886, a concession that especially removed much of the impetus for independence among Afro-Cubans.[18] The Cuban sugar crisis of the 1880s significantly weakened the country's economy and with it the Creole plantocracy on which Spain's control of the island depended, yet exile groups continued to display little appetite for renewed hostilities or faith in those who called for them.[19]

During this interregnum Martí busied himself with a range of writing projects, including two book-length translations for New York publisher D. Appleton and Company and columns for several newspapers in the United States and abroad. In the spring of 1886 Manuel Mercado secured for him a much-sought position as foreign correspondent for the Mexico City newspaper *El Partido Liberal*.[20] Despite the plentiful work and Carmita's consoling presence, Martí began to feel the chasm of separation from his family in Cuba. His health, which had stabilized somewhat during his first years in New York, now declined as the sarcoidosis that had plagued him intermittently since adolescence became a more constant companion.[21] It was a fatigued, embittered Martí who wrote to Mercado of his anguish at living away from his loved ones: "Everything binds me to New York, at least for the next few years of my life: everything binds me to this poisoned cup" where

> every day, when night falls, I feel myself consumed from within by a grief that compels me onward, overturns my soul, and bids me come out of myself. . . . From within me comes a fire that burns me, like a fever, eager and dry. A death in stages.[22]

Correspondence between Martí and his family—with Carmen the only notable exception—flowed freely now. Pepito sent his first letter, as Martí once penned his first letter to Leonor as a boy:

> Papá, I love you very much. I will like anything that you send me very much. Mamá knows that a day never passes without me remembering you. They say that I am your very portrait and that makes me happy. Many kisses from your son,
> Pepe[23]

Martí's mood darkened further upon learning of the death of his childhood mentor, Rafael María de Mendive, in November 1886. Many gathered in Havana to mourn his passing and celebrate a decorated life devoted to the education of Cuba's youth; but the exiled Martí, his most distinguished pupil, could not join them. But what most troubled Martí was the rapid decline of his father. Leonor wrote of his falling ill in late November, and by the new year it was clear that Mariano was nearing his last days.[24] The news of Mariano's death on February 2, 1887, was no less a blow for having been anticipated. Martí's sorrow flowed freely in several letters from this time, perhaps most poignantly in his February 28 letter to longtime friend Fermín Valdés Domínguez:

> My sorrows, which it seemed could not be any greater, have become so, now that I can never, as I had wished, love and celebrate him for all to see, and reward, in the last years of his life, that proud and forceful virtue that I myself could not appreciate until my own was put to the test.[25]

As immeasurably as Mariano's death added to Martí's sense of guilt and estrangement, it also indirectly set in motion the events that would return Martí to the revolutionary fold. After the wedding of Martí's last remaining unattached sister, Antonia, two years before, Mariano and Leonor lived in a small apartment owned by sister Amelia's husband, José.[26] Mariano's stay in New York raised for Leonor the possibility that she might also visit her son there one day; with Mariano's death the opportunity arose for the grieving widow to do so. Martí was already edging cautiously toward a reconciliation with Gómez, as the general had by now abandoned the idea of heading the movement on his own. But it was Leonor's visit to New York in November 1887 that may have finally spurred Martí to rededicate himself to his revolutionary calling.

By the time of Leonor's visit Martí already had made an enthusiastic return to revolutionary activity. His organizing efforts now took on an added urgency due to his growing awareness of the United States as a burgeoning hemispheric power that could threaten Cuba's prospects for freedom. He returned to the Cuban cause spurred by the dual pressures of a disorganized movement unprepared to take action and the fear that U.S. intervention in Cuba in the form of annexation or outright conquest would preempt the movement if they did not act soon, thus ending any chance for a successful revolution. Compounding and abetting the U.S. threat was the rising popularity among the exiles of annexationist and autonomist groups, which in the absence of visible revolutionary activity were moving to fill the political vacuum. The United States had been attempting to purchase Cuba as far back as 1808 under the Jefferson administration and as recently as 1869 with the Ten Years' War already under way.[27] Now, with weakened Spanish and Cuban economies and an ascendant United States in an increasingly expansionist mood, Martí did not doubt that Cuba's northern neighbor would take any opportunity to capture, whether by purchase or force, the island its successive leaders had long coveted.

It was with these many pressures in mind that Martí made his public return at Manhattan's Masonic Temple on October 10, 1887, at the annual commemoration of the launch of the Ten Years' War. With his speech that evening Martí effectively relaunched the revolutionary movement and served notice to friend and foe that he was back for good. While paying homage to Cuba's war heroes and appealing to the audience's sense of duty and debt to their *patria*, however, Martí implicitly criticized Gómez's recently failed efforts by acknowledging the "many sensible men" among them who "prefer to allow time for historical events to culminate in all their natural force, to precipitating them to satisfy their own guilty impatience, to jeopardizing them with premature action."[28] His criticisms of Gómez were much more pointed in his response to an October 10 letter from General Juan Fernández Ruz seeking his support for a new initiative. In his October 20 reply Martí counseled patience, describing an exile community "already tired of serving ill-advised heroes" but "not incapable . . . of understanding and helping a worthy movement at the proper time."[29] Martí's advice that the war "should not be attempted today, without sufficient size and before its natural time" illustrates that for him, the time for revolution was nigh but not quite now.[30]

Martí continued his organizing activities in the weeks before his mother's arrival, forging ahead despite his misgivings and following in his own revolutionary work his advice to Ruz: "Prepare yourself, but not for today."[31] Ruz persisted, however, and during a November visit to New York persuaded Martí to bring his proposal to the attention of the city's exiles. As Ruz's desire to move ahead coincided to some degree with Martí's own organizing efforts, they agreed to hold a meeting of politically minded exiles at the home of fellow conspirator Enrique Trujillo to determine the most viable course for action. The consensus among those attending the November 11 meeting was that any new insurrection would require full and methodical preparation beforehand. The assembled group then named a committee charged with developing a detailed plan of action.[32] After three years in the political wilderness, Martí was once again at the forefront of a movement to liberate Cuba.

It was not only Martí who experienced a change of heart; his mother also had been reconsidering her opposition to his chosen cause and even to the cause itself. Over the seven years since Martí's second deportation, Leonor's position had evolved from disapproval to a grudging resignation. More recently, however, she had grown into an acceptance of her son's devotion to country; the island's economic hardships and ongoing political tensions were leading her to realize that her son's cause was a necessary and righteous one.

By the time Leonor arrived in New York on November 22, that transformation was all but complete. She brought a gift with her: a ring forged from a link of the chain Martí had worn as a teenager in prison, now prominently engraved "CUBA." It was Martí's idea to use the link, which he had delivered to artisan Agustín de Zéndegui nearly ten years earlier in hopes that his friend could fashion a ring from it. Leonor finally had the ring made before departing the island, and she presented it to her son as a token of solidarity with both him and his — now their — cause.[33]

Leonor's two-month visit buoyed Martí physically as well as emotionally; he happily avers in his December 9 letter to Mercado that her presence was the cause for his "sudden [return to] health that everyone has noticed."[34] She did not seem to mind the limited time they could spend together, although it very much bothered Martí: "With this life of work that I lead, I barely have time at night to see her; but this is enough for me to feel less cold in my hands, and to return more energized each morning to my task."[35] Martí worked continually during his mother's visit, by day writing and by night finalizing a plan he hoped would set in motion the revolution that would liberate his country. Toward the end of November he called a group of military leaders including Emilio Núñez to a November 30 meeting at which he and his fellow conspirators would present their plan for the military men's approval. He reached out to Cuban revolutionaries in Key West, a crucial constituency as yet untapped by previous efforts, whose support for independence had, unlike their counterparts in New York, remained constant. On November 29 he wrote to José Dolores Poyo, leader of the Key West contingent, to share his ideas and ask for their support.[36]

Martí hoped the November 30 meeting would serve to build a consensus between the civilian Comisión Ejecutiva (Executive Commission) he had charged with formulating a plan and the veterans whose support he would need in order to fulfill his final objective: to persuade Gómez to return to the revolutionary fold, but on Martí's terms. Martí knew that Gómez had struggled mightily in his attempts to build a successful movement on his own, and he believed that the general would be much more likely to join him if he had a detailed plan in place, money to carry it out, and the support of key military leaders. All went according to plan, as the assembled exiles ratified the Comisión Ejecutiva's plan and agreed to draft a group letter inviting Gómez and Maceo, among others, to join them.[37]

The length of time Martí worked on the resulting joint letter—more than two weeks—suggests how crucial it was for his hopes and ambitions. The price for getting it wrong—for producing a document that one or more members refused to sign or that put off Gómez or Maceo—would be more than just another setback. It would mean the end of his own credibility as civilian head of the movement and perhaps for the very idea of a civilian-run government for the future state.

On December 16 Martí signed his name at the bottom of the 2,800-word letter to his "Distinguished Compatriot" Máximo Gómez. Twenty others added their signatures, including two military officers, Emilio Núñez and José Rodríguez Camino. Three co-signers withheld their names, signing as "A Cuban" or "A Camagüeyan." And as a further testament to Martí's achievement, one co-signer, Ramón Rubiera, was among those whose vocal denunciations of Martí had compelled him to organize the air-clearing event at Clarendon Hall two years earlier.[38] As a co-signer, Rubiera now stood with Martí as part of a united front offering to welcome Gómez, Maceo, and other generals as equal partners in the great work.

The letter makes a straightforward case for war, but only under a united leadership enacting the will of Cubans on the island and in solidarity with exile communities in New York and elsewhere. Martí could now demand this from the generals because he had built the power base that they could not; he had organizational infrastructure, broad popular support, and money to make the revolution a reality. Martí's position of relative strength also explains the letter's language and tone: collegial but firm, maintaining the tone of comradeship while defining unequivocally the revolution's goals, how it must proceed, and how it would be presented to the outside world. Although the plan outlined in the December 16 letter represented a group consensus reached via a lengthy process, the letter itself very much bears the stamp of its author and animating spirit. Gómez's acceptance of its terms would thus also constitute his recognition of Martí as the architect of the revolution.

No longer "the childish and ignorant people who took to the field" in 1868, the heirs of the Ten Years' War generation were ready to fight but only for "a grand plan worthy of their sacrifice." That plan had to offer not only a military strategy but a clear political goal that transcended the personal designs of individual leaders seeking to "advance interests or satisfy personal hatreds."[39] To meet this standard, the revolution would adhere to five main goals: (1) to justify to the island's population the need for a "revolutionary solution" and assuage misgivings, proceeding "by virtue of a recognized democratic end"; (2) to "proceed without delay to organize" a military strategy, one coordinated by both "outside" (exile) and "inside" (island) generals; (3) to unite the various exile organizations under a single democratic structure; (4) to prevent any single interested party or group from dominating the revolution and subsequent state "for the preponderance of a single social class, or the disproportionate authority of a military or civilian faction"; and (5) to impede or otherwise blunt the circulation of annexationist ideas that would threaten the revolution's momentum.[40]

These five principles essentially amounted to two overriding imperatives: to unite Cubans on the island and in exile behind a single plan or platform and to ensure that no individuals or subgroups would bend the revolution to their own ends. To achieve these goals, the movement had to accomplish what none before ever managed: to bring structure and party discipline to an unruly, profoundly disorganized group of sometimes conflicting interests. The letter bemoans the revolution's present state in a somewhat scolding tone, noting disapprovingly that Cuba "does not yet have, as it should with the war coming so soon, a plan to unite it and a political program to reassure it."[41]

With the generals' cooperation, the letter's signatories asserted, the plan before them would provide that way forward if all interested parties — including the military — agreed to sublimate their personal interests to the greater good. The revolution's leaders had to, in the letter's words, "for their own credibility and authority, demonstrate by their unity abroad and their submission to the public good, that rather than the scourge of the nation they are its greatest hope."[42] Their ultimate directive is contained in the letter's final word, *fundar* — "to found."

JANUARY 1888 MARKED GÓMEZ'S AND MACEO'S RETURN TO the fold. Neither man wholly accepted the commission's terms; in a January

15 letter Maceo shared his own views on how best to proceed, and in Gómez's reply ten days later he agreed in principle to "occupy my combat post to fight for the independence of Cuba" but wrote that the time for war had not yet arrived.[43] Time evidently had not assuaged Gómez's anger toward Martí; in an otherwise warm and encouraging reply, the general's letter avoided any mention of his once and future collaborator. Martí at first took offense but soon was persuaded by Flor Crombet to overlook the general's slight.[44] The generals' responses were sufficiently positive that Martí felt justified in moving ahead with plans to launch a revolution in the near future. In the meantime, other commanders, including General Francisco Carrillo, indicated their readiness to join the war as soon as everything was in place.[45]

Coinciding with Gómez's and Maceo's return was the departure of Leonor Pérez, who by late December had seen enough of the United States. In an undated letter to Chata she laments the life her son is leading and states her desire to go home:

> [L]ife for him in this land is terrible, as it would be for me if I had to live in it, despite its greatness, it is disagreeable [*antipática*] to those of us born in other climates and other customs.[46]

The birth in Havana of Antonia's second child—Leonor's eleventh grandchild—on January 22, 1888, provided the necessary pretext for her departure. On January 27, the eve of her son's thirty-fifth birthday, Leonor ended her two-month stay in New York and boarded the steamer *City of Washington* bound for Havana.[47]

Even with the generals' pledged cooperation, the dream of solidarity among exiles remained elusive. The biggest practical hurdle for Martí's New York group was the active presence of at least three other major organizations in Tampa and Key West, each raising money independently and approaching the idea of insurrection somewhat differently from the rest. The Key West group, working under the umbrella name Convención Cubana (Cuban Convention), shared neither the New Yorkers' democratic structure nor their goal; convention members did not seek to develop their own revolutionary plans but made funds available to any expeditionary plan they found viable. In contrast to the New Yorkers' emphasis on democratic governance and transparency, the Key West Convención Cubana was not a single organization at all; it was an agglomeration of cells that had little contact with each other.[48] This structure was calculated to frustrate Spanish attempts to infiltrate the groups, but it had the collateral effect of making coordinated activity nearly impossible.

One immediate consequence of this divergence among exile groups was the tendency for rogue commanders to launch their own expeditions. Juan Fernández Ruz, who was dissatisfied with the New Yorkers' decision to wait, forged ahead with his own plan for an immediate invasion. In early February Martí was forced to act, sending Crombet to intervene with the Key West exiles to stop Ruz.[49] In a February 12 letter to Emilio Núñez, Martí describes a "quieting down" due to Ruz's disappointment that "the exiles could not be organized, as he had dreamed, to act in private concert with him as supreme chief of the war."[50]

Differences between the military and civilian leadership also persisted, primarily over who would control the increasingly plentiful funds now being raised by groups like Los Independientes, a New York group dedicated to funding the revolution. The influx of money convinced many, including close Martí ally Crombet, that the decision to wait was a mistake.

These tensions among the revolution's dozen or so central players boiled over at a July 15 meeting of Los Independientes at Manhattan's Pythagoras Hall. The majority of those present agreed that the time for small, disparate expeditions had passed and that only the methodical construction of a single, coordinated movement would achieve their shared goal of liberating Cuba. Crombet, one of a vocal dissenting minority, presented his own plan for immediate action; when Martí rose to rebut Crombet and reaffirm the majority position, the two came nearly to blows.[51] This and other such incidents lent credibility to annexationist claims that the revolutionaries remained in disarray and fueled speculation more generally that the attempt to form a united revolutionary front had failed.[52]

Martí responded to these and other dangers by working himself nearly to death, spending long hours at his tiny office at 120 Front Street and seeing Carmita and María hardly at all. Longtime friend Blanca de Baralt described Martí's office as a "pigeon-coop" that one reached "by climbing four floors by a narrow iron staircase." The office's spartan furnishings included "shelves . . . replete with books, a table, a few chairs, a portrait of him by the artist [Herman] Norman," and a few personal effects, notably the famous "prison ring."[53] With Leonor having returned to Havana after a two-month visit, Martí could devote himself completely to his work. He spent nearly every waking hour at the small Front Street office writing on Cuba-related topics for the exile papers and on the United States for his more lucrative international clients; his translation of Helen Hunt Jackson's novel *Ramona* appeared in July. Martí also returned to diplomatic work, accepting a position as interim consul of Uruguay and listing the Front Street office as the consulate's address.[54]

The demands of all these tasks, combined with the seemingly endless one of negotiating among warring exile factions, together took a toll on his already fragile health; on July 26, when Martí shipped one thousand copies of *Ramona* to Mercado, he described himself as emerging from "a lengthy prostration, full of remorse for having abandoned during it all work that did not require a firm deadline, or that demanded any concentration of spirit."[55] Shortly afterward a physically and spiritually exhausted Martí withdrew, first to a spa in Brooklyn's Bath Beach from which he made daily trips to Manhattan, then more completely to a retreat in the Catskill Mountains in hopes of replenishing himself for the struggles to come.

By the fall Martí had sufficiently recovered from his latest bout of sarcoidosis to help plan the upcoming October 10 commemoration of the start of the Ten Years' War.[56] These celebrations had by now passed into tradition for Cubans in New York and elsewhere, and were especially important for raising funds and awareness of the homeland's ongoing plight. Martí's October 10 speech was not as long or fiery as in previous years, perhaps due to residual weakness after the recent illness. The speech is important, however, for Martí's broaching the subject of race, which had long beset the Cuban cause and been partly responsible for its unraveling at the end of the Ten Years' War. Martí framed his praise of former revolutionary president Tomás Estrada Palma, who was in the audience, and his fellow hero Ignacio Agramonte explicitly in terms of race, noting their loyalty to the black Cubans who had fought alongside them: "We will tell [Afro-Cubans] . . . what in the majesty of his tent Ignacio Agramonte used to say of the mulatto Ramón Agüero: 'This is my brother.'"[57]

Although the problem of racism and its divisive influence on previous revolutionary projects was not news to Martí, its potential to unravel what could now be his last, best chance to liberate Cuba from Spanish rule compelled him to address it directly. Racism had certainly been on Martí's mind in the weeks before the October 10 commemoration; in a September 26 letter to Núñez, he noted disapprovingly "how around here there lurk those evil passions, and how blacks are considered little more than beasts."[58] Martí would later tackle the problem of racism at greater length in essays such as "Mi raza" (My Race) and his classic "Nuestra América" (Our America). But is clear from both this letter and his October 1888 speech at the Masonic Temple that from early on in his leadership of the revolution he considered its resolution crucial to the mission's success.

Beyond his personal distaste for racism, Martí had a more pragmatic reason for taking such a stand. Despite the movement's recent successes and renewed momentum, New York's exiles had long waxed and waned in their support for revolution; seeing the potential danger of having the revolution's objectives relying solely on them, Martí decided to reach out to other Cuban communities that might prove more receptive to the revolutionary solution. And the most steadfast and dedicated revolutionary community, the one seemingly most compatible with his vision, was not in New York but among the more politically engaged cigar workers of Tampa and Key West, the majority of whom were black or mixed-race Cubans. If the revolution was ever to overcome the final obstacles to building a lasting, united front, its future must lie not with New York elites but among the ranks of working-class black Cubans.

AFTER THE ANNIVERSARY CELEBRATIONS OF OCTOBER 1888, Martí and his fellow conspirators carried on the daily work of preparing the eventual revolution. The enthusiasm with which his speech was received by key figures confirmed what was hardly in question before the event: that Martí was now the de facto face and voice of the revolution.[59] Now when he published editorials or wrote to defend the movement against disparaging portrayals, as he did in the pages of *El Avisador Cubano* in response to the disgruntled Juan Fernández Ruz, he was no longer another pundit, however well-known, but the spokesman and representative voice of Cuban independence.[60]

Martí's heightened profile gave him a bully pulpit from which to further consolidate the forces he had marshaled in support of his vision. It also brought him to the attention of a new audience of young Cubans galvanized by his speeches and writings and eager to fight for his vision of a free Cuba. Among this new generation of revolutionaries were Benjamín Guerra and Gonzalo de Quesada y Aróstegui, who soon became two of Martí's most skilled and loyal lieutenants.[61]

With the movement gaining momentum and his health stable for the moment, Martí continued to speak out and write for the next several months. On March 25, 1889, he achieved another breakthrough, with the publication of a lengthy letter to the editor of the *Evening Post* bringing the cause of Cuban independence to a broader English-language readership. During his first decade in New York, Martí had seen the United States rise from the ashes of war and Reconstruction to become a strong and prosperous nation. He now watched with growing alarm as the nation that had reached the limits of outward expansion "from sea to shining sea" turned its gaze outward, toward its southern neighbors. The national mood was becoming decidedly expansionist, with a new generation eager to continue the glorious exploits of its forebears. Manifest Destiny was making a political comeback in the new dream not of expanding the nation's own borders but of spreading American values and capitalism to territories beyond them. Cuba's rich resources and strategic location, combined with Spain's economic troubles and ongoing difficulties in maintaining control of its unruly colony, made the island a prime focus of expansionist speculation.[62]

In his work as a foreign correspondent Martí had long followed economic and political developments in the United States, writing on topics ranging from the 1888 presidential election and the rise of organized labor to the nation's burgeoning expansionist ambitions. It was this last issue that most informed Martí's shifting attitude toward his adopted country. The sometimes uneasy combination of admiration and wariness that marked his earlier writings on the United States had morphed into a sense of foreboding at both its increasingly disdainful treatment of its southern neighbors and its imperial designs on the hemisphere. This shift in Martí's attitude toward the United States is visible as far back as his 1886 writings on "The Great Workers' Strikes in the United States," in which he compares the unions to revolutionary figures, from Christ to Luther to those of the French Revolution, arising to challenge systemic oppression. Thus the appearance in the March 16 issue of the Philadelphia paper *The Manufacturer* of an editorial titled "Do We Want Cuba?" that broadly insulted the island's population and openly questioned its capacity for self-government offered Martí a golden opportunity to challenge American assumptions of moral superiority and assert the independence movement's competence and viability.[63]

Martí encountered "Do We Want Cuba?" as it was reprinted five days later in the *Evening Post* of New York with added commentary applauding and embellishing the original essay's slanders against the Cuban people.[64] He composed his response under the title "Vindication of Cuba" and mailed it to the *Evening Post* that day. Martí's rebuttal in the March 25 edition of the *Post* is from its opening words a marvel of controlled indignation:

> Sir: I beg to be allowed the privilege of referring in your columns to the injurious criticism of the Cubans printed in the *Manufacturer* of Philadelphia, and reproduced in your issue of yesterday.
>
> This is not the occasion to discuss the question of the annexation of Cuba. It is probable that no self-respecting Cuban would like to see his country annexed to a nation where the leaders of opinion share towards him the predjudices excusable only to vulgar jingoism or rampant ignorance. No honest Cuban will stoop to be received as a moral pest for the sake of the usefulness of his land in a community where his ability is denied, his morality insulted, and his character despised. There are some Cubans who, from honorable motives, from an ardent admiration for progress and liberty, from a prescience of their powers under better political conditions, from an unhappy ignorance of the history and tendency of annexation, would like to see the island annexed to the United States. But those who have fought in war and learned in exile, who have built, by the work of hands and mind, a virtuous home in the heart of an unfriendly community . . . who have raised, with their less prepared elements, a town of workingmen where the United States had previously a few huts in a barren cliff; those, more numerous than the others, do not desire the annexation of Cuba to the United States. They do not need it. They admire this nation, the greatest ever built by liberty, but they

dislike the conditions that, like worms in the heart, have begun in this mighty republic their work of destruction.[65]

This fiery opening is followed by a lengthy, point-by-point rebuttal of the original article interspersed with Martí's expressions of offense at its authors' "ignorance of history and character" in making such "wanton assertions" regarding Cuba's struggle for freedom.[66] After comparing the Cuban revolution in its ideals and historical scope to that of the United States itself, Martí concludes with the ironic observation that among the very obstacles facing Cubans are "the just fears of [some] that our dead . . . would be but the fertilizers of the soil for the benefit of a foreign plant, or the occasion for a sneer from the *Manufacturer* of Philadelphia."[67]

In its intellectual rigor and rhetorical fire, Martí's letter served notice to English-language readers that, far from being "helpless, lazy, deficient in morals, and incapable by nature and experience of fulfilling the obligations of citizenship in a great and free republic," Cubans had both the capacity and inherent right to aspire to the same benefits of freedom and self-government as their disdainful northern neighbors.[68] Martí's subsequent circulation of his letter in Spanish, along with translations of the original articles, in a pamphlet titled "Cuba and the United States," dealt a major blow to the annexationists, who had been gaining in numbers and credibility. It also made him the toast of the exile community, as his Front Street office was besieged with congratulatory mail from across Latin America and visits from those wishing to praise him in person for his courageous stand.[69] Most importantly, Martí's "Vindication of Cuba" cemented among exiles the conviction that American imperialism was as dangerous an enemy as the Spanish Empire they sought to overthrow in Cuba.

IN THE MONTHS THAT FOLLOWED MARTÍ'S "VINDICATION," he continued to busy himself with writing projects, notably the short-lived children's magazine *La edad de oro*.[70] He helped found La Liga, an organization that offered classes in literacy and basic education at no charge to working-class, mostly Afro-Cuban exiles.[71] A recurrence of symptoms of Martí's chronic sarcoidosis slowed him for much of August, but he recovered in time for the first International Conference of American States in October.

The conference was the brainchild of secretary of state and onetime presidential aspirant James G. Blaine as part of his "big brother" policy, a refinement of the Monroe Doctrine to consolidate U.S. power in the hemisphere by extending its influence among Latin American states.[72] For Martí, the conference was U.S. imperialism incarnate, the very embodiment of the movement's worst fears regarding its rapacious northern neighbor. From his position as consul for Uruguay, he occupied a perfect vantage point from which to closely observe the conference—and do whatever he could to undermine and frustrate its thinly veiled designs. Martí immediately set to work raising the exiles' awareness of the conference's implications for the prospects of Cuban independence and rallying Latin American public opinion against its aims. Beginning with an August 31 interview for the magazine *Export and Finance* and his interactions with the arriving delegates from Argentina and Uruguay the following months, Martí worked tirelessly in his capacity as Uruguayan consul to alert participants and the broader public to the conference's underlying political motives. He published in the Buenos Aires newspaper *La Nación* the first of twelve essays spanning nine months and focusing on the conference proceedings.[73] With his publication of the final issue of *La edad de oro* in October, Martí planned to turn his full attention to the conference.[74]

The International Conference of American States convened in Washington, D.C., on October 2, in advance of the delegates embarking on a six-week tour by rail that took them as far west as Chicago. Eight days into the conference, Martí gave his annual keynote speech in New York at the October 10 commemoration of the first Cuban insurrection by beating the war drums as loudly as ever, invoking Admiral Nelson at Waterloo and Imam Schamyl, who led the resistance against Russian annexation of the Caucasian nations, alongside Cuba's own heroes.[75] The speech's final image of a Cuban nation raised "in the arms of a free America" indicates both Martí's opposition to U.S. hegemony and his renewed hemispheric vision of "Our America" as a pan-Hispanic independence movement.[76]

With the October 10 festivities over, Martí focused almost exclusively on the proceedings of the International Conference of American States in Washington. In his regular columns for *La Nación* he revealed U.S. machinations for Latin American readers while working behind the scenes to influence the proceedings whenever possible. On October 29 he alerted Gonzalo de Quesada, whom he had placed as secretary to the Argentinean delegation, to annexationist plans to be presented by anti-independence elements.[77] In his November 2 column he exposed the U.S. plan to impose binding arbitration on the conference member-states as a way of resolving international disputes. The U.S. proposal, which would have any such disputes adjudicated by a tribunal in Washington, understandably drew the ire of the Latin American delegates and led to the adoption of an alternative plan. Martí reported in *La Nación* that arbitration

> would be an excellent thing, if it did not mean submission of America's principal issues, which are soon to be, if they are not changed in time, those of its relations with the people of the United States, with different interests in the world, and contrary ones on the continent, from those

of the [Latin] American peoples, to a tribunal in which, by those wonders that helped Cortez triumph in Mexico and Alvarado in Guatemala,
there were not cause to fear, by the power of the purse, or of dazzle-
ment, that the lion may have more votes than the courageous colt or the
trusting buck to oppose the chorus of sheep.[78]

Martí made the most of the opportunity to directly influence conference
delegates who spent the Christmas holidays in New York by organizing a
December party at which he delivered one of his most renowned speeches,
known informally as "Mother America": "However great this land may be,"
Martí declared to the assembled delegates, "for us, in the secret of our hearts
. . . the greater land, because it is ours and because it has suffered more, is the
land of [Benito] Juárez's birth."[79] Although the conference would resume after
the holidays and continue for another four months, Martí resolved to remain
vigilant to what he considered a clear and present danger to his hopes for a free
Cuba.

But Martí's singular focus on the International Conference of American
States in addition to his ongoing writing deadlines and consular duties created
a vacuum in the revolutionary ranks that others eventually moved to fill. The
closed two-party system adopted in Restoration Spain in 1881, known as the
"peaceful turn," dictated that power alternate every two years between conservative and liberal prime ministers. What this meant for Cuba was a decadelong
game of *fort-da*, with liberal reforms followed by their revision or withdrawal
under the succeeding conservative regime. When in January 1890 the Spanish
government under liberal Prime Minister Práxedes Mateo Sagasta announced
the removal of prohibitions for exiles to travel to Cuba, Antonio Maceo took
immediate advantage. Maceo arrived at Santiago de Cuba on January 30 for the
purpose of gauging the island's capacity and appetite for a new war.

Maceo's arrival in Santiago, his hometown, created a near-riot among the
townspeople who had long considered him a national hero. A few days later
the rebel general traveled to Havana, where admirers including Flor Crombet,
who had himself come to Cuba under the new amnesty, organized a banquet
in his honor. The incredulous pair, disbelieving their luck at not having to filibuster or otherwise invade the island to launch an insurrection, proceeded to
plan an uprising later in the year. Unfortunately for them, the prime minister's
office changed hands in July, and the new colonial governor appointed by the
incoming conservative government was alarmed at the sudden convergence of
former insurgents and the uproar their presence was causing. He promptly had
Maceo and Crombet deported on August 30.[80]

Shortly after their expulsion from Cuba, Maceo and Crombet returned to
New York with news of their enthusiastic reception on the island. Martí im-

mediately organized an event for the unexpected arrivals, but to his great surprise the war heroes received a relatively cold welcome, with many prominent exiles staying away from the gathering. Maceo mistakenly interpreted the
exiles' absence as indicative of the community's "glacial indifference" toward
revolution; he had not considered that many exiles, committed to the comprehensive, incremental plan that received Gómez's blessing, no longer had any
interest in the spontaneous expeditions of individual generals—or those that
did not include Gómez's direct participation.[81]

Maceo's sparsely attended event was not the first hint for Martí that enthusiasm was again waning in New York. A similar event earlier in the year featuring Emilio Núñez and other Ten Years' War veterans had drawn a significantly
smaller crowd—and payday—than either man expected.[82] With the notable exception of the annual October 10 celebrations, exile interest in revolution had
declined considerably from its high-water mark of March 1889, when Martí's
"Vindication of Cuba" for a time galvanized popular support. What was missing, he knew, was Gómez, who although pledged in principle continued to
evade any specific commitment. This malaise preceded Maceo's failed New
York visit by several months, yet by June 1890, when Martí wrote of his frustrations to fellow conspirator Juan Bonilla, he was disheartened, once again ill, and
alarmingly close to giving up:

> My discouragement is great, and I stumble along, as one who is falling
> apart along the way and carries on, retrieving fallen pieces of himself. I
> have but one faith and it is in a few hearts. If they fail me, or do not see
> me,—then, Juan, we must throw in the towel ...
>
> I have not fought badly, my dear Juan, these last few months, despite
> my feeling sometimes of impending death [*moridera*].[83]

With the revolution at an apparent impasse and Gómez showing no sign
of ending his Hamlet act, Martí's own involvement for a time diminished significantly. By mid-June he had wrapped up his popular series on the recently
concluded International Conference of American States,[84] and in late July he
accepted not one but two additional consular positions, for Argentina and Para-
guay. But by then Martí had grown so debilitated by overwork that his sarcoidosis returned, and at Carmita Mantilla's insistence he withdrew to the Catskills
for nearly a month to recuperate.[85]

Martí's only notable revolutionary activities for the rest of 1890 were the unsuccessful Maceo-Crombet event and his keynote speech at the annual October 10 commemoration. Aside from these and a few smaller speaking engagements, he retreated to his journalistic work and consular duties. Martí began
work on two of his most widely celebrated and enduring writings: the volume

of poems that would become his *Versos sencillos* and the canonical essay "Nuestra América."

Foremost on Martí's mind, however, was his impending appointment as Uruguay's representative at the Monetary Conference of the American Republics, a major gathering to be held in Washington starting in January 1891 that promised to occupy much of his time during the last months of 1890.[86] After the mixed outcome of the previous year's pan-American gathering, the monetary conference was Secretary of State Blaine's latest move to consolidate U.S. power in the hemisphere; its primary agenda was a holdover proposal from the previous year's international conference for the establishment of a common silver-based currency to be printed in each country but accepted among all American states.[87] Beyond Blaine's foreign policy agenda, the Harrison administration saw the proposal as a way of stabilizing the U.S. dollar, which was at its weakest point since the adoption of a bimetallic (gold and silver) monetary policy in 1878. Over the next decade the price of gold remained relatively stable, but that of silver dropped sharply due to its increased production in western states. The surplus without a viable outlet was seriously undermining the value of the dollar; Blaine's proposal, if adopted at the monetary conference, would alleviate the glut by putting silver coins into circulation all across the hemisphere.[88] But for Martí, the silver issue was another U.S. attempt to dictate economic policy to the rest of the continent and wield power over its southern neighbors for its own benefit. The monetary conference and the threat that Martí believed it posed would require his full attention in the coming months. The revolution, if it was ever to happen at all, would have to wait.

"NUESTRA AMÉRICA" APPEARED IN PRINT FOR THE FIRST time on New Year's Day 1891, an appropriate date for an essay that in many ways marked the turn of a new era for both Martí and the revolution.[89] With the upcoming monetary conference very much on his mind, Martí channeled his deep apprehension regarding U.S. hemispheric ambitions into a clarion call for resistance across the southern continent. His long-held dream of a united Mother America emerges in "Nuestra América" with the added urgency of a rallying cry, as Martí urges his fellow Latin Americans to look beyond their own borders and narrow self-interests to see the larger threat that faced them all:

> The conceited villager thinks the entire world to be his backyard, and so long as he remains its mayor, or torments the rival who stole his girlfriend, or his savings continue to grow, believes all is good in the world, ignorant of giants with seven-league boots who can bring that boot down upon him, or of the battle of comets in the heavens that traverse the dormant skies swallowing entire worlds. What is left of the village in

America had better awaken. These are not times for sleeping in a head-
sock, but for sleeping with our weapons . . .

We can no longer be a people of leaves adrift on the air, with our cup
full of flowers, crackling or humming according to the caress of capri-
cious sunlight, or the beating or slashing of the storm; the trees must
hold the line, that the seven-league giant may not pass! It is the hour
of reckoning, and of the united march, and we should close ranks, as
closely as veins of silver in the Andes.[90]

Having had his fill of lukewarm commitments and conditional half-measures,
a furious Martí also lashes out at the ambivalent in the very language that was directed at him during his withdrawal from the revolution, tarring the uncommit-
ted as Europeanized effeminates with "painted nails and bracelets" and "seven-
month" weaklings who, "lacking valor, deny [that of] others."[91] In a throwback
to the earlier vision of his Guatemalan writings on Mother America, however,
Martí reserved the essay's most memorable language for a loving portrait of
Latin America's indigenous peoples and their founding role in its present nations. "Of what country can a man be so proud," he asks, "as of our afflicted
republics of America, raised among the silent masses of Indians . . . upon the
bloodied arms of a century of apostles?"[92]

Beyond his saber rattling and denunciations of others' inaction and self-
interest, Martí's larger thesis in "Nuestra América" is directed squarely at his
fellow delegates to the upcoming monetary conference. As captured most con-
cisely in the declaration that "the imported book in America has been defeated
by the natural man," he presents his long-held vision of a Latin America that
depends for its viability on its own unique cultural and political institutions, not
those artificially grafted from European models. The key to proper governance
of its nations thus becomes clear: "To govern is to create" and the process of
governing "the analysis of those elements peculiar to the peoples of America."[93]

For Martí the continent's greatest threat came not from within but from an
impending confrontation "with an enterprising and vigorous nation that does
not know us yet scorns us."[94] Although Martí explicitly linked the obsolete "imported book" with Europe, his invocation of that other, northern America as
the looming "seven-league giant" could not be more ominous. The continent's
only hope to "confront and divert" the looming giant was to reveal itself as a
united equal: "our America's urgent duty is to show ourselves as we are, one in
soul and purpose. . . . By its ignorance, it may, perhaps, set upon her its greed.
Out of respect, once it knows her, it may stay its hand."[95] Emerging from the
seemingly hyperbolic language and apocalyptic imagery of "Nuestra América"
is delegate Martí's stark memo to his counterparts: for Latin America's young
republics to survive the threat of cultural, political, and economic subjugation

under the northern boot heel, they had to embrace policies together that were specifically tailored to the needs and aspirations of their own peoples. To act in mere imitation of the United States or otherwise submit to its imperatives in the governance of their own countries was to invite disaster.

With the publication of "Nuestra América" in New York and its later reprinting in Mexico's *El Partido Liberal*, Martí offered an unmistakable preview of his mindset entering the monetary conference. Delays in processing Martí's request for credentials for the conference kept him away from its inaugural session on January 7, but when the conference reconvened on the morning of February 4, Martí was in attendance. The delegates did not discover until reading the next morning's papers that while they were in session, the U.S. Senate passed a bill authorizing the free coinage of silver. The timing of the bill dismayed many delegates, for whom it revealed the U.S. government's true motives for a common silver currency.[96] For Martí, it further confirmed that the continent's northern "big brother" was not operating in the best interests of its fellow nations. As the House had yet to vote on the bill, conference delegates opted to table discussion of the common-currency proposal until March.[97]

For the conference's next session, on March 23, the United States adjusted its strategy somewhat; its delegation moved for immediate discussion of a new proposal for a subsequent conference in London at which delegates would ratify a common bimetallic policy for all American states that would fix the value of gold and silver. But many delegates balked at assessing the new proposal and voted to table discussion until the following week.

Throughout the conference Martí sought to keep abreast of Cuba-related developments, especially any that signaled U.S. interest in annexation. He was thus dismayed to read newspaper accounts of Blaine's visit to the island following the March conference meeting. The presence on the same trip of John Watson Foster, a high-ranking State Department official and expert on Latin America, alarmed Martí, as it confirmed the United States' growing interest in annexing Cuba at a time when neither the revolutionary movement nor the broader exile community was prepared to fight. With the conference soon to end, he now faced the possibly futile task of returning to New York to launch by necessity the kind of premature intervention the movement was designed to prevent. And if he could not persuade Gómez to lead the new uprising, its prospects looked grim indeed.

There first remained the matter of defeating Blaine's monetary scheme. If Martí could not prevent the United States from dooming his efforts to liberate Cuba, he reasoned, he could at least help slow its hegemony over the rest of the hemisphere. He also hoped that the monetary conference's failure would deal "a death blow to Blaine's candidacy" for the presidency in 1892, which if not averted would mean a much more aggressively expansionist United States.[98]

When the monetary conference reconvened on March 30, it was Martí who made the motion to defer indefinitely a decision to arrange the U.S.-proposed London monetary conference. After lengthy discussion, Martí's motion passed, essentially killing U.S. hopes of establishing a common hemispheric currency.[99]

That evening Martí attended a dinner hosted by Matías Romero, the Mexican diplomat who served as president of the monetary conference. There Romero briefed Martí on the rapidly deteriorating situation in Cuba, advising him that it was the deeply indebted Spanish government, not the Cubans themselves, who were trying to negotiate the island's annexation. According to Romero, this was not an attractive prospect for the United States, which wanted no part of governing against their will a population so prone to armed resistance.[100] If Romero was right, conditions were considerably more propitious for insurrection than Martí had imagined. A jubilant Martí immediately wrote to Gonzalo de Quesada: "The way is clear! Clear at last, clear and better positioned than ever, to prepare, if we wish, the revolution, ordained in Cuba, and with arms open wide!"[101] With a successful rebellion suddenly within his grasp, Martí had no desire to attend the conference's final session on April 4 and returned immediately to New York. The time to fight seemed finally to be at hand.

UPON HIS RETURN TO NEW YORK, A REINVIGORATED MARTÍ plunged into his work, continuing to prepare the revolution while maintaining a busy writing and speaking schedule. The news that his wife was preparing a return to New York with Pepito heartened Martí, who was cautiously optimistic that they might achieve some sort of reconciliation.[102] It is not clear why Carmen chose this moment to return to New York or indeed whether the decision was unilateral on her part. But Martí had long pined for his son, whom "Carmen [had retained] in Cuba for longer than is fair," and the prospect of seeing Pepito again may have overridden his misgivings about the reunion.[103]

In the six years since Carmen had left him the second time, Martí had found in Carmita Mantilla the home and partner denied him by her departure. Daughter María Mantilla affirmed in a 1935 letter to her own son, the actor Cesar Romero, that Martí "found in [Carmita] all the comfort, support, love and warmth that he never found in his own wife."[104] Martí's mother also came to embrace Carmita and value her presence in his life; Leonor was already corresponding with her "dear Carmita" before meeting her during her New York visit, and the two enjoyed a familial rapport vastly different from Leonor's relations with the more guarded and circumspect Carmen.[105] Martí's abandonment by Carmen and ongoing relationship with Carmita was common knowledge among the New York exiles, most of whom thought of them as a de facto married couple. Those close to Martí knew that his enduring bond with Carmita had been a source of comfort and strength through difficult times.

Since Carmen's March 1885 departure the couple had not only physically separated but had grown truly estranged. Martí never faltered in his financial obligations to Carmen and Pepito, and his contributions to them increased in proportion to his successes as a writer. But the two had exchanged letters only twice in the previous four years and not at all in the nine months preceding Carmen's June 30 arrival in New York.[106] Despite this apparent absence of any real affinity remaining between them and the contentment of Martí's relationship with Carmita, it pained him deeply to think of his son growing up without him. He also, more out of a sense of duty than any hope of rekindling the flame, did not want to give up on his marriage so long as it stood any chance of redemption. So in June 1891 Martí left his home of six years with Carmita Mantilla and took up residence at the Hotel Phoenix in Upper Manhattan, where he awaited the arrival of Carmen and Pepito.

The reunion went badly. Much had changed in Martí's life since he and Carmen last met; he had gained considerable fame as a journalist, poet, and political pundit, and he now enjoyed a growing reputation as a skilled negotiator and diplomat. But the core dynamic driving the couple's discord was unaltered by the years apart; Martí was as committed to revolution as he had ever been, and Carmen had, if anything, grown even more entrenched in her opposition. Shortly after her arrival with Pepito, the Martís took a short holiday on Bath Beach in a bid to avoid the summer heat and, perhaps, insulate Carmen for a time from Martí's daily political activities.[107] Upon their return to the city, however, the truth of Martí's immersion in revolutionary politics would have been inescapable for Carmen. It is also inconceivable for her not to have learned of her husband's cohabitation with Carmita Mantilla, although given Martí's romantic history and her own long absence, the fact should have come as no surprise.

But the tipping point for Carmen may have been the publication during her stay of Martí's *Versos sencillos*, a virtual autobiography of his inner life and emotional history that exposed his feelings of resentment and regret toward her. It was not the first time Martí had assailed her in print, as his 1885 novel *Amistad funesta* constituted a veiled indictment of their marriage and her responsibility for its failure. But *Versos sencillos* laid bare the bitterness and despair of the "tortured soul" that inhabits its pages—as well as the underlying cause and source of its agony:

XXXVII

Here is my chest, woman,
Which I know you will wound;
Larger it should be,
That you may wound it all the more!

Because I note, tortured soul,
That in my miraculous chest,
The deeper the wound,
The more beautiful my song.[108]

The knowledge that Martí had read aloud from these poems, perhaps this one, at a gathering the previous winter attended by many of the couple's mutual friends would only have added insult to the grievous injury.[109]

By August Carmen had seen enough. We do not know why she chose to leave New York with Pepito without a final confrontation, without even saying goodbye; perhaps her sense of betrayal and humiliation drove her to leave Martí in the most hurtful possible manner. He was away at Sea Cliff in Long Island, helping to care for a former colleague's widow who had fallen ill, when Carmen made her move. She went to the office of Martí's fellow revolutionary Enrique Trujillo, imploring him to intercede with the Spanish consulate to grant expedited passports for her and Pepito. Trujillo shared Martí's desire for a free Cuba and had participated in his early revolutionary efforts, but the two had a serious falling-out in 1887, when Trujillo chose not to invite Carmita Mantilla to a gathering in honor of Leonor Martí's birthday.[110] It is not clear whether Carmen chose Trujillo because she knew of his enmity with her husband or if she had learned of the incident that ended their friendship. What we know is that Trujillo acted swiftly on Carmen's behalf and that on August 27 she and Pepito left New York—and Martí—for good.

Upon his return to the Hotel Phoenix, an astonished Martí learned of his family's escape from downstairs neighbor Clara Pujals, whom Carmen had charged with breaking the news. Pujals later recalled that he visibly blanched upon hearing the news and on his way up to his apartment turned suddenly and said: "There was a man who was crucified once, but I am crucified every day." He did not sleep at all that night, the muffled tap of his pacing feet punctuating the air above the Pujalses' bed.[111] Martí left the Hotel Phoenix shortly afterward and went home to Carmita. He never saw his wife or son again.

CARMEN'S SUDDEN DEPARTURE DEVASTATED MARTÍ NOT only emotionally but physically, triggering a recurrence of his symptoms that debilitated him intermittently for several months.[112] The timing of this most recent episode was especially inauspicious, as having largely avoided revolutionary activities during Carmen's abortive stay he strove to redouble his efforts in advance of the October 10 commemorations. Conscious of both the time wasted and the window of opportunity that seemed to be opening, Martí saw his upcoming speech as a chance to rally himself as well as his fellow exiles to the task of revolution.

Martí's address at Hardman Hall at the October 10 celebration returned him to the rhetorical fire of former years, indicating his own sense of urgency and a desire to rouse his audience. In sometimes confrontational language he commanded the crowd to snap out of its complacency and chided the unwilling: "The habit of yielding," he declared, "blunts the capacity to dare. Let the timid and the sterile make way for those with the sense to respect it!"[113] Denouncing those "timid" Cubans who still hoped to avert bloodshed via annexation or autonomy, Martí's words left no room for conciliation or compromise with the colonizer: "What are we here, Cubans or enemies of Cuba? Adventurers or pirates? Marauders or redeemers?"[114]

The Cubans who witnessed Martí's speech that night were not the only ones stirred to action. One of the several Spanish spies who attended the gathering filed a lengthy report that their employer at New York's Spanish consulate circulated widely, including to Governor Camilo de Polavieja in Havana and Spain's U.S. ambassador in Washington.[115] The report's author describes a Hardman Hall "full to the brim, to the point that many ladies and young girls had to stand in the back, and others, for lack of space, had to leave."[116] Nor was Martí the only draw or most warmly received figure present that evening; the Spanish agent reports that Martí's protégé Quesada also wowed the audience as the opening speaker, and war hero General Francisco Carrillo was singled out from the crowd and received an ovation "that lasted by the clock a quarter of an hour."[117] Martí apparently read aloud, "amidst a frightful clamor," a telegram sending greetings from their counterparts' October 10 celebrations in Key West.[118] The Spanish spies identified "more than ten peninsulars" (native Spaniards), among the seven hundred in attendance, "who applauded incessantly."[119]

Neither Martí's insurrectional activities nor his diplomatic work were news to the Spanish consulate or the various agents who shadowed him. As late as September 18, Spain's consul in New York had dismissed published newspaper reports of exile plans for another revolution as "intentionally hyperbolic" and of "scarce importance."[120] The resounding success of the October 10 event greatly alarmed Spain's official representatives and the pro-Spanish press in New York. They immediately denounced in the press and the embassies of the countries Martí represented his participation in such an openly seditious event. Martí responded by immediately resigning all his diplomatic positions, explaining that he did not wish his revolutionary affiliations to be the cause of strained relations between them and Spain.[121] As he had prematurely done once before, Martí again sacrificed his livelihood to devote himself fully to the revolution he was now certain must come.

Yet Martí could not realistically move without Gómez, and Gómez had shown no desire to rejoin the movement. With exile support for the revolution at its peak following the October 10 gathering, Martí believed the movement to be in danger of squandering its greatest opportunity. The waxing and waning of the New York exiles' appetite for revolution had long vexed Martí, who dreamed of the kind of unyielding support enjoyed by separatist groups in Florida. Cubans in Tampa and Key West were committed supporters of independence and its most reliable underwriters. As the older of the two, Key West had since the Ten Years' War been a required stop on the itinerary of any would-be revolutionary seeking to finance the next filibuster. Tampa's Cuban community had actually started in the mid-1880s as an offshoot of the older group, as some Key West cigar businesses relocated northward to enjoy the advantages of a new railroad. The Cuban-built suburb of Ybor City was now home to the city's thriving cigar industry and predominantly black Cuban population.[122] Key West and Tampa were hotbeds of revolution, prosperous Cuban enclaves that would make much more reliable partners than New York's more fickle and divided community—if he only had the chance to win them over.

That opportunity followed closely the resounding success of October 10, when on November 16 a thrilled Martí received—and quickly accepted—an invitation from Néstor L. Carbonell, president of Tampa's Ignacio Agramonte Club.[123] Here at last was his chance to sell his vision to the city's engaged and energized cigar workers. If he could convince them, and especially Key West's workers, to unite behind a single, overarching revolutionary project that would serve all of their interests, the squabbling New Yorkers—and more importantly, Gómez—would have no choice but to fall in line.

Although Martí knew Tampa's exiles to be fervent advocates for independence, he could not have been prepared for the enthusiasm and sheer raucousness of their welcome. His train reached Ybor City late at night on November 25, and despite a torrential downpour, hundreds of Cubans awaited him. Bands playing, people jostling for the chance to shake his hand, the jubilant crowd formed a procession that more or less spontaneously conducted their pleasantly bewildered guest to the nearby Liceo, where an even greater and more jubilant crowd burst into boisterous applause as he climbed the Liceo steps. Accounts describe the crowd falling into stone silence as Martí briefly spoke. Then the mass of happy Cubans converged upon him again in a blur of ovations and handshaking and back-slapping; after a time they carried Martí off literally on their shoulders through the streets of Ybor City in the early hours of a Thursday morning singing the Ten Years' War–era hymn of independence known as the "Bayamo Anthem" and eventually delivering him to the door of host Néstor Carbonell.[124]

It was more than he could have dared hope for. Here at last were the revolutionaries of his dreams, Cubans who did not need firing up, whose commitment and ardor were a match for his own. On this night Martí glimpsed the revolution's future—and it was not in New York.

The next three days were a whirlwind of activity for Martí, with well-wishers and supporters at every turn and crowds packing the Liceo for his speeches. On November 26 Martí met with representatives from Tampa-area revolutionary clubs to help draft a manifesto they called "Resolutions," which the group then ratified as representing their groups' collective beliefs and principles.[125] He gave his first Tampa speech at the Liceo before a crowd that filled every seat and spilled into the aisles and onto the stage around the podium. That night Martí delivered one of his most famous speeches, which has come to be known by its indelible closing phrase, "With all, and for the good of all."[126]

Martí's first address to Tampa's Cubans skillfully distilled a decade of revolutionary speeches into a single, cogent call for solidarity and support. From his opening portrayal of Cuba "as an altar on which to offer our lives, not a pedestal on which to raise ourselves," Martí announced his revolution as a collective one, inviting all into a partnership of equals sacrificing for the common good.[127] He offered a virtual catalogue of potential problems and contradictions raised by the revolution's opponents, from waning enthusiasm to self-interest, from a diminished appetite for bloodshed to fears of racial discord, and he dismissed each with the phrase "They lie."[128] The end of Martí's speech triggered a reprise of the previous evening as the impassioned Cubans again carried their new champion on happy shoulders through the Tampa streets as they sang hymns to the revolution.[129]

The following day marked the twentieth anniversary of the wrongful execution in Havana of eight medical students whom Martí had helped enshrine as the revolution's first martyrs. In keeping with the anniversary's somber nature, Martí traded the rhetorical fire of the previous night for a solemn, even reverent tribute to the students' "beautiful and useful deaths," which he urged his audience to celebrate as contributions to a better future: "Death gives lessons and examples, death guides our finger across the book of life: from such enduring invisible ties are woven the soul of a nation!"[130] Martí's November 27 speech came to be known by its closing image of young revolutionaries as "new pines" (*pinos nuevos*):

> Let us sing today, before their unforgettable tomb, the hymn of life. Yesterday I heard it from the earth itself, as I came, through the darkening day, to this faithful town. . . . Up toward those tattered clouds stretched a single pine tree, defying the storm, raising its crown to the sky. The sun broke suddenly over a clearing, and there, by that sudden flash of light, I saw arising from the yellowed grass, from among the blackened trunks of the fallen, the joyful shoots of the new pines. That is what we are: new pines![131]

For the revitalized Martí the revolution was no longer the sole province of a generation of veterans. It would now fall to a new generation to take up the mantle of the Ten Years' War without repeating its mistakes or succumbing to fear or divisiveness or personal ambition or greed. What Martí saw in Tampa convinced him that the new pines were up to the task.

UPON RETURNING TO NEW YORK ON NOVEMBER 30, A RE-energized Martí immediately moved to arrange a visit to Key West, whose exile community of nearly ten thousand quadrupled Tampa's Cuban population.[132] He did not, however, want to go to Key West as merely the latest in a long line of would-be expeditionaries stumping for funds; it was crucial to the task of uniting the exiles that he be received, as he was in Tampa, as speaking for a larger movement that encompassed all Cubans. "I burn in my desire to see the Key with my own eyes," wrote Martí to fellow organizer José Dolores Poyo, publisher of Key West paper *El Yara*. "But how can I come of my own volition, as a beggar for fame seeking friends?"[133] What he needed was an invitation. "But send for me," he wrote, a request that Poyo readily granted.[134]

In the weeks that it took to arrange Martí's visit, his health again began to flag; by the time he stepped off the train in Tampa on Christmas Eve, he was suffering from an acute bronchial laryngitis and could barely speak. Upon arrival there, his telegram notified Gonzalo de Quesada that he was "sick, but nearing the noble Key."[135] Again an enthusiastic crowd gathered to accompany Martí to the Key West–bound steamer *Olivette* when it docked on Christmas Day. Another seeming multitude awaited his arrival at the dock, cheering and waving flags and banners as they followed the local representatives who escorted the exhausted and feverish visitor.

Spanish spies present at the scene in Key West reported on Martí's arrival to an alarmed Spanish consul, who in turn informed his superior of the "great number of Cubans who greeted the approaching steamer with shouts of 'Viva Cuba libre'" and gathered to meet Martí, some two hundred of whom followed him to the door of his hotel.[136] Despite his diminished state, Martí managed to give a brief talk to the leaders gathered at the Hotel Duval and another at the banquet they had organized in his honor.[137]

By the next morning Martí's condition had deteriorated sufficiently to require medical attention. Dr. Eligio Palma, a fellow Cuban, prescribed bed rest and insisted that Martí receive no visitors—an order that the patient completely disregarded. From his bed he wrote to Quesada, describing himself "surrounded by guards of love," as over the next seven days a stream of organizers, conspirators, and well-wishers passed through his rooms at the Duval.[138] Although a public event scheduled for December 27 had to be canceled, he

FIGURE 11.1. *Martí in Key West with the other founding members of the Cuban Revolutionary Party. Standing, left to right: Genaro Hernández, Serafín Bello, Aurelio Rodríguez, José G. Pompez, Frank E. Bolio, Francisco M. González. Seated, left to right: Gualterio García, José Martí, Ángel Peláez. From Gonzalo de Quesada y Miranda,* Iconografía martiana *(Havana: Oficina de Publicaciones del Consejo de Estado, 1985).*

continued to work, notably on the important documents he was drafting for ratification by the assembled Key West leaders. He was sufficiently recovered by January 3 to present for discussion his "Bases of the Cuban Revolutionary Party" and "Secret Statutes" (figure 11.1). That evening he returned to public view at a gathering of the exile leaders, and on January 4 he felt well enough to tour the key's cigar plants and address the workers at Eduardo Hidalgo Gato's factory, the largest in the area. Wherever he went that day Cubans hailed the debilitated Martí as Cuba's future liberator, and home and business owners set out banners and decorations in the colors of the Cuban flag. The workers at Gato's factory greeted Martí with strains of the "Bayamo Anthem" and festooned him with gifts. The outpouring of support was unlike anything he had ever experienced in New York, rivaling even Tampa's welcome in its show of warmth and solidarity.

Martí departed Key West for Tampa on January 6, 1892, carrying the ratified Cuban Revolutionary Party platform that the Tampa contingent also approved two days later. On the evening of January 9 he left for New York, having accomplished in less than six weeks what no individual or movement had come close to managing in twenty-three years: he had united, at least on paper, the vast majority of Florida's Cuban exiles behind the platform of a single Cuban Revolutionary Party. Martí's achievement is all the more remarkable given the maze of revolutionary clubs simultaneously at work in Key West alone. These numerous clubs, each founded by a member of a Central Cuban Convention, all communicated to some degree with the parent convention, indicating that Key West's exiles had made significant progress toward unification before Martí's visit.[139] But it was only with Martí's intervention, through both his own personal leadership and charisma and the production of a common statement of purpose, that the loosely coordinated groups melded into a single, powerful voice for change.

Martí's visits to Tampa and Key West at the end of 1891 and beginning of 1892 made him a champion of Florida's predominantly black cigar workers, whose engagement and fervor energized a revolution that had largely slumbered through the previous four years. But more important than even the workers' solidarity was their collective financial strength, which far surpassed that of New York's exile community in its level and reliability of commitment. After decades and the squandering of untold hundreds of thousands of dollars on dozens of failed uprisings, that prodigious source was harnessed by Martí to function as a single economic engine that would drive a revolution—with Martí's the primary determining voice on how and when it would be spent. After two decades spent pursuing dreams of Cuba *libre*, he had nearly everything he needed to make his dream a reality, save for one final piece.

Now it was time to rouse that final piece, Generalísimo Máximo Gómez, his own personal Cuban Achilles, out of his tent.

CHAPTER TWELVE

New York (4)

THE FINAL PUSH

Nothing can oppose now the realization and conclusion of our plans.

"TO THE PRESIDENTS OF THE CLUBS," JULY 1893

WITH THE TRIUMPHS OF TAMPA AND KEY WEST, THE New York contingent began finally, if in some cases grudgingly, to converge under Martí's leadership.[1] The most visible sign of this solidarity came in late January 1892, when Los Independientes, New York's most powerful exile organization, signed onto the Cuban Revolutionary Party "Bases" and "Secret Statutes" previously ratified in Tampa and Key West, effectively forming a single, unified revolutionary organization for the first time.[2] Martí's ascent as the revolution's civilian leader began to attract the attention of the U.S. government and thus only compounded the ongoing surveillance by Spanish agents and the Pinkerton Agency. He continued to face resistance from annexationists and a smaller pro-Spanish faction advocating a continued autonomous relationship with the mother country.

But some of Martí's harshest critics hailed from within the revolutionary ranks, as he now faced a string of attacks from political rivals wary of a suspected power grab. The rebukes of prominent veterans who accused Martí of warmongering for his own personal gain and upbraided him for not having fought in the Ten Years' War were the most threatening politically, as they might sow seeds of doubt regarding the movement's readiness and Martí's own motives. Neither the failure to respond nor a public war of words held any upside for Martí, as neither approach would accomplish the needed neutralization of such public criticisms.

The most potentially damaging of these public skirmishes began with Martí's "With All and for the Good of All" speech in Tampa in which he implicitly dismissed as lies the assessment in a recent book that Cubans were unwilling to enter another bloody conflict.[3] Ten Years' War veteran Ramón Roa then persuaded fellow war hero Enrique Collazo and two other veterans who had returned to Cuba to publish a scathing editorial in the Havana newspaper *La Lucha* portraying Martí as a cowardly opportunist sending others off to die for his own personal aims. Known as the "Roa-Collazo letter," it indicted the civilian leader as one who "did not discharge his duty as a Cuban when Cuba appealed for the efforts of her children" and who now chose to "live on the savings of Tampa's cigar workers."[4] Harshest of all was the authors' assertion that in a future war they could not "shake [Martí's] hand in the field" because he would choose to "continue giving lessons on patriotism from abroad, in the shadow of the U.S. flag."[5]

Even in their unusual brazenness such attacks were not out of the ordinary, especially coming from Cuba itself. The nicknames "Cristo Inutil" (Useless Christ), "Capitan Araña" (Captain Spider, a name for one who would send others off to fight but not go himself), and others that dogged Martí throughout his political life did not originate in the Roa-Collazo letter; he had suffered these same insults twenty years earlier in his first skirmishes with pro-Spanish newspapers in Madrid.[6] But they resounded more painfully as Martí became more widely known as a revolutionary leader and as his rivals and enemies began to mark him as someone to defeat.

This public rebuke by respected military veterans, however, posed a real threat. The circulation of such a high-profile attack on both the revolution's efficacy and moral justification had the potential to undo all its recent gains, and thus it simply had to be addressed. Yet to personally impugn the war heroes' own motives or reputations could backfire, causing a rift between civilian and military factions that Martí had long sought to avoid.

Martí's January 12 response successfully walked that rhetorical tightrope, honoring the generals' service but deploring their current position, defending the exiles' role — and his own — in the revolution while questioning his critics' choice to live and work under Spanish rule. The letter's parting shot, an open invitation to meet Collazo immediately "at the time and place you deem convenient," captures all of these rhetorical points in a marvel of passive-aggressive control: "It may be," Martí avers, that at the moment of shaking hands "the patriotic spirit that radiates from your letter . . . will allow me to forget, when I extend mine, that yours is that of a man who has slandered another."[7]

Martí's efforts to build a unified revolutionary movement paid dividends in the showdown with Collazo, as the exile community stood united behind him; even Enrique Trujillo, who was no longer on speaking terms with Martí since helping his wife leave the country, wrote in a latter to the New York paper *El Porvenir* that "everything Collazo says [in his letter] is a lie."[8] Martí ally Manuel

Sanguily wrote from Cuba to assure the exiles that José María Aguirre, one of the letter's supposed co-authors, signed it "without really knowing to what he had signed his name."[9] Although *La Lucha* did not publish Martí's response to the Roa-Collazo letter, its broad circulation beyond Havana assured that the authors were widely rebuked by the exile community.

Public attacks on the revolution lost their momentum after the Collazo incident, but the experience bolstered for Martí and his inner circle their long-held conviction that the revolution needed an official publication for the dissemination of ideas. Such a newspaper would enable optimal control and management of the movement's public positions while more effectively countering the attacks of annexationists and others. The ubiquity of Cuban newspapers in Key West had particularly impressed Martí during his December visit as a clear sign of the exiles' political vigor.[10] With the broad political and financial support of cigar workers in Florida and New York, he could now afford to publish and widely circulate a paper that would serve as the revolution's official voice. That this desire was very much on Martí's mind in January 1892 is evident in his exhortations to Key West colleague Ángel Peláez to "publish, publish. To Cuba at every opportunity," as revolutions "advance on paths of paper."[11]

His advice to Peláez neatly captures Martí's thinking behind the founding of the newspaper *Patria* in March 1892. Martí's writing had always been his weapon, both in hostile combat and as a persuasive rhetorical tool among his friends. But it was the outcry from the exile community in the aftermath of the Collazo incident that finally persuaded Martí that the time had come to launch an official paper of the revolution. At a January 21 meeting in New York of La Liga, the organization Martí had helped found for the education of working-class Cubans, the members resolved to raise the necessary funds for the new paper. The subsequent fund-raising initiative made *Patria* a reality.[12] Beginning with its first issue, on March 14, Martí served notice that the revolution would now be fought as much with words as with bullets and machetes.

Martí wasted no time in using *Patria* as the bully pulpit it was designed to be, deploying it to circulate a message of freedom and revolution well beyond New York to Cubans across the United States and the Caribbean. Unbeknown to the Spanish, who noted the paper's appearance, Martí had also arranged to circulate *Patria* clandestinely among Cubans on the island.[13]

WITH THE CONSOLIDATION IN EARLY 1892 OF THE NEW York exiles, Martí finally stood as the revolution's unquestioned civilian leader. He had engineered his ascent by successfully shifting the movement's political and economic balance of power from New York southward to Florida, where no rival had a comparable foothold. Mindful of suspicions voiced by Collazo and still nursed by some exiles that Martí was building the revolution as a springboard for his own personal gains, Martí moved to preempt such criticisms by emphasizing the movement's rigorously democratic process and by avoiding any appearance of official power. Although he was elected on April 8 by the collective membership of the New York and Florida clubs to head the party, Martí rejected the title of president in favor of that of delegate, whose powers were only those specifically vested in him by the membership. He emphasized that the Cuban Revolutionary Party itself was not designed as a permanent political organization but would disband once the revolution succeeded, to make way for parties organized by Cubans on the island.[14] Token opposition remained, mostly from Martí nemesis Trujillo and his newspaper *El Futuro*; with Martí's selection as delegate and the establishment of *Patria* as the party's official publication, the few remaining dissenters were outvoted and outmaneuvered.[15]

Nearly everyone involved saw Máximo Gómez as essential to the revolution's success. To impel Gómez's return, Martí had to demonstrate that this new and unprecedented coalition would last, that it would maintain its coherence in the face of the heightened scrutiny and unrelenting efforts of Spain and others to unravel it. Having been the sole agent and animating spirit for the revolution's solidarity, Martí now found himself obliged to enforce party unity through constant personal contact with all the major exile communities. Martí especially employed his fellow leaders to orchestrate a groundswell of support for Gómez's return, a collective clamor that the general would be unable to refuse.

Martí accomplished these crucial tasks via constant correspondence with regional party leaders but even more through a punishing travel schedule among all the centers of revolutionary activity. His successes helped fuel a proliferation of revolutionary clubs, including those in Philadelphia, New Orleans, and two more in Tampa. Exiles in Jamaica alone founded five new clubs.[16] An overlapping Puerto Rican movement began to converge with the Cuban movement, and Martí welcomed it into the fold as a partner in the fight for independence from Spain.[17] The upsurge required even more coordination and extensive travels than Martí anticipated. Over the next two years he made 135 visits to cities across the eastern United States and the Caribbean, shuttling constantly as he wove together from disparate strands the fabric of a revolution.[18]

As he entered this final, grueling phase of preparations, Martí used *Patria* to alert exiles of what would surely be Spain's greater efforts to undermine the revolution by means of espionage and propaganda, to unravel the war from within before it could materialize on the island. In the May 28 issue of *Patria*, Martí counsels Cubans to beware "the seeming friendliness" of "the enemy that seizes upon the discord that arose in the aftermath of a too-long and sluggish war"; he assures readers that in that moment of solidarity "this espionage is useless."[19] Despite these assurances, however, he remained convinced that only through constant effort and unrelenting vigilance could the Spanish threat be averted.

The question was whether his body would betray him. Martí's health had remained precarious after his December 1891 illness in Key West, and for five months afterward he suffered intermittently from various symptoms. In 1892 Martí was thirty-nine years old, but he had inherited none of his father's physical vigor; the symptoms of sarcoidosis that had occasionally weakened him in his youth—joint pain, labored breathing, and a propensity to fevers—had by now become chronic conditions. In January he rarely visited his Front Street office, leaving his bed only for revolutionary gatherings and to teach his evening classes at La Liga: "From class to bed," he writes to Rafael Serra. "I do not write, because my lung burns, and will not permit it."[20] He recovered somewhat in February, but an April 20 letter to José Dolores Poyo reveals another setback: "I am still unable to leave my bed, from which I write this. . . . Not even the best doctor knows now what ails me: my intestines broken, and a weakness that will not allow me to lift my hand."[21] During such times Martí was reduced to dictating his *Patria* articles to Gonzalo de Quesada from bed, as he was too weak to lift a pen.[22] Only through force of personality and sheer will did he manage these increasingly frequent episodes, concealing his illness from all but his inner circle and soldiering on for the cause: "'Dead' hardly describes my condition. But for my country, I live."[23]

By early July Martí was finally well enough to travel for a series of meetings across Florida. The twenty-four-day journey took Martí and his delegation, which included Poyo and Generals Serafín Sánchez and Carlos Roloff, from the established Tampa and Key West clubs to new ones in Ocala, St. Augustine, and Jacksonville.[24] In an important departure from previous insurrections, however, the generals and Martí concurred that the insurgents should also determine the existence of political and military support in Cuba and plan for a coordinated and simultaneous launch of forces on the island and from the sea. To that end, and with the Cuban Revolutionary Party's backing, on August 4 Martí sent an emissary, Gerardo Castellanos, to Cuba on a mission to establish contact with key conspirators who would assist in preparing the coming war.[25] Key to this mission was his old friend Juan Gualberto Gómez, who since Martí's 1879 deportation had remained at the center of revolutionary activity on the island.

But the main purpose of Martí's Florida sojourn was to assess the clubs' level of coordination and readiness for action. Before departing he directed the leaders of all exile organizations to take a vote among "all military veterans of the war in Cuba" to select the revolution's supreme military head in charge of "the military ordination of the Party."[26] Martí assumed, correctly, that their choice would be Máximo Gómez. In anticipation of an eventual and inevitable meeting with the general, he wanted the party's invitation to come with the full backing of Gómez's fellow veterans and the assurance that the civilian exile population had fulfilled its share of the bargain in organizing the necessary financial and political support for the decisive war.

Shortly after returning to New York, Martí published news in *Patria* of his Florida trip and the revolution's progress, notably a moving essay on his visit to the St. Augustine tomb of Félix Varela, the Cuban priest exiled in 1823 for advocating Latin American independence.[27] On August 8 he reported on his activities to the assembled New York members, who with few exceptions welcomed the good news.[28] More substantial resistance, however, was arising from without; the Spanish government, alerted by Spanish agents to the flurry of revolutionary activity, feared the possibility of a new uprising.[29] Apparently unaware of any coordination with island elements, Spain focused on the Cuban Revolutionary Party and appealed to U.S. officials to help quash the hostile forces the United States was harboring. On the one hand Spain's representatives in Washington assured Madrid that the Cubans' activities amounted to no more than "shouting, with the goal of attracting public attention to their own importance, their only means of winning the independence of Cuba."[30] Tellingly, an August 8 report from Washington describes a meeting at which U.S. Secretary of State Blaine, despite his assurances that the United States would stop the launch of any expeditions from its own shores, "regarded [the revolutionaries] as having no credibility whatsoever" and "considered them an absurdity."[31]

Spain's machinations and the mutterings of a small minority within the party notwithstanding, on August 18 the military leadership unanimously selected Máximo Gómez "to head the revolutionary military organization."[32] Martí immediately wrote to Serafín Sánchez with the news that he was now ready to meet with Gómez "to see how to adjust his situation to the general convenience, and how it may be arranged *without delay and without alarm*."[33] Martí's emphasis on avoiding both delay and alarm reveals the importance of the trip's timing and its logistics; it was crucial to avoid a long delay that might stall momentum or fuel rumors of the general's refusal while concealing Martí's visit with him from vigilant Spanish agents. He succeeded on both counts, arranging a trip to Gómez's family farm in the Dominican Republic and managing to dodge Spanish spies for several weeks.[34] After a brief retreat to Newport, Rhode Island, to prepare and rest up for the journey, Martí left New York on August 30 for the meeting that would determine the fate of the revolution.[35]

HIS SEEMING RELUCTANCE DID NOT MEAN GÓMEZ WAS UN-interested in the revolution's development. He had been closely monitoring it for some time and remained in touch with fellow veterans who had served with him in the Ten Years' War. They kept him apprised of Martí's progress and were now encouraging him to lead the burgeoning insurrection. News of the

Cuban Revolutionary Party's establishment and of Martí's unprecedented success in uniting the disparate exile clubs into a single revolutionary force raised the general's hopes; yet he still harbored reservations about working with his fiery civilian counterpart. He said of Martí that "his purity is immaculate" and acknowledged that Martí could "go to the battlefields of Cuba and fight with valor" equal to its greatest heroes. Gómez also said Martí "lacks self-restraint and is inexorable" in his grudges against slights real or imagined.[36] But the encouragement of so many fellow exiles finally persuaded Gómez to attempt a reconciliation with his erstwhile ally.

Martí arrived in the Haitian port town of Gonaives on August 7 and reached Gómez's ranch outside the town of Montecristi in the Dominican Republic four days later. The two began a conversation that unfolded over the next four days. By the time Martí presented Gómez with the party's official letter on September 15 inviting him to assume military leadership of the revolution, the once and future *generalísimo* was ready to accept.[37]

His primary objective fulfilled, Martí planned to remain on Hispaniola for several more days, meeting with exile leaders and clubs in the Dominican Republic and Haiti. A temporary ban on incoming vessels due to a cholera epidemic extended his stay in Port au Prince unexpectedly, but on October 4 he embarked on the next leg of his journey. With Gómez now reconciled to the revolution — and to Martí's equal part in it — Martí turned his attention to General Antonio Maceo.

Martí arrived in Kingston, Jamaica, on the afternoon of October 8 to visit the city's exile community, which numbered several hundred Cubans and dated back to the start of the Ten Years' War. He also paid a visit to Maceo's ranch on the outskirts of Kingston; although the general was away in Costa Rica, Martí met with the general's wife and his mother, Mariana Grajales.[38] It is not clear whether Martí notified Maceo of his intended visit or indeed whether he planned it at all before his reconciliation with Gómez. Maceo had been, if anything, even more recalcitrant than Gómez regarding Martí's leadership, an attitude he never fully relinquished. The Afro-Cuban general still held a grudge against white leaders of the Ten Years' War over their ambivalence toward abolition, which had played a strategic role in the rebels' defeat. Even with Gómez's embrace of the party and Martí, Maceo's participation remained crucial to the revolution's success. Spanish observers heartily agreed with this assessment; one surveillance report even called Maceo "the Negroes' idol" without whom "the movement would absolutely fail."[39] The Spanish knew that only Maceo could mobilize the island's black population to fight in sufficient numbers, and Martí understood that the black cigar workers' current level of support for the party would plummet if Maceo rejected its authority. Although Martí did not meet with Maceo on this trip, he believed that his presence among the Kingston workers was important enough to remain in Kingston for the revolution's October 10 commemoration of the start of the Ten Years' War.[40]

The last months of 1892 saw Martí continue his revolutionary shuttle diplomacy. He returned to New York on October 19 and three weeks later departed again for Florida with news of Gómez's return to his place at the front of the revolution. Martí spent the next six weeks in Florida spreading the word in Tampa, Key West, and Ocala and raising funds for the now-certain war of independence.[41] Energized by the revolution's momentum and the raucous ovations of supportive Cubans who greeted him at every stop, he dismissed the concerns for his safety expressed by his inner circle, perhaps underestimating how far Spanish agents or internal enemies might go to stop him.

That Martí had been too sanguine about his personal safety became clear on December 16 when a plot to poison him narrowly failed. His itinerary of the previous two days was a busy if not particularly momentous one. He and his delegation received the customarily enthusiastic welcome upon arrival in Ocala, where they attended the dedication of a new Cuban housing development named Martí City in his honor. Martí tended to other ceremonial functions in Ocala including presiding over Martí City's first wedding and accepting an honorary membership in its revolutionary club.[42] The next day's only significant event was a public speech—in English, a language with which he had grown comfortable in public—to an overflow crowd at the Marion Opera House, whereupon he received yet another honorary club membership.[43] The Martí contingent departed Ocala late that evening and arrived in Tampa in the early hours of December 16. Martí found the hotel where he had stayed on previous visits too noisy for his needs and opted this time for a quieter, private apartment where he could better rest and work between engagements. Already exhausted from weeks of work and travel, Martí gamely delivered a series of memorable public speeches over the next several days.[44]

Unbeknown to him, Spanish agents were again tailing him on this trip and noting where he stayed and with whom. The agents in turn hired two local young Cubans to infiltrate Martí's inner circle, and they offered their services as personal assistants. This was not an unusual occurrence for Martí, as workers sought his company wherever he traveled. After one particularly grueling afternoon, a drained Martí went back in his room with only the two young Cubans to attend him. Due to his precarious health and punishing schedule, Martí had come to rely on the occasional boost from Vin Mariani, a cocaine-infused wine that many legally used in those days as a stimulant.[45] He sent one of his new aides for a glass of Mariani but immediately detected an odd taste and spit it out. In the time it took him to do so, the two young men disappeared.[46] A local doctor, Miguel Barbarrosa, brought in as a precaution, confirmed that the wine had indeed been poisoned, likely with some kind of acid.

Martí's close brush with assassination shook his advisors more than it did Martí himself. Local leaders Ruperto and Paulina Pedroso insisted that Martí move to their home in Ybor City, where they could keep close watch on him. Ruperto Pedroso took to sleeping by the front door of Martí's bedroom, and other Cubans established rotations to guard the house around the clock. Martí swore Dr. Barbarrosa to secrecy and insisted that the perpetrators not be pursued or punished. But news of the assassination attempt soon spread throughout the city.

Within a few days of the failed attempt, one of the would-be assassins, whose name was Valentín, came to ask Martí's forgiveness. Over the Pedrosos' violent protests, Martí received the chastened young man, whom he took to his rooms for a private conversation. When the young Cuban left, Ruperto Pedroso again protested Martí's credulity. According to legend, Martí dismissed his guardian's fears, predicting that the would-be killer would be "among the first to fire a shot in Cuba." He was right. When the war came, the young man was among the first to join it. And by war's end the repentant young Cuban in Martí's bedroom had become war hero Commander Valentín Castro Córdoba.[47]

THE LAST WEEK OF MARTÍ'S TAMPA STAY TRANSPIRED WITH-out further incident, and by December 24 he was back in New York. Despite the life-saving instinct to spit out that first mouthful of poisoned wine, he had apparently ingested enough to weaken him considerably, and he remained for a time under medical supervision.[48] Martí wrote to Serafín Sánchez that his "illness in Tampa was not natural" and that he still suffered "the consequences of an evil that could have been averted in time."[49]

Even in his weakened condition, it was now time to begin final preparations for war. This meant the recruitment of volunteers from all the exile clubs as well as the acquisition of arms and supplies and a final fund-raising push. It also required a strategy for coordinating the insurrection's launch from both the U.S. mainland and on the island and determining a point of departure for the first expeditionary forces. Before any of this, he would need to report to the New York clubs regarding his most recent trip to Florida and announce the start of this final phase of preparations.

Political developments in Spain left the revolution little room for error. Facing worsening economic conditions and burgeoning unrest in Cuba, it became clear in Madrid that neither the surveillance of exiles nor continued appeals for help to an unsympathetic U.S. government would be enough to avert an insurrection. The Spanish government in Madrid thus embarked on a last-ditch effort to reform its relation to Cuba. In January 1893 the Ministro de Ultra-mar (Minister of Overseas Territories) Antonio Maura proposed a series of constitutional changes, including the acceptance of the Autonomists as a legiti-

mate opposition party. Maura hoped to replace the island's colonial administration with an autonomous government run by Cubans, a move calculated to
undermine the revolutionaries.[50] Martí dismissed the proposed concessions in
the pages of *Patria*, calling those clinging to autonomist hopes "guilty of a be-
ginner's romantic politics, and of a benevolent blindness."[51] But he understood
that the only sure way to avert the threat of Spanish reforms was to launch the
war before they could happen.

In February Martí received word that an emissary was coming from Cuba
with money collected for the war who also apparently brought important information relevant to the impending war. Travel had become more crucial for
Martí's work and at the same time more uncertain; after the assassination attempt he began taking great pains to conceal his whereabouts from the Spanish agents he knew shadowed his every move. He would travel at night if at all
possible, seldom stay in the same place on consecutive nights, and depart before
dawn. Only Gonzalo de Quesada, Martí's personal assistant and most trusted
aide, would know his travel routes or precise locations. These precautions made
his proposed meeting with the emissary especially complicated, as Martí could
not leave New York until he was sure to dodge enemy agents and could not reveal the location of the rendezvous to the Cuban visitor until shortly before his
arrival.[52]

Martí arrived in Savannah, Georgia, on February 13 or 14 and upon arrival
moved the meeting some 130 miles south to Fernandina, a seaport just across
the border on Florida's Amelia Island.[53] Three or four days passed before Martí
finally met the Cuban envoy, who turned out to be General Julio Sanguily, a
hero of the Ten Years' War. Upon seeing Fernandina Beach, the two agreed that
it would be an excellent place from which to launch the exile forces.[54]

Although by subterfuge Martí managed to temporarily throw Spanish
agents off the trail, word of his presence in Fernandina soon spread. To avert
speculation regarding the seaport as a possible departure point for the war, he
proceeded to make the rounds of the various Florida clubs in hopes of making
Fernandina appear as just another fund-raising stop.[55]

Upon returning to New York on March 9, Martí worked relentlessly to raise
the funds necessary to launch the war. Despite years of such efforts and the selfless contributions of thousands of Cubans, by its own calculations the Cuban
Revolutionary Party remained many thousands of dollars short of the amount
necessary to arm and support the thousands of men preparing to fight.[56] Thus
in late April Martí moved to expand his field of operations, making fund-raising
visits to exile clubs in Philadelphia, Atlanta, and New Orleans. He spent no
more than a day in each city, hoping with his multicity itinerary to evade Spanish agents before departing for his other crucial objective: to meet in Costa Rica
with General Antonio Maceo, the revolution's last important holdout.

On April 29 Martí was set to depart New Orleans to meet Maceo when news broke of a rogue uprising in Cuba led by brothers Manuel and Ricardo Sartorius in the eastern province of Holguín. In truth, the incident hardly qualified as a rebellion, as it consisted at its peak of no more than sixty badly armed men.[57] Yet precisely because of its disorganized, impromptu nature, the surprise rebellion threatened to damage the true revolution's credibility, providing an unwelcome reminder of Cuba's long history of revolutionary futility and inviting renewed calls for a negotiated settlement. It could also potentially heighten the urgency in Madrid to introduce reforms that would further undermine the revolutionary rationale. Most crucially, the uprising could encourage others to abandon Martí's carefully wrought movement to join the Sartorius brothers or strike out on their own, thus diffusing the party's fund-raising apparatus and endangering the cohesiveness of the revolution itself.

Martí immediately abandoned his Costa Rica plans and moved swiftly to control the damage, writing Quesada with instructions to quickly and publicly disown the rogue offensive.[58] Arriving in Tampa to meet with exile leaders, Martí found Cubans in a celebratory mood, unaware that this was not the revolution he and his colleagues had planned. A public meeting was hastily convened in a bid to quell the exiles' ill-informed exuberance and to counsel patience. Martí then rushed to Key West to continue the damage control, only to learn that the last remnants of the uprising had accepted a pardon and surrendered to the Spanish authorities.[59]

Although the abortive rebellion was a serious distraction for Martí and continued to cause problems for the revolution in its aftermath, it did not at all dampen the exiles' enthusiasm. It also failed to hinder Martí's fund-raising initiative; on May 6 he wrote Máximo Gómez with the news that he had raised $30,000 (more than $750,000 in 2012 dollars) for the war despite "the intrigues of the Spanish government" that he believed had encouraged the credulous Sartorius brothers in hopes of discrediting the real movement.[60] The windfall came at a propitious time, as a larger threat loomed in the form of an international economic crisis that seriously endangered the revolution's strongest backers in the United States as well as on the island. Florida's cigar factories were especially hard hit by the so-called Panic of 1893; with several factories closing and others forced to reduce their workforce, the workers who had largely underwritten the revolution could no longer maintain anything close to their accustomed level of support.[61]

As much as these unforeseen obstacles troubled Martí, he could take some small comfort in knowing that 1893 was treating Spain no better. Maura's plan for an autonomous Cuban government did not sit well with the peninsula's conservatives, who considered it too extreme, and it found scant support among Cubans themselves. Unrest in the northern Spanish city of San Sebastián led to a series of riots fomented by Basque autonomists, who Maura's opponents argued were emboldened by talk of Cuban autonomy.[62]

With fund-raising potentially imperiled, Martí found himself under increasing pressure to bring the revolution to fruition. On May 20 he was back in New York, but he stayed only five days before departing again to meet with Gómez in an effort to develop plans for the war. He hoped on this trip to fulfill his earlier objective of meeting as well with Maceo, who continued to dissociate himself from the party but briefly considered joining the Sartorius rebellion.[63] Before departing, Martí completed work on "The Cuban Revolutionary Party to Cuba," a lengthy manifesto disowning the party's role in the recent uprising and outlining its plan for a legitimate war of independence.[64] The essay appeared in the May 27 issue of *Patria* and circulated as a pamphlet beyond that, and it was reprinted almost in its entirety in Havana's autonomist paper *La Igualdad*.[65]

With *Patria* in Quesada's hands during his absence, Martí met with Gómez on June 3. During the next two days the pair developed a general plan for the war's inception based on the party's commitment to a coordinated simultaneous launch from the island and abroad. They agreed to name Maceo head of the rebel forces in the eastern province of Oriente, which they determined should be the starting point for the island's first offensive.[66] The decision to place Maceo in such a prominent role was a political one; the leaders of the previous war had refused to do so to assuage some white Cubans' fear of an eventual black-led government. Maceo harbored a grudge nearly fifteen years later, and Martí understood that Maceo would only join a revolution that treated Cubans of all races equally. Martí's explicit support of racial equality in essays such as "Mi raza," with its declaration that "Cuban [means] more than white, more than mulatto, more than black," was no idle abolitionist gesture; in the context of his politics, it signaled his acknowledgment of both Maceo and the Afro-Cuban population that revered him as crucial to the revolution's success.[67]

Martí left Gómez's Montecristi farm on June 5 for the four-day journey to Port-au-Prince, from which he planned to depart for Costa Rica. On June 9 he reached Haiti's capital city, where he remained for the next two weeks. The cause of Martí's extended stay in Port-au-Prince is not clear but may well have been health-related. In his absence *Patria*'s May 27 issue stated that he was "not yet recovered from the pains that afflict him" when he left to see Gómez; its July 8 issue announced that despite his health being "on the whole not satisfactory," Martí had a successful journey.[68]

A somewhat recovered Martí reached Panama on June 27 and met with exile groups before proceeding to San José, Costa Rica. His first meeting with Maceo occurred on July 1, during which Martí imparted the war plans he had developed with Gómez. Maceo agreed fully with the proposed strategy; in fact, he saw no need to raise more money for the war, arguing that his own needs were modest. "Maceo does not want a large expedition, nor a ship," Martí later wrote to Gómez. He added that Cubans in Costa Rica had already raised $5,000 for Maceo, "about a third of what we had budgeted."[69]

The rest of Martí's weeklong stay in Costa Rica was eventful even by the standards of his Florida visits. Crowds of loud and ardent supporters followed him and Maceo wherever they went, at one point bursting into wild applause upon their entrance to the city's law school to attend someone else's lecture. Maceo took Martí to meet Costa Rican President José Joaquín Rodríguez, a moment that perhaps reminded him of the heady days of his tenures in Mexico and Guatemala.[70] After several days of celebratory events and speeches, Martí left Costa Rica with the conviction that his work was nearly done.

Upon returning to New York on July 13, Martí declared to a gathering of the city's exile leaders that despite the ongoing economic crisis the moment to act had arrived: "Nothing can now stop the realization and conclusion of our plans. . . . Everything is ready, everything is done."[71] In what was by now a discernable pattern, an exhausted Martí then retreated for a time to Bath Beach "to recover, if possible, the necessary health for the enormous final campaign."[72] August found a reconstituted Martí back at work, assuring the readers of *Patria* that the United States' continuing economic troubles would not stop the revolution: "The greater the foreign land's agony becomes, the harder we must work to conquer, and soon, our own land."[73]

In late August Martí sent a lengthy and detailed report to Gómez outlining conditions on the island, arrangements in progress for the expeditions, and the purchase and projected distribution of arms. With everything seemingly ready, Martí assured his partner that the revolution awaited only his order to proceed.[74] Certain of Gómez's approval, Martí headed to Florida to rally the troops and await the order from the revolution's commander-in-chief.

It was not forthcoming. In his September 18 reply Gómez disagreed with Martí's assessment, informing him that he could not manage the necessary coordination between the exile and island contingents without additional time and money. Following Gómez's clarification that he would not act before preparations were completed to his satisfaction, Martí redoubled his efforts in a desperate bid to complete preparations. By October 21 he had amassed enough money for a major arms purchase and continued fund-raising in hopes that neither unforeseen developments nor the lingering economic downturn would further hinder their plans.[75]

In the coming months, Martí's worst fears nearly came to pass. November brought news of another rogue uprising in Cuba, this time in the province of Las Villas. Martí's contacts on the island reported that the premature insurrection occurred due to a faked order to engage, a ruse calculated by Cuban autonomists or the Spanish themselves to sow confusion and disrupt communications between exiles and the Cuban forces. Martí himself came to believe that the tactic's true aim was to uncover revolutionary cells on the island awaiting orders from abroad.[76]

Martí vehemently decried the Spanish ruse in speeches and on the pages of *Patria*, dismissing it as a last-ditch effort to avert what was now an inevitable war.[77] He moved to assure unnerved collaborators, including Serafín Sánchez, that Spain had failed in its attempt to "provoke an incomplete uprising, and perturb me, that I may in error and by piecemeal send our disorganized reinforcements. None of this will be accomplished."[78]

Privately, however, Martí understood that if he did not move swiftly to preempt such tactics, they could well undermine the real offensive; even his own communications with Gómez, he realized, were vulnerable to Spanish trickery. He thus wrote to Gómez with a set of instructions — essentially a code — by which the *generalísimo* was to read all future communications from him.[79]

Although the Las Villas misfire did little actual damage to the independence movement or plans, it reinforced Martí's conviction that delaying the war any longer than necessary would expose it to more unforeseen duplicities. Yet without Gómez's final approval, he could do nothing but wait.

THE NEW YEAR BROUGHT MORE CONFIRMATION THAT DE-ferring the war left the revolutionary movement a sitting duck for its enemies. On January 3, 1894, Martí received word of another Spanish-orchestrated crisis, one that directly threatened a core constituency and the heart of the party's livelihood. The Florida cigar factories that closed or lowered production had mostly recovered from the country's economic malaise and returned to full capacity by fall 1893. This did not, however, augur a return to good times; seizing on the continuing economic uncertainty as a pretext, many Cuban employers told returning workers that they would have to accept lower wages. Although this had long been a successful tactic among U.S. employers, it was a nonstarter for Key West's skilled, highly organized workers, who immediately announced a strike.[80]

Key West's cigar workers had a long history of strikes, the most recent serious stoppages coming shortly before Martí's first visit in 1891. For most of the Ten Years' War they had avoided work stoppages for the sake of the cause, which they were largely financing. That support gradually waned as workers recognized that employers were taking advantage of their unwillingness to strike, and it dwindled with the rebel leadership's ambivalence regarding abolition. Workers first walked off the job in 1875 and by 1890 had staged four more major strikes, signaling that Cuban independence was no longer their first priority.[81] Martí's arrival in 1891 changed all that for a time, his more broadly democratic, racially progressive vision inspiring the workers to again believe in both the possibility of a free Cuba and their own enfranchisement. But now the employers' collective action threatened to undo that progress, in effect daring workers to strike at a time when the movement's apparent inertia gave them no reason not to do so.

Beyond the temporary interruption of contributions to the Cuban Revolutionary Party, the Key West strike of 1894 also created an opening for a Spanish government eager to neutralize the revolution's most crucial funding source. During previous disputes, the workers had held all the cards; as the workers comprised an organized labor force and a skilled, essentially irreplaceable commodity, factory owners had no choice but to concede to their demands.[82] This time, though, the owners made a deal with the Spanish government to import non-union Spaniards from Cuba to replace the strikers.[83]

Martí immediately notified Gómez of the "serious disturbance that the Spanish have managed to foment in the Key," then moved to thwart it by legal means. He quickly hired a young American attorney named Horatio Rubens and dispatched him to Key West to investigate the situation and determine possible remedies. Martí initially intended to accompany Rubens, but the attorney persuaded him that his presence among the strikers—as well a group of hostile, loyal Spaniards—could well inflame the already tense situation and reflect badly on the revolutionary movement.

The delegate nevertheless made his presence felt from the pages of *Patria*, roundly denouncing the Spanish ploy but training most of his ire on "the North Americans complicit in the attempt" to betray the very Cuban exiles who had founded Key West.[84] Only privately, as in his January 8 letter to Maceo, did Martí acknowledge his fear that "the Key's revolutionary capacity has begun to come undone and will not last long."[85]

In his public statements, the party's delegate remained defiant. Of his writings during the Key West crisis, Martí's January 29 editorial "To Cuba!" offers the most substantive indictment of the United States as an enemy of the Cuban revolution. An indignant Martí, thinking perhaps of his own early admiration for the United States, expressed regret for the exiles' history of trust in their adopted country and faith in its leaders: "Excessive trust and gratitude were the foremost, and perhaps only, errors of that nascent partnership."[86] Cubans, he argued, had been blinded by their admiration for the founding fathers and for Lincoln and overlooked how badly the nation's current leaders, particularly President Cleveland and Secretary Blaine, had abandoned that founding spirit in favor of "the republic of privilege and the unjust monopoly."[87] The most recent manifestation of that betrayal in Key West, Martí averred, proved conclusively that there could be no true peace for Cubans except in their own country:

Who desires a secure nation, let them conquer it. Who does not conquer
it, let them live by the whip and by exile. . . . There is no firmer ground
than that on which one was born. To Cuba! cries out one's entire soul,
after this deception in Key West.[88]

If the United States of 1891's "Our America" was for Martí a giant to be feared,
here it revealed itself as an enemy of Cuban independence.

Meanwhile in Key West, Rubens soon discovered that the strikebreakers
were hired in Havana, not on U.S. soil. This technicality allowed him to successfully argue that their importation violated federal law prohibiting such practices, specifically the Contract Labor Law of 1885. U.S. Treasury officials agreed
to prosecute the cases, and after some legal wrangling eventually the more than
one hundred Spanish workers were deported.[89] The Cuban workers' victory
was thus also a triumph for the party, which through its timely intervention
managed to reignite its most important political and financial base. That base
nevertheless declined significantly in the aftermath of the strike, with factories
and two thousand workers believed to have quit Key West for Tampa in 1894
alone.[90]

Despite the Key West crisis, Martí considered preparations for the war to be
nearly complete, and on March 3 he again tried to persuade Gómez to green-
light the war. Martí's letter assured the *generalísimo* that the expeditionary forces
would be ready to deploy in "six weeks to two months, and no more, or less."[91]
Martí was buoyed by the arrival in New York of his childhood friend Fermín
Valdés Domínguez, whom he had excommunicated for writing in the Havana
autonomist paper *El Cubano*. The price of forgiveness and reconciliation was
Fermín's public disavowal of Cuban autonomy and embrace of the revolution.[92]
This done, Martí arranged a hero's welcome for his old friend, even organizing
a February 24 event in his honor.[93]

Gómez's response to Martí's entreaty was as receptive as Martí had ever received from him; the old general wished only to return to New York and assess
for himself the level of preparedness and enthusiasm among the exiles before
making a firm commitment to deploy. In Martí's reply of March 24, he insisted
that it was he who should travel covertly to Montecristi, citing as crucial "that
the government . . . see no movement of chiefs that may presage—in time to
disrupt it—an immediate mobilization, nor use it as a pretext for persecutions
or atrocities on the island."[94] But Gómez would not be dissuaded and began
preparations for his arrival.

Another setback, the confiscation by Cuban authorities of a major arms
shipment to the island, only briefly lowered the exiles' heightened hopes in
anticipation of Gómez's New York visit.[95] He and his eldest son, Francisco

(known as Panchito), arrived in New York on April 8, initiating a nearly two-week period of private discussions punctuated by exile gatherings. Aware of the constant surveillance to which he, and now Gómez, were subjected, Martí suffered great anxiety about private meetings that included the commanders; he had not wanted Gómez to come to New York precisely to avoid the appearance of serious military planning. But Gómez came to New York with the intention of holding just such meetings, which he insisted were the only way he could accurately assess the exiles' readiness for war. Blanca de Baralt included in her memoirs this childhood memory of one such meeting held at her home during Gómez's stay:

> One time, with the aim of eluding Spain's henchmen, [Martí] chose our house for a very important gathering of the Cuban chiefs. It was on an evening in mid-April 1894. . . .
>
> Out of an abundance of caution, we — the family, — remained in our bedrooms and gave our servants the night off.
>
> The conspirators started arriving, and Martí, in person, would open the door for them. Some would enter by the back door, others by the front. Among those present were Máximo Gómez and his son Panchito, the cripple [José] Mayía Rodríguez, Loynaz del Castillo, Martí, and two or three others: seven or eight in all.
>
> In the drawing room by the front they sat around the table, those men in whose hands lay Cuba's fate.
>
> A profound silence filled the house, and they left late, one at a time, and with the same stealth with which they had arrived, by both doors.[96]

On April 21 Gómez departed the city convinced of the party's readiness for the long-awaited war, leaving Panchito behind to accompany the now chronically ailing Martí on his remaining travels in advance of the war.

With Gómez's explicit authorization and a deployment plan in place, Martí could now arrange the final logistics for the war's launch. He threw himself into the labors, working nearly around the clock for the next several months to raise money while diverting Spanish attention. Martí's requests for money from the exile clubs took on added urgency. In a May 10 fund-raising letter to the heads of one New York club he set a deadline of "within six weeks, or sooner if possible"; in another, dated May 3 to a Mexican national, Rodolfo Menéndez, Martí implores him to "convene as many collaborators — Cuban and Mexican — as you can find where you live" to raise money.[97] In a third letter, dated June 22, Martí refers to an old friend's wife who apparently sold off her jewelry for the cause: "I hope she is not angry over the theft I am committing, — for the bracelet that Cuba is taking from her."[98]

Contributions from Key West dwindled in the aftermath of the January strike; on July 7 Martí wrote to Serafín Sánchez that the party treasury contained "not a single dollar from the Key" and urged him to send at least two-thirds of the pledged money at once: "Less, is not possible."[99] The Key West labor unrest continued, with owners more willing to relocate to Tampa rather than accede to workers' demands. On May 18 Martí wrote to organizers George Jackson and Salvador Herrera in hopes of averting another potentially damaging strike, this time over a factory owner's refusal to host a visit by Martí. "The point may be right," he argues, "but the occasion is wrong."[100]

Identifying and culling suspected informants and traitors from the Cuban ranks also became a priority, as the deployment would depend for its success on secrecy. Spain would surely move to expose any seemingly imminent launch, and Martí now understood that the United States would act on any credible leads from Pinkerton agents or the Spanish themselves. It thus became imperative to remove from their plans anyone who might have been planted by the Spanish or who might turn to them for money or out of fear. A May 27 letter to Sánchez in Key West instructs him to remove a certain "Ramirez," whose "contradictory and unnecessary conduct" had aroused his suspicion, "from all knowledge of the real action that at any moment may be required." Martí suggests that "Ramírez" may yet be useful as a means of feeding false information that would divert the Spanish from assessing the true progress of preparations.[101] In a June 18 letter to Antonio Maceo, Martí continued to fret over the security of communications during his travels, and he established a code with Maceo similar to the one he had previously sent to Gómez.[102]

Martí's primary weapon in the emerging information war was *Patria*, which he consistently used to divert the Spanish from the revolution's true activities and manipulate public opinion.[103] During one of his many trips he specifically instructed Gonzalo de Quesada to keep the paper "totally silent . . . in all matters regarding the autonomists, hammering very hard on the sin, but without ever naming the sinners."[104] This strategy of denouncing the policy while withholding the names of its supporters was designed to block autonomists from gaining a following through exposure in the paper; it also allowed *Patria* to attack the autonomists without providing them an opening to directly respond. Martí instructed his surrogates in the press to present the revolution not as the latest exile invasion but as a movement prepared to aid Cuba in its struggle, standing ready "not to go ourselves, but to help her if, against what would be our wishes, she is provoked. . . . We must repeat this at all hours: furtively in the press, firmly and to the best of our ability in private conversations."[105] Martí's propaganda war against the Spanish, which was being fought on the island and among the exiles, emerges clearly at such moments.

This atmosphere of intense surveillance and pressure made travel more complicated than ever during the crucial final stage of preparation. On May 12 Martí set out with Panchito Gómez to finalize plans for the war. In addition to the many precautions employed to ensure secure communications and his own personal safety, he now took pains to conceal as much as possible the true purpose for the journey. This would require stops in several Florida cities to give the appearance of a routine fund-raising trip and perhaps throw Spanish agents off his trail. On June 5 Martí wrote from the steamer *Albert Dumois* about to dock in Costa Rica to brief his hosts in San José regarding this ruse. In the letter he asks that they circulate news of his impending visit, "but not with too much anticipation, as if I were on a propaganda tour."[106]

Spanish observers were not fooled by Martí's attempted sleight of hand; they had reliable information regarding plans to launch the war "within two months, at the latest" and knew Martí's itinerary and travel companions.[107] This information, combined with earlier intelligence regarding the large sums of money being raised, compelled Spain to lodge a formal protest in Washington regarding the continued presence of Cuban revolutionary forces apparently planning to attack the island from U.S. soil. Martí learned of the Spanish protest in the midst of a three-month period of almost frenzied travel during which he barely spent a week at home.[108] Martí again used *Patria* to respond to the Spanish action, instructing staff member Serafín Bello to assert in its pages the party's "right to propaganda, so long as it does not *extend toward action. The visible organization of a war against an ally country falls clearly within the law.*"[109] With the onset of the war at best only months away, he could only hope that the U.S. government would agree—or at least vacillate long enough for Cuban forces to strike.

IN SEPTEMBER MARTÍ FINALLY RETURNED FROM HIS THREE-month odyssey, having met with exiles and raised funds in several countries. Beyond the routine Florida stops, Martí visited and spoke in New Orleans, Costa Rica, Panama, Jamaica, San Antonio, and—for the first time as party delegate—Mexico City and Veracruz.[110] With all preparations apparently in place and awaiting only Gómez's order, Martí notified Maceo to be "absolutely ready" to deploy by mid-October.[111]

That did not happen, as a series of miscommunications and disruptions orchestrated by the Spanish managed to repeatedly delay the deployment. Eleventh-hour fires were now appearing faster than Martí could extinguish them, threatening to throw the entire operation into disarray. Rogue elements joining the fray compounded the problem, with commanders Martí had never heard of issuing statements and taking actions that sowed confusion among the ranks: "Who is this Carlos Aguirre?" asks a clearly exasperated Martí in the midst of the chaos. A September 5 dispatch to generals in the field instructing them not to act without explicit orders only partly salvaged the situation, and by the planned mid-October launch date commanders in Santiago and Camagüey were preparing to petition Gómez to delay deployment indefinitely.[112]

The extended frustration of the war's onset exacerbated Martí's fears that the Spanish were trying to hold off the revolution long enough to introduce last-minute concessions on the island. News of dissension within the Cuban ranks, he reasoned, would only create momentum on the island and in the Spanish Parliament for reforms that would undermine support for the war.[113] With the military offensive frustrated for the moment, Martí returned to the information war with the September 22 publication in *Patria* of "The Recent Language of Certain Autonomists."[114] Martí's editorial railed against elements among the island's upper classes who supported autonomy as the last, best chance to preserve the existing social hierarchy; these unnamed individuals, Martí argued, "could impede, even after independence, the just equilibrium of diverse elements on the island and the recognition . . . of all their political capabilities and powers," without which Cuba would be ripe for annexation by "the annihilating and rapacious Yankee."[115] Thus for Martí, affluent Cubans who supported autonomy to save their own socioeconomic privileges were playing into the hands of not only the Spanish colonizer but the more dangerous, because more powerful, United States.

Even as Martí urged exiles to hold the line, a combination of money woes and the ongoing confusion in Cuba compelled Gómez to delay the deployment until mid-November.[116] By then he had traveled to Fernandina to meet with Nathaniel Barnett Borden, an American who supported the revolution despite working for Spain among a half-dozen other countries as vice consul in Jacksonville. More important for the Cubans was the fact that Borden operated a successful shipping business out of Fernandina.[117] A November 10 assassination attempt on Maceo in San José, however, necessitated a second postponement. By early December Martí had managed through unrelenting efforts to restore order and a clear chain of command for the deployment, opening the way for co-signers Martí, Gómez's representative Colonel José Mayía Rodríguez, and General Enrique Collazo, who had mended fences with Martí to become military chief of the island forces, to issue the official plan of deployment on December 8 and distribute it to the collective military command.[118]

The waiting was over.

THE FAILURE OF THE SO-CALLED FERNANDINA PLAN, THE ill-fated expedition that presaged the revolution's successful launch in April 1895, has since become the stuff of Martí legend. More than a century of scholarship has portrayed its unraveling as the work of traitors abetted by U.S. and Pinkerton agents. But contrary to such accounts of a deployment besieged by "a swarm of federal agents, police, [and] spies,"[119] the U.S. government had no presence in the area at all beyond a single, disabled vessel stationed a hundred miles away in Savannah.[120] In truth, the Fernandina Plan failed due to the Cubans' own mistakes and lapses of judgment at crucial moments.

The plan called for three vessels to take different routes from Fernandina Beach and ultimately converge on the island. The ships were to be charters contracted in the United States under assumed names and false pretenses; the Cubans would then reveal their true intentions to the respective captains and offer bribes of $1,000 to change course and were prepared to take the ships by force if the bribes failed. The ships would then head to different destinations — the Dominican Republic, Costa Rica, and Key West — to collect the generals and their troops before landing at different points in Cuba.[121]

Martí contacted Nathaniel Borden immediately upon issuing the deployment plan and arranged to meet him at the Hotel St. Denis in New York, where Martí took a room under the name "D. E. Mantell." Borden arrived on December 12 and went about the business of contracting the three vessels, arousing suspicion when one South Brooklyn captain noticed that Borden was hiring multiple crews.[122]

The mission was further compromised by the blunders of Colonel Fernando López de Queralta, a Ten Years' War veteran who was to lead one of the three expeditionary vessels. The colonel refused to sail upon discovering that his vessel had been contracted under false pretenses. López de Queralta offered instead to secure a vessel with the explicit intention of sailing to Cuba, insisting that he had already revealed their plans to a broker who agreed to help them. Martí reluctantly agreed to the change, accompanying López de Queralta to a supposedly secret meeting with the broker that actually took place in a busy public office. After the meeting Martí insisted that they let Borden book the remaining vessel as originally planned. Martí later replaced López de Queralta after a second incident, when the colonel listed arms being shipped for the expedition as "military articles," in direct contravention of Martí's instructions. Rail workers refused to load the weapons, which were eventually sent by steamer, delaying their delivery by eleven days.[123] The colonel disappeared shortly thereafter, leaving Martí to wonder whether he had compromised the mission out of "cowardice, or perhaps ill intent."[124]

Despite these slip-ups, the plan did not hit its first snag until December 24, when Captain John Dahl of the yacht *Amadis* refused to board the expeditionary leaders on the grounds that the ship's charter prohibited additional passengers. Borden quickly replaced Dahl with Captain David S. Weed, who suspected his clients of smuggling and notified the yacht's owners.[125]

Rumors soon spread of unusual activity along the Eastern Seaboard and eventually reached a reporter for the *New York World*, who received confirmation from the *Amadis*'s broker that its clients were possibly engaged in a filibustering expedition. An account of another vessel transporting "$30,000 worth of small arms" seemed to corroborate the broker's story, and on January 9, T. A. Hall, the *World*'s correspondent in Fernandina, notified U.S. Customs Officer George L. Baltzell of the suspicious activity.[126] Martí, who was in New York tending to last-minute preparations, was astonished to read a January 11 article in the *New York World* titled "Off on a Secret Cruise," which not only exposed all of Borden's recent activities for public consumption but revealed that insurance companies had canceled coverage on the vessels. The article's subheading, "Old Salts Think They Are off to Filibuster or Smuggle," left little doubt that the game was up.[127]

The plan now began precipitously to unravel. On the same morning that the *World* article appeared, a Captain Griffin of the *Lagonda* notified Baltzell that "a number of suspicious boxes had been put on the yacht the night before."[128] Baltzell promptly sent deputy collector W. B. C. Duryee to board the *Lagonda*; Duryee spotted the suspicious shipment below deck but was refused permission by Borden to examine it. Frustrated by Borden's stonewalling, Baltzell wired the Treasury Department for instructions on how to proceed. Orders from Washington to board the vessel came the next day, but the courier entrusted with delivering the telegram to the local authorities brought it instead to Borden, whether by coincidence or design. Whichever the case, the intercepted telegram gave Borden the advance notice he needed to avert disaster. At that point Manuel Mantilla, Carmita's son who had joined the expedition with her blessing, panicked and threw a number of rifles and other arms overboard in the presence of Captain Griffin. The captain later recovered the contraband from the river bottom and turned it over to the customs house.[129]

Subsequent searches of all three vessels turned up nothing more dangerous than a box containing thirty machetes; however, Borden was forced to confess when Griffin reported to Baltzell what he had seen. By the time the authorities raided Borden's Fernandina warehouse and confiscated 140 crates containing hundreds of firearms and thousands of cartridges, the Fernandina Plan's catastrophe was complete.[130]

The fruits of nearly seven years of organizing and fund-raising were suddenly in immediate and catastrophic peril. Martí monitored the plan's demise from the Hotel Travellers in Jacksonville, where he had registered on January 13 under a false name. There an emergency meeting of the available conspirators was hastily convened at which a distraught Martí alternated between blaming López de Queralta for the plan's failure and taking complete responsibility for it. With arrest and imprisonment a real possibility, any further action and certainly any public appearance by anyone in the room were out of the question. The assembled leaders thus agreed to summon attorney Horatio Rubens to determine whether the confiscated arms could be recovered. If they were in fact lost in addition to the money wasted on the charters, it was far from certain when — or whether — they could again raise the funds for another try. Only after Rubens returned on December 15 to assure the Cubans that the weapons could be recovered, as in the absence of direct evidence of filibustering there were no grounds for retaining them, did Martí and his advisors agree to regroup for a second try.[131] Having been saved by Rubens's intervention, the revolution lived to fight another day.

MARTÍ'S GREATEST FEAR IN THE AFTERMATH OF THE FAILED Fernandina Plan was that the revolution's enemies would cite it as proof of the ultimate impossibility of armed rebellion. Such an argument, if accepted by Cubans on the island and abroad, would pave the way for Cuban autonomy or annexation by the United States and would doom the independence movement for the foreseeable future.

To Martí's great surprise, the opposite happened. Far from the Cuban Revolutionary Party being dismissed as incompetent, the exposure of the Fernandina Plan paradoxically raised the party's stature in the eyes of its adherents and its enemies, observers on both sides expressing surprise at such a precarious and complicated plot having come so close to fruition. News of the Florida and federal officials' role in unraveling the plan also heightened the enmity toward the United States that Cubans on the island and in exile had been nurturing since the previous year's Key West strike. In a January 1895 letter to Gómez, Martí expressed his wonder at "the discipline and respect of the island, astonished at this effort, — and the love of the diaspora, inflamed by this patent villainy."[132] His January 17 letter to Juan Gualberto Gómez in Cuba likewise took a comforting tone, assuring his friend that even the failure of such an ambitious plan "serves to further unite all of our supporters, heightens public respect, and leaves intact all our powers, with no more real damage than the restorable loss."[133] He went on to reassure Gualberto Gómez that the party would be prepared once again to deploy in "one or two months."[134]

In order to succeed, the new offensive would have to overcome the additional obstacles of increased Spanish vigilance and a more engaged United States. Whatever its shortcomings, the Fernandina Plan had the advantage of surprise; the U.S. State Department had dismissed the revolutionaries as rank amateurs, and even Spanish agents who closely monitored their every move were shocked by the operation's scope and ambition. Those advantages now forfeited, the insurrection would have to fashion a plan that would allow expeditionary forces to land in Cuba despite the combined and now relentless surveillance of Spain, the Pinkerton Agency, and the U.S. Coast Guard. No one was underestimating them any more.

On January 29 Martí fulfilled his promise to Gualberto Gómez with the renewed deployment plan, again co-signed by himself, Collazo, and Mayía Rodríguez.[135] The launch was now a certainty and once mobilized would come within weeks. Two days later Martí left New York, never to return.

MARTÍ SPENT HIS LAST TWO WEEKS IN NEW YORK AS A MAN besieged, constantly on the run from Spanish and Pinkerton agents. He adopted the same security measures that had served him during his many travels, both for his own safety and to protect anyone who might be linked to him. He was also forced to abandon the house he had shared for a decade with Carmita Mantilla and stayed instead in the homes of fellow Cubans, seldom spending more than one night at the same address. During his final days in New York, Martí avoided going out in the daytime, traveled exclusively in closed carriages, and almost never used the front doors of the places he frequented.[136]

The timeline set in motion by the deployment plan left Martí with less than forty-eight hours in New York. Not knowing when, or whether, he would return, he left the running of *Patria* and the daily business of the party in the hands of his most trusted lieutenants, Gonzalo de Quesada and Benjamín Guerra. He also said his last goodbyes, making the rounds of his closest friends and collaborators in the city. Although his parting moments with Carmita Mantilla are not documented, this would surely have been the most poignant and bittersweet farewell of all.

Carmita and Martí had barely seen each other for months due to his travels and his desire to shield her as much as possible from the harassment of spies. As his single most loyal supporter and companion over the years, Carmita more than anyone had helped Martí reach this crowning moment of a lifetime's ambition. She was also without a doubt the love of his life, and he hers. Thus in Carmita's final gesture, in the very act of letting him go, we find perhaps the highest expression of her devotion.

AMONG MARTÍ'S LAST STOPS ON THE MORNING OF JANUARY 31 was the home of Luis and Blanca de Baralt, loyal friends whose brownstone on 55th and Broadway had covertly hosted revolutionary gatherings and, more recently, Martí himself. Blanca de Baralt later wrote of the last time she ever saw him:

> I was in my dining room having breakfast. The doorbell rang and I heard Martí's voice ask the maid who was opening the door: "Is the gentleman at home?" — and moments later he entered the dining room.

"They tell me that Luis has already left: what a shame. I came in a hurry hoping to catch him, since I didn't want to leave without saying goodbye. God knows when we will see each other again."

After talking with me for a few minutes: "Say goodbye to Adelaida and Fico [her parents] for me. I'm leaving now and I can't be late. Goodbye. I don't have a moment to lose." I walked him to the front door and he bolted out into the cold morning air.

Days later we noticed a brown overcoat that had been left hanging on the hatstand. It did not belong to any of us. Perhaps a friend had left it there? A strange thing to forget in the middle of winter.

My sister-in-law checked the pockets to see if there was some sign of its owner. Imagine our astonishment to find them bursting with letters and papers addressed to Martí.

Poor man, in his rush to leave, he forgot his coat in the vestibule, and went out into the freezing cold without even noticing. How worried he must have been![137]

Martí did in fact have a world of worry on his mind in those final hours, but preeminent among them was the need to leave the city unnoticed. Shortly after leaving the Baralts' without his coat, a carriage came to fetch them at the home of Ramón Luis Miranda, the last of several safe houses where Martí had been staying. Miranda also has the distinction of having been Martí's last personal physician as well as one of the few close friends who helped celebrate his last birthday at a small gathering at Delmonico's steak house.[138] Miranda's son, Luis Rodolfo Miranda, later offered this recollection of Martí's final minutes in New York:

> To elude the surveillance to which [he] was subjected . . . Martí and Gonzalo de Quesada entered a closed carriage that, stopped on the street in front of our house, was awaiting them, and taking the appropriate precautions in order to not be seen, made no further stops and headed straight to the harbor to board the steamer that would carry them to the Dominican Republic.[139]

Waiting at the dock were three of his closest allies: General Enrique Collazo, Colonel José Mayía Rodríguez, and Carmita's son Manuel Mantilla. Together the four of them boarded the Haiti-bound steamer *Athos* as architects of a war to free their people from centuries of economic, cultural, and political slavery.

CHAPTER THIRTEEN

Farewells and Rowboats

I have just learned that these Cuban gentlemen have purchased a schooner ... taking a route that I suppose will lead them to the Island of Cuba....

[S]o it would be appropriate, for our gunboats along that coast, to remain alert and keep close watch per these reports, should this come to pass.

DISPATCH TO THE GENERAL CONSUL OF SPAIN
IN SANTO DOMINGO, MARCH 31, 1895

W HEN MARTÍ QUIT NEW YORK HE LEFT BEHIND A dozen letters for Gonzalo de Quesada to forward to various collaborators, a flurry of memos and directives in advance of the imminent deployment.[1] But once aboard the Haiti-bound steamer *Athos*, he could write to the two people who had become the emotional center of his life: Carmita and María Mantilla. Leaving the fourteen-year-old María was especially painful, as regardless of his biological paternity he had become her dearest friend and father in all but name. Martí begins his February 2 letter to María: "Your little anguished face is still before me, and the pain of your parting kiss. Let us both be good, I to deserve that you embrace me again, and you that you may be as beautiful in my eyes as you were that day."[2] In his letter of the same day to Carmita, he worries that it will be difficult to stay in touch: "I still do not see how it will be possible, due to the unknown nature of our path. . . . Nevertheless, it does not matter. — I see you when the sun sets and when the sun rises."[3]

Martí wrote to the Mantillas only sporadically over the next two months and to his mother not at all. Even before Fernandina, Martí corresponded very little with his loved ones. Now, in the frenzy to set everything in place for the imminent launch, farewells would have to wait.

MARTÍ'S MOST PRESSING UNRESOLVED BUSINESS, AND THE most delicate, was with Antonio Maceo. Martí faced a potentially sticky situation with the mercurial general, to whom he had promised $5,000 that Maceo insisted was necessary before embarking. Several wealthy supporters had stepped up to donate or lend funds to the party to replace the money spent on the failed Fernandina Plan; but the collaborators could not fully recoup the lost funds, and Martí had raised less than half — $2,000 — of the promised amount. He now faced the delicate task of explaining his situation to Maceo and somehow appeasing him at this difficult moment. After a brief but carefully worded explanation, Martí wrote to the general:

> You can well see where I am headed [with this]. The island jumps with anticipation and will wait a little longer. . . . We need only arrive. Then there are ample supplies *already purchased* for three expeditions. This I have done. What will you not do? And what would I not help you do, within [the island] or without?[4]

Hoping Maceo would be appeased, the rebel leaders forged ahead. On February 7 they reached Montecristi, where General Máximo Gómez awaited them to begin final preparations. With Spanish forces on the island and the U.S. Coast Guard on heightened alert for an invasion, the rebels opted to have the uprising begin from within Cuba and expeditionary forces arrive afterward. Everything depended on the leaders on the island determining a date. Soon after arriving in Montecristi, they received word from Juan Gualberto Gómez, Martí's main contact in Cuba, that at a recent summit in Havana the deployment was set for February 24.[5] That gave the exiles a little over two weeks to collect men and supplies and find vessels that would take them to Cuba.

Maceo's angry rejection of Martí's request to deploy with diminished funds and his intimation that he might not come at all complicated an already tight timeline. Getting all available forces to the island as soon as possible after the uprising began — and before Spain could get reinforcements there — was crucial; they could ill afford any delay, especially of an entire expeditionary force. Maceo knew this and used it to pressure the others to grant his demands. But he was not counting on Flor Crombet, whom Martí had sent to intercede with Maceo, offering to lead the force in Maceo's place. Effectively underbid by Crombet, an outraged Maceo dug in his heels rather than lose face.[6]

Preparations for Máximo Gómez's expeditionary group continued over the coming days, with the most important objective being to secure a suitable vessel.[7] On February 14 Gómez and Martí dispatched Mayía Rodríguez, General Gómez's top assistant, to Santo Domingo to monitor developments on the island from the Dominican capital and notify them when the island troops deployed. Rodríguez returned ten days later with both good and better news; in one hand he carried an envelope from Dominican President Ulises Heureaux containing his personal contribution of $2,000; the other held a telegram confirming that in the early morning hours of February 24, rebel forces in Cuba had risen up against Spain.[8]

The welcome news meant that it was time for some final decisions, most pressingly regarding Maceo's continued intransigence. With no time for further negotiations and at the risk of losing Maceo for good, the rebels were left no choice but to accept Crombet's offer to replace him. A clearly irritated Martí notified Maceo of the change, expressing disbelief that a "patriotism that overcomes bullets" would "allow itself to be defeated by our poverty—by our poverty, which is nevertheless sufficient for our obligations."[9] He reminded the general of his indispensability at this "moment of true greatness" and urged him to embark with his men "in a shell or a leviathan . . . as soon as that shell comes."[10]

Part of Martí's impatience with Maceo undoubtedly stemmed from the enormous material price he personally had paid for the revolution. For all the hundreds of thousands of dollars he had raised and managed, Martí himself was penniless; he left New York with the clothes on his back and the few things that fit into the weathered leather valise he took with him to Montecristi. So threadbare were the clothes Martí took to Montecristi that he spent the remainder of his time there in borrowed attire; on March 1 he sent Gómez regrets that he could not return his son Panchito's cape or a pair of his "beloved and well-loved trousers."[11] Two weeks earlier he had written half-jokingly to Gonzalo de Quesada that the needed repair of his only pair of shoes allowed him "a half hour's rest."[12] General Enrique Collazo later wrote of Martí's vagabond existence during his final years:

> He lived as a nomad, with no home, no trunk, and no clothes; he would stay at the nearest hotel wherever sleep happened to overtake him; he ate wherever he could find the cheapest good food; he could order a meal like no one else; yet he himself ate little to almost nothing, living for days on Vin Mariani.[13]

If anything, Collazo underestimated the degree to which Martí had by 1895 abandoned any notion of a conventional life. As the head of an organization actively engaged in gun running, money laundering, and other activities necessary to the violent overthrow of a government, Martí crossed over the line from mere nomad to outlaw. And he found this new outlaw's life invigorating, even liberating, in kinship with the smugglers he observed on March 2 in a Haitian border town: "In the smuggler we see the brave [man], who risks himself; the astute [one], who fools the powerful; the rebel, in whom others see and admire themselves. [Thus] contraband comes to be loved and defended, as true justice."[14] It is among the most revealing moments in Martí's diaries; he clearly "sees" and "admires" himself in his romanticized portrait of the smuggler who to the authorities is a mere criminal. But the portrayal also reveals Martí's keen awareness of his own idealized public and self-image as a border-crossing outlaw persecuted by governments yet beloved by his people.

Martí's final transformation into a gun-wielding revolutionary was more than mere public posturing. By his final days in Montecristi, Martí's intellectual break with the European "imported book" of "Our America" parlance and the bourgeois life he had come to associate with it was all but complete. In his diary entry of March 3 Martí wrote of an elaborately bound and gilded volume he encountered "in a pile of books forgotten under a table" in a house where he was staying; browsing the series of French biographical profiles within its pages, he reflected that its "contents, more than for the book, are of a society, now hollow, that is finished."[15] It was precisely that "society" of tired class hierarchies, bourgeois letters, and especially liberal careerism, that Martí now wholeheartedly rejected:

> Career: the open and facile cause, the great temptation, the satisfaction of needs without the original effort that unleashes and develops a man, and rears him, through the respect for those who suffer and produce as he does. . . . He is useless, and generally harmful, who enjoys a well-being that he has not created: he is a prop for injustice, or timid friend to reason, who by the undeserving use of a level of comfort and pleasure out of proportion with his own individual effort and service, loses the habit of creating, and respect for those who create.[16]

Having turned his back on the European education that had largely created him, Martí felt a truer kinship with the black barber cutting his hair who, born in St. Thomas of Danish, English, and Spanish ancestry, declared himself itinerant and a Haitian by default, or the beggar woman outside his shop who likewise had chosen a poverty of independence over one of oppression.[17]

Although Martí had suffered major financial setbacks in his life, by now his state of poverty was very much a choice. He spent nearly a decade giving every dollar that passed through his hands to the revolution, his devotion to the cause total and complete. Unmoored from allegiances to class or caste or ancestry,

Martí had at last become as he had once portrayed himself, a man "without a country, but without a master"; he could land in Cuba secure in the knowledge that he had literally nothing to lose but his life.[18]

LANDING IN CUBA, HOWEVER, WAS NOT SOMETHING THAT Máximo Gómez was prepared to have him do. With the matter of Maceo and Crombet decided, the *generalísimo* turned to his other main point of concern: keeping the civilian Martí out of harm's way. With no military training and the additional burden of a chronic illness, it would be the height of folly, reasoned Gómez, to expose the revolution's most valuable public asset, its very face and voice, to death on a battlefield. Martí would contribute far more to the cause by returning to New York and continuing to raise funds for what could be a lengthy war.[19]

General Enrique Collazo, who was present at the meeting with Martí, Gómez, and Mayía Rodríguez, explained that with a launch vessel apparently secured, the revolution's military head was prepared to proceed without Martí:

> General Gómez proposed to embark immediately for Cuba with [General Paquito] Borrero, Rodríguez, [Ángel de la] Guerra, Collazo, and another eight or ten men, while Martí and M. Mantilla would return to New York to agitate among the exiles and organize a greater expedition that he might bring later on.
>
> Martí opposed this plan, his self-respect driving the idea of accompanying Gómez and disembarking with him on the coast of Cuba.[20]

Martí eventually yielded to the greater wisdom of his compatriots, perhaps partly in the interest of maintaining a united front and not allowing dissension among them so near their deployment.[21]

And he may well have stood by that decision were it not for the appearance on March 9 of news reports, originating with the *New York Herald* and rapidly reprinted across the hemisphere, that he and Gómez were already in Cuba.[22] In the days after Martí agreed to return to New York, it was decided that he should make a final round among supporters in the Dominican Republic and Haiti to raise additional funds. On March 8 he may have been planning to visit the Dominican president and Cuban sympathizer Ulises Heureaux to ask his permission to deploy an expeditionary force from Dominican shores.[23] The understanding was that Martí would return home shortly thereafter.

The appearance of the false story in Santo Domingo's *Listín Diario* the following morning reversed Martí's calculations. The apocryphal story crystallized for Martí the political necessity of his presence, if only as a figurehead, among the men who would sacrifice their lives for Cuba at his behest. The discovery that the *New York Herald* story was false, he reasoned, could hurt morale during the war's crucial first days. It was clear to him that he had to go.

His companions were astonished. Martí was, at forty-two, an old man, frail and suffering a range of chronic symptoms that required ongoing medical care. The long hours and punishing travels of the previous several years had taken a noticeable toll, and his chronic insomnia and poor eating habits only exacerbated his ills. In addition to the constant aches and pulmonary difficulties caused by sarcoidosis, Martí had now aggravated the inguinal ulcers he had incurred twenty years earlier in prison. The pain in his groin was bad enough to send him to a doctor in Cap Haïtien, Ulpiano Dellundé, who, according to a March 2 letter from Gómez's son Panchito to his father, "ordered a box of medicines for [Martí's] ulcers."[24] Correspondence between Martí and Gómez confirms that he had been seeing Dellundé since his first visit to Montecristi in May 1893.[25] He apparently suffered from a fever at the same time; a March 1 diary entry notes that a medical student named Salcedo gave Martí "a dose of antipyrine," a drug commonly prescribed for aches and fevers before the development of aspirin.[26]

Thinking that Martí's return to New York had been settled, Gómez and Collazo implored their colleague to reconsider his reversal, explaining that the rigors of the Cuban jungle were no place for someone in his diminished physical state. More importantly, Gómez argued, the delegate's death would deal an insurmountable symbolic blow to the revolution. But Martí would not be moved. Collazo later wrote that the false reports of Martí's presence in Cuba "overthrew Gómez's plan and from that moment it was impossible to deter Martí."[27]

So on March 18 it was Collazo, not Martí, who along with Manuel Mantilla boarded the New York–bound steamer *Clyde*. Both would eventually reach Cuba as part of later expeditions.[28] After their departure, Gómez and Martí began negotiations for another schooner, the *Mary John*, whose owner promised to hire a captain and crew for the journey to Cuba.[29]

Believing their departure to be imminent, Martí spent the next week bidding his loved ones farewell. On March 18 he wrote to assure Carmita Mantilla of his safe return—"You will see me again"—adding darkly that he had "yet much left to suffer."[30] Martí also addressed a final bit of personal business during this week, arranging for his doctor and by now fellow conspirator Ulpiano Dellundé to finance María Mantilla's enrollment at Le Petit Français, a private school in New York.[31] On March 25 he wrote to his mother that

> on the eve of a long journey, I am thinking of you. And ceaselessly I think of you. You are offended, in the anger of your love, by this sacrificing of my life; and yet why was I born of you with a love of sacri-

fice? . . . A man's duty is there where he may be most useful. But with me goes always, in my growing and necessary agony, the memory of my mother.[32]

Martí's letter of the same day to Gonzalo de Quesada and Benjamín Guerra is considerably less loquacious, opening with the terse announcement: "Partimos" (We depart).[33]

But they did not depart. A week of negotiations with the owner of the *Mary John* went nowhere, as the crew hired for the voyage refused to go to Cuba.[34] The revolution's two preeminent leaders found themselves stranded in Montecristi even as the battles raged on the island. A major concern for the absent chiefs was that other generals would fill the vacuum on their own, perhaps moving independently to form a provisional military government in direct contravention to the revolution's stated goals. Martí had shared these fears with Tomás Estrada Palma, who would become president, imploring him in a March 16 letter to use his influence to avoid the suppression in Cuba of "any organization of the war that would bring with it a republic, that would not be the absolute submission to military rule, to which the country is beforehand and by nature opposed."[35] In their absence, Martí had reason to fear just such a takeover by generals he considered much less trustworthy than Gómez.

Although no such plots seemed to emerge in the revolution's first days, initial reports from the island were not altogether encouraging. Forces in the east won significant early victories, but Spanish authorities managed to arrest leaders of the western contingent, including Martí's primary contact, Juan Gualberto Gómez, in Havana. The exile chiefs were somewhat heartened by reports out of Madrid that the Spanish were forced to send an additional nine thousand men, apparently ill-trained conscripts, to the island, as its sixteen thousand troops were struggling to contain the rebels.[36]

With no other immediate prospects for embarkation, Martí again turned to the only weapon at his disposal: his writing. On March 25 he and Gómez co-authored what is now considered the revolution's defining document, the equivalent of the U.S. Declaration of Independence. Known as the Montecristi Manifesto, it stands as the final, definitive statement not only of the war but of Martí's entire hemispheric political vision as developed and refined over two decades and countless speeches and letters. The entire document, and especially its closing declaration of "a war worthy of the respect of its enemies and the support of the [world's] peoples, for its rigid conception of the rights of man, and its abhorrence of sterile vengeance and useless devastation," was conceived as a public statement to be disseminated among newspapers and embassies across the hemisphere; Martí's March 28 letter to Quesada contained detailed instructions to do exactly that.[37] Martí's dream of fighting in Cuba may have been momentarily frustrated, but his mastery of the information war remained unrivaled.

By March 30, Gómez finally managed to secure an old schooner whose owner demanded that Gómez purchase the ailing vessel and pay him and his crew a separate amount. Owner John Bastian also stipulated that the passengers should not be seen boarding the vessel at port; instead they would take a smaller craft out to sea where the schooner *Brothers* would be waiting.[38]

They left at midnight. Gómez embraced his wife and children one last time before departing, and Martí hastily composed two last letters. The first, to Quesada, is essentially Martí's last will and testament; having no money to speak of, most of the letter focuses on directions for the posthumous organization and publication of his writings. The other is Martí's farewell to José Francisco Martí, the son he had not seen for four years who was now being raised as a loyal Spaniard. The April 1 note is as terse as it is heartbreaking:

> Son:
>
> Tonight I leave for Cuba: I leave without you, when you should be by my side. As I depart, I think of you. If I disappear along the way, you will receive with this letter the watch chain [*leontina*] that your father used in life. Farewell. Be fair.
>
> Your
>
> José Martí

THE VOYAGE FROM MONTECRISTI TO CUBA WAS A CIRCU-itous and perilous one: ten days spent alternately at sea or in hiding, under constant threat of discovery and capture. That they reached Cuba at all was due to improvisation, the timely intervention of friends, and on at least one occasion, dumb luck.

Gómez, Martí, and four of their fellows set out at sunrise on April 1. Within hours the Spanish vice consul in Montecristi wired the news to his counterpart in Santo Domingo, who in turn notified the Cuban authorities. The rebels were reported traveling westbound toward Haiti, and the Haitian consulate was also notified.[39]

Due to a lack of wind, it took the schooner *Brothers* thirty-three hours to cover less than 140 miles, reaching the Bahamian island of Great Inagua in the early evening of April 3 to take on supplies. This first stop confirmed for the revolutionaries and their hired crew just how dangerous this trip was going to be; while docked the Cubans narrowly missed being discovered when a port official demanded to search the vessel. A later customs search actually uncovered a cache of revolvers, which Martí managed to persuade officials were for the passengers' personal protection. The vessel's owner, John Bastian, had suspiciously disappeared during all this, returning only to inform the passengers that the crew had deserted. Martí and Gómez spent the next twenty-four hours trying to hire a replacement crew, to no avail.[40]

Bastian had clearly lost his nerve, yet the Cubans could not risk a falling-out with him lest he betray them to the authorities. They had bought the craft, but without a crew they were effectively stranded—and a sitting duck for Spanish spies. The best Martí and Gómez could do was coerce Bastian into returning part of the money they had paid him and hope for an opportunity to escape the island before being captured.

It is not clear how Martí managed to send word of their predicament to a sympathetic diplomat, a man named Barbes who served as Haiti's consul at Great Inagua. Without Barbes's timely intervention the Cubans' departure would have been significantly delayed and their risk of capture dramatically increased. The Haitian consul put Martí in touch with Captain Heinrich J. Löwe of the German cargo ship *Nordstrand*, who agreed—for a significant sum—to carry the expedition to Cuba.

The *Nordstrand* had stopped in Great Inagua to deliver cargo from Mobile, Alabama, and take on additional crew for stops in Cap Haïtien and Jamaica. The plan was like something out of an adventure novel: after its scheduled stop in Haiti the ship would navigate off the southern coast of Cuba in the dead of night, whereupon the Cubans would head for the beach in a rowboat they had purchased for the purpose. Consul Barbes provided the group with false passports, as they would need to travel under assumed names.[41] Every Spanish and Pinkerton agent between Montecristi and Cuba would be looking for them; any contingency, from bad weather to a suspicious customs agent to an ill-timed encounter with the Spanish navy, would spell disaster.

The *Nordstrand* made its scheduled stop in Cap Haïtien on April 6. It would not leave for another four days—ample time for Spanish agents to discover the Cubans' presence and have them arrested. To avoid detection the six men agreed to separate and stay at different locations—Martí at the home of Ulpiano Dellundé and the others at various hotels and safe houses in town—only regrouping onboard the *Nordstrand* on April 10. In the meantime they stayed indoors and waited.

Martí used the unexpected opportunity to write once again to his beloved María, a longer, more personal letter than his previous farewell to the family. In his April 9 letter he revels in the daily intimacies of their life together, fussing over her studies and touting the virtues of two books that accompanied the letter. In its closing words of fatherly advice, however, we see Martí's realization that he may never see her again:

Feel yourself clean and pure, like the light. Leave to others the frivolous world: You are worth more. Smile, and pass them by. And if you never see me again . . . place a book, the book I have requested, — on my grave. Or upon your breast, because there will I be buried should I die where no man can find me. — Work. A kiss. And wait for me.

But before Martí could stand down the fear of dying on the battlefield, he would have to safely depart Cap Haïtien. And that almost did not happen.

A NARROW ESCAPE — AND ONE
LAST LETTER FOR HIS *PATRIA*

*T*HAT SAME DAY, PERHAPS EVEN AS MARTÍ WAS WRIT-
ing to María, the order arrived for the Cubans' arrest. Their
presence had been detected despite their best efforts, and at
12:05 p.m. on April 9 the arrest order arrived in Cap Haïtien along
with news that a Spanish warship had been sent to collect the
Cubans. The expeditionaries were saved by the unlikeliest of heroes:
part-time telegraphist José Arán, who happened to be on duty when
the order came — and happened to be Ulpiano Dellundé's godson.
Arán immediately ran to his godfather's house to alert Martí; that
evening the Cubans gathered onboard the *Nordstrand*, where they
hid until the ship departed at 2 p.m. the next day. Arán did not deliver the telegram to its destination until the next day, when the
danger had passed.[1] The six remained concealed in their cabins even
after the *Nordstrand*'s departure for fear of being spotted by a passing vessel or crew member who might alert the authorities.[2]

During their last thirty hours on board the *Nordstrand*, Martí
tended to one last bit of business that had eluded him during the
previous days' excitement, that of writing to Quesada and Guerra
regarding the management of *Patria* during his absence. The April
10 letter gave his lieutenants important guidelines for the "war of
thoughts" they would be waging from New York:

> And always the same main points: Cuba's capacity for self-
> government, — the reasons for this capacity, — the inability of
> Spain to further develop these capacities in Cuba, — Cuba's fatal
> decadence, and the alienation from its destiny, under continued
> Spanish dominion, patently obvious differences between the

actual conditions in Cuba and those in the emancipated American republics,—the moderation and patriotism of black Cubans, and the proven certainty of their peaceful and useful collaboration,—our loyal affection for the respectful Spaniard—the clear and democratic concept of our political reality and the enlightened war by which we will secure it. This every day, in various forms and throughout the paper.[3]

The letter's methodical sense of purpose is perhaps most remarkable for its coming in the final, tumultuous hours before Martí's arrival in Cuba. Neither the ongoing perils to the expedition nor the danger they posed to his own life distracted Martí from his singular focus on the work that had to be done. It would be difficult to find, in all of his vast body of work, a more explicit statement of editorial intent and mission.

But the time for letters soon ended. Clouds started swirling well before nightfall on April 11, the seas growing rough enough to rock even the *Nordstrand*'s substantial bulk. General Gómez and Captain Löwe had agreed that the ship would come no closer to shore than three miles, from which point the invaders would proceed in a smaller boat. The *Nordstrand* soon reached the agreed-upon limit but under a downpour so torrential that the small boat was unlikely to reach the shore. The heavy cloud cover left them in a near-pitch darkness that Gómez later described as "a black funeral shroud that might envelop us forever."[4] Captain Löwe then took the ship closer, to within a mile of Cuba's southern coast.

From there the six revolutionaries lowered their rowboat into the rampaging waters. They loaded their guns and supplies, then themselves, into the boat, and started rowing for their lives. Gómez later described the journey's horrific final mile:

The steamer departed at once and we are left, abandoned to the horror that envelops us. None of us are seamen, but we take to the oars with everything we have. Martí and César [Salas] at the prow, [they] row very badly, but with desperation; the other three in the center, I have taken the wheel that I barely know how to operate, which the wind tears from my grip and I finally lose control of it.

The darkness is deep and the rains grow stronger. We have lost our way and can barely discern the land. Two figures on shore, who we figure may well be Spanish guards, serve as landmarks, and with extraordinary effort and labor we head toward them.[5]

After more than an hour the storm relented, allowing the fatigued crew to approach the shore. But by 10 p.m. they had not yet found a place to land along the crags and cliffs that lined the shore. Eventually a small strip of beach, known simply as La Playita, offered an opening at the foot of a steep cliff. There they landed, soaked, exhausted, and lucky to be alive.

CHAPTER FOURTEEN

"My Life for My Country"

I am now every day in danger of giving my life for my country and for my duty—given that I understand it and have the strength to fulfill it.

MARTÍ, UNFINISHED LETTER TO MANUEL MERCADO, MAY 18, 1895

A S THE MEN FINALLY—AND SOMEWHAT MIRACU- lously—reached the beach, General Gómez's worries were only just beginning.[1] Shortly past 10 p.m. on April 11, 1895, Gómez, Martí, and their four companions stepped out of their rowboat and onto the beach. Having survived the pelting rainstorm, tumultuous waves, and their own lack of nautical experience, they now had to confront the even greater perils that awaited them on land.

If Martí did not yet grasp the physical difficulties or risks to his personal safety that he would face, General Gómez surely did. A veteran warrior with intimate knowledge of the island's tropical forests, he well knew that their party—and especially Martí, as their only civilian member—had at least as much to fear from the punishing terrain and the daily grind of life in the Cuban bush as they did from Spanish troops. He also knew that until they could join a larger Cuban force somewhere inland, they could be captured or killed at any moment by the Spanish troops who would come after them as soon as they learned of the Cubans' landing. For this same reason, Cuban forces in the area would be looking out for their arrival. But Gómez had, of necessity, told almost no one of the logistics of their journey, and in fact, he himself was unsure of their exact landing point until their final approach to the island. He determined that their party should land at night to minimize the chance of being sighted. Although these measures ensured the party's safe arrival, they now presented a different and more pressing problem: no one knew where they were—or that they had arrived at all.

Gómez's diary entry of April 11 offers this terse account of the difficulties that the six men faced upon landing:

> After unloading all of our very heavy equipment, each of us taking weapons and over 2,000 rounds—clothes, etc., etc.—and setting the boat adrift, we distributed that immense load among ourselves and set off inland over terribly tangled terrain.[2]

The difficult conditions—rain, darkness, unfamiliar terrain—weighed all the more heavily on Gómez as he considered his civilian charge. The prospect of braving the east's tangled landscape during the rainy season, when weeklong downpours made trails and conventional roads impassable, was daunting even for the most seasoned fighters. Although nearly sixty, Gómez was physically strong and long accustomed to the hardships of jungle warfare. If the situation was discouraging for the group as a whole, it would be that much more trying for the inexperienced Martí, a man utterly unprepared for the rigors of life in the Cuban bush.

Thus began a journey that would see Martí cover nearly 245 miles—a third of it on foot—in thirty-eight days over some of the most forbidding terrain in the Caribbean, the Oriente Province of Cuba (table 14.1). Martí had spent the previous fifteen years in New York City and aside from childhood travels with his father knew little of the island beyond Havana. At 145 pounds, he was physically slight and weakened by the galaxy of ailments he had suffered since his prison days. Gómez knew that beyond sparing Martí as much physical hardship as possible, he had to protect his civilian charge at every moment because the loss of Martí would constitute a political and spiritual blow from which the nascent revolution might not recover. For these and other reasons, Gómez worried that Martí's presence among the troops, whatever its value as a morale booster or political validation of Martí's preeminence within the movement, would prove at best a distraction. At worst, Gómez feared that his civilian counterpart's decision to come to Cuba would prove disastrous. As the small group strode ashore on that rainy Tuesday night, all of the fears and misgivings that Gómez had shared with Martí back in Montecristi, where he had tried to dissuade his friend from coming, weighed on him like the damp darkness of the Cuban night.

The immediate problem facing the expeditionary group was where to spend the night. This would at first glance seem a simple enough matter; certainly the island had no shortage of sympathetic local Cubans with whom the revolutionaries might find shelter. But Gómez had made no advance arrangements

TABLE 14.1. DISTANCE OF MARTÍ'S TRAVELS DURING HIS FINAL
THIRTY-EIGHT DAYS IN CUBA

Segment	Site	Distance covered (mi)
1	Playita to Cajobajo	1.7
2	"The Temple" (cave)	7.1
3	Tavera	7.5
4	Vega Batea	10.7
5	Palmarito	6.2
6	Pozanco	12.6
7	Palenque	4.3
8	Madre Vieja	6.6
9	Los Ciguatos	6.2
10	La Yuraguana	18.3
11	Malabé	23.1
12	Iguanabo	6.8
13	Vuelta Corta	2.6
14	Aguacate	14
15	Kentucky	7.4
16	Rita Perdomo	16.2
17	La Yaya	9.1
18	La Mejorana	6.2
19	Jagua	9.1
20	La Güira de Miranda	10.7
21	Bío	11.6
22	Altagracia de Venero	15.4
23	Travesía	12.8
24	Dos Ríos	4.6
25	Vuelta Grande	4.8
26	Dos Ríos	4.8

for their shelter, as doing so would expose them to possible capture or assassination. The Spanish government had known for months that an invasion was
imminent; several New York papers published the false rumor that Gómez had
been in Cuba for several weeks.[3] Any information that fell into Spanish hands
at this delicate early stage, whether by accident or deliberate betrayal, could
prove deadly.

Whatever the wisdom of Gómez's precautions, his group now found itself
on a secluded beach in the middle of the night, drenched from the landing and
the rain, and lacking any immediate prospects for food or shelter. What they

did each have was a rifle, two thousand rounds of ammunition, and a backpack for their clothes and personal items. After the initial euphoria of landing subsided, the group quickly realized that they could not stay in the open for long. Each man hoisted his allotted load, and they headed inland to the safety of the hills. They marched for about an hour before stopping to rest, wet, weary, and afraid of being caught in the open by Spanish soldiers. They planned to march farther inland in the morning toward the outskirts of Cajobabo, a nearby town, to find a larger contingent of their comrades or at least a sympathetic home to offer them food and shelter. But now they were hungry, exhausted, and facing the prospect of a dangerous night outdoors.

They spotted an apparently occupied homestead and decided to take their chances there rather than risk capture in the open. Less than an hour after the group's arrival, Gómez had to make his first crucial decision. They could remain in the open and risk capture or death, or approach an inhabited home unannounced and hope the occupants would be sympathetic to the cause — or at least their plight. Fortunately, the home belonged to a peasant named Gonzalo Leyva, and he and his family were enthusiastic supporters. Gómez's April 11 diary entry captures both the urgency of the situation and the utter randomness to which the men had surrendered themselves: "We resolved to call, to risk it, and luckily we were greeted by good Cuban people."[4]

After a tense initial encounter, Leyva welcomed the men into his house. They were deeply grateful for Leyva's hospitality, for they knew that his decision to harbor the insurgents was not made lightly. Gómez knew from their recent cat-and-mouse games with various naval authorities en route to the island that the Spanish would have been alerted and that the area would be thoroughly searched by Spanish troops. The general and his host knew that the revolutionaries' presence in a Cuban home, were it discovered, would mean certain death for all of them. Because of this, Gómez determined that the group could not stay in the Leyvas home. They would have to find a shelter that would keep them safe from a Spanish ambush without endangering the lives of their hosts.

Gonzalo Leyva knew just the place. Leyva called on a young Cuban named Silvestre Martínez, a family friend, to lead the group to a small nearby cave. Martínez promised to return the next day with food and to send word to Cuban forces in the area of the group's arrival. The shelter turned out to be less a cave than a sort of covered eave notched into a hillside, which offered protection from the elements but not much else. Nevertheless, years later Gómez would affectionately refer to this first refuge on the island as "the temple," a title that suggests both the hideout's crucial importance on that first night and its almost mystical place in Cuban national lore.[5]

As promised, Martínez returned to the revolutionaries' temple the following day, bringing food and a scout — Gonzalo Leyva's son Jesús, to serve as a guide until they could join their fellow insurgents. Martínez also managed to contact a Cuban commander, Félix Ruenes, who dispatched two of his troops to meet Gómez. The soldiers soon returned to Ruenes with Gómez's directions for a rendezvous the following day. On April 14, after a second night in the cave, the men met Ruenes's troops near the neighboring town of Vega Batea at Tavera, the ranch of Gómez ally Miguel Aguirre.

MARTÍ WAS LITTLE MORE THAN AN OBSERVER TO THESE initial events on the island, deferring to Gómez in all matters from the moment of their landing. Martí had to limit his writing during the perilous journey to the island, and no entry appears in his diary between April 7 and 11. However, his uncharacteristically terse entries for April 11–13 offer small yet telling glimpses into Martí's state of mind during his first days back in Cuba. In his brief entry for April 12, Martí expresses relief and gratitude for the simple shelter of the cave and the man who led them to it, in a few heartfelt words: "We sleep—dry leaves.... Silvestre [Martínez] brings me leaves."[6]

His entry of April 14 then reveals a man delighted to finally experience the "natural life" whose virtues he had extolled for so long in his poetry. Or perhaps this and other early entries portray a man so intoxicated by the metaphorical significance of the physical space he has entered that he has yet to realize the toll it is already taking on his body. Whatever the case, Martí dubs April 14 his first day as a true *mambi*, as the Cuban insurgents called themselves.[7] Once his small group merged with Ruenes's force of fifty men, Martí seemed comfortable among the troops. Although Gómez remained the supreme military leader, Martí felt more at ease once he began to live among the rank and file: wading across rivers, chatting with the men, trading stories at meals. Despite the obvious physical hardships and his precarious health, Martí very much enjoyed the march-and-camp routine that punctuated his final days. Martí's April 14 entry reveals a man filled with wonder at everything he encountered, reveling in the flora and fauna of his long-lost home as well as the camaraderie of his fellow insurgents:

> We set out at five. Waist-high we crossed the river—and recrossed it—
> *bayás altos* [tall bushes and berries] along the shore. Later, in our new
> shoes and heavy packs, the highest hill, with the fine leaves of the ya-ya
> [tree], Cuban majagua, and the cupey with its star-shaped cones. We
> spy, curled up in [the roots of] a lechero tree, our first jutía.[8] Marcos
> [Colonel Marcos del Rosario, one of the five men who landed with
> Martí at Playita and the only Afro-Cuban in that group] removes his
> shoes and climbs over the mangroves. With the first stroke of his ma-
> chete he cuts open its throat.... We eat wild oranges, which José picks:

"How sweet!" Uphill. Climbing together makes men brothers. Over the hills we reach the Sao del Nejesial: a beautiful little mountain clearing, with old palm, mango, and orange trees. José goes. Marcos comes, his bandana filled with coconuts. . . . I rest in the camp. César sews my *tahalí* [machete belt]. The first task is to gather fronds, spread them on the ground. Gómez takes his machete and cuts fronds for himself and for me. . . . All of them, some shredding coconuts, Marcos, helping the general, skinning the jutía. They season it with orange and salt.[9]

Martí's portrayal of the men under Ruenes's command is no less glowing, its author overjoyed to find himself among them:

Suddenly, men: "Ah, brothers!" I jump to attention. Ruenes's guerrillas, Félix Ruenes, Galano, Rubio, all 10 — Their eyes resplendent.

Embraces all around. Each of them carrying a rifle, machete, revolver. . . . And all through the day, what light, what air, how full my chest was, how light my anguished body! Looking out from the ranch, I see, at the top of the crest behind it, a dove and a star.[10]

Gómez notes Martí's's surprising acclimation to the insurgent life in his diary entry of the same day:

The path is difficult, traipsing over tall and very steep mountains; the march is terribly fatiguing and loaded down as we are, we walk by sheer effort.

We are impressed, we old warriors accustomed to these hardships, by Martí's resilience — that he keeps up with us without any sign of slacking through these extremely steep mountains.[11]

Yet the Cuban rain forest was not Martí's home. Before this trip Martí had not set foot in Cuba for more than fifteen years and had spent most of his adult life as an exile in New York. Likewise, his Cuban childhood had been spent amid the relative comfort of bourgeois Havana, far from the harshness and uncertainty of rural life. By now Martí was more cosmopolitan New Yorker than rugged Cuban *mambi*. Much of his spiritual, almost visceral ecstasy during these first days on the island grew paradoxically from an awareness of his own foreignness there. Martí's sense of exile in his own land, among those he would embrace as his people, was likely not experienced as a shock or even a new sensation but as the logical outcome of his lifelong struggles as an outsider among both civilian and military exiles. Martí also felt deeply his own alienation from the culture of machismo that he knew was an indispensable element of the new

Cuban nationalism but which he did not nearly embody. These contradictory convictions heavily influenced Martí's ill-advised decision, over all objections, to return to Cuba with the insurgency. During these first days on the island, however, all Martí saw and felt was the warmth and affection of a long-delayed homecoming.

On the morning of April 15 Martí awoke to the chaos and commotion of the *mambi* camp. In many ways the day was unremarkable, even domestic, in its activities: a group of men was sent to a nearby town to buy provisions for the evening meal; Martí describes them returning with "salt, capers, a package of sweets, three bottles of liquor, chocolate, rum and. . . pigs."[12] As an outsider neither familiar with nor skilled in the many tasks necessary for the maintenance of the camp, Martí received no assignment for the day. Amid the bustle of the camp, as his newfound comrades set to work, Martí occupied himself with party business and correspondence. Although Martí did not regret his decision to join the insurgents on the island, he often found himself strangely displaced amid the daily hubbub. Such tasks as slaughtering a jutía or fashioning a shelter from the fronds of yagua trees seemed as natural—even banal— to Martí's companions as they were wondrous to him.[13] Martí's keen awareness of the chasm of experience and consciousness that separated him from the *mambis* for whom he had so much affection and upon whom his dream of a free Cuba utterly depended only exacerbated his lifelong—and until now, long-suppressed—desire to stand as an equal with the world's hard men.

If in his own mind Martí would never rid himself of a certain gnawing sense of inadequacy, if he never lived to feel himself completely emerging from the shadow of the revolution's military leaders, the events of April 15 nevertheless brought him the satisfaction of knowing that his love and admiration for his military counterparts was finally requited. The commanding officers' decision to award Martí the (almost entirely symbolic) rank of major general so moved him that he wrote of the event twice that evening: in a brief diary entry and a longer, more emotive description in a letter to his New York confidants Gonzalo de Quesada and Benjamín Guerra.[14] In both versions, Gómez asks Martí for his permission to meet with the other commanders—but without him. Martí consents to Gomez's request with a mixture of resignation and apprehension, fearing that this will set a precedent for his removal from any significant discussions among the leadership. Gómez and the others return to inform Martí of his new rank and title.

From its opening sentence, the longer letter displays a powerful affect absent from the diary entry, a terse eloquence unusual in a writer known for his often turgid prose: "I write to you in free Cuba, at sunrise on the 15th of April, from a low clearing in the hills of Baracoa."[15] This greeting and Martí's further description of his surroundings—in the camp, among palm trees, with the commingled voices of the men in the background—reveal Martí's continued sense of wonder at finding himself there. What follows is a barely restrained declaration of joy at this culmination of all his revolutionary efforts—and the resolution of a lifelong inner struggle: "Until today I have not felt myself a man. I have lived in shame, dragging behind me the chains of my fatherland, all my life."[16]

As profound as Martí's suppressed sense of inadequacy had been in the company of Gómez and his fellow "old warriors," he marveled all the more at being awarded the rank of "Major General of the Liberation Army": "With a single embrace, they rendered my poor life equal to their ten years [of armed struggle]! They held me long in their arms. . . . I am filled with tenderness at this sight, of such serene abnegation all around me."[17] Thus for Martí, the crowning moment of his validation as a revolutionary leader also fulfilled a long-held fantasy—at last, to be accepted, even embraced, by the military men as one of them. Martí's lifelong dream of standing as an equal with the revolution's old warriors—tempered by his equally deep-seated complex as a frail, learned man among hearty, wizened, macho revolutionaries—found resolution at this moment of acceptance by men he had paradoxically loved and resented his entire life.

The commanders' symbolic gesture of validation did little, however, to quell the exile community's growing impatience and discomfort with Martí's leadership. Even as Martí strove to rally both the military and civilians around the dream of liberating Cuba, he was keenly aware of divisions within the leadership as well as his enemies' efforts to undermine him. The exile press was regularly turning out editorials that questioned his place among the movement's leadership and his presence on the island. But at least exile pundits did not display the open contempt that typified the island's newspapers, which mocked Martí as absurdly out of place "in his little master's outfit" among the *mambis*.[18] Such attacks compelled Martí to fight a multifront political war of his own, not only against hostile publications on the island and abroad but also, and more dangerously, against elements within the military leadership. Chief among these was General Antonio Maceo, who had never agreed to Martí's and Gómez's plans to establish a civilian government and who advocated a more authoritarian military state.

It is thus not surprising that in his letter of April 15 to Guerra and de Quesada—the same letter in which he giddily describes his symbolic military appointment—Martí includes "two essential declarations upon which our campaign ought to turn." The first of these directives was to accept nothing short of "absolute independence"; the other was to see the struggle through to its end and maintain exile support throughout. Martí reminded the letter's recipients that "for the Spanish the first campaign is the political campaign," and he urged them to meet "one push with another."[19]

Martí's letter of April 15 underscored his deep concern—virtually absent from his diaries and other correspondence of the time—that his ongoing presence in Cuba among the *mambis* created a zero-sum game: whatever boost to morale or other gains might come from his symbolic leadership, his absence in New York made it more difficult to effectively wage the ideological and political war of words to which he was far better suited. His biggest immediate limitation on the island was that he could contact his collaborators only via irregular, hand-delivered messages. The reliability of these missives depended on the contingencies of the march and the battlefield, and even successfully sent letters faced possible interruption or interception by the enemy. Beyond these practical obstacles, Martí feared that although de Quesada, Guerra, and other surrogates could dutifully transmit his words and act on his strategic imperatives, they could not be expected to do so as effectively or in as timely a manner as if he were present. Martí thus found himself paradoxically receiving symbolic decoration as a general in a war in which he played no substantive role—while his absence in New York limited, perhaps even hampered, his effectiveness in the equally crucial battles he was actively managing there.

The days that followed were hard but relatively uneventful, the dreary routine of marching and camping punctuated by occasional news of battles fought and of movements made by an unseen enemy. Martí continued to write not only in his diary but in a steady correspondence with allies and others on the outside. He also apparently found time to read, noting in his April 17 entry the copy of Plutarch's *Life of Cicero* he kept "in the same pocket in which I carry 50 rounds."[20] Martí often turned to great thinkers and writers of the past when facing difficult circumstances, and he had a special admiration for Cicero that dated from his days at law school in Zaragoza. Martí especially admired the first-century Roman thinker for his ability to adapt his political strategies to fit shifting, often unpredictable situations—a skill that Martí knew he would need as he faced the first real test of his political vision. On the morning of April 18, Martí, Gómez, and the rest of their original expeditionary group left Ruenes's troops, taking only six of Ruenes's men with them. The twelve headed inland toward Camagüey, the site of a planned summit with the assembled heads of all the insurgent forces. At Camagüey the assembled leaders planned to officially declare the existence of the new republic-at-arms and appoint its first official representatives, who would in turn select Cuba's first president. Unlike Cicero, who struggled through civil wars and a dictatorship, Martí believed his political and cultural vision flexible enough to respond to wartime exigencies without bowing to them. He knew, however, that the Camagüey summit would bring the first test of that vision.[21]

Martí and Gómez were impatient to reach Camagüey and christen the new state as quickly as possible. They also feared being intercepted by Spanish troops, who knew of their presence on the island, and they had serious concerns about Maceo's explicit disagreement over the desirability of a civilian government. Both men surely worried that a sufficiently angered Maceo might withdraw his three thousand troops—or even turn them on other Cuban units commanded by more democratically minded generals. Although these worst-case scenarios seemed unlikely, especially given Maceo's financial dependence on Martí and the Cuban Revolutionary Party, even the threat of dissension on such a scale would cripple the coalition that Martí had so carefully aligned in the years leading up to the war. Reaching Camagüey and achieving consensus among the revolutionary leaders—with the help of Martí's soaring rhetoric and growing reputation as the insurgency's preeminent leader—would perhaps preempt any dissension that Maceo's opposition might pose for the Gómez-Martí republican plan.

But traveling through the Cuban bush—wading across rivers, hiking up and across mountains, opening trails in the underbrush with machetes—was slow and difficult work that taxed the novice *mambi* more than it did the elder *generalísimo*. Gómez, after all, had spent a decade in these same backwoods and swamps during the failed Ten Years' War of 1868–1878. If Martí had not seriously considered how the war's physical rigors would wear on him, he would certainly have realized it by now. Yet his diary makes little mention of its author's personal discomfort, focusing instead on the Cuban landscape, flora and fauna, and people throughout. Martí's wonder at the natural beauty that surrounded him is again palpable in his entry of April 18 after a long day of marching and climbing:

> The beautiful night won't let me sleep. The crickets chirp; a lizard clicks, and its chorus responds; the cupey and the paguá, a short, spiny palm tree; the fireflies hover slowly among the noisy nests, I hear the music of the jungle composed and soft, as if of the finest violins; the music undulates, it embraces and unbinds, spreads its wing and perches, titillates and elevates, ever subtly and quietly. It is the emergence of the fluid *son* [a style of Cuban music and dance step]: What wings brush the leaves? What diminutive violin, and waves of violins, draw the *son*, and soul, from the leaves? What dance from the souls of the leaves?[22]

As in his earlier diary entries, Martí's utter joy at walking and sleeping on his beloved island seemed for a time to outweigh whatever personal discomforts he was suffering, suggesting the solace and strength he drew from the environment during his trying final days.

Yet greater and more immediate dangers faced Martí and his small retinue. They learned from their scouts that Spanish troops were en route to intercept them as part of a larger strategy to decapitate the insurgency by capturing or killing its leaders.[23] And if they managed to evade their Spanish pursuers and reach Camagüey, they would face a potentially greater obstacle in the continued recalcitrance of Antonio Maceo, who preceded Martí and Gómez into the field with three thousand men — a formidable force that the wily general could easily use to his advantage in any political confrontation. Maceo's standing as the highest-ranking Afro-Cuban in the revolutionary forces presented an additional level of complexity, as any perceived slight to him might undermine the multiracial coalition Martí had painstakingly built over many years and render viable once again the divide-and-conquer racialist strategy that Spain had so effectively employed in previous struggles.[24]

Maceo knew that his military might and wide renown among exiles would give him considerable bargaining power in any negotiation regarding Cuba's future. At worst, he could simply refuse to coordinate his operations with Gómez, withhold his forces à la Achilles, or even turn them against his counterparts in a bid to secure power for himself. It is possible, given Maceo's prominence as a military leader and high regard among Afro-Cubans, that personal ambition played at least some role in his resistance to the Martí-Gómez plan.

Maceo's letters and published statements suggest that his contrary posture also stemmed at least partly from a sense of belittlement and insult at the civilian leadership's hands, the final straw having been his subordination to Martí ally Flor Crombet in the military and administrative hierarchy. Maceo may have perceived this final snub as confirmation of the leadership's own lingering, latent racism despite Martí's many and passionate denunciations of racial prejudice. Maceo had long and willingly consented to occupying a subordinate role in the military hierarchy, as he was keenly aware of Spain's desire to use the Afro-Cuban's prominence as proof of the revolution's underlying racial agenda. Such gestures on his part may have fueled a heightened, if suppressed, sensitivity to real or perceived slights from the cause to which he had devoted his life. Maceo's internalized struggle, exacerbated by the daily, even hourly pressures and dangers of the military campaign, can only have sharpened his sense of disparagement and quickness to anger.

In Maceo's defense, the general's long-standing devotion to the cause of Cuban independence was beyond question, and he had only recently — and narrowly — survived an assassination attempt himself.[25] Yet Martí and Gómez were beginning to regard Maceo as a potent but unstable asset to be managed very carefully, an assessment that Maceo's erratic behavior in the coming days would amply confirm.

Maceo's brush with death was far from the only anecdotal evidence Martí would receive of the dangers all around him. The days that followed Martí's nighttime idyll of April 18 brought many troubling omens, among them the news of Flor Crombet's death in battle shortly after arriving in Cuba.[26] Crombet, along with brothers Antonio and José Maceo, was among a group that landed in Cuba on March 30 to help lead the war effort. Antonio Maceo, wary of the group being discovered before reaching insurgent forces, split it into smaller units and sent them along different routes to ensure that at least some would evade capture. One of Crombet's scouts defected and alerted Spanish forces to his group's location. Only José Maceo survived the ensuing battle on April 10 and wandered alone in the Cuban bush for nearly two weeks before finding a Cuban unit led by Pedro "Perico" Pérez. The other five members of that group, including Crombet, were killed in the ambush. Crombet was among Martí's closest friends and most devoted partisans, making news of his death a political as well as personal loss for the civilian leader.

More importantly for Martí's growing sense of peril, the fall of Crombet and narrow escape of Antonio Maceo—both skilled generals and accomplished warriors—boded ill for the prospects of an inexperienced, physically fragile writer and poet. Nor were civilians or even women spared the wrath of the vindictive and increasingly desperate Spanish forces: Caridad Pérez y Piñó, in whose home Martí's group stopped to rest and eat on April 19, told them the story of her husband's murder by Spanish troops for helping the insurgents. Pérez and her three children escaped with their lives, but she bore a long scar on her back from the machete wound she had received in the struggle. Martí later recounted how Pérez y Piñó got her *machetazo*:

> Her husband killed the betraying *chino* [Chinese Cuban] from his
> ranch, and one more—Caridad was wounded in the back; the husband
> fell dead—the Spanish soldiers fled—Caridad takes up her daughter
> in one arm, and spurting blood, chases after them: "If only I'd had a
> rifle." She returns, calls her people, they bury the husband, she sends for
> [General Bernabé] Boza: "see what they have done to me!" The troops
> jump up: we want to go find that captain. . . . Caridad was showing them
> her wound. And continued living, preaching, motivating in the camp.[27]

Even as Martí admired this intrepid Cuban woman and her enduring support of the insurgents—cooking, mending their torn clothes—he may well have reflected on the riding tide of blood and betrayal that until now he had only known second-hand and wondered when his own time might come. With the violence that his revolution had unleashed now raging all around him and Spanish troops close on his trail, surely that moment was not far off.

The days that followed Crombet's death and the attempt on Maceo were largely uneventful. The small Martí and Gómez group fell into a tedious, wearying routine of early mornings, long marches, and brief stops for rest or food, punctuated by a few hours of troubled, exhausted sleep. The boredom and physical weariness of the march belied the creeping sense of danger that permeated their every move and thought. They had been on the march for nearly a week and seen no action but received constant and discouraging news of hard-fought battles, fallen comrades, and Spanish troops on their trail, as Martí notes in his diary entry of April 24: "we carry our load, from sun to sun, along the fatiguing trail. One senses the danger . . . they have been close on our tracks."[28] Although nearby commander Perico Pérez sent eighteen of his men to supplement the group, Gómez was still in no position to engage their pursuers. The would-be conquerors had themselves become the quarry. Martí was a target, and the ongoing efforts to protect and shield him from harm were becoming a drain on men and resources and a distraction for Gómez. Before the *generalísimo* could turn his full attention to defeating the Spanish, he had to safely deliver his civilian charge to Camagüey and secure Cuba's political future.

On the morning of April 25 Martí heard for the first time the sounds of combat, as his group was close to the fierce battle at Arroyo Hondo: "The combat unfolds as if at our very feet; three bullets bore, heavily, into the tree trunks."[29] Thanks to José Maceo's victory in that skirmish, Martí and his group gained a boon that until then had eluded them, the horses Maceo's men took from the fallen Spanish. Even in victory, there was no time for rest or celebration. Martí, Gómez, and the others, joining José Maceo's men, rode eight hours before finally stopping at midnight to rest and tend to the wounded. Despite the dangers and exhaustion, Martí's letter of the following day to Carmita Mantilla expresses hope and resilience in the face of great personal difficulty:

> [W]e came and from a few paces away the great battle raged for two hours: there the first bullets crossed above our heads; the enemy having been rebuffed moments later, we fell into our people's arms: there horses, jubilation, and we continued the admirable march, by torchlight; eight more hours of marching on our feet, after two of combat and four from the day's march, the entire night, without stopping to eat day or night. I lay down at three in the morning, [after] aiding the wounded. Back on our feet at five, all happily; later they sleep, talk among themselves, come by carrying potatoes and beef, they bring my new horse and mount; and will we fight today? We pack up and are on our way; our soul is one: some arms taken from the enemy.[30]

Of the four other letters Martí wrote on April 26, the most important went to Antonio Maceo, whose forces were camped nearby and with whom Gómez and Martí requested a meeting. They agreed that meeting with Maceo in advance of their anticipated Camagüey showdown would be crucial to the summit's success. That Martí's entreaty to Maceo did not immediately succeed in persuading him suggests as much Maceo's continued recalcitrance as the difficulties of arranging such a high-level meeting. Although Maceo remained a ferocious fighter and audacious tactician after the attempt on his life, he grew increasingly circumspect about his personal movements, revealing his whereabouts and anticipated locations only to his closest advisors. April 29 and 30 brought another near-miss with Antonio Maceo, the attempted rendezvous postponed this time due to his involvement in what he cryptically called "urgent operations." Whether Maceo suspected others within the ranks of plotting against him or was simply dodging Spanish pursuers, he remained an elusive quarry for Martí and Gómez, citing military maneuvers and other contingencies as his reasons for avoiding the pair.[31]

In the days that followed, Martí and Gómez simultaneously played hunter and hunted, staying a step ahead of their Spanish pursuers as they labored to persuade Maceo to meet them. In the interim Martí busied himself with war business. His correspondence to Quesada and Guerra consisted largely of directions for managing the home front, while a series of circulars and memos—all co-written with Gómez—to the military leadership focused on broader strategy and the coordination of the Camagüey summit where the government-in-arms' political representatives (many of them proxies for their civilian counterparts in exile) would meet to determine and ratify the laws and broader constitutional framework of the future Cuban state. As was his custom, Martí weathered hard times, both personal and political, by delving deeper into his work.

The first week of May brought the promise of gratification on the island and exile fronts for Martí's efforts. The opportunity of a one-on-one interview on the evening of May 2 to be published in the *New York Herald* and the lengthy letter to the *Herald*'s editor dated that same day that Martí co-authored with Gómez gave the revolution's best-known public figure favorable press at a time when his enemies were seeking to discredit him and by extension the independence movement.[32] Even more encouragingly, he and Gómez finally managed to arrange their long-sought meeting with Antonio Maceo. Maceo made more claims of engagement in unspecified operations but finally agreed in writing to meet his counterparts on May 5, with the time and place to be determined.[33] Martí's letters to Maceo betray no particular frustration beyond an affectionate, if somewhat disingenuous, disappointment at their extended separation: "I have had one true regret here, among so many reasons to be pleased: not having seen you," he wrote on May 2; in the next day's letter he considered it "good fortune and a pleasure to have you so near us."[34] Privately, however, he and Gómez had grown increasingly frustrated with Maceo's antics, as Gómez's terse diary entry of April 28 amply demonstrates: "The shameful peripeties of General Antonio Maceo since his landing deserve their own separate chapter."[35] Their deep concerns regarding Maceo's history of recalcitrance and his current erratic behavior notwithstanding, his newfound willingness to meet now gave them reason for guarded optimism.

ON THE AFTERNOON OF MAY 5 ANTONIO MACEO ASSEMBLED a small group of his most trusted men and rode out to his arranged rendezvous with Gómez and Martí. He did not, however, ride to their agreed-upon meeting point, choosing instead to intercept the others along the trail. Given the recent failed assassination attempt against him, it is clear that Maceo was wary of any leaked intelligence that might allow his enemies to set a trap for him.

From the available accounts, Maceo and his men most likely rode to a predetermined spot along the trail to wait for the others—Gómez, Martí, José Maceo, and the roughly hundred men who accompanied them. Upon their approach, Maceo and his men charged suddenly onto the trail from the surrounding thickets, the sudden stirring and clatter of horses' hooves momentarily startling Gómez and his troops. At the head of his men, Maceo halted his charge directly before Gómez, announced that they were "on the move," and demanded that the location of their meeting be changed to a nearby deserted plantation called La Mejorana.[36] Maceo offered no explanation for the sudden change and never revealed the nature or aim of the maneuvers in which his men were engaged. If Maceo's erratic and aggressive behavior since arriving in Cuba had worried Gómez and Martí, this new confirmation of his growing volatility only underscored the precariousness of their relationship at this crucial moment.

Given the relatively spartan conditions under which Antonio Maceo's guests had been living, they must have been impressed, if not stunned, by the feast that Maceo had prepared for them. Upon their arrival at La Mejorana, Antonio Maceo ordered food and drink from his camp for the whole contingent. José Maceo, like most of the Cuban field commanders, was barely managing to keep his troops clothed and fed, much less produce a lavish moveable feast on such short notice. Given the context, the recipients of Antonio Maceo's largesse could hardly miss its underlying boastfulness and displaced aggression. The feast was a gesture that simultaneously honored Gómez and Martí and showed off Maceo's power and resources. Antonio Maceo's message to his supposed allies, as they prepared to negotiate the war's strategy and the distribution of troops and territory for the foreseeable future, was unmistakable.

As the feast was prepared, Maceo and Gómez turned quickly to business. The two generals excluded Martí from their initial discussions, which centered on a planned westward offensive and the assignment of troops and objectives among the various generals.[37] Martí's apparent lack of suspicion at this exclusion suggests that he knew the topics under discussion did not directly concern him. Given the meeting's high stakes and the growing tension between them and Maceo, Martí's marked lack of anxiety most of all reflected his implicit trust in Gómez by this point: whatever disagreements the two had over a decade of organizing and fighting for Cuba, their recent months of close collaboration and constant travel—and now the launch of the war—cemented a bond that Martí believed would withstand Maceo's clumsy attempts at a Cuban realpolitik. The dread that filled Martí three weeks earlier, during his previous exclusion from military deliberations, seems to have left him. The intervening weeks of living and working among the *mambis* seemingly infused in him a sense of having found his place among them, a feeling of belonging that by now had less to do with his symbolic rank as general than with his lived experience among the men and his personal bond with Gómez.

It was precisely this sense of belonging that Maceo was at that moment working to undermine. Aside from the strategic and administrative business of managing the war, Maceo's primary objective for this meeting was to relegate Martí—and the civilian leadership he represented—to a secondary role in the future Cuban state and if possible to send him back to New York for the rest of the war. Martí's May 5 diary entry tersely describes Maceo's position as mediated by Gómez:

> [T]hey call me before long, from the porch where they stand: Maceo has other ideas about governing: a junta of generals, with authority vested in their representatives,—and a General Secretariat:—the country, then, and all its offices, which create and animate the army, as subordinate to the Army. . . . I insist on presenting myself before the representatives who will convene to elect the government. [Maceo] doesn't want each chief to send their own, under their own authority: he will send the four from Oriente: "within 15 days they will be with you—and they will be people who will not be bamboozled by Doctor Martí."[38]

Martí wondered not only at the substance of Maceo's proposals but also at his manner:

> At the table, opulent and laden with chicken and suckling pig, he returns to the subject: he wounds me, and repulses me: I realize that I should shake off the part, with which I am being marked, of civilian defender of forces hostile to the military movement. I maintain, rudely: the Army, free,—and the nation, as a nation and with all of its dignity represented. I display my discontent at such an indiscreet and forced conversation, at the table, as Maceo makes haste to leave . . .
>
> On horseback, a quick goodbye: "You go that way."[39]

José Maceo and his five hundred troops split from Gómez and Martí immediately after their meeting with the elder Maceo, riding off toward their assigned territories in Santiago. José Maceo's departure temporarily left Martí and Gómez with only twenty men as an escort, as it would take several days for them to join up with General Quintín Banderas and his nearly one thousand troops. The two men's accounts of Maceo's departure and their own suddenly dispiriting situation suggest a deep, shared disillusionment. Martí wrote in his May 5 diary entry:

> [We] rode on with our vengeful escort; at day's end, without our scouts, who stayed with José [Maceo], our direction unknown, to a shed on the trail, where we did not dismount. They send for the scouts: we ride on, to another muddy ranch, away from the camps, open to attack. G. sends for meat, from José's camp: the scouts bring it. And so, like outcasts, with our sad thoughts, we slept.[40]

Gómez's May 5 diary entry echoes Martí's sense of abandonment and of their putative host's disdain: "Afterward, at about four in the afternoon he led us to the outskirts of the camp, where we spent the night alone and abandoned, barely escorted by 20 inexperienced and poorly armed men."[41] Both descriptions are consistent with their respective authors' narrative styles and psychological processes, Martí's "open to attack" and "like outcasts, with our sad thoughts" contrasting instructively with Gómez's terse, disapproving reference to the "inexperienced and poorly armed men" escorting them. The entries depict their profound disappointment with the meeting but also their growing dread at the prospect of a divisive, potentially destructive showdown with Maceo's proxies at Camagüey. The general's spiteful, even bizarre behavior clearly signaled that he would not let his financial dependence on Martí's fundraising machine — or his subordinate rank to Gómez as the revolution's military head — override his distrust for civilian rule and desire for a ruling military junta. However valuable Maceo might still be as a military ally, he now loomed as a potential and formidable obstacle on the path to a truly democratic Cuba.

The days following Martí and Gómez's summit with Antonio Maceo brought a flurry of military activity, if not in actual battles then certainly in terms of troop movements. The coordinated distribution of troops under the various commanders, each assigned a specific region, suggests that Gómez and Antonio Maceo decided upon this strategy at their May 5 meeting. Although Gómez and Martí found themselves practically alone in the meeting's immediate aftermath, their path soon intersected with several insurgent units en route to their various destinations. Quintín Banderas and his army of a thousand so-called *orientales*, a primarily Afro-Cuban unit, joined Gómez and Martí on May 7 on their way to Sancti Spíritus in the center of the island. Ángel Guerra, one of the four men who had landed with Gómez and Martí and had accompanied them ever since, departed the following day with a few hundred men. On May 9 Banderas's forces continued on to Sancti Spíritus, and Gómez and Martí subsequently joined Colonel José Miró and his four hundred men. Through it all, Martí remained troubled by the tense confrontation with Antonio Maceo and wondered how many other commanders agreed with Maceo's desire for military rather than civilian rule in a free Cuba.

Martí's fears, as he would soon learn, were not unfounded, as others among the military leadership clearly shared Maceo's aversion to civilian rule. Martí's May 9 diary entry emphasizes his awareness of the increasingly heated polemic surrounding his potential leadership of the future state. Martí wove separate anecdotes featuring Colonel Miró, a Martí loyalist, into a single narrative illustrating the divisiveness that threatened the revolution's success:

> [Miró] tells me of the efforts of Galvez, in Havana, to belittle the revolution: of the great hatred with which Galvez speaks of me and of Juan Gualberto [Gómez]:[42] "it is you, you whom they fear": "at the tops of their lungs they would claim that you would not come, and that is what will now confuse them."—It surprises me, here as everywhere else, the affection shown us, and the unity of soul, *which will be condescended to, and which will go unrecognized, and which will be superseded, to the detriment, or at least the detriment of delay, of the revolution, in its first year of impetus.* The spirit that I planted is the one that has taken root, and that of the island, and with it, and guided by it, we would triumph shortly, and with a greater victory, and for a better peace. I foresee that, for a certain period at least, the revolution will be divorced by force from this spirit,—it will be deprived of enchantment and pleasure, and the power to conquer this natural consortium,—it will be robbed of the benefit of this conjunction between the activities of these revolutionary forces and the spirit that animates them.—A detail: *President* they have called me, all of the men, since my arrival at camp, despite my public repulsion [of the title], and at every camp at which I arrive, the respect is reborn, and a certain warm enthusiasm of general affection, and demonstrations of the people's reveling in my presence and simplicity.—And at the approach of one [who addressed me as]: President, and at my smiling acknowledgement: "Do not call Martí President: call him General: he comes here as a General: do not call him President." "And who would contain the people's impulse, General," says Miró: "that which is born from all of their hearts?" "Well: but he is not yet President: he is the Delegate."—I kept quiet, and noted the embarrassment and displeasure among all present, and among some almost aggravation.[43]

The "General" in the May 9 incident was clearly Gómez, who had been influenced by Maceo's views in ways Martí did not anticipate. Although Martí describes his disappointment in terms of the larger political struggle, Gómez's ambivalence, even caginess, regarding Martí's role in the future Cuban state is the greater emotional and psychological blow.

Gómez's apparent hedging of his bet on Martí as the head of a civilian-led state soon escalated into outright rejection and denial. In a heated argument the following day with Colonel Serafín Bello, another Martí supporter, Gómez declared that "Martí will not be President while I am alive. . . because I don't know what happens to presidents, that once they arrive they go bad, except for [Benito] Juarez, and even he did a little, and Washington."[44] In both cases, Gómez avoided direct criticism of Martí, at least while the latter was in earshot, yet something obviously had changed in the general's thinking even in the few hours that separated the two incidents. On May 9 Gómez did not necessarily oppose the idea of Martí as president but only his being hailed as such before the fact ("he is not yet the President: he is the Delegate"). By the next day, however, Gómez was arguing against the entire idea of a civilian head of state—indeed, the only two presidents of which he explicitly approved had been successful generals.

Gómez's potential defection to those opposing civilian leadership troubled Martí much more than he let on in his May 9 and 10 diary entries. Without Gómez's active support, Martí could not reasonably hope to overcome the growing opposition to his leadership or to civilian rule. He would have to again secure Gómez's backing or at least persuade him to withhold judgment until after the Camagüey summit.

On May 11 Miró and most of his troops set off for their assigned operations in the neighboring province of Santiago, leaving Martí and Gómez with roughly fifty men. The next day, this smaller unit rode about thirteen miles inland to the outskirts of the town of Jatía. They spent the next week in that general area awaiting the arrival of General Bartolomé Masó and his three hundred cavalrymen, despite the very precarious situation in which they found themselves: without Miró, Banderas, Guerra, or either Maceo, pursued by Spanish troops, and unwilling or unable to make progress toward Camagüey without Masó's protection.[45]

As the record of Martí and Gómez's travels across the island indicates, their weeklong wait for Masó was entirely uncharacteristic of their movements. Their slower progress during the week after their May 5 meeting with Maceo was partly due to bad weather, as the group faced a heavy downpour and steadily deteriorating conditions on the ground; Martí's diary notes rainfall and a difficult landscape of mud and high or turgid rivers every day from May 10 through May 17.[46] Gómez may have fallen ill and thus been indisposed to traveling longer distances.[47] Nevertheless, the extended wait for Masó not only departed radically from Gómez's movements to that point but flew in the face of the *generalísimo's* own larger strategic imperatives. Gómez understood that due to Spain's greater numbers and superior firepower, the *mambis* had to stay constantly on the move and avoid engaging the enemy in the field, to strike quickly and only when the situation and numbers favored them.[48] All of this suggests that Gómez and Martí's extended wait for Masó was both an unplanned and undesirable one.

And yet they waited, for reasons that had as much to do with politics as they did with strategy or tactics. Martí's May 12 letter to Masó requested his help with military and more broadly political matters: "Now, by your side, the work can be broadened, *and more can be said to the country*, without ceasing our movements."[49] "The work" refers specifically to the anticipated coordination of Masó's substantial cavalry power with Gómez's strategic command, a union that would create a stronger military force as well as provide cover for Martí's safe arrival at the Camagüey summit. The statement's broader meaning, however—especially the hope that Masó's arrival would say something more "to the country"—suggests Martí's awareness that Masó's renown among the Cubans as a veteran of the Ten Years' War and status as a leading voice for independence on the island made him a valuable political ally and might make him an effective counter to those who dismissed Martí as a naïve radical out of touch with the natives' true interests. As a white Creole from a respected Cuban family, Masó visibly joining Martí and Gómez would provide political cover against Spain's assertion as well that the revolution was really the first stage of a race war against whites.

Martí had for some days suspected that Masó was engaged with Maceo, as he indicates in his May 10 diary entry: "For word from Masó we wait. Could he have gone to concentrate his forces with Maceo's?"[50] The available historical records are not clear on the question of the concentration to which Martí and Gómez refer in their respective diaries from this time, but the fact that Martí did not know Masó's whereabouts suggests that the general was not moving according to the plans Gómez had agreed upon with Maceo at their May 5 meeting. By May 12 Martí and Gómez had confirmed that Masó was carrying out operations with Maceo as part of this concentration of forces in the east that Gómez apparently countermanded: "[Masó] is marching... obeying orders for the concentration, which no longer has reason to continue."[51]

Plotting military strategy and distributing short-term duties and objectives among the field commanders constituted an important part of the business that Gómez and Maceo had discussed at their meeting at La Mejorana the previous week. No indication exists of Gómez having explicitly cancelled such a concentration before his mention of it in his May 13 diary entry, nor is there on the other hand any evidence that he and Maceo agreed to or even discussed this change at their meeting. It is highly unlikely, however, that Gómez would not have stated his intention to Maceo, as the entire point of their May 5 meeting was to coordinate efforts in order to avoid precisely this kind of confusion. The fact that Masó was with Maceo, then, suggests not a miscommunication but rather an act of insubordination and defiance: Maceo may well have chosen to keep Masó with him in pursuit of his own military objectives and in contradiction of Gómez's orders. Whether by accident or design, however, the consequences of Masó's delay in reaching Gómez and Martí would soon become all too clear.

IF MARTÍ REALIZED THE DANGER TO HIS LIFE AND THE VERY real possibility that he would not survive the war only after arriving in Cuba, he came to embrace the prospect as part of his duty to the revolution he had set in motion. Whatever the impact of recent events on the revolution's fortunes and however much anguish and uncertainty they may have caused Martí, his final writings reveal a palpable sense of clarity and even serenity. Although Martí had immersed himself in the daily administrative and strategic concerns of the war effort since arriving on the island, his May 18 letter to Mercado demonstrates that his larger duty went beyond simply liberating Cuba from Spanish rule. One of Martí's greatest strengths as a political thinker was his ability to grasp Cuba's fight for independence as part of a larger struggle fought over a rapidly shifting terrain as the older empires slowly but inexorably yielded to the United States as the Western Hemisphere's preeminent power. It was this vision of a postcolonial Latin America perched precariously between a faltering Spain and a rising American empire that fueled his determination that the new Cuban republic help lead a larger pan-American and anticolonial movement in the new century. His duty, as he explained it to Mercado, was "to impede in time with the independence of Cuba that the United States extend itself throughout the Antilles and fall with ever greater force upon the lands of our America."[52] Once Cuba gained its freedom, it had to work to prevent "the annexation of the nations of our America to the turgid and brutal North that despises us."[53]

However much Martí might have vacillated between respect for the founding democratic principles of the United States on the one hand and contempt for its materialism and racism on the other, by the time of his final letter to Manuel Mercado he understood it as the greatest threat to Cuban independence. And in what has since become the letter's most celebrated sentence, he clearly saw himself as his country's protector and future leader: "I lived inside the monster, and know its entrails—and my sling is David's."[54] Yet the mixed biblical metaphors reveal the ambivalence that had always marked Martí's relation to the "brutal" North he could not bring himself to despise. For if the David-and-Goliath reference depicts Martí's view of himself as a confident if outgunned adversary of empire, his nod to the parable of Jonah and the whale in the same sentence reveals a much more complex relation to the American "monster." As Jonah, who defied God's order and attempted to escape his judgment, remained a grudging instrument of divine will even after God delivered him from the belly of the whale, so did Martí struggle to the end of his life against U.S. domination even as he conceded its influence and power.[55]

Martí did not live to finish his final letter to Mercado. We do not know why he stopped where he did, what circumstances compelled him to do so. The otherwise unremarkable act of leaving a task to be finished later takes on an added poignancy and complexity, however, when we consider the sense of urgency and peril that permeates the letter. "This is life or death," Martí wrote toward the end, "and there is no room for error."[56] Given the improvised, often haphazard nature of the Cuban insurgency, the statement stands in hindsight as an ominous portent of the series of errors and miscalculations that would soon cost Martí his life.

BARTOLOMÉ MASÓ AND HIS CAVALRY UNIT OF THREE HUN-dred men finally met Martí and Gómez on May 19 at a nearby ranch called La Vuelta Grande. Martí had not seen Gómez for nearly two days, having stayed behind with perhaps a dozen men as the others rode to intercept an anticipated Spanish supply convoy in the area. Raiding such convoys was an important part of the *mambís'* war strategy, as they used captured arms, ammunition, and food to bolster their own inadequate supplies. This particular raid presented for Gómez two considerable problems. First, he needed to leave a few men behind at camp to protect Martí in their absence. Doing so meant completing the mission with fewer men than he would have liked while still leaving Martí vulnerable to attack. A second and no less significant hazard was that while such raids were ideal for an insurgent force on the move, they posed considerable risk for a unit returning to a base camp. With the help of their native scouts, Spanish troops could easily pick up their trail and follow it back to the camp—and to Martí.[57] As an experienced field commander, Gómez would have understood both of these potential pitfalls and would not have lightly made the decision to pursue the convoy. He did so likely out of sheer necessity, due to an immediate lack of ammunition or food.

In Gómez's absence Martí continued to correspond with field commanders and various others. The anticipated convoy never materialized, and Gómez returned to camp around midday on May 19 to find Martí with Masó and his cavalry unit. Martí and his small retinue had left camp at 4 a.m. that day to meet Masó's forces, which had camped a few miles away at La Vuelta Grande. Exhausted after several days' hard riding from La Sabana, Masó's horses were too tired to cover even the few miles to Gómez and Martí's camp, much less embark on the men's desired journey to the Camagüey summit. Martí sent a brief letter to Gómez informing him that Masó had finally arrived, noting that the general "had been greatly upset by the useless trip to La Sabana" and urging Gómez to return as soon as possible.[58]

That May 19 letter—two short paragraphs, totaling eighty-seven words—is Martí's last known piece of writing, not, as is widely believed, his interrupted letter from the previous day. The point is not merely an academic one, as it provides a small but important insight into the myth-building that began in earnest soon after Martí's death and has continued now for more than a century. The May 18 letter is rightly recognized as an important document not only for historical reasons but for its concise, powerful distillation of Martí's political thinking at the end of his life—a sort of political last will and testament for those who would inherit his work and continue it.[59] And as the final statement of a life lived in service to a revolutionary ideal, it is tempting to want to enshrine the May 18 letter as the ultimate image of Martí as national patriarch and heroic icon—his famous final words, as it were, before charging off to an equally heroic death. Yet the expansive, inspired May 18 letter was interrupted, thrust aside by some more immediate concern directly related to the exigencies of life in wartime. It is this more urgent, more anxious Martí that we find in his final letter to Gómez, his last, terse, hastily written words utterly bereft of the rhetorical flights and expansive vision of his incomplete letter to Mercado. Although Martí does not mention his own state of mind in the last letter, it is easy to read his description of the men's exhaustion and Masó's frustration as his own.

Despite the trying circumstances of their meeting, Masó's reunion with Gómez and Martí brought a much-needed boost to morale. As Gómez notes in his May 19 diary entry, however, the euphoria proved fleeting:

> We enjoyed a time of genuine enthusiasm.
> We rallied the troops and Martí spoke with genuine ardor and a warrior's spirit; unaware that the enemy had followed my trail and that disaster awaited us and for Martí, the greatest catastrophe of all.[60]

The only detailed description of Martí's last speech comes from Colonel José Miró, according to whom Martí spoke "with the fervor of an apostle" and declared that "for the cause of Cuba I would be crucified!"[61] About two hours after Martí's final speech, he lay dead on a battlefield, according to some reports the only Cuban casualty of what is now known as the Battle of Dos Ríos.[62]

Gómez, Masó, and Spanish Colonel José Ximénez de Sandoval, among others, later published wildly divergent, even mutually incriminating accounts of what happened that day—and how the revolution's preeminent leader died there. Gómez became especially notorious for giving different, sometimes conflicting versions of both Martí's death and his own actions during the Battle of Dos Ríos.[63]

If no single person is responsible for the circumstances that led to Martí's death at Dos Ríos, it nevertheless resulted from a combination of bad luck, miscommunication, a high concentration of Spanish forces in the area, and significant missteps by Cuban leaders. Two such decisions especially contributed to the circumstances that led to Martí's death: Masó's lost week with Maceo and Gómez's decision to chase a Spanish convoy that never came. Whatever material needs for food or arms necessitated the attempted raid, it enabled Spanish troops to follow the trail back to Gómez and Martí's camp. Likewise, the decision to sit and wait for Masó gave Sandoval, who knew the Cubans' general whereabouts but not their precise location, time to concentrate Spanish forces in the area in anticipation of an eventual confrontation.

Maceo's failure either to realize Gómez's need for Masó or to communicate it to his fellow general contributed indirectly to Martí's death at Dos Ríos. Masó spent several days following orders that Gómez had explicitly contravened, which he may or may not have done at his May 5 meeting with Antonio Maceo. Regardless of whether Gómez stated on May 5 his desire to meet with Masó's unit, he and Martí made it clear that they were headed for the Camagüey summit. No known evidence shows that Maceo made any attempt to inform Masó of Gómez's desires during their joint operations or that Masó had any idea how badly he was needed at Dos Ríos until receiving Martí's and Gómez's urgent entreaties. Curiously, none of Maceo's biographers discuss the period of May 12–20 in any detail, leaving an uncharacteristic and conspicuous gap in an otherwise richly researched life.[64] The week that Masó thus lost as a consequence of Maceo's neglect or insubordination made it possible for Sandoval's Spanish troops to locate Gómez, which in turn led directly to Martí's tragic — and needless — death in battle.

THE MYTH OF JOSÉ MARTÍ'S HEROIC DEATH AT DOS RÍOS IS central to his standing as Cuba's preeminent national icon, so much so that at least one Martí scholar has wondered what, indeed, would be left of his myth of martyrdom if it were ever proven less than glorious. Yet there is no historically significant event in Martí's life about which less is concretely known or that has been subjected to more speculation and outright invention. Perhaps the very fact of the historical vacuum surrounding Martí's death — of the impossibility of confirming beyond a reasonable doubt what exactly happened — has enabled and encouraged these fabrications: historical contingency molded into myth and hardened over time into unquestioned orthodoxy.

Power, influence, and access to journalists also played crucial roles in the establishment of a "consensus" narrative that became the official account of Martí's death. And, not coincidentally, this generally accepted account largely echoes Gómez's version of events. As a highly respected figure who achieved something close to mythic status himself, the deferential treatment Gómez enjoyed from journalists and biographers, along with his considerable political skills, allowed him to both disseminate the story of Martí's heroic death and suppress any version that would render him culpable for it.[65] Gómez also enjoyed the support of key surrogates such as José Miró, whose published account of Martí's death confirms Gómez's in nearly every detail. Yet the available evidence regarding Martí's death at Dos Ríos simply does not support the myth of a heroic ride into martyrdom and glory. In fact, the historical record suggests a death remarkable primarily for the identity of the fallen — and for having been utterly unnecessary.

All we know for certain is that on the afternoon of May 19, Cuban and Spanish forces clashed at Dos Ríos, and Martí died in combat. From these sketchy facts has grown the myth of Martí's heroic, even glorious martyr's death, a composite of which might read like this: On the afternoon of May 19, Gómez's and Masó's combined troops, more than three hundred men, came under surprise attack by a Spanish force greater than twice its size. Unprepared for the sudden assault, Gómez hastily assembled a counterforce and charged into the fray. Before riding off, Gómez admonished Martí to stay behind and out of danger, but the latter disobeyed the order and followed him into battle.[66] With revolver in hand, Martí charged a Spanish position, at which point he was fatally shot and fell from his horse. A young officer named Ángel de la Guardia, who had been accompanying Martí and was riding close behind him, escaped injury but was unable to either prevent Martí's death or retrieve his body. After Gómez's own failed attempt to rescue his fallen comrade, Martí's body was carried off by Spanish soldiers, who did not immediately know the victim's identity but suspected they had killed someone important.[67] And thus, unwilling to stand on the sidelines while others risked their lives, Martí chose spontaneously to lead by example, leaving his own death as the greatest, highest model of Cuban patriotism and nationalist ardor.

Other, competing versions of this story circulated in the immediate aftermath of Martí's death that far surpass this one in their disregard for basic historical accuracy, although in the years that followed, the above composite account became conventional received wisdom, legend, and national myth. The most widely circulated of the "alternative" versions had Martí killed while on his way to depart the island after he agreed to return to the United States and his role of expatriate civilian leader. This version seems to have arisen from an interview attributed to Gómez in the *New York Herald* of June 11, 1895, but which he denied giving. In this apocryphal story, recounted here in a 1920 history of Cuba, Martí and a small group of fellow *mambis* lived to make a romantic last stand against a larger force that surrounded them:

> While Gómez set out for Camaguey, Martí turned toward the southern coast, intending to go first to Jamaica, whence he could take an English steamer for New York or any other destination he might select. Martí had with him an escort of only fifty men, and soon after parting company with Gómez he was led by a treacherous guide into a ravine where he was trapped by a Spanish force outnumbering the Cubans twenty to one.[!] The Cubans fought with desperate valor, Martí himself leading a charge which nearly succeeded in cutting a way through the Spanish lines. But the odds were too heavy against them, and without even the satisfaction of taking two or three Spanish lives for every life they gave, the Cubans were all slain, Martí himself being among the last to fall. Word of the conflict reached Gómez, and he came hastening back, just too late to save his comrade, and was himself wounded in the furious attack which he made upon the Spaniards in an attempt at least to recover Martí's body.[68]

Along with the story of Martí's "last stand," several other rumors circulated regarding the circumstances of his death at Dos Ríos: that Martí had been shot while asleep in his hammock; that he had been gunned down from behind; that he and de la Guardia had run into the enemy fire utterly by accident, riding casually "with an air of tourists." Colonel José Ximénez de Sandoval, commander of the Spanish forces at Dos Ríos, vehemently decried all such representations of Martí's death in a July 4, 1908, letter to Gonzalo de Quesada to which he attached some of the false reports. Sandoval wrote a detailed, point-by-point rebuttal of Gómez's account that appeared in 1911.[69]

The consistency among these accounts—in effect, the constant repetition of a single, unvarying mythic narrative—has come to eclipse the historical record. In a rare contemporary example of agreement between Havana and the U.S.-based exile community, the official Cuban accounts of Martí's heroic death that Cuban schoolchildren read in their textbooks to this day find their counterparts in identical versions published in New York and Miami for Cuban American children.[70] Although widely accepted, this account of Martí's death has little basis in historical fact, and much evidence exists that calls it—and the motivations of its leading disseminators—into question. Regardless of whether Martí charged to his death because he felt ashamed at having incited others to fight without doing so himself or was, consciously or not, actually courting death due to his long-held fantasies of martyrdom, or simply got caught up in the fervent moment and forgot his own lack of military training and skills—in short, whether it was a snap decision or some deeper desire that drove Martí onto the battlefield, his death was not nearly as heroic or picturesque as the myth. In its suddenness and utter banality it actually stands as a poignant anticlimax to a life filled with truly eventful and heroic moments: a relative whimper compared to his short but outsized life.

The single most overlooked element in the many examinations of Martí's death has been the role played by his would-be protector Ángel de la Guardia, eyewitness to the chaotic moments preceding Martí's fatal charge. (In perhaps the most poignant irony surrounding Martí's death, de la Guardia's name in Spanish literally means "guardian angel.") For most commentators, de la Guardia has been little more than a youthful foil for Martí's final heroic moments, following his brave leader into the breach only to witness his death— and conveniently positioned to testify to Martí's last, selfless act of courage and patriotism.[71] Gómez's own initial account even suggests that the young man's place in Cuban history was entirely a product of happenstance: Gómez states in his May 19 diary entry that Martí "had found himself alone, with a child who had never seen combat: Miguel [*sic*] de la Guardia."[72]

The available evidence contradicts the *generalísimo*'s assertion. Far from a novice, de la Guardia had joined Masó's troops six weeks earlier and in his first combat experience led forty *mambís* to capture a Spanish convoy and defeat the more than one hundred Spanish troops escorting it. Impressed with his bravery and skill in battle, Masó immediately promoted him to officer status, and Ángel de la Guardia joined his older brother Dominador as one of the general's personal assistants. Thus by the time of Ángel de la Guardia's arrival in Gómez's camp, as his biographer Enrique Gay-Calbó affirms, "he had experience and knew well the sound of gunfire."[73] However reliable Gómez's claim of ignorance regarding Ángel de la Guardia's military skills and experience, then, the fact is that by the time of the Battle of Dos Ríos the young man had established a reputation as a formidable fighter.

What de la Guardia's superiors did not yet know about him, which would become apparent only after Martí's death, was that his passions on the battlefield often overrode his sense of self-preservation, sometimes to the point of insubordination. Gay-Calbó presents this element of de la Guardia's personality in a relatively sympathetic light:

> [Because] he was convinced of the need to fight, he considered wasted those moments in which there was no fighting. His notion of war found itself in contradiction to that of his commanders. . . . Ángel de la Guardia obeyed [his superiors] with his rigid sense of discipline, although he took advantage of every opportunity to make war as he conceived it, and then he was at the head of his favorite machete charge, at

the head of his men, the first to strike, the most tireless in battle, always the conqueror.[74]

Unbeknown to Gómez and Masó, then, de la Guardia was far from the ideal candidate to keep Martí away from the fighting. In the commanders' defense, de la Guardia's love of danger and disregard for orders did not fully emerge until after Dos Ríos. But on at least three occasions after Martí's death—the last of which cost him his own life—de la Guardia charged on Spanish positions in direct contradiction of his superior's orders.[75] By the time of his death, at least one general, Calixto García, had privately counseled the young officer to temper his passions so that he might live to serve his country longer. De la Guardia promised to thenceforth be more prudent, but his promised discretion continued to fail him at crucial moments.[76] This was partly because de la Guardia's seemingly spontaneous battlefield decisions did not stem entirely from youthful exuberance or love of country. On at least one occasion the young *mambi* shared with his comrades his desire to reach the rank of general. He longed to wear the ceremonial belt that signified the general's rank and distinguished its wearers from their troops. De la Guardia's favorite slogan was known to be "La faja, o la caja," or in English, "the belt or the box"—to make general's rank or die trying.[77] And for a time, this approach served him well: Ángel de la Guardia rose quickly through the Cuban ranks and had reached the rank of colonel by the time of his death in 1897.

It is thus less than likely that, as the legend has it, de la Guardia was either persuaded by Martí to charge with him or followed helplessly behind his impassioned civilian leader. Yet for all the discrepancies in the conflicting accounts of Martí's death, none has disputed that Martí chose to charge into battle. One might expect that Ángel de la Guardia's subsequent history of impulsive, even foolhardy aggressiveness on the battlefield would have led them to question how Martí came to find himself charging straight into enemy fire while supposedly in de la Guardia's care—to wonder whether Martí's fatal charge resulted not from his own stirred-up passions but from de la Guardia's. Yet no such statements of doubt have ever appeared.

To ask such questions, then as now, is to cast doubt upon the most indispensable component of the most central story in the Martí myth: that he died a hero's death. If Martí did not choose to charge into battle—if instead he was simply following the ill-advised whim of his supposed guardian—then his death was not the final testament of a hero but the sad and untimely end of a man whose final epiphany—that the battlefield was really not his place—came too late.

THE QUESTION OF WHAT REALLY HAPPENED DURING MARTÍ'S final moments will likely never be definitively resolved. His associates and contemporaries had little motivation to present the unvarnished truth, in some cases because of the roles they may have played in the tragedy. More importantly, Martí's death created both the need and the opportunity for a central enabling and ennobling story, one that might sustain the movement through the difficult times to come and shield it from the material and psychological blow it suffered with the loss of its chief architect and motivational leader.

Perhaps for that reason, the only reliable written eyewitness account of Martí's death was deliberately destroyed. Miguel de la Guardia later confessed to having burned the letter from his son that explained what happened in those final moments. His explanation for destroying the letter was that as a known sympathizer, he was under constant surveillance by Spanish authorities and subject to unannounced searches of his person and property at any moment. Miguel de la Guardia's situation was so precarious as to have once narrowly escaped execution only by the intercession of a Spanish priest.[78] The risk of being caught holding such a letter, he reasoned, was thus too great, so he chose to burn it.

This explanation seems perfectly reasonable at first, especially given that the only surviving correspondence between Miguel and Ángel de la Guardia, as well as letters to and from other Cuban leaders, dates from after his 1897 exile to Santo Domingo. Ángel de la Guardia's son donated these and other letters to the Academia de la Historia de Cuba to encourage a biography of his father.[79] Ángel de la Guardia himself never wrote another account of Martí's death, although several second-hand anecdotal accounts survive.[80] But the destruction of the letter does not explain why Miguel de la Guardia never divulged its contents in any other venue. If doing so after 1897 would no longer have placed him or his family in danger, why did he remain silent regarding such a crucial matter?

We will never know. Miguel de la Guardia took the contents of his son's letter to the grave — he never himself wrote down what Ángel de la Guardia revealed in that letter, nor did he ever divulge the circumstances of Martí's death to any interviewer, biographer, or journalist.

Why would the only known reader of the only known firsthand account of Martí's death suppress that information? One strong possibility would be that it might have portrayed Martí's death in a less-than-flattering light or at least in a way that contradicted Gómez's by-then well-known account. Given how hard Spanish ideologues and apologists had for years worked to discredit Martí in the eyes of Cubans both at home and in exile, evidence that his death had been less than heroic — and that insurgent leaders knowingly suppressed that evidence — would have constituted a significant victory in the war of public opinion and would have significantly undermined the authority and public reputation of its supreme military commander.

In the absence of definitive testimony from Ángel de la Guardia, the most complete single account of Martí's death remains Gómez's. His initial telling does not address the question of whether Martí led the charge that killed him. It does otherwise serve as a first draft of what became the accepted narrative:

> [We] were desperately battling a column of over 800 men, at a league's [three miles'] distance from our camp; at Dos Ríos.[81]
>
> Never had I found myself in a more compromising position—our first approach swept away the enemy vanguard but immediately slackened, then of course the enemy stood firm with strong firepower; and Martí, who did not stand by my side, fell injured or dead at a point where he could not be recovered and remained in the enemy's power.
>
> When I learned of this I advanced alone up until I could see him.
>
> This loss of a friend, a companion, and a patriot; the slackening and little brio of my people, all of this crushed my spirit to such an end that leaving a few shooters upon an enemy that we could no longer defeat, I retired with my soul saddened . . .
>
> When Martí fell, he had abandoned me and found himself alone, with a child who had never before seen combat: Miguel [*sic*] de la Guardia. And this, despite that when we were about to confront the enemy, I ordered him to stay behind; but he did not want to obey my order and unable to do anything else, but march ahead to drag my people along, I could no longer occupy myself with Martí. I soon found myself nearly alone, 50 paces from the enemy on our left flank; and turning toward the Center I find Guardia retiring with his horse injured, and he gives me the sad news of Martí dead or injured.[82]

Whatever Gómez's later prevarications, he steadily maintained that Martí died because he disregarded Gómez's order to stay behind at camp. In later versions Gómez elaborated upon this basic sequence of events, always implicitly blaming Martí's death on his own insubordination and ill-advised choice to "abandon" him.[83] Curiously, Gómez never specifically addressed his story's apparent inconsistencies, not the least of which is the paradoxical claim that Martí abandoned Gómez even as the latter rode ahead and instructed him to stay out of the fight—in effect abandoning Martí. Even more confusing is the question of how, if in fact Gómez left Martí behind, Martí and de la Guardia could have charged so far ahead of Gómez that he had to mount his own charge into enemy fire in his attempt to retrieve him. Given the distance between the Cuban camp at La Vuelta Grande and the battleground at Dos Ríos—"a league," according to Gómez, roughly equivalent to three miles—the idea that Martí and de la Guardia somehow ended up as much as fifty meters in front of Gómez's charge is at best questionable.[84]

Beyond these internal inconsistencies, other eyewitness accounts flatly contradict each other on the veracity of Gómez's claim of having ordered Martí to remain behind. José Miró's account supports Gómez's assertion, but others contradict it. According to Cuban officers Dominador de la Guardia and José Masó Parra, Martí rode in front with the other leaders and their assistants; Masó Parra takes special pains in his narrative to place Martí by Gómez's side at the head of 150 riders.[85]

Nor are these the only inconsistencies that suggest the unreliability of Gómez's account. The *generalísimo* continued in later accounts to call Martí's fellow rider Miguel de la Guardia even long after his true identity was widely known. While it is plausible that Gómez initially might not have known the young officer's first name, it is curious, given the general accuracy of names, dates, and other facts in his diary, that he would describe de la Guardia as "a child who had never seen combat" if in fact he did not know him. Along with his undisputed expertise as a military strategist and field commander, Gómez was a savvy enough politician to have immediately grasped the danger of being scape-goated for Martí's death. He was also sufficiently powerful within the Cuban leadership — and influential enough among both the Cuban population and the exile community — to persuade or compel others to disseminate his preferred version of events. This small but curious discrepancy in Gómez's initial account thus signals a desire to distance himself from Ángel de la Guardia and more importantly, given the young man's later reputation as a headstrong and erratic fighter, from any responsibility for having placed Martí in his care. More so than the larger misrepresentations of time and distance, this smaller discrep-ancy indicates Gómez's keen awareness of the importance of shaping the story of Martí's death — and especially of who would be blamed for it.

GIVEN THE FORMIDABLE FIGURE THAT GÓMEZ BECAME IN Cuban war and politics during his lifetime, it is perhaps not surprising that the most substantial rebuttal of his account of Martí's death did not surface until after Gómez himself died. Dominador de la Guardia waited until 1911, six years after Gómez died a national hero, to write down his eyewitness account of Martí's death in a letter to Martí's former doctor Eligio Palma, an account that directly contradicted much of Gómez's by-then canonized version. Dominador de la Guardia explicitly denied that Martí had stayed behind at camp and that Gómez had asked him to do so. In Dominador de la Guardia's account, Martí rode at the head of the troops alongside Gómez and General Paquito Borrero. After describing the Cubans' difficult and ill-advised crossing of the Río Con-tramaestre, during which they were forced to break formation, and their initial successful attack of the Spanish vanguard, de la Guardia describes Martí's fatal charge:

At General Gómez's order, we halted our advance; at that moment General Masó was at General Gómez's side. Gómez said to Martí: "Here!" and gestured behind himself, as if to guard him with his own body. I was next to General Masó, with my brother Ángel with me and next to Martí; when they opened fire against the column, Martí invited my brother Ángel to continue with him ahead, and so they did. With the smoke from the gunfire we did not notice their advance and they rode about 50 meters ahead of us. At that distance they made a magnificent target for the Spanish forces and these fired upon them at close range.

Martí took a bullet in the neck and fell to the ground, and my brother Ángel's horse was shot three times. Angelito tried to carry Martí; but he could not manage it: he was too much of a boy and Martí too heavy. Then he gestured for me to come to where he was, and I, not understanding what he was doing that far ahead, insisted he come back to where we stood in the firing line. Barely had Ángel turned his back on the enemy to come to us, when the Spanish began their advance. It took Ángel some time to get back to us, as his horse could barely walk, so by the time he gave Gómez the news of Martí's death and where he had fallen, the Spanish at those very moments were arriving at where Martí was.[86]

Given that others, most notably his erstwhile commander Bartolomé Masó, did publish divergent accounts, it is not clear why de la Guardia shared his memory of the event only in private correspondence rather than a more public venue or why he waited until 1911—six years after Gómez's death—to do so. Perhaps he wished to avoid a public confrontation with Gómez for political or personal reasons. Or perhaps he simply did not want to tarnish the iconic aura of Cuba's greatest national hero.

Whatever his reasons, Dominador de la Guardia's account contradicts Gómez's on at least two important points. First, it does not mention Gómez's claim—crucial to both the myth of Martí's heroic death and Gómez's lack of implication in it—that the *generalísimo* ordered Martí to refrain from battle. This point is partly assuaged by de la Guardia's emphasis on Gómez's "Here!" command, which though at variance with Gómez's version at least allows that he made some attempt to protect Martí. De la Guardia's description of the confusion of the battle scene as well as the smoke and sound of gunfire that surrounded the fighters also allows for the possibility that Gómez's order went unheard by Martí, who according to de la Guardia's account was far enough away to have perhaps missed it. De la Guardia's own positioning would seem to undermine that possibility, however, as he himself would have been close enough to hear both Martí invite his brother Ángel to advance and Gómez's "Here!" command.

De la Guardia's second divergence from Gómez's account is more troubling. For regardless of whether or when Gómez ordered Martí to keep himself out of danger, de la Guardia's account emphasizes that Martí not only did not remain at the camp but was among the first few fighters to arrive at the battle scene and that Gómez did nothing to prevent or discourage his doing so. Nor is de la Guardia's account the only one to make this claim, as Masó Parra concurs that the first group to reach the battleground included "Gómez, Masó, and Borrero. ... Martí was with that group and was among the first to fall."[87] De la Guardia's account also confirms that "Borrero and Martí went with General Gómez. No one stayed behind in any prefecture."[88] Moreover, the three miles between Dos Ríos and the Cuban camp at La Vuelta Grande and the presence of the Río Contramaestre between the camp and the battleground—higher than usual that day due to heavy rains—would seem to contradict Gómez's claim that he ordered Martí back before advancing. It is at the very least unlikely that the relatively inexperienced Martí, having initially stayed behind, would have overtaken the more experienced riders' charge, much less crossed a swollen river without the guidance of even Ángel de la Guardia, whom by all accounts he did not encounter until just before his final charge.

Much more than the question of Gómez's alleged order to Martí or his actual words, then, it is Dominador de la Guardia's and Masó Parra's assertion that Martí rode with the initial group that more seriously calls into question the veracity and reliability of Gómez's canonical version of Martí's death. These discrepancies, combined with evidence of Gómez's undeniable status and influence in postwar Cuba—and his documented attempts to distance himself from the event—cast a long shadow over the myth of Martí's heroic death in battle.

Although we will never know with any certainty the exact circumstances of Martí's death, the available evidence strongly suggests that Cuba's most beloved national hero did not die the glorious death of legend. If "lie" seems too strong a word, then perhaps "myth" will have to do. For as Martí himself once wrote, "Fame is a useful myth."[89] The sentence appears near the end of his April 17, 1884, column in *La Nación* on the funeral procession for the crew of the USS *Jeannette*, which perished during a polar expedition. Martí goes on to assert that duty, "which brings pleasure, rules men. It guides, it saves, and it is enough."[90] The words "useful" and "duty" appear often in Martí's work, words that signaled his commitment to a life not just of thought but of thoughtful action. If Martí's final act in this world was not a thoughtful one, and if because of it he died less a martyr than a victim, those facts could never diminish what was by any measure a useful—and heroic—life.

A Hero's Afterlife

At press time we received the cruel confirmation that the exemplary
Apostle, the beloved master, the selfless José Martí, is no more.

PATRIA, JUNE 17, 1895

ON MAY 19, 1895, IN THE MIDST OF WHAT IS NOW KNOWN
as the Battle of Dos Ríos, José Martí rode his horse directly in
front of an enemy position and was immediately shot dead. General Máximo
Gómez, who for the rest of his life claimed that he had advised Martí against
entering the fray, risked his own life and that of his men to retrieve his comrade's body. Despite Gómez's efforts, Spanish troops retained Martí's body in
an advance begun within minutes of his fall. The Spanish soldiers who recovered the body did not know whom they had found, but they could tell by his
clothes and the papers and money he was carrying that he was someone important. Only later that evening, after the fighting subsided, did Spanish Captain
Enrique Satue positively identify the body as Martí's.[1]

WHEN WORD OF MARTÍ'S DEATH REACHED THE COLONIAL
government in Havana, authorities moved to display his remains as quickly
and publicly as possible. From Captain-General Arsenio Martínez Campos on
down, the island's Spanish leaders shared the Cubans' conviction that news of
Martí's death would demoralize the rebels and perhaps bring the insurgency
to a swift end. Martínez Campos held public ceremonies in Havana to deco-
rate and promote those involved in the battle at Dos Ríos, and the archbishop
Manuel Santander went as far as performing a *te deum*, a brief celebratory service, to give thanks to God for Martí's death.[2] Most importantly, Martínez
Campos sent word from Santiago de Cuba to Colonel José Ximénez de San-

doval, commanding officer of the Spanish forces at Dos Ríos, to preserve the body for a public burial:

> Friend Sandoval: Martí's death has been much debated. To remove all doubt it is indispensable that the body be transferred here. This would have a great effect on morale and add resonance to the great service [to the cause] done by yourself and your troops. Please make use, then, of whatever resources you have at your disposal to preserve the body and conduct it here as quickly as possible. Tend to this matter above all else. I am attaching the photograph and news regarding Martí, so that you may confirm that the captured body is his, before sending it here. Congratulations again from your friend M.[3]

Before receiving these instructions, Sandoval had done little to preserve Martí's body or belongings. Taking care to retrieve Martí's papers, including his now-famous final, unfinished letter to Manuel Mercado, the Spanish colonel had the body stripped naked, distributed the money Martí was carrying among his men, and had the corpse loaded saddlebag-style across the back of a mule. The next day, the body was buried in a shallow grave, without the benefit of clothes or a coffin, in the cemetery of a village called Remanganaguas. Only upon receiving orders from Havana did Sandoval send for a Spanish military doctor, Pablo A. de Valencia y Forns, to exhume the body and conduct a formal autopsy.[4]

In his report on the May 23 autopsy, Dr. Valencia formally confirmed the identity of the deceased as Martí and recorded the cause of death as blunt trauma caused by gunshot wounds to the chest and throat. Valencia's final task was perhaps the most difficult: embalming and preparing for burial a body that had received sustained exposure to the elements and gratuitously shoddy treatment for over four days.[5]

It would be another four days before Martí's body would reach its final resting place. Not until May 27 — eight days after his death at Dos Ríos — did Martí's hastily preserved body reach niche #134 of Santa Ifigenia cemetery in Santiago de Cuba. Before the burial, Sandoval made sure to have a photographer take pictures of Martí's body, by now in an advanced state of decay; these included the infamous head shot that Spanish authorities circulated to the newspapers as proof of the Cuban hero's death. Sandoval himself presided over the funeral service, which he concluded by inviting — challenging, really — anyone present who knew Martí to say a few words. Unsurprisingly, given that anyone who admitted knowing, much less admiring the insurgent leader would be subject to immediate arrest or worse, Sandoval found no takers.[6]

IN THE QUARTER-CENTURY THAT FOLLOWED HIS DEATH, the name of the man who would almost certainly have been Cuba's first president was little circulated on the island. This was partly because the cause for which he had fought and died did not immediately come to fruition; the war in Cuba dragged on for another three years before U.S. intervention brought the Spanish Empire to an ignominious and humiliating end, and the island did not achieve even nominal independence until 1902. By then it had become obvious that the United States delivered the island from Spain only to bring it under U.S. influence. The clearest evidence of the U.S. intention to keep Cuba under its control was the addition to the General Treaty of 1901, signed by the two countries, of the infamous Platt Amendment:

ARTICLE III

The government of Cuba consents that the United States may exercise the right to intervene for the preservation of Cuban independence, the maintenance of a government adequate for the protection of life, property, and individual liberty, and for discharging the obligations with respect to Cuba imposed by the treaty of Paris [1898, which ended the Spanish-American War] on the United States, now to be assumed and undertaken by the government of Cuba.[7]

The Platt Amendment, introduced by the United States in 1901 and accepted into the Cuban constitution a year later, allowed unilateral U.S. involvement in Cuban domestic matters and mandated the sale or lease of Cuban territory for U.S. military bases on the island. It denied voting rights to Cubans who were not property owners, effectively excluding most of the Afro-Cubans who had fought so bravely and in such numbers for a free Cuba. Tomás Estrada Palma, soon to become Cuba's first president, lamented the injury to his "dignity as a Cuban" but acknowledged that acceptance of the U.S. demands was necessary in order to "give full expression to our gratitude."[8] So if there was now a country called Cuba, with its own flag, borders, and constitution, it was paradoxically the very independence for which Martí had fought and died that was threatened by imperialist U.S. policies.

Another reason for Martí's delayed enshrinement as Cuba's national hero was simple unfamiliarity; he had spent most of his life and done all of his most important work in exile, and the Spanish government was keen to restrict circulation of his name and writings among the civilian population for obvious reasons. Only with the nationalist revival of the 1930s and the abrogation of the notorious Platt Amendment in 1934 did Martí's name begin to be associated with those of others — Generals Gómez, Maceo, Masó — long acknowledged as the revolution's heroes. In this context, it is not surprising that Martí would not be the subject of a book-length biography until 1932, when Jorge Mañach's *Martí, el apostol* (Martí, the Apostle) introduced the revolutionary's life and work to a generation of Cubans who had grown up hardly knowing his name.[9]

Curiously, the Cuban communists who emerged in the 1930s in opposition to the new republican movement did not embrace Martí as the Marxist Castro regime does today. The earlier communists rejected Martí as a misguided optimist and a capitalist stooge who by fighting Spain had only played into the hands of an avaricious, imperialist United States. Such dismissals of Martí by prominent Cuban Marxists persisted right up until the Castro revolution's embrace of Martí as its intellectual cornerstone in the 1950s.[10]

Martí's legend grew through the 1940s and 1950s, and a proliferation of published articles, tributes, and hagiographies followed that outdid even Mañach's 1932 biography in their reverential treatment of the Cuban hero. Politicians took special notice of Martí's newfound emotional resonance among Cubans, and successive governments increasingly embraced him as the island nation's undisputed national hero and invoked his name in defense of their actions and policies. By the 1940s the activist Martí ideologically exhumed by student groups and labor unions had been effectively appropriated by ruling elites, and a more official, mythologized version of the man was deployed for the purpose of maintaining power. The 1940s saw the first phase of the "statuesque" Martí, with busts erected in practically every Cuban town, official tributes on national holidays, and what soon became obligatory references and quotations at public events. Official interest in Martí soon became a virtual industry and the circulation and management of his name and image an important function. Successive Cuban governments took to subsidizing and sponsoring publications on Martí and funding the work of state-sponsored scholars to oversee their dissemination in print as well as in school curricula at every level.[11]

The enshrinement of Martí as Cuba's national icon reached its first apogee in the 1950s, with at least one prominent Martí scholar, Félix Lizaso, becoming a minister in Fulgencio Batista's cabinet.[12] Batista, Cuba's de facto ruler since 1933 who formally seized power in a 1952 coup, took special pains to align himself with the name and image of Cuba's greatest national hero. It was Batista who presided over the nationalist frenzy surrounding the 1953 centennial celebration of Martí's birth that culminated in the unveiling of an enormous stone monument erected directly across from the presidential palace. The monument remains today the centerpiece of the rechristened Plaza de la Revolución.

Thus by 1953 Martí's name and image had become synonymous with Cuban nationalism and independence—a fact that was not lost on Fidel Castro and his insurgent movement to topple the Batista dictatorship. Castro cannily embraced Martí, whom Cuban Marxists only a generation before had dismissed as a capitalist tool, as the very inspiration for the "Centennial Generation" he declared as the true heirs of the nineteenth-century hero's revolutionary vision. With Castro's 1954 manifesto "La historia me absolverá" ("History Will Absolve Me"), the Cuban Revolution marks the start of a concerted effort to recast Martí's revolutionary vision in its own twentieth-century image:

> We are proud of the history of our country. We learned history in school and we have grown up hearing of liberty, justice, and human rights. We were taught from a young age to venerate the glorious example of our heroes and our martyrs. Céspedes, Agramonte, Maceo, Gómez, and Martí were the first names engraved on our brains.[13]

During the more than half-century that the Castro regime has ruled the island, it has institutionalized Martí studies to a degree unimaginable even to Batista's battalion of state-sponsored scholars. Havana's Center for Martí Studies has published thousands of pages in books and articles on the Cuban hero, and his name and image are, if anything, even more ubiquitous than they were before 1959. Not to be outdone, since the 1950s the Cuban diaspora has published untold thousands of pages on Martí, in whose history of exile they see their own hopes of a future Cuba that better reflects their hero's revolutionary vision. If the two warring sides agree on nothing else — including their interpretations of Martí's life and works — they share a deep and lasting reverence for a common national hero, their "Apostle of Freedom."

ON MAY 27, 1895, THE SAME DAY — POSSIBLY THE VERY hour — of Martí's belated funeral in Santiago de Cuba, María Mantilla received in New York the farewell letter her father had written more than two months earlier. By now the news of his death had reached New York and the Cuban exile community, whose desperate denials of the story were stilled by the graphic photographs of the autopsy that soon appeared in the New York papers. In his letter, the dead man assured his daughter that he carried over his heart a small book of quotations that she had given him as a gift, as a shield against bullets: "you will see how it will protect me from all danger."[14]

It would be another seven years before the Cuban national flag would fly over the island. But as fourteen-year-old María Mantilla read his letter, she was probably not thinking of that far-off day. More likely she was thinking that the man she had come to think of as her father, the man her mother had loved for fifteen years, was dead.

Notes

Preface

1. Agramonte (1841–1873) was a general in the Ten Years' War, the first failed war of independence against Spain. Lolo Villalobos was a longtime Cuban politician and mayor of Guanabacoa during pre-Fidel times.

2. "Latino" and "Latina" are twentieth-century terms for U.S.-born descendants of Latin American immigrants. As an ethnolinguistic rather than a racial category, it more broadly includes Latin Americans in the United States who self-identify as Latino/a. The newer terms have largely displaced the older "Hispanic," although they are still sometimes used interchangeably. See Luis Ricardo Fraga, *Latino Lives in America: Making It Home* (Philadelphia: Temple University Press, 2010), 145; Robert H. Holden and Rina Villars, *Contemporary Latin America: 1970 to the Present* (Hoboken, NJ: John Wiley, 2012), 18.

3. Alberto Baeza Flores, *Vida de José Martí: el hombre íntimo y el hombre public* [Life of José Martí: The Private Man and the Public Man] (Havana: Comisión Nacional Organizadora de los Actos y Ediciones del Centenario y del Monumento de Martí, 1954); Luis Toledo Sande, *Cesto de llamas: biografía de José Martí* [Basket of Flames: Biography of José Martí] (Havana: Editorial de Ciencias Sociales, 1996); Jorge Mañach, *Martí, el apostol* [Martí, the Apostle] (Madrid: Espasa-Calpe, 1933); Félix Lizaso, *Martí, místico del deber* [Martí, Dutiful Mystic] (Havana: Losada, 1952).

4. Gonzalo de Quesada y Miranda, *Martí, hombre* [Martí, the Man] (Havana: Seone, Fernández, 1940); Raúl García Martí, *Biografía familiar* [Family Biography] (Havana: Cárdenas, 1938).

5. Carlos Márquez Sterling, *Biografía de José Martí* (Barcelona: Manuel Pareja, 1973).

6. José Martí, *Obras completas de José Martí* [Complete Works of José Martí] (Havana: Centro de Estudios Martianos, 2001), 4:168. Hereafter, the 2001, twenty-six-volume set of *Obras completas* is cited as JMOC. All translations are my own unless otherwise specified.

Introduction. Mariano and Leonor

1. "Nuestras ideas" was one of four Martí essays published on the occasion of the inaugural issue of *Patria*, the newspaper he founded and ran until his death. *JMOC*, 1:321. All epigraphs are from Martí's work unless otherwise specified.

2. Several sources corroborate that the weather that morning, and indeed during all of January 1853, was unseasonably cold and damp. Although forecasting as we know it today did not exist, newspapers typically published the previous day's weather. U.S. papers in cities with major ports published regular shipping reports, which typically included arrivals and departures as well as wrecked or sunken vessels and known storms. *El Diario de La Habana*, January 28 and 29, 1853; *New York Times*, "Marine Intelligence" column, January 4 and February 7, 1853, 8.

3. Adys Cupull and Froilán González, *Creciente agonía* [Growing Agony] (Havana: Editorial José Martí, 2009), 16–17.

4. Ibid.

5. Ellen Churchill Semple, *American History and Its Geographic Conditions* (San Francisco: Houghton Mifflin, 1903); Felipe Fernández-Armesto, *The Canary Islands after the Conquest* (Oxford, England: Oxford University Press, 1982); Daniel Jay Browne, *Letters from the Canary Islands* (Boston: G. W. Light, 1834).

6. Cupull and González, 17.

7. Ibid., 18–19.

8. Stanley G. Payne, *Politics and the Military in Modern Spain* (Stanford, CA: Stanford University Press, 1967), 5–82; Wayne H. Bowen and José E. Alvarez, introduction to *A Military History of Modern Spain: From the Napleonic Era to the international War on Terror*, ed. Bowen and Alvarez (Westport, CT: Praeger, 2007), 1–14.

9. E. Christiansen, *The Origins of Military Power in Spain* (Oxford, England: Oxford University Press, 1967), 10–22; Payne, 5–14.

10. Adrian Shubert, *A Social History of Modern Spain* (London: Routledge, 1990), 172–177; *New York Times*, "The Naval and Military Forces of Spain," January 13, 1862, 2.

11. Cupull and González, 21.

12. M. Tuñon de Lara, *La España del siglo XIX* [Spain of the Nineteenth Century] (Barcelona: Editorial Laia, 1977), 1:99–104, 1:137–139.

13. Cupull and González, 22.

14. Tom Chaffin, *Fatal Glory: Narciso López and the First Clandestine U.S. War against Cuba* (Baton Rouge, LA: LSU Press, 2003); Robert Granville Caldwell, "The López Expeditions to Cuba," PhD diss., Princeton University, 1915.

15. Although declared in 1817, the ban would not take effect in Spain's remaining colonies until 1820. Hugh Thomas, *Cuba; or, The Pursuit of Freedom*, 1971 (updated ed., New York: DaCapo, 1998), 94; David Brion Davis, *The Problem of Slavery in Western Culture* (Ithaca, NY: Cornell University Press, 1966), 360–363.

16. Rafael E. Tarragó, *Experiencias políticas de los cubanos en la Cuba española: 1512–1898* [The Political Experiences of Cubans in Colonial Cuba: 1512–1898] (Barcelona: Puvill, 1996); Thomas, 197–198.

17. Thomas, 211–214.

18. Chaffin, 44–71.

19. Thomas, 211–215; Caldwell, 91–113.

20. Cupull and González, 22.

21. Mariano Martí was approximately five feet two inches tall, an average height among Spanish men of the time but slightly shorter than average among men from the country's Mediterranean coastal region encompassing his native Valencia. For a more thorough overview of height and its relationship to socioeconomic class status in nineteenth-century Spain, see John Komlos, *Stature, Living Standards, and Economic Development* (Chicago: University of Chicago Press, 1994), 16–19.

22. Cupull and González, 23–26.

23. Chaffin, 215–216; Caldwell, 111–113.

24. Thomas, 218–219.

25. Ibid., 93–105, especially 96.

26. *El Diario de La Habana*, January 28 and 29, 1853.

PART ONE. BEFORE THE FALL (1853–1870)

Chapter One. An Unlikely Prodigy

1. Epigraphs: *JMOC*, 20:404, 458. Martí's reference to a copy of his *Versos sencillos* that accompanied the letter indicates that he wrote and sent it shortly after the book's publication in 1891. Citations are from José Martí, *Versos sencillos/Simple Verses*, reprint with translation and introduction by Manuel A. Tellechea, Recovering the U.S. Hispanic Literary Heritage (Houston: Arte Público, 1997).

2. Ricardo Hodelín Tablada, *Enfermedades de José Martí* [Illnesses of José Martí] (Santiago, Cuba: Oriente, 2007), 18–19.

3. Thomas, 218–233; Louis A. Pérez Jr., *Cuba: Between Reform and Revolution* (New York: Oxford University Press, 1988), 110–111.

4. Chaffin, 24–25; Robert E. May, *John A. Quitman: Old South Crusader* (Baton Rouge: LSU Press, 1995), 284n46.

5. Tuñon, 170–174; Thomas, 224–225.

6. Cupull and González, 28–29; Ibrahim Hidalgo Paz, *José Martí 1853–1895: Cronología*, 2nd ed. (Havana: Centro de Estudios Martianos, 2003), 16.

7. Cupull and González, 30–31.

8. Ibid., 31–32; Hidalgo Paz, *José Martí 1853–1895*, 17.

9. Samuel Hazard, *Cuba in Pen and Pencil* (Hartford, CT: Hartford, 1871), 256.

10. Ibid., 256–257.

11. Fermín Valdés Domínguez, "Ofrenda de hermano" [Brother's Offering], 1908, reprint, *Opus Habana* 7.1 (2003): 8.

12. Although a great deal of demographic and life-expectancy information for Cuba and Spain exists for the 1880s and later, data for earlier periods is less useful due to unreliable burial and other records. Nevertheless, average life expectancy among nonslave males is believed to be less than forty years, a figure consistent with other Caribbean

locations. The available data suggest some divergence between urban and rural populations for both Spain and Cuba. See Stanley L. Engerman, "A Population History of the Caribbean," in *A Population History of North America*, ed. Michael R. Haines and Richard Hall Steckel (Cambridge, England: Cambridge University Press, 2000), 483–528; and James C. Riley, *Low Income, Social Growth, and Good Health* (Berkeley: University of California Press, 2007), 88–90.

13. It is likely that the Martís conceived at least two of their three children up to this point shortly after the previous children were weaned or perhaps even during a transitional stage of less frequent breast feedings combined with solid foods. Breastfeeding, which has long been known to retard ovulation in nursing mothers, was still the norm for women in Europe and the United States in the mid-nineteenth century, as supplies of cow's milk were notoriously unsafe and commercial formulas had not yet come into use. While women who were affluent enough to hire wet nurses or acquire slaves for the purpose generally did so, Leonor obviously could do neither. The Martís' second- and fourth-born, Leonor Petrona and María del Carmen, were conceived when the previous child was approximately nine months old. This indicates that Leonor became pregnant in both cases almost immediately upon the onset of ovulation, which would have occurred as nursing slowed or ceased entirely. Graziela Caselli, Jacques Vallin, and Guillaume Wunsch, *Demography: Analysis and Synthesis* (New York: Academic Press, 2006), 421–422; Valerie A. Fildes, *Breasts, Bottles, and Babies: A History of Infant Feeding* (Edinburgh, Scotland: Edinburgh University Press, 1989).

14. Mariano apparently retained his interest in La Fuente de la Salud café he co-owned with a relative, Francisco Martí. Cupull and González, 22.

15. Although transatlantic steamships had operated for several years from Britain and the United States, Spain did not build its first steamship until 1858. The Spanish polacre *Magdalena* was the only vessel that made the crossing to Valencia at the time. Ibid., 33.

16. Ibid., 32; Hidalgo Paz, *José Martí 1853–1895*, 17.

17. Cupull and González, 33.

18. William D. James, Timothy G. Berger, and Dirk M. Elston, *Andrews' Diseases of the Skin: Clinical Dermatology* (Amsterdam: Saunders Elsevier, 2006), 22–26.

19. Cupull and González, 33–34.

20. Ibid., 33.

21. This kind of tension would have been informed by a much longer history of peninsular-born versus Creole discrimination dating back to at least the sixteenth century. See, for example, José Antonio Mazzotti, "Epic, Creoles, and Nation in Spanish America," in *A Companion to the Literatures of Colonial America*, ed. Susan P. Castillo and Ivy Schweitzer (New York: Wiley-Blackwell, 2005), 480–499; and Jorge Cañizares-Esguerra, "Racial, Religious, and Civic Creole Identity in Colonial Spanish America," *American Literary History* 17:3 (2005): 420–437.

22. Cupull and González, 33.

23. Ibid., 35–36.

24. Ibid., 37.

25. Richard Henry Dana, *To Cuba and Back: A Vacation Voyage* (London: Smith, Elder, 1859), 23.

26. Several U.S. and European travel writers from this time describe the phenomenon of Cuban ladies seated in parlor windows. Hazard, 161–162; Dana, 26.

27. Cupull and González, 41.

28. In Garcia Márti, 36–39.

29. Ibid.

30. Ibid.

31. In Cupull and González, 41.

32. Pamela María Smorkaloff, *Readers and Writers in Cuba: A Social History of Print Culture, 1830s–1990s* (London: Taylor and Francis, 1997), 4–11.

33. Thomas, 94–95.

34. Christopher Lloyd, *The Navy and the Slave Trade* (London: Longmans Green, 1949), 163–183.

35. Cupull and González, 42–43.

36. Ibid., 47.

37. *JMOC*, 22:189. The passage comes from no. 286 of 430 unpublished and undated fragments Martí wrote during his last ten years in New York, 1885–1895.

38. The regulation of slavery in Cuba provided for a range of legal punishments for slaves from public whippings to execution by garrote. Any slave found hanging in the woods in the way Martí describes was almost certainly lynched illegally by his owners or someone else. Reinaldo Suárez Suárez, "José Martí contra Alphonse Karr, en defensa de la vida, contra la pena de muerte" [José Martí versus Alphonse Karr, in Defense of Life, against Capital Punishment], in *Biblioteca Jurídica Virtual*, ed. Margarita García Castillo and Oscar Montoya Pérez (Mexico City: Instituto de Investigaciones Jurídicas, Universidad Nacional Autónoma de México, 2006), 45–47.

39. Martí, *Versos sencillos/Simple Verses*, 89. For the original poem in Spanish, see *JMOC*, 16:106.

40. In his widely read biography of Martí, Jorge Mañach mentions neither incident in discussing Martí's time in Hanábana. More recent scholars like Paul Estrade and Oscar Montero present the stories of young Pepe's encounters with slaves as established fact but do not cite sources to support their claims. Jorge Mañach, *Martí, el apostol* [Martí, the Apostle] (Madrid: Espasa-Calpe, 1933), 18–20; Paul Estrade, *José Martí: los fundamentos de la democracía Latinoaméricana* [José Martí: The Foundations of Latin American Democracy] (Madrid: Casa de Velasquez, 2000), 212; Oscar Montero, *José Martí: An Introduction* (London: Palgrave Macmillan, 2004), 59–60.

41. Herbert S. Klein, *The Atlantic Slave Trade* (Cambridge, England: Cambridge University Press, 1999), 131–133.

42. For a more thorough discussion of Martí as a writer of chronicles and how the chronicle genre differs significantly from conventional reportage of the time, see Susana Rotker, *Fundación de una escritura: las crónicas de José Martí* [Foundation of a Genre: The Chronicles of José Martí] (Havana: Casa de las Américas, 1992).

43. Cupull and González, 43–44.

44. Ibid.

45. Ibid., 43–47.

46. Ibid.

A Boy's First Letter

1. *JMOC*, 20:243.

Chapter Two. The Teacher Appears

1. Epigraphs: *JMOC*, 17:13; Rafael María Mendive, *Poesias de Rafael María de Mendive*, 3rd ed. (Havana: Miguel de Villa, 1883), 93.
2. *El Diario de La Habana*, January 28, 1853, 1.
3. For a concise overview of Mendive's life and work, see Vidal Morales y Morales's introduction to Mendive's *Poesias*.
4. Valdés Domínguez, "Ofrenda," 8.
5. Cupull and González, 47.
6. *JMOC*, 19:104.
7. Carlos Ripoll, *La vida íntima y secreta de José Martí* [The Intimate and Secret Life of José Martí] (Miami: Dos Ríos, 1995), 4.
8. Donald C. Simmons Jr., *Confederate Settlements in British Honduras* (Jefferson, NC: McFarland, 2001), 22–23. Twenty-five years later, in 1888, the price for arable land in British Honduras still hovered around twenty pounds, at the time equivalent to $4, per acre. Lindsey W. Bristowe and Philip B. Wright, *The Handbook of British Honduras for 1888–89* (Edinburgh, Scotland: William Blackwood and Sons, 1888), 80–82.
9. Cupull and González, 48.
10. Hidalgo Paz, *José Martí 1853–1895*, 20.
11. Ibid.
12. Cupull and González, 49.
13. Ibid.
14. *JMOC*, 22:285.
15. Quoted in Ripoll, *La vida íntima*, 1.
16. Cupull and González, 49; Hidalgo Paz, *José Martí 1853–1895*, 20.
17. Hidalgo Paz, *José Martí 1853–1895*, 21.
18. Victor Pérez Galdós, *José Martí: visión de un hombre universal* [José Martí: Vision of a Universal Man] (Barcelona: Puvill, 1999), 27–29; Cupull and González, 56–57; Hidalgo Paz, *José Martí 1853–1895*, 22–23.
19. For the full text of Rita Cabrera's will in Spanish, see Cupull and González, 53–57.
20. Ibid., 58–59.
21. *JMOC*, 17:14.
22. Cupull and González, 59; Hidalgo Paz, *José Martí 1853–1895*, 24–25.
23. Ibid.
24. Thomas, 235–236; Clifford L. Staten, *The History of Cuba* (New York: Palgrave Macmillan, 2005), 27–28.
25. Ibid.
26. Thomas, 245–253; Staten, 32–34.
27. Thomas, 248.
28. *JMOC*, 1:31–38.

29. For the most thorough and systematic debunking of Valdés Domínguez's claim, see Carlos Ripoll, *Martí y el fin de una leyenda* [Martí and the End of a Legend] (New York: Dos Ríos, 2007), 9–12.

30. Thomas, 248–250.

31. Ibid., 249–250; Cupull and González, 61–62.

32. For the full text of Martí's play, see *JMOC*, 18:11–24.

33. Cupull and González, 62.

34. *JMOC*, 18:18–19.

35. Cupull and González, 67–68.

36. Hidalgo Paz, *José Martí 1853–1895*, 26–27.

37. Cupull and González, 68–69.

38. *JMOC*, 1:116. Martí got the date wrong in this early account, as the Villanueva massacre transpired on the night of January 24, not 22.

39. *JMOC*, 16:102–103.

40. Cupull and González, 247.

41. Valdés Domínguez refers here to both of Martí's parents, Mariano and Leonor. Quoted in Ripoll, *La vida íntima*, 1.

42. Letter by Miguel F. Viondi y Vera, who befriended Martí in 1879 when the latter came to work for his Havana law practice. Quoted in Ripoll, *La vida íntima*, 1.

43. *JMOC*, 20:245.

Chapter Three. Trial by Fire

1. Epigraphs: *JMOC*, 1:40; Francisco Pí y Margall and Francisco de Pí y Arsuaga, eds., *Historia de España en el Siglo XIX: Sucesos politicos, económicos, sociales y artísticos* [History of Spain in the Nineteenth Century: Political, Economic, Social, and Artistic Events] (Madrid: Segui, 1902), 7.1:126.

2. Hidalgo Paz, *José Martí 1853–1895*, 27–28.

3. Fermín Valdés Domínguez, *Diario de soldado* [Soldier's Diary], 1895 (reprint, ed. Hiram Dupotey Fideaux, Havana: Universidad de La Habana, Centro de Información Científica y Técnica, 1972), 1:12. See also Joan Casanovas, *Bread or Bullets: Urban Labor and Spanish Colonialism, 1850–1898* (Pittsburgh, PA: University of Pittsburgh Press, 1998), 78–79.

4. Luis Navarro García, *Las guerras de España en Cuba* [Spain's Wars in Cuba] (Madrid: Encuentro, 1998), 45.

5. Hidalgo Paz, *José Martí 1853–1895*, 28.

6. *JMOC*, 17:20.

7. Thomas, 248–249.

8. Ibid., 252.

9. Hidalgo Paz, *José Martí 1853–1895*, 28.

10. Ana Cairo Ballester, *José Martí y la novela de la cultura cubana* [José Martí and the Novel of Cuban Culture] (Santiago de Compostela, Spain: Universidad Santiago de Compostela, 2003), 119.

11. Thomas, 251–252.

12. Ibid.

13. Antonio Martínez Bello, *La adolescencia de Martí* [Martí's Adolescence] (Havana: P. Fernández, 1944), 50; Cupull and González, 70–71; Hidalgo Paz, *José Martí 1853–1895*, 28.

14. Cupull and González, 71–72.

15. Ibid.

16. Hidalgo Paz, *José Martí 1853–1895*, 28.

17. Fermín Valdés Domínguez changed important details in his several published versions of the story, in one instance even within the same book. *Diario*, 1:13–14, 273. See also Cupull and González, 72–73.

18. Ibid.

19. *JMOC*, 1:45.

20. *JMOC*, 20:245–246.

21. Cupull and González, 74–75.

22. *JMOC*, 1:39.

23. Ripoll, *Martí y el fin*, 22–28.

24. Centro de Estudios Martianos, "Documentos sobre José Martí" [Documents Regarding José Martí], *Anuario del Centro de Estudios Martianos* 2 (1979): 37.

25. Ibid., 44.

26. Cupull and González, 75.

27. *JMOC*, 1:40.

28. Ibid.

29. Cupull and González, 77–78.

30. Sellén and one other suspect, Santiago Balbín, were declared innocent of all charges and released on December 22. Hidalgo Paz, *José Martí 1853–1895*, 30.

31. Ripoll, *Martí y el fin*, 22–28.

32. Valdés Domínguez, "Ofrenda," 10.

33. Martí's nephew Raúl García Martí presents this more dramatic version as fact in his 1938 biography of Martí (67). The account has since been reproduced unquestioningly in many Martí studies, including several otherwise reliable ones.

34. Quoted in Vidal Morales y Morales, *Iniciadores y primeros mártires de la revolución cubana* [Initiators and First Martyrs of the Cuban Revolution] (Havana: Moderna Poesía, 1901], 3:556–557.

35. José Robles Pozo, *Derecho procesal de España. . . : Las leyes y la jurisprudencia vigentes del enjuiciamiento criminal* [Procedural Law of Spain. . . : The Laws and Jurisprudence of Criminal Prosecution] (Madrid: Revista de Legislación, 1890), 309–310.

36. N. Ponce de León, trans., *The Book of Blood: An Authentic Record of the Policy Adopted by Modern Spain to Put an End to the War for the Independence of Cuba (October 1868 to November 10, 1873)* (New York: N. Ponce de León, 1873), vii.

37. Cupull and González, 78.

38. For a useful overview of Spain's colonial prison system in the nineteenth century, see Carlos Aguirre, "Cárcel y sociedad en América Latina: 1800–1940" [Prison and Society in Latin America: 1800–1940], in *Historia social urbana: espacios y flujos* [Urban Social History: Ebbs and Flows], ed. Eduardo Kingman Garcés (Quito: 50 Años

FLACSO, 2009), 209–252. See also Fernando Picó, *El día menos pensado: historia de los presidiarios en Puerto Rico (1793–1993)* [When Least Expected: A History of Prisoners in Puerto Rico (1793–1993)] (Rio Piedras, Puerto Rico: Huracán, 1994).

39. Schubert, 9–55.

40. Fernando Cadalso y Manzano, *Estudios penitenciarios: presidios españoles, escuelas clásica y positiva y colonias penales, con un breve compendio de la legislación, costumbres jurídicas y prácticas penitenciarias que rigen en los establecimientos* [Penitentiary Studies: Spanish Prisons, Classical and Positivist Schools, and Penal Colonies, with a Brief Compendium of the Legislation, Juridical Customs, and Penitentiary Practices that Govern These Establishments] (Madrid: F. Góngora, 1893), 217–219. See also Picó, 101–109.

41. Enrique Sanz Delgado, "Disciplina y reclusion en el siglo XIX: criterios humanizadores y control de la custodia" [Discipline and Imprisonment in the Nineteenth Century: Humanizing Criteria and the Control of Custody], *Anuario de Derecho Penal y Ciencias Penales* 55 (January 2002): 109–201; Picó, 79–91.

42. Picó, 155–163.

43. Aguirre, 236–237.

44. Picó, 139–140.

45. Cupull and González, 84.

46. Hidalgo Paz, *José Martí 1853–1895*, 31–32; Cupull and González, 78.

47. *JMOC*, 1:46.

48. Picó, 61–62.

49. Ibid., 139–140.

50. Quoted in García Martí, 70.

51. Cupull and González, 85.

52. Spain, *Ordenanza General de los Presidios del Reino 1834* [General Ordinance of Prisons in the Kingdom], section 3, Del Ayudante, article 98 (Madrid: Ministerio de Ultramar, 1834), 19a. Archivo Histórico Nacional.

53. *JMOC*, 1:58.

54. Centro de Estudios Martianos, 43–44.

55. Ibid., 44.

56. Ibid., 44 and 46, respectively.

57. *JMOC*, 17:29.

58. Cupull and González, 88.

59. Ibid., 89–90.

60. Tablada, 38.

61. Quoted in Emilio Roig de Leuschsenring, *Martí en España* [Martí in Spain] (Havana: Cultural, 1938), 89.

62. Centro de Estudios Martianos, 48.

63. Cupull and González, 91.

Havana Farewell

1. *JMOC*, 20:47.

2. For the full text of "El presidio político en Cuba," see *JMOC*, 1:45–74.

PART TWO. EXILE (1871–1880)

Chapter Four. Spain

1. Epigraph: "La República Española ante la revolución cubana," *JMOC*, 1:89.

2. *JMOC*, 17:27.

3. Cupull and González, 91; Hidalgo Paz, *José Martí 1853–1895*, 34.

4. Guillermo de Zéndegui, *Ámbito de Martí* [Martí's World] (Bogotá: Departamento de Publicaciones, Sociedad Colombista Panamericana, 1954), 49; Hidalgo Paz, *José Martí 1853–1895*, 34.

5. Cupull and González, 92; Hidalgo Paz, *José Martí 1853–1895*, 34.

6. Tablada, 42.

7. Shubert, 46–47.

8. Peter Pierson, *The History of Spain* (Westport, CT: Greenwood, 1999), 14–15; Shubert, 47.

9. Alejandro Lapunzina, *Architecture of Spain* (Westport, CT: Greenwood, 2005), 131–132; Juan Antonio Gaya Nuño, *Historia del Museo del Prado: 1819–1976* [History of the Museo del Prado: 1819–1976] (León, Spain: Everest, 1976), 9–10, 104–123.

10. William D. Phillips Jr. and Carla Rahn, *A Concise History of Spain* (Cambridge, England: Cambridge University Press, 2010), 222; Pierson, 105–107.

11. Carlos Márquez Sterling, *Martí, ciudadano de América* [Martí, Citizen of America] (New York: Las Américas, 1965), 55–56; Tablada, 43. Regarding Sauvalle's editorship of *El Laborante* and Martí's possible contributions to that publication, see Cesar García del Pino, El Laborante *y otros temas martianos* [*The* Laborer and Other Martí Topics] (Havana: Unión, 2006), 7–28.

12. Samuel Sánchez Gávez, *Martí ciñó el mandil: prueba documental de su filiación masónica* [Martí Wore the Apron: Documented Proof of His Masonic Affiliation] (Havana: Biblioteca Nacional José Martí, Ediciones Bachiller, 2007), 32–46, 59–60.

13. Márquez Sterling, *Martí, ciudadano*, 55–56; Tablada, 43–44.

14. Echevarría may be the mysterious woman, identified in her letters only as "M," with whom Martí had an affair during this period. Esteemed Martí scholar Carlos Ripoll does not raise that possibility in his own work on the letters; *La vida íntima*, 26–36. Nonetheless, her closeness to the young Martí from his earliest days in Madrid make her a very strong circumstantial candidate.

15. Tablada, 45–46.

16. Ibid., 48–49.

17. Ibid., 48–49, 169–170.

18. Hidalgo Paz, *José Martí 1853–1895*, 35.

19. Nicolás del Castillo's great-great-niece Elena García Casanova confirmed in a 2010 interview that Castillo had just turned sixty when he was released from prison. *Ecured*, "Martí y los espirituanos" [Martí and the People of Sancti Spíritu], October 25, 2010, http://www.ecured.cu/index.php/Mart%C3%AD_y_los_espirituanos, accessed July 31, 2013.

20. *JMOC*, 1:68.

21. Ibid., 45.

22. Ibid., 61.

23. Ibid., 74.

24. Ibid., 49.

25. Daniel 5:23–28. Quotations and citations are from *The New Oxford Annotated Bible*, rev. standard ed., 1962.

26. Daniel 5:30.

27. *JMOC*, 1:56.

28. Hidalgo Paz, *José Martí 1853–1895*, 35.

29. For the full text of the anonymous letter signed "Various Cubans" dated September 17, 1871, to the *Jurado Federal*, see *JMOC*, 1:77–78. For the September 22 letter co-signed by Martí and Carlos Sauvalle, see 78–80.

30. Márquez Sterling, *Biografía*, 86.

31. Germán Rodas Chaves, *José Martí: aproximación a sus primeros 20 años de vida* [José Martí: Overview of His First Twenty Years] (Quito: Abya Yala, 2001), 42; Hidalgo Paz, *José Martí 1853–1895*, 35.

32. Carlos Ripoll, "Los estudiantes de 1871" [The Students of 1871], 1986, in *Escritos cubanos de historia, política y literatura* [Cuban Writings on History, Politics, and Literature] (Miami: Dos Ríos, 1998).

33. Ibid.

34. Ibid.

35. Tablada, 52–55.

36. *JMOC*, 17:32.

37. Ripoll, "Los estudiantes."

38. Valdés Domínguez, "Ofrenda," 15–16.

39. Tablada, 56–57.

40. Hidalgo Paz, *José Martí 1853–1895*, 37.

41. *JMOC*, 17:34–41.

42. *JMOC*, 1:83–85.

43. Hidalgo Paz, *José Martí 1853–1895*, 38.

44. Ibid.

45. Ibid., 81; Cupull and González, 95–96.

46. Ripoll, *La vida íntima*, 37–46.

47. Pierson, 106.

48. Hidalgo Paz, *José Martí 1853–1895*, 39.

49. *JMOC*, 1:89–98.

50. Ibid., 91.

51. Ibid., 93.

52. Ibid., 99–107 and 108–111, respectively.

53. Cupull and González, 95–96.

54. *JMOC*, 16:74.

55. Ripoll, *La vida íntima*, 37–38.

56. Ibid. See also Manuel García Guatas, *La Zaragoza de José Martí* [José Martí's Zaragoza] (Zaragoza, Spain: Institución Fernando el Católico, 1999), 24–28.

57. García Guatas, 21–24, 57–58.

58. Ibid., 21–28.

59. Ibid., 38–46.

60. Hidalgo Paz, *José Martí 1853–1895*, 41.

61. *JMOC*, 18:25–76.

62. Hidalgo Paz, *José Martí 1853–1895*, 41.

63. Ibid.

64. Luis García Pascual, *Destinatario José Martí* [Letters to José Martí] (Havana: Abril, 2005), 93.

65. Ibid., 108–111.

66. Cupull and González, 99.

67. García Pascual, 106–108.

68. Cupull and González, 99.

69. Bowen and Alvarez, 29–32.

70. Thomas, 262–263.

71. Bowen and Alvarez, 29–32; Thomas, 263.

72. *JMOC*, 4:391.

73. Hidalgo Paz, *José Martí 1853–1895*, 42.

74. Ibid.; Cupull and González, 101.

75. Ripoll, *La vida íntima*, 41–43.

76. Hidalgo Paz, *José Martí 1853–1895*, 42–43.

77. Ibid.

78. *JMOC*, 21:77.

79. Hidalgo Paz, *José Martí 1853–1895*, 44–45.

80. Ibid., 44.

81. *JMOC*, 1:121–123.

82. Ripoll, *La vida íntima*, 45–46.

83. Quoted in García Pascual, 16.

84. Cupull and González, 102–104.

85. Hidalgo Paz, *José Martí 1853–1895*, 45.

86. Ibid., 46; Cupull and González, 105.

Chapter Five. A Young Man's Travels

1. Epigraph: *JMOC*, 17:107.

2. Ibid., 23:168.

3. Constant Mews, ed. and trans., *The Lost Love Letters of Héloïse and Abelard: Perceptions of Dialogue in Twelfth-Century France* (Basingstoke, England: Palgrave Macmillan, 2001).

4. García Pascual, 11–12.

5. *JMOC*, 17:108–109.

6. For the full text of Montalvo's December 26, 1874, letter sent to Paris and her final letter to Martí, dated March 16, 1875, and sent to Mexico City, see García Pascual, 11–12 and 40–41, respectively.

7. *Le Rappel*, "Les on-dit" [The Hearsay], December 23, 1874, 2.

8. Patrick H. Hutton, Amanda S. Bourque, and Amy J. Staples, eds., *Historical Dictionary of the Third French Republic, 1870–1940* (New York: Greenwood, 1986), 215; Albert León Guerard, *France: A Modern History*, 2nd ed. (Ann Arbor, MI: University of Michigan Press, 1969), 327–329.

9. Guerard, 328–329; William L. Shirer, *The Collapse of the Third Republic* (New York: Simon and Schuster, 1969), 36–39.

10. José Martí, *Obras completas. Edición crítica* (Havana: Centro de Estudios Martianos, 2000), 3:22–23. For some reason, this essay is not included in *JMOC*, the 2001 *Obras completas*, though it does appear in the 2000 and earlier editions.

11. *JMOC*, 6:352.

12. *JMOC*, 19:115.

13. U.S. National Archives and Record Service, Passenger Lists of Vessels Arriving in New York, 1820–1897, microfilm, roll 396, January 1–March 10, 1875, Washington, DC, 1958.

14. *New York Times*, "Rough Weather on the Atlantic," January 9, 1875, 3.

15. *JMOC*, 19:16.

16. *JMOC*, 7:173.

17. *JMOC*, 22:150.

18. Timothy Rives, "Grant, Babcock, and the Whiskey Ring," *Prologue: Quarterly of the National Archives and Records Administration* 32.3 (Fall 2000), http://www.archives.gov/publications/prologue/2000/fall/whiskey-ring-1.html, accessed June 30, 2012; Mary E. Seematter, "The St. Louis Whiskey Ring," *Gateway Heritage*, Spring 1988, 32–42.

19. James Wilford Garner, *Reconstruction in Mississippi* (New York: Macmillan, 1902), 335–336; Warren A. Ellem, "The Overthrow of Reconstruction in Mississippi," *Journal of Mississippi History* 54:2 (1992), 175–201.

20. George C. Rable, *But There Was No Peace: The Role of Violence in the Politics of Reconstruction* (Athens: University of Georgia Press, 2007), 140–142; Charles Vincent, *Black Legislators in Louisiana during Reconstruction* (Carbondale, IL: SIU Press, 2011), 187.

21. James Brewer Stewart, *Wendell Phillips: Liberty's Hero* (Baton Rouge, LA: LSU Press, 1998), 308–311; *The National Cyclopedia of American Biography* (New York: J. T. White, 2012), 10:513.

22. Ibid.

23. *JMOC*, 19:17.

24. The Mexican silver peso circulated as legal currency in the United States alongside the dollar late into the nineteenth century despite Congress's official abolition of the practice in 1857. At the time of *La Iberia*'s collection for the Martís, the peso's value would have been roughly equivalent to the U.S. dollar. Assuming equivalence between the Mexican silver peso and the U.S. dollar in 1875—a fair assumption based on available data—the Martís' $72.50 windfall would have been worth $1,422.19 in 2010. W. A. Shaw, *The History of Currency 1251–1894: Being an Account of the Gold and Silver Moneys and Monetary Standards of Europe and America, together with an Examination of the Effects of Currency and Exchange Phenomena on Commercial and National Progress and Well Being*, 1896 (reprint, New York: G. P. Putnam's Sons, 1967), 328–333.

Chapter Six. Discovering America (1): Mexico

1. Epigraph: *JMOC*, 20:18.

2. Roberto Terrero, "Apuntes para una biografía: Manuel Mercado, íntimo amigo de José Martí" [Notes toward a Biography: Manuel Mercado, Intimate Friend of José Martí] (Havana: Universidad de Ciencias Pedagógicas Blas Roca Calderío, September 27, 2011).

3. Manuel Mercado, *Discurso inaugural pronunciado en la Academia de Jurisprudencia Teórico-Práctica el día 19 de enero* [Inaugural Lecture Given at the Academy of Theoretical-Practical Jurisprudence on January 19] (Mexico City: Ignacio Cumplido, 1860).

4. Roderic Ai Camp, *Mexican Political Biographies, 1884–1935* (Austin: University of Texas Press, 1991), 144–145.

5. *JMOC*, 17:43–44, 47.

6. Ibid., 18–19.

7. Ibid., 88–89. For the full text of Martí's poem "Y es que mi alma" (And So My Soul), see 87–89.

8. Michele Cunningham, *Mexico and the Foreign Policy of Napoleon III* (London: Palgrave Macmillan, 2001); Gene Smith, *Maximilian and Carlota* (New York: William Morrow, 1974).

9. Jaime Hugo Talancón Escobedo, *Benito Juárez: la educación y el estado* [Benito Juárez: Education and the State] (Mexico City: Universidad Nacional Autónoma de México, 2006).

10. Albert G. Robinson, *Cuba Old and New*, 1915 (reproduced, Project Gutenberg, 2004, http://gutenberg.org/ebooks/11464).

11. Daila Antonia Muller, "Cuban Emigrés, Mexican Politics, and the Cuban Question, 1895–1899," PhD diss., University of California–Berkeley, 2007, 59–61. For examples of Martí's writings, including correspondence, regarding Macías, Menendez de la Peña, and Domínguez Cowan, respectively, see *JMOC*, 5:239–241, 3:171–174, and 20:254–258.

12. Muller, 58–59.

13. José Ortiz Monasterio, *México eternamente: Vicente Riva Palacio ante la escritura de la historia* [Mexico Forever: Vicente Riva Palacio before the Structure of History] (Mexico City: Fondo de Cultura Económica, 2004), 255–258; Carlos Ripoll, *José Martí: nuevas obras completas* [José Martí: New Complete Works] (Miami: Dos Ríos, 2001), 11.

14. *Obras completas* (*JMOC*) contains a number of unsigned items that appeared in the *Revista Universal* posthumously attributed to Martí. Ripoll, *José Martí: nuevas obras completas*, 3–8. Other articles appearing under the pseudonyms Anáhuac and Orestes are less problematic because corroboration from other texts confirms Martí's authorship.

15. Quoted in José de Jesús Núñez y Domínguez, *Martí en México* (Mexico City: Mexico, Secretaría de Relaciones Exteriores, 1933), 23.

16. *JMOC*, 7:133.

17. *JMOC*, 17:79–80.

18. Balzac's affinity for coffee was well known and documented in his essays "Traité des excitants modernes" (Treatise on Modern Stimulants) and "Propos sur le café"

(About Coffee). Baudelaire, for his part, published his celebratory "Poéme du ha-schisch" in 1860 and in the 1840s was a member in good standing, along with Gautier, of Paris's Club des Haschischins. Honoré de Balzac, *Traité des excitants modernes* (1845, reprint, Paris: Edicions de Boucher, 2002); Charles Baudelaire, *Les paradis artificial, opium et haschisch* [The Artificial Paradise: Opium and Hashish] (Paris: Poulet-Malassis et de Broise, 1860), 1.

19. To be fair, Martí was a fan of coffee before he was arrested and imprisoned in 1869. In a letter from prison he bemoaned the lack of money for coffee, suggesting that its absence pained him second only to that of his own family. *JMOC*, 1:41.

20. García Martí, 116.

21. Richard Everett Boyer, "Mexico City and the Great Flood: Aspects of Life and Society, 1629–1635," PhD diss., University of Connecticut, 1973; Enrique Florescano and Susan Swan, *Breve historia de la sequia en México* [Brief History of Drought in Mexico] (Veracruz, Mexico: Universidad Veracruzana, Dirección Editorial, 1995).

22. García Martí, 116–117.

23. Tablada, 80.

24. *JMOC*, 6:305.

25. *JMOC*, 17:12–17 and 1:116, respectively.

26. *JMOC*, 6:305–308.

27. Hidalgo Paz, *José Martí 1853–1895*, 48–49.

28. In his March 25, 1876, *Revista Universal* article "La fiesta masónica" [The Masonic Party], Martí documents his participation as a speaker at an event held at a Masonic lodge he identifies as Toltecas. The article does not appear in *JMOC*, the 2001 edition of *Obras completas*, but Martí does identify himself as its author in correspondence with a reader who objected to his name appearing as a participant. Reproduced, Portal José Martí, http://www.josemarti.cu/, accessed July 1, 2012.

29. *JMOC*, 1:128.

30. Alfonso Herrera Franyutti, *Martí en México: recuerdos de una época* [Martí in Mexico: Remembrances of an Era], 1933 (reprint, Mexico City: Consejo Nacional para la Cultura y las Artes, 1996), 55.

31. Guadalupe Loaeza, "La puerta falsa/El poeta suicida" [The False Door/The Poet's Suicide], *Fondo de Cultura Económica*, January 6, 2008, http://www.fondode culturaeconomica.com/editorial/prensa/Detalle.aspx?seccion=Detalle&id_desplegado =12610, accessed July 16, 2012.

32. *JMOC*, 17:169, 171.

33. Ibid., 169.

34. *JMOC*, 20:251.

35. Ibid., 252–253.

36. Ibid., 253.

37. *JMOC*, 17:170–172. Another poem with the same title had appeared in *Revista Universal* a month earlier, in the March 11, 1875, issue.

38. *JMOC*, 1:130.

39. Both women continued to write to Martí after his arrival in Mexico, the later cor-respondences reproaching him for not replying. The last known letter from "M," con-

sidered to have been Barbarita Echevarría, dates from July 1875, while Blanca de Montalvo continued to write to Martí until March 1876. No record exists of Martí having responded to any of these letters. Ripoll, *La vida íntima*, 43–44.

40. *JMOC*, 6:417–420 and 227, respectively.

41. Ripoll, *La vida íntima*, 49–50.

42. Paul Royet and Patrice Mériaux, *Surveillance, Maintenance, and Diagnosis of Flood Protection Dikes: A Practical Handbook for Owners and Operators* (Versailles: Quae, 2007), 18; Cornelius Walford, *The Famines of the World, Past and Present* (Manchester, NH: Ayer, 1970), 35.

43. *JMOC*, 6:296–298.

44. In García Pascual, 23.

45. For the texts of Agüero's second and third letters to Martí, undated but sent on consecutive days sometime in September, see García Pascual, 24 and 24–25, respectively.

46. Ibid., 25.

47. Apparently conflicting accounts from at least two sources are easily reconciled by this timeline. Guasp was a passenger on the *City of Merida*, the ship that brought Martí to Mexico, though only on the Havana-Veracruz leg of its journey; thus it is plausible that the two became reacquainted via Azcárate's introduction. For examples of the two differing accounts of their meeting, see Ripoll, *La vida íntima*, 47, and García Martí, 120.

48. Ripoll, *La vida íntima*, 47; Enrique de Olavarría y Ferrari, *Reseña histórica del teátro en México, 1538–1911* [Historical Summary of the Theater in Mexico, 1538–1911], 1914 (3rd ed., Mexico City: Porrúa, 1961), 2:917.

49. Herrera Franyutti, 119. Padilla's words become dialogue for her character early in the play: "I do not ask for such a high thing: / I want a modest work, / Plaything, practice, proverb." *JMOC*, 18:110.

50. True to the play's self-reflexive nature, its protagonist, who is a playwright, reveals, "In the morning it was commissioned, / And conceived that morning; / More frivolous than elegant, / That afternoon it was done." *JMOC*, 18:126.

51. The closest English-language equivalent for the Spanish proverb "Quien espera, desespera" may be "A watched pot never boils," although this lacks the economy and poetic charm of the Spanish. To compare Agüero's quote from her letter with the play's ironic, somewhat snarky paraphrase, see García Pascual, 23, and *JMOC*, 18:114.

52. *JMOC*, 18:126–127. Due to the complex structure of the play's closing speech, I have taken the liberty of changing the literal translation of the play's antepenultimate and penultimate lines "Imaginando que al menos / Entre públicos buenos" [Imagining that at least / Among good publics (or audiences)] to "Thinking that here tonight, if nowhere else" to maintain something of the verses' rhythm and rhyme scheme while preserving as much as possible of the text's original language. My translation of these closing lines remains true to what I believe to be the character's literal point, which would be consistent with the play's larger metafictional (self-referential) structure.

53. *JMOC*, 17:107–110.

54. In García Pascual, 25.

55. *JMOC*, 18:124.

56. Ripoll, *La vida íntima*, 48.

57. Ibid.

58. Jorge Mañach, "La hermana de Martí" [Martí's Sister], part 1 of 2, *Diario de la Marina*, January 11, 1924, 1–3.

59. In García Pascual, 27.

60. *JMOC*, 1:128.

61. Ibrahim Hidalgo Paz, *Incursiones en la obra de José Martí* [Incursions in the Work of José Martí] (Havana: Centro de Estudios Martianos, 1989), 87.

62. The *Usted/tú* distinction has no parallel in English.

63. García Pascual, 32.

64. Ibid., 28.

65. Ibid., 29.

66. Herrera Franyutti, 159. For more on Ignacio, see Emiliano Tejera, "Gobernadores de la Isla de Santo Domingo, siglos XVI–XVII" [Governors of the Island of Santo Domingo, Sixteenth–Seventeenth Centuries], 1915, reprint, BAGN: *Boletín del Archivo General de la Nación*, http://www.bagn.academiahistoria.org.do/boletines/boletin18/BAGN_1941_No_18-04.pdf, accessed July 1, 2012, 375. On Cristóbal Zayas Bazán, see Thomas, 44–45.

67. García Martí, 138.

68. Hidalgo Paz, *Incursiones*, 51.

69. For the text of Zayas Bazán's letter and the footnote that contains Agüero's rather catty remarks, see García Pascual, 32.

70. Ibid., 31.

71. Ibid.

72. Ibid., 31–32.

73. Ibid., 30.

74. Ibid.

75. Ibid., 33.

76. Ripoll, *La vida íntima*, 52.

77. Cupull and González, 117; García Martí, 136.

78. In García Pascual, 32.

79. Herrera Franyutti, 120–121; Cupull and González, 117; García Martí, 137.

80. Quoted in Ripoll, *La vida íntima*, 52.

81. Martí was officially inducted into the society on December 21 during another of its regular Tuesday-night gatherings. Hidalgo Paz, *José Martí 1853–1895*, 51.

82. Quoted in Herrera Franyutti, 122.

83. García Martí, 138.

84. Cupull and González, 117.

85. Gloria Delgado and Harim B. Gutiérrez, *Historia de México* (New York: Pearson, 2006), 1:496; Francie R. Chassen de López, *From Liberal to Revolutionary Oaxaca: The View from the South, Mexico 1867–1911* (University Park, PA: Penn State University Press, 2004), 355–356.

86. Delgado and Harim B. Gutiérrez, *Historia de México* (New York: Pearson, 2005), 2:21–23; Will Fowler, *Gobernantes mexicanos: 1821–1910* (Mexican Heads of State: 1821–1910; Mexico City: Fondo de Cultura Económica, 2008), 339–357.

87. Paul Garner, *Porfirio Díaz*, Profiles in Power (White Plains, NY: Longman, 2001), 246.

88. Jim Harter, *World Railways of the Nineteenth Century: A Pictorial History in Victorian Engravings* (Baltimore, MD: Johns Hopkins University Press, 2005), 199.

89. Fowler, 344–354.

90. John Mason Hart, *Revolutionary Mexico: The Coming and Process of the Mexican Revolution* (Berkeley: University of California Press, 1987), 105; Delgado and Gutiérrez, 1:499–500.

91. Julia Preston and Samuel Dillon, *Opening Mexico: The Making of a Democracy* (London: Macmillan, 2005), 45; Delgado and Gutiérrez, 1:500–501.

92. Ignacio Altamirano, "Letter to Concepción Quiros P.," February 29, 1876, in vol. 21, *Epistolario (1850–1899)*, of Altamirano, *Obras completas* (Mexico City: Secretaría de Educación Pública, 2001), 377.

93. Martí's January 14, 1876, essay "La civilización de las indígenas" [The Civilization of the Indigenous] appears in the 1985 edition of Martí's *Obras completas* (2:254) but not the 2001 edition.

94. Neftali G. García, *The Mexican Revolution: Legacy of Courage* (Mexico City: Xlibris, 2010), 36; Hart, 6, 105.

95. Herrera Franyutti, 127–133.

96. Hidalgo Paz, *José Martí 1853–1895*, 51–52; Herrera Franyutti, 137–138.

97. Hidalgo Paz, *José Martí 1853–1895*, 52–53.

98. Martí, *Obras completas*, 1985, 2:266–270.

99. Hidalgo Paz, *José Martí 1853–1895*, 53.

100. *JMOC*, 17:133. Curiously, given his otherwise prodigious output in Mexico, "Carmen" was Martí's only publication in May and one of only two poems he published in 1876.

101. *JMOC*, 20:15.

102. Quoted in Herrera Franyutti, 160.

103. Tablada, 86–87; Herrera Franyutti, 160–161.

104. Herrera Franyutti, 61, 77.

105. Ibid., 142.

106. García Martí, 139.

107. Martí, *Obras completas*, 1985, 2:274.

108. Hidalgo Paz, *Incursiones*, 87.

109. Herrera Franyutti, 165–166.

110. P. Garner, 63.

111. Herrera Franyutti, 171–173.

112. Frank Averill Knapp, *The Life of Sebastián Lerdo de Tejada, 1823–1889: A Study of Influence and Obscurity* (Austin: University of Texas Press, 1951), 254–256.

113. Cupull and González, 120; Herrera Franyutti, 173.

114. P. Garner, 63–65.

115. Forensic historian Ricardo Tablada speculates that the congenital heart defect from which Ana and Antonia suffered may have been a weakness in one or more ven-

tricles. This would in turn have made them vulnerable to the demands that Mexico City's altitude of nearly 8,000 feet could place on the heart (76).

116. Tablada, 95; Cupull, 120.

117. *JMOC*, 6:359–360.

118. This unsigned essay does not appear in any edition of Martí's *Obras completas*, though it is generally believed to be his. José Martí, "La situación" [The Situation], *El Federalista*, December 10, 1876.

119. *JMOC*, 20:17.

120. For examples of crossing European borders, see Eugene M. Avrutin, *Jews and the Imperial State: Identification Politics in Tsarist Russia* (Ithaca, NY: Cornell University Press, 2010), 127–128.

121. *JMOC*, 20:16.

122. In his January 1, 1877, letter to Mercado, Martí explains that with this name he commits "but a minor treason" against himself, further offering that "it is always good to be, even in the most serious cases, as little of a hypocrite as possible." *JMOC*, 20:16.

123. *JMOC*, 6:361, 362.

124. Ibid., 363.

125. Ibid.

126. *JMOC*, 20:20–21; Herrera Franyutti, 185.

127. *JMOC*, 20:16.

A Secret Mission

1. Iglesias's remaining forces, under the command of General Florencio Antillón, surrendered at Los Adobes near Guadalajara. Iglesias then fled with his cabinet members to the western port of Manzanillo, where he sailed for San Francisco. Diego Arenas Guzmán, *El periodismo en la revolución mexicana, 1876–1908* [Journalism during the Mexican Revolution, 1876–1908] (Mexico City: Biblioteca del Instituto Nacional de Estudios Históricos de la Revolución Mexicana, 1966), 1:26–27; Hidalgo Paz, *José Martí 1853–1895*, 57.

2. Cupull and González, 125.

3. Hazard, 256–257.

4. *JMOC*, 20:20.

5. Hidalgo Paz, *José Martí 1853–1895*, 58.

6. Tablada, 91.

7. Ibid., 92–93, 228.

8. Ibid., 173–174.

9. Here as elsewhere in Martí's letters, the Spanish word *paquete* is idiomatic for the packet ship, which in the nineteenth century was a common method of delivering mail internationally as well as domestically via rivers and canals. By the 1870s almost all packets were steamships. John M. Dobson, *Bulls, Bears, Boom, and Bust: A Historical Encyclopedia of American Business Concepts* (Santa Barbara, CA: ABC-CLIO, 2007), 101–102; Mariano Velázquez de la Cadena, *A Dictionary of the Spanish and English Languages* (New York: D. Appleton, 1877), 715.

10. *JMOC*, 20:21–22.

11. Spencer Tucker, ed., *The Encyclopedia of the Spanish-American and Philippine-American Wars: A Political, Social, and Military History* (Santa Barbara, CA: ABC-CLIO, 2009), 1:648.

12. Duvon C. Corbitt, "Mercedes and Realengos," *Hispanic American Historical Review* 19 (1939): 280; Thomas, 264–266.

13. García Martí, 141–142.

14. *JMOC* 20:22.

15. Ibid.

16. Ibid., 24.

17. Ibid., 25–26.

18. Hidalgo Paz, *José Martí 1853–1895*, 58.

19. Herrera Franyutti, 198.

Chapter Seven. Discovering America (2): Guatemala

1. *JMOC*, 20:23–24.

2. Ibid., 258.

3. Ibid., 259.

4. Cupull and González, 129.

5. *JMOC*, 20:26.

6. Ibid., 27.

7. *Diario de Yucatán*, "El paso de Martí por Progreso y Mérida en 1877: 'Porque no dejó nunca huella'" [Martí's Path through Progreso and Mérida in 1877: "Why He Never Left A Footprint"], July 6, 1969, n.p.

8. *JMOC*, 21:359.

9. Herrera Franyutti, 198–199.

10. *JMOC*, 18:288.

11. Although work on the Interoceanic Railroad started in 1877, the capital, Guatemala City, did not have rail service until 1884. Delmer G. Ross, "The Construction of the Interoceanic Railroad of Guatemala," *The Americas* 33 (January 1977): 430–456; Delmer G. Ross, *Development of Railroads in Guatemala and El Salvador, 1849–1929* (Lewiston, NY: Edwin Mellen, 2001), 12–15; Alejandro Prieto and R. Piatkowski, *Ideas generals sobre el ferrocarril interoceánico de Guatemala* [General Ideas Regarding the Interoceanic Railroad of Guatemala] (Guatemala City: Taracena e Hijos, 1880).

12. *JMOC*, 19:115–116.

13. Ibid., 25.

14. Ibid., 29.

15. Cristóbal Colón, "Carta de Cristóbal Colón a Sr. Rafael Sánchez" [Letter from Christopher Columbus to Mr. Rafael Sánchez], April 25, 1493, in *Viajes de Cristóbal Colón: Con una carta* [Travels of Christopher Columbus: With a Letter], ed. Martín Fernández de Navarrete (Barcelona: Calpe, 1922), 201–209; Bernal Díaz del Castillo, *Historia verdadera de la conquista de la Nueva España* [True History of the Conquest of New Spain] (Madrid: Emprenta del Reyno, 1632), 1–3.

16. *JMOC*, 19:31.

17. Ibid., 32.

18. Ibid., 29.

19. *JMOC*, 19:30. Le Plongeon died, discredited and penniless, in Brooklyn in 1908. Lawrence Gustave Desmond, *Yucatán through Her Eyes: Alice Dixon Le Plongeon, Writer And Expeditionary Photographer* (Albuquerque: University of New Mexico Press, 2009), 324–326.

20. *JMOC*, 19:32–33.

21. *JMOC*, 22:177.

22. *JMOC*, 19:37; the full text appears on pages 37–39.

23. Ibid., 39.

24. Ibid., 58.

25. David Vela, *Martí en Guatemala* [Martí in Guatemala] (Guatemala City: Guatemala, Ministerio de Educación Pública, 1954), 53–54; Hidalgo Paz, *José Martí 1853–1895*, 60.

26. *JMOC*, 19:44.

27. Ibid.

28. Ibid.

29. Ibid. Martí misidentified "Izabal mountain," which was probably part of the Sierra de Santa Cruz at Lake Izabal. William Tufts Brigham, *Guatemala, the Land of the Quetzal: A Sketch* (London: T. Fisher Unwin, 1887), 6.

30. *JMOC*, 19:45.

31. Ibid.

32. Augustus Henry Keane, *Central America: The West Indies and South America* (London: E. Stanford, 1878), 99–100.

33. Keane, 100.

34. *JMOC*, 19:47.

35. Ibid., 48.

36. Keane, 100–101.

37. Robert Glasgow Dunlop, *Travels in Central America: Being a Journal of Nearly Three Years' Residence in the Country: Together with a Sketch of the History of the Republic, and an Account of Its Climate, Productions, Commerce, Etc.* (London: Longman, Brown, Green, and Longmans, 1847), 118.

38. Accounts in travelogues and geographical journals of the time mostly agree that six to seven leagues, roughly eighteen to twenty-one miles, was typical progress for a full eight- to ten-hour day, barring additional difficulties. See, for example, E. Legh Page, "Notes on a Journey from Belize to Guatemala, and Return by the River Polochic in 1834," *Journal of the Royal Geographical Society of London* 8 (1838), 318.

39. Hidalgo Paz, *José Martí 1853–1895*, 60.

40. Martí notes in the travelogue's final entry that he was writing at midday, presumably during a rest stop, as the noonday sun "penetrates the thick branches of the trees." *JMOC*, 19:62.

41. Ibid.

42. *JMOC*, 7:119.

43. Curiously, Macedo went on to become an important advisor for the Díaz regime and one of Mexico's best-known public intellectuals during Díaz's tenure. Alfonso María y Campos, "Porfirianos prominentes: orígenes y años de juventud de ocho integrantes del Grupo de los Científicos, 1846–1876" [Prominent Porfirians: Origins and Childhood of Eight Members of the Group of Scientists, 1846–1876], *Historia Mexicana* 34.4 (April–June 1985): 610–661.

44. Vela, 50–51.

45. On April 24 Guatemala's Office of Public Education officially recognized Martí's degrees, thus removing the final barrier to his employment. Hidalgo Paz, *José Martí 1853–1895*, 61, 62.

46. Vela, 56.

47. José María Izaguirre, "Martí en Guatemala," *Revista cubana: homenaje a Martí en el centenario de su nacimiento* [Cuban Journal: Homage to José Martí on the Centennial of His Birth] (Havana: Ministerio de Educación, Dirección General de la Cultura, 1953), 333–334. Izaguirre misremembered the essay's setting as Africa; Martí's memoir instead recounts his experience in a labor camp in Havana. *JMOC*, 1:45–74.

48. Izaguirre, 334.

49. Jim Handy, *Gift of the Devil: A History of Guatemala* (Boston: South End, 1984), 36–40; James D. Cockroft, *América Latina y Estados Unidos: historia y política país por país* [Latin America and the United States: History and Politics Country by Country] (Mexico City: Siglo XXI, 2001), 164.

50. Richard F. Nyrop, *Guatemala: A Country Study*, 2nd ed. (Washington, DC: Department of the Army, 1984), 14–20.

51. Regina Wagner, *The History of Coffee in Guatemala* (Bogotá: Villegas y Asociados, 2001), 85–95.

52. W. George Lovell, "The Century after Independence: Land and Life in Guatemala, 1821–1920," *Canadian Journal of Latin American and Caribbean Studies* 19.37–38:243–260.

53. Máximo Soto-Hall, *Martí y el General Justo Rufino Barrios* (Guatemala City: Biblioteca de Cultura Popular, 1952), 6.

54. Antonio S. Coll, a government official and later secretary of the Treasury, quoted in Vela, 253.

55. *JMOC*, 20:28.

56. Hidalgo Paz, *José Martí 1853–1895*, 60.

57. Ibid., 61; Vela, 56–57.

58. Martí's letter to Macal the next day opens by referring to the minister's request. *JMOC*, 7:97.

59. Ibid.

60. Ibid., 97–98.

61. Some scholars, among them Robert Huish and W. George Lovell, place this event in mid-June 1877, while Ibrahim Hidalgo Paz argues that it occurred within Martí's first month in Guatemala. Given Hidalgo Paz's general reliability and the presence of a few minor errors in Huish and Lovell's essay, I find Hidalgo Paz the more credible source on this point. Robert L. Huish and W. George Lovell, "Under the Volcanoes: The In-

fluence of Guatemala on José Martí," *Cuban Studies* 39.1 (2008): 35; Hidalgo Paz, *José Martí 1853–1895*, 61–62.

62. *JMOC*, 20:476.

63. Hidalgo Paz, *José Martí 1853–1895*, 62.

64. Huish and Lovell assert that the interview occurred in March 1877, while Hidalgo Paz and others place the meeting sometime in April. Given the April 11 date of Martí's letter to Joaquín Macal, who helped arrange the meeting, Martí is unlikely to have met Barrios before mid-April. Huish and Lovell, 33; Hidalgo Paz, *José Martí 1853–1895*, 62.

65. Izaguirre emigrated in 1874 and thus had been in Guatemala about three years by the time Martí arrived. Izaguirre's brother, Manuel José, was among the first Cubans captured after the onset of the 1868 war; he was deported and sentenced to hard labor at the Spanish work camp on the island of Ceuta and came to Guatemala after escaping to Cádiz. Vela, 56.

66. Antonio S. Coll explains in a note to scholar David Vela, to whom he entrusted an unpublished account of the meeting, that he compiled it from the eyewitness accounts of others who were present. Vela, 253.

67. For a fuller overview of Coll's account, see Vela, 253–254.

68. *JMOC*, 7:158.

69. Hidalgo Paz, *José Martí 1853–1895*, 63.

70. *JMOC*, 16:78–79.

71. Several sources confirm the medical cause of María Granados's death, albeit with some speculative variations. See, for example, Sande, 109, and Nohely S. Broderman, *José Martí: patriota y poeta* [José Martí: Patriot and Poet] (Havana: Ediciones Geminis, 1973), 19.

72. Soto-Hall, 149. Regarding Miguel García Granados's death, see his obituary in *The Numismatist* 63 (1950): 145.

73. José Antonio Portuondo, *Martí y el diversionismo ideológico* [Martí and Ideological Diversionism] (Havana: Centro de Estudios Martianos, 1974), 9.

74. Martí said as much in an 1891 letter to friend Gonzalo de Quesada bemoaning his rejection of Maria for Carmen after the latter definitively left him and returned to Cuba with their son. Blanca Z. de Baralt, who knew Martí at the time, affirms that he expressed similar regrets to her and in writing to their mutual friend Miguel Viondi. Neither letter appears in *JMOC*, the 2001 *Obras completas*, although the one to Quesada survives in Quesada y Miranda's *Martí, hombre* (195). See also Blanca Z. de Baralt, *El Martí que yo conocí* [The Martí I Knew] (Havana: Trópico, 1945), 164.

75. Izaguirre, 338.

76. Ibid.

77. The editorial interpolation in brackets replaces the phrase "a los dos días de haber llegado a Guatemala" (two days after arriving in Guatemala). Since the grammar of the sentence makes it unclear whether the phrase refers to Martí's arrival or Manuel Izaguirre's, I have replaced the indeterminate phrase with an approximation of when the ball would have occurred.

78. Quoted in Ripoll, *La vida íntima*, 68.

79. Ibid.

80. Izaguirre, 338–339. I translated the original Spanish word *nasa* as "creel," a kind of wicker basket used to catch fish. I note this here only to draw attention to it as a delightfully apt metaphor.

81. *JMOC*, 20:29.

82. *JMOC*, 16:79.

83. García Pascual, 47.

84. Hidalgo Paz, *José Martí 1853–1895*, 63–64.

85. In García Pascual, 45–46.

86. Izaguirre, 340.

87. Ibid., 340–341.

88. Hidalgo Paz, *José Martí 1853–1895*, 64.

89. Ibid.

90. *JMOC*, 20:32.

91. Ibid.

92. Ibid.

93. Ibid.

94. Vela, 270–272.

95. Pedro Tobar Cruz, "Crónica de la conspiración de Antonio Kopesky en 1877 y el gobierno liberal de Justo Rufino Barrios" [Chronicle of the 1877 Conspiracy of Antonio Kopesky and the Liberal Government of Justo Rufino Barrios], *Antropología e historia de Guatemala* 1 (1979): 127.

96. Hernández de León, 194.

97. Barrios later claimed to have been repelled by the bloody but—for him— necessary actions that he believed protected Guatemala from the threat of reactionary elements. Paul Burgues, *Justo Rufino Barrios: Una biografía* (Guatemala City: Editorial del Ejército, 1971), 160–161. See also Hernández de León, 194–195.

98. Tobar Cruz, 132, 136.

99. For example, the magazine *El Pueblo* continued to honor the November 7 anniversary even in 1891, six years after Barrios's death in 1885.

100. Tobar Cruz, 136.

101. Hidalgo Paz, *José Martí 1853–1895*, 65.

102. *JMOC*, 20:37; the full text of the letter appears on pages 37–38.

103. Ibid.

104. *JMOC*, 7:111. Pages 110–112 have the full text of Martí's letter to Valero Pujol, editor of *El Progreso* and eventual publisher of his book on Guatemala.

105. *JMOC*, 20:33.

106. Ibid., 35.

107. Ibid.

108. The nineteenth-century travel literature regarding Mexico almost uniformly confirms the ubiquity of bandits on the roads and the need for travelers to hire armed escorts for their own safety. See, for example, S. S. Hill, *Travels in Peru and Mexico* (London: Longman, Green, Longman, and Roberts, 1860), 2:270–275; and John Lloyd

Stephens, *Incidents of Travel in Central America, Chiapas, and Yucatan* (New York: Harper and Brothers, 1871), 2:40–41, 164–165.

109. Herrera Franyutti, 221–222; Hidalgo Paz, *José Martí 1853–1895*, 65–66.

110. Herrera Franyutti, 223; Hidalgo Paz, *José Martí 1853–1895*, 66.

111. Quoted in Herrera Franyutti, 223.

112. Herrera Franyutti, 224–225; Hidalgo Paz, *José Martí 1853–1895*, 66.

113. The letter is quoted in Herrera Franyutti, 225.

114. Ibid., 229.

115. Martí wrote his speech on what appears to be a woman's stationery bearing the monogram "C," more than likely Carmen's, and read it at the ceremony. *JMOC*, 22:85–86.

116. Herrera Franyutti, 229–230.

117. Forty years after the Martís' journey on the Tlalpan Road, Edith O'Shaughnessy wrote of the Pedregal, a prehistoric lava stream along the Tlalpan, as having been "for centuries, with its caves and retreats, the beloved of bandits and all shades of delinquents." Edith O'Shaughnessy, *Diplomatic Days* (New York: Harper and Brothers, 1917), 279–280. See also Samuel Salinas Alvarez, *Historia de los caminos de México, época prehistórica, época colonial* [History of the Roads of Mexico, Prehistoric Times, Colonial Times] (Mexico City: Banco Nacional de Obras y Servicios Públicos, 1994), 235.

118. Herrera Franyutti, 234; Hidalgo Paz, *José Martí 1853–1895*, 67.

119. *JMOC*, 18:385.

120. *JMOC*, 20:38.

121. *JMOC*, 7:147.

122. Herrera Franyutti, 239.

123. Ibid. See also Hidalgo Paz, *José Martí 1853–1895*, 67–68.

124. Tablada, 96.

125. *JMOC*, 20:39.

126. For a more thorough description of the Sierra Madre, see Antonio García Cubas, *Mexico: Its Industry, Trade, and Resources*, trans. William Thompson (Mexico City: Departamento de Fomento, Colonización y Industria, 1893), 128–130.

127. *JMOC*, 7:157.

128. Herrera Franyutti, 243–244; Hidalgo Paz, *José Martí 1853–1895*, 68.

129. *JMOC*, 20:40.

130. Ibid.

131. Ibid., 19. Martí's letter appears out of sequence in the *Epistolario* volume of *Obras completas*. The original letter lists the date only as January 9, and the editors added 1877 as the likely year of its writing. But Martí refers in the letter to both the remainder of the book and his travels with Carmen; thus the actual date of the letter must be 1878, not 1877.

132. Tobar Cruz, 135–136.

133. Thomas, 265–267.

134. Estimates of total casualties range from 150,000 to 200,000, including at least 50,000 Cubans. Some scholars, such as Hugh Thomas, include Cuban casualties from the subsequent Little War (1879–1880) in their estimates. Thomas, 269; Antonio Pirala,

Anales de la Guerra de Cuba [Annals of the War in Cuba] (Madrid: Felipe González Rojas, 1898), 3:683; Byron Farwell, ed., *The Encyclopedia of Nineteenth-Century Land Warfare: An Illustrated World View* (New York: W. W. Norton, 2001), 838.

135. Thomas, 267–268.

136. Ibid., 269–271.

137. Hidalgo Paz, *José Martí 1853–1895*, 69.

138. *JMOC*, 20:41.

139. Ibid., 43.

140. Vela, 206; Hidalgo Paz, *José Martí 1853–1895*, 70.

141. *JMOC*, 20:45.

142. Ibid., 46.

143. Ibid., 45.

144. Regarding these never-completed projects, see *JMOC*, 20:41 (coffee plantation) and 45 (magazine).

145. Ibid., 41.

146. References to Voltaire are plentiful in Martí's works. Especially noteworthy is his brief portrait of the French writer in the 1889 essay "Músicos, poetas y pintores" (Musicians, Poets, and Painters). *JMOC*, 18:396–397.

147. For the full text of Martí's essay, essentially a prospectus for the magazine, see *JMOC*, 7:104–106.

148. Hugo Meltzl de Lomnitz, "Present Tasks of Comparative Literature," 1877, in *Comparative Literature, the Early Years: An Anthology of Essays*, ed. Hans-Joachim Schultz and Philip H. Rhein (Chapel Hill: University of North Carolina Press, 1973), 56–62. For a fuller discussion of Martí's proposed *Revista Guatemalteca* and the founding of comparative literature, see Alfred López, "Hugo Meltzl and That Dangerous American Supplement; or, A Tale of Two 1877s," special issue, *The Americas, Otherwise*, ed. Lois Parkinson Zamora and Silvia D. Spitta, *Comparative Literature* 61.3 (Summer 2009): 220–230.

149. *JMOC*, 7:104–105.

150. Ibid., 105.

151. Hidalgo Paz, *José Martí 1853–1895*, 71.

152. *JMOC*, 7:106.

153. Vela, 206–207; Herrera Franyutti, 249; Hidalgo Paz, *José Martí 1853–1895*, 70.

154. Izaguirre, 339–340.

155. Hidalgo Paz, *José Martí 1853–1895*, 71.

156. *JMOC*, 20:48.

157. Ibid., 49.

158. Ibid.

159. Rubén Pérez Nápoles, *José Martí: el poeta armado* [José Martí: The Armed Poet] (Madrid: Algaba, 2004), 133–134.

160. García Pascual, 47.

161. Tuberculosis was notorious through most of the nineteenth century for being a sort of opposite number to the century's other deadly disease, cholera. While cholera manifested rapidly and overwhelmingly, often killing its victims within twenty-four hours, tuberculosis characteristically brought a slow, agonizing death six months or

more after the first appearance of symptoms. Suellen Hoy, *Chasing Dirt: The American Pursuit of Cleanliness* (London: Oxford University Press, 1996), 62; J. N. Hays, *The Burdens of Disease: Epidemics and Human Response in Western History* (New Brunswick, NJ: Rutgers University Press, 2010), 155–178.

162. Izaguirre, 342.

163. Vela, 346–347.

164. *JMOC*, 16:78.

165. Hidalgo Paz, *José Martí 1853–1895*, 71.

166. *JMOC*, 20:52–53.

167. Ibid., 55. Carmen's letter to Lola Mercado accompanied Martí's July 6 letter to Manuel Mercado.

168. Ibid., 52.

169. Ibid.

170. Ibid., 53.

171. Herrera Franyutti, 250.

Chapter Eight. Homecoming, Interrupted

1. Epigraph: *JMOC*, 20:59.

2. Shipping records show that the Martís departed Honduras for Havana on August 28. They traveled by horse or mule rather than a more public conveyance such as a train or hired coach that would leave a record, and Martí himself kept no journal of the trip; thus, no definitive information exists to fix their actual date of departure from Guatemala City or arrival in Trujillo. Herrera Franyutti, 250; Hidalgo Paz, *José Martí 1853–1895*, 72.

3. Herrera Franyutti, 250.

4. Cupull and González, 140.

5. *JMOC*, 20:56–57.

6. Hidalgo Paz, *José Martí 1853–1895*, 72–73.

7. Ibid.

8. Ibid., 73–74.

9. *JMOC*, 5:252.

10. Ballester, 119–120.

11. Tablada, 98–99.

12. *JMOC*, 20:59. The earlier letter to which Martí refers, presumably written shortly after his son's birth, does not appear among Mercado's collected letters and most likely was lost.

13. Hidalgo Paz, *José Martí 1853–1895*, 74.

14. *JMOC*, 5:87.

15. Ibid.

16. Hidalgo Paz, *José Martí 1853–1895*, 76.

17. According to some scholars Martí started teaching in private settings in January 1879, although official certification of his credentials was necessary for him to hold a regular position in Havana schools. On January 29 Martí submitted his credentials and

applied for a position at the Instituto Provincial of Havana. The school's petition to hire Martí was granted on February 21 pending presentation of his diploma. Hidalgo Paz, *José Martí 1853–1895*, 75–76.

18. Ibid., 77–78.

19. Ibid., 78.

20. Ibid., 78–79.

21. Here in his letter of January 12, 1892, to Enrique Collazo, Martí paraphrases his 1879 response to party head Sánchez Hechevarría. *JMOC*, 1:293.

22. Hidalgo Paz, *José Martí 1853–1895*, 79.

23. Rafael Soto Paz, *Antología de periodistas cubanos* [Anthology of Cuban Journalists] (Havana: Empresa Editora de Publicaciones, 1943), 74–75.

24. *JMOC*, 4:178–179.

25. Ibid., 179.

26. Ibid.

27. Ibid., 180.

28. García Martí, 152.

29. Ibid.

30. *JMOC*, 15:369–380. Martí's admiring tribute to Charles Darwin upon the naturalist's death in 1882 demonstrates that he was quite familiar with Darwin's work. Martí's regular attendance at the Liceo's roundtables on naturalism and evolution indicates his interest in these subjects and suggests that he would have made a fine advocate for Darwin's theories.

31. César García del Pino, *"El Laborante:* Carlos Sauvalle y José Martí" [*The Laborer:* Carlos Sauvalle and José Martí], *Revista de la Biblioteca Nacional José Martí* 60.2 (May–August 1969): 165–194.

32. Hidalgo Paz, *José Martí 1853–1895*, 81–82.

33. Pérez, 11–12; Thomas, 268–269.

34. Thomas, 269.

35. Pérez, 11–12.

36. Ibid., 12; Thomas, 269; Hidalgo Paz, *José Martí 1853–1895*, 89, 91.

37. Cupull and González, 145; Hidalgo Paz, *José Martí 1853–1895*, 82.

38. Hidalgo Paz, *José Martí 1853–1895*, 82; García Martí, 153–154.

39. García Martí, 153.

40. Hidalgo Paz, *José Martí 1853–1895*, 83.

41. Ibid., 85; Cupull and González, 146.

42. *JMOC*, 5:366. Martí included this reminiscence as part of an essay that appeared in the May 21, 1892, issue of his New York newspaper, *Patria*.

43. José Martí, *Epistolario* [Letters], edited, introduction, and notes by Gonzalo de Quesada y Miranda (Havana: El Siglo XX, 1948), 1:150. Martí's October 13, 1879, letter to Viondi does not appear in *JMOC*, the 2001 *Obras completas*.

44. An extensive search of the Archivo Histórico Nacional in Madrid and its counterpart in Cantabria Province, where Setién's supposed hometown of Laredo is situated, turned up no documentation to support his standing as a delegate. A further

search resulted in no birth or death records or related documentation of anyone by the name of Ladislao Setién.

45. Cupull and González, 146.

46. Hidalgo Paz, *José Martí 1853–1895*, 84–86.

47. Ibid., 85.

48. Ibid.

49. Ibid., 86.

50. Martí, *Epistolario*, 1:157. Martí's November 28 letter to Viondi does not appear in the 2001 *Obras completas* (*JMOC*).

51. *JMOC*, 21:124–130.

52. Phillips, 225; García Martí, 154.

53. Carlos Ripoll, "Martí y Francia" [Martí and France], *Trazos de Cuba* 14 (1996): 18–19; Hidalgo Paz, *José Martí 1853–1895*, 86.

54. *JMOC*, 20:281.

55. Hidalgo Paz, *José Martí 1853–1895*, 86.

PART THREE. THE GREAT WORK (1881–1895)

Chapter Nine. New York (1): A False Start

1. Epigraph: *JMOC*, 19:103.

2. U.S. National Archives and Records Service, Passenger Lists of Vessels Arriving at New York, 1820–1897, roll 422, January 2–February 24, 1880 (list nos. 1–190), Name of Vessel: *France*. Point of Departure: Havre. Date of Arrival: January 3, 1880.

3. Ripoll, *La vida íntima*, 148; Cupull and González, 147.

4. Ripoll, *La vida íntima*, 148–149.

5. Cupull and González, 147; Hidalgo Paz, *José Martí 1853–1895*, 87.

6. Hidalgo Paz, *José Martí 1853–1895*, 87.

7. Nydia Sarabia, *Noticias confidenciales sobre Cuba 1870–1895* [Confidential Reports on Cuba 1870–1895] (Havana: Editora Política, 1985), 85.

8. Ibid., 86–88.

9. Paul Estrade, "La Pinkerton contra Martí" [Pinkerton versus Martí], *Anuario del Centro de Estudios Martianos* 1 (1978): 209–211.

10. Sarabia, *Noticias*, 91.

11. "La Pinkerton contra Martí," 209–211; Raúl Rodríguez, *Los escudos invisibles: un Martí desconocido* [The Invisible Shields: An Unknown Martí] (Havana: Capitán San Luis, 2003), 38–41.

12. Ibid., 41. See 40–41 for a more extensive list of various agents' expenses during this period.

13. José Miguel Oviedo, *La niña de New York: una revisión de la vida erótica de José Martí* [The Girl from New York: A Revision of the Erotic Life of José Martí] (Mexico City: Fondo de Cultura Económica, 1989), 61.

14. Ibid., 60, 116–117.

15. Ibid., 61–62.

16. Ripoll, *La vida íntima*, 109.

17. Martí, *José Martí: Epistolario*, 1:446–448.

18. Ibid.

19. María Mantilla, letter to Cesar Romero, February 9, 1935, http://www.latin americanstudies.org/marti/maria-mantilla-1935.pdf, accessed August 1, 2013.

20. Nydia Sarabia, *La patriota del silencio: Carmen Miyares* [The Silent Patriot: Carmen Miyares] (Havana: Ciencias Sociales, 1990), 94–95.

21. De Baralt, 52–53. Also see Mary Cruz, *El hombre Martí* [The Man Martí] (Havana: Centro de Estudios Martianos, 2007), 111–112.

22. Andrew Wang and Thomas M. Bashore, eds., *Valvular Heart Disease*, Contemporary Cardiology (Berlin: Springer, 2009) 399; Michael Y. Henein, *Valvular Disease in Clinical Practice* (Berlin: Springer, 2008), 13–14.

23. Cupull, 147.

24. *JMOC*, 20:282.

25. Ibid., 284.

26. Ibid., 60.

27. Ibid., 61.

28. Pérez, 12.

29. García Pascual, 77–78.

30. Cupull and González, 148.

31. Pérez, 12–13; Thomas, 268–269.

32. Ibid., 163.

33. Sarabia, *Noticias*, 93; Sarabia, *La patriota*, 40–41.

In the Land of Bolívar

1. Nicanor Bolet Peraza, "Discurso en Chickering Hall, 19 de mayo de 1897" [Speech at Chickering Hall, May 19, 1897], in *Venezuela a Martí* [Venezuela to Martí] (Havana: Lex, 1953), 41–42; Salvador Morales, *Martí en Venezuela, Bolívar en Martí* [Martí in Venezuela, Bolívar in Martí] (Caracas: Ediciones Centauro, 1985), 10–11.

2. George Schneiweiss Wise, *Caudillo: A Portrait of Antonio Guzmán Blanco* (New York: Columbia University Press, 1951), 95–97; Paul H. Lewis, *Authoritarian Regimes in Latin America: Dictators, Despots, and Tyrants* (Lanham, MD: Rowman and Littlefield, 2006), 61–62.

3. Martí would have been familiar with Ten Years' War instigator Carlos Manuel de Céspedes's public declarations of solidarity with Venezuela and gratitude for Guzmán Blanco's support of the rebels. See, for example, his August 10, 1871, letter to General José R. Monagas, in Carlos Manuel Céspedes, *De Bayamo a San Lorenzo* [From Bayamo to San Lorenzo] (Havana: Ministerio de Educación, 1944), 149–150. See also Morales, 12–14.

4. *JMOC*, 18:304.

5. Hidalgo Paz, *José Martí 1853–1895*, 92.

6. Ibid., 92–93.

7. Ibid., 93.

8. Ibid.

9. Cupull and González, 153.

Chapter Ten. New York (2): No Country, No Master

1. Epigraph: *JMOC*, 16:100.

2. The titular "Ismaelillo" refers to the Old Testament figure Ismael, son of Hagar. In Genesis, Abraham's barren wife, Sara, directs Hagar to conceive a child with him but then banishes her and the infant. Hagar, left to wander in the desert, cries out to God in her anguish and is comforted with the knowledge that her son, to be named Ismael (Hebrew for "God has heard"), will become a great hero who will fight for right and freedom. Ismael later fulfills the prophesy, becoming a central founding figure for the tribes that would form the Islamic peoples. This history explains Martí's multiple references to the child in *Ismaelillo* as *guerrero* (warrior) and as "Árabe."

3. *JMOC*, 16:17.

4. Ibid., 42.

5. Ibid., 48.

6. Hidalgo Paz, *José Martí 1853–1895*, 94.

7. Edwin G. Burrows and Mike Wallace, *Gotham: A History of New York to 1898* (Oxford, England: Oxford University Press, 1999), 1020–1038.

8. *JMOC*, 22:150.

9. Burrows and Wallace, 1041–1042.

10. Ibid., 1074, 1147–1148.

11. Ibid., 1089–1090.

12. Ibid., 1111–1131.

13. *JMOC*, 9:9.

14. The Bogotá newspaper *La Pluma* also sought, unsuccessfully, to publish new work by Martí. Hidalgo Paz, *José Martí 1853–1895*, 95.

15. *JMOC*, 9:73–81.

16. Ibid., 277–283.

17. Hidalgo Paz, *José Martí 1853–1895*, 98; Sarabia, *Noticias*, 96.

18. *JMOC*, 20:78.

19. *JMOC*, 19:121.

20. Ibid., 122.

21. Ibid., 123.

22. *JMOC*, 9:17.

23. *JMOC*, 16:161–162 and 196–197, respectively.

24. Sarabia, *Noticias*, 94–95.

25. *JMOC*, 1:170.

26. Ibid., 172.

27. Hidalgo Paz, *José Martí 1853–1895*, 98.

28. Sarabia, *Noticias*, 96.

29. Cupull and González, 150–154.

30. García Pascual, 84–85.

31. *JMOC*, 21:180 and 287, respectively.

32. Ibid., 275–276.

33. *JMOC*, 18:179.

34. Ibid., 179–180.

35. In García Pascual, 94.

36. Ibid., 102.

37. Ibid., 93.

38. *JMOC*, 9:17.

39. Hidalgo Paz, *Jose Martí 1853–1895*, 99–100.

40. Ibid.

41. Hidalgo Paz, *Jose Martí 1853–1895*, 101.

42. For the translation of Jevon's work, see *JMOC*, 25:213–355.

43. Hidalgo Paz, *Jose Martí 1853–1895*, 102–104.

44. *JMOC*, 9:253–254 and 353–355, respectively.

45. *JMOC*, 10:29–38, 10:170–180, 10:459–464, 11:65–78, and 11:186–187, respectively.

46. *JMOC*, 10:33, 11:186–187, and 10:459, respectively.

47. Richard S. Lowry, *"Littery Man": Mark Twain and Modern Authorship* (Oxford, England: Oxford University Press, 1996), 47, 64–65.

48. Rotker, 62.

49. Ibid., 33–36.

50. Ibid., 17–18.

51. Sarabia, *Noticias*, 99, 247; Hidalgo Paz, *José Martí 1853–1895*, 102.

52. Sarabia, *Noticias*, 101; Hidalgo Paz, *José Martí 1853–1895*, 103.

53. That expedition, led by General Ramón Leocadio Bonachea, actually reached Cuba on November 29, 1884. It failed, and Bonachea was executed in Havana on March 7, 1885. Sarabia, *Noticias*, 99–101, 247.

54. Quoted in Sarabia, *Noticias*, 101–104. The text of Martí's October 10, 1883, speech does not appear in *Obras completas* and seems to be lost.

55. Cupull and González, 189–190. Mariano's letters are from the personal archive of Cuban scholar Luis García Pascual.

56. Quoted in Cupull and González, 192–193.

57. For the letter—in verse—in which Martí sends his regrets, see *JMOC*, 16:347.

58. García Martí, 15–16.

59. Hidalgo Paz, *José Martí 1853–1895*, 104.

60. Sarabia, *Noticias*, 106; Hidalgo Paz, *José Martí 1853–1895*, 104–105.

61. Hidalgo Paz, *José Martí 1853–1895*, 105.

62. Ibid.

63. *JMOC*, 1:177–179.

64. Ibid., 180.

Chapter Eleven. New York (3): The Great Work Begins

1. Epigraph: *JMOC*, 1:217.

2. Máximo Gómez, *Diario de Campaña 1868–1899* [War Diary 1868–1899] (Havana: Instituto del Libro, 1968), 180.

3. Hidalgo Paz, *José Martí 1853–1895*, 107.

4. Sarabia, *Noticias*, 107.

5. Gómez, 184.

6. Carlos Ripoll, *José Martí: letras y huellas desconocidas* [José Martí: Unknown Letters and Traces] (Miami: Eliseo Torres, 1976), 89.

7. This and other letters from the period penned by Gómez and Maceo are from the personal collection of Carlos Ripoll, who has published them in both facsimile and transcription. For the text of Gómez's January 20 letter to Arnao in Spanish, see Ripoll, *José Martí: letras*, 89–90.

8. Hidalgo Paz, *José Martí 1853–1895*, 107.

9. Ripoll, *José Martí: letras*, 91–92.

10. *JMOC*, 20:80. The letter is undated, as are several other Martí letters to Mercado at about this time. Martí's references to Carmen's departure and intimations that he suspended revolutionary activities suggest that he wrote this letter after March 1885.

11. Hidalgo Paz, *José Martí 1853–1895*, 108.

12. *JMOC*, 1:181.

13. Bernardo Vega, *Memorias de Bernardo Vega: contribución a la historia de la comunidad puertorriqueña en Nueva York* [Memoirs of Bernardo Vega: A Contribution to the History of the Puerto Rican Community in New York], ed. César Andreu Iglesias (Rio Piedras, Puerto Rico: Ediciones Huracán, 1977), 83.

14. Vega, 84.

15. Ibid., 85.

16. *JMOC*, 1:184.

17. Ibid., 185.

18. Thomas, 279–292.

19. Ibid., 271–280.

20. Hidalgo Paz, *José Martí 1853–1895*, 111–112.

21. References to Martí's chronic pains and ailments stemming from his sarcoidosis occur regularly in his letters to Mercado and other trusted friends beginning in the spring of 1884; although their frequency varies over time, arguably peaking in 1892, they persisted to the end of his life. See, for example, *JMOC*, 1:299, and *JMOC*, 20:72, 92, 106, and 495. For a helpful overview of Martí's sarcoidosis and its impact on his health during these years, see Tablada, 102–141.

22. *JMOC*, 20:80.

23. In García Pascual, 178.

24. Ibid., 179–180; *JMOC*, 20:102–104.

25. *JMOC*, 20:321. For the full text of Martí's February 28, 1887, letter to Fermín Valdés Domínguez, see *JMOC*, 20:321–322.

26. Cupull and González, 206.

27. Thomas, 88–90, 211–217, 225–232, 251–253.

28. *JMOC*, 4:222.

29. *JMOC*, 1:200.

30. Ibid., 204.

31. Ibid.

32. Delfín Rodríguez-Silva, *Cronología martiana: la ruta apostólica de José Martí 1853–1895* [Martí Chronology: The Apostolic Route of José Martí 1853–1895] (Miami: Ediciones Universal, 1996), 193–194; Hidalgo Paz, *José Martí 1853–1895*, 116.

33. Cupull and González, 222; Hidalgo Paz, *José Martí 1853–1895*, 116.

34. *JMOC*, 20:120.

35. Ibid.

36. Hidalgo Paz, *José Martí 1853–1895*, 116–117.

37. Ibid., 118.

38. *JMOC*, 1:222.

39. Ibid., 217.

40. Ibid., 218–219.

41. Ibid., 221.

42. Ibid.

43. García Pascual, 209–211 and 212–214, respectively.

44. Rodríguez-Silva, 195–196.

45. Hidalgo Paz, *José Martí 1853–1895*, 120.

46. Quoted in Sarabia, *La patriota*, 101.

47. Cupull and González, 232.

48. Hidalgo Paz, *Incursiones*, 110–111.

49. Rodríguez-Silva, 196; Hidalgo Paz, *José Martí 1853–1895*, 119.

50. *JMOC*, 1:225.

51. Vega, 87.

52. Rodríguez-Silva, 196–197.

53. De Baralt, 151.

54. Hidalgo Paz, *José Martí 1853–1895*, 119–120.

55. *JMOC*, 20:127.

56. Hidalgo Paz, *José Martí 1853–1895*, 123.

57. *JMOC*, 4:231. During the Ten Years' War, Palma was named president of the "Republic in Arms," a largely ceremonial title that nevertheless gave him great stature among the exiles.

58. *JMOC*, 1:227.

59. Hidalgo Paz, *José Martí 1853–1895*, 124.

60. For the full text of Martí's November 7, 1888, letter to the editor, see *JMOC*, 1:228.

61. Rodríguez-Silva, 198–200.

62. Burrows and Wallace, 1209–1211; Thomas, 310–313.

63. For the full text of the editorial "Do We Want Cuba?" see Philip S. Foner, ed., *Our America: Writings on Latin America and the Struggle for Cuban Independence* (New York: Monthly Review, 1977), 228–230.

64. For the original article as reprinted in the *Evening Post* under the title "A Protectionist View of Cuban Annexation," see Foner, 230–234.

65. Ibid., 234–235.

66. Ibid., 239.

67. Ibid., 241.

68. Ibid., 239.

69. Rodríguez-Silva, 213–214.

70. *JMOC*, 18:295–303.

71. Rodríguez-Silva, 223; Hidalgo Paz, *José Martí 1853–1895*, 126.

72. Sidney Lens and Howard Zinn, eds., *The Forging of the American Empire: From Revolution to Vietnam, A History of U.S. Imperialism*, Human Security Series (London: Pluto, 2003), 464–465.

73. *JMOC*, 6:33–40.

74. Hidalgo Paz, *José Martí 1853–1895*, 127–128.

75. *JMOC*, 4:250.

76. Ibid., 255.

77. Hidalgo Paz, *José Martí 1853–1895*, 128.

78. *JMOC*, 6:55.

79. Ibid., 134. Martí's speech appears in *Obras completas* as "Discurso pronunciado en la velada artístico-literaria de la Sociedad Literaria Hispanoamericana, 19 diciembre 1889" [Speech Given at the Artistic-Literary Evening of the Hispanoamerican Literary Society, December 19, 1889].

80. Rodríguez-Silva, 241–242; Hidalgo Paz, *José Martí 1853–1895*, 130.

81. García Martí, 262–263; Rodríguez-Silva, 243.

82. Rodríguez-Silva, 239–240.

83. *JMOC*, 20:369.

84. For the concluding column on the conference, see *JMOC*, 6:106–111. See also Hidalgo Paz, *José Martí 1853–1895*, 131.

85. Rodríguez-Silva, 244; Hidalgo Paz, *José Martí 1853–1895*, 132.

86. Hidalgo Paz, *José Martí 1853–1895*, 133–134.

87. David Healy, *James G. Blaine and Latin America* (Columbia: University of Missouri Press, 2000), 154–155.

88. Gary M. Walton and Hugh Rockoff, *History of the American Economy*, 2nd ed. (Boston: South-Western College Publishing, 2010), 347–350.

89. Ibid.

90. *JMOC*, 6:15.

91. Ibid., 16.

92. Ibid.

93. *JMOC*, 6:17.

94. Ibid., 21.

95. Ibid., 22.

96. Rodríguez-Silva, 250–251.

97. Ibid.

98. *JMOC*, 6:182.

99. Rodríguez-Silva, 250–253; Hidalgo Paz, *José Martí 1853–1895*, 139.

100. Rodríguez-Silva, 253–254.

101. *JMOC*, 6:181.

102. Cupull, 239.

103. *JMOC*, 20:139.

104. Mantilla death certificate.

105. See, for example, Leonor's June 15, 1887, letter to Carmita in *Papeles de Martí* [Martí's Papers], ed. Gonzalo Quesada y Miranda (Havana: Academia de la Historia de Cuba, 1933), 3:177–178.

106. For Carmen's letters to Martí of April 30, 1887, and September 1, 1890, see García Pascual, 177–178 and 188–189, respectively.

107. Hidalgo Paz, *José Martí 1853–1895*, 142.

108. *JMOC*, 16:115.

109. Ripoll, *La vida íntima*, 238.

110. Ibid., 173–174; Vega, 82. Trujillo himself did not write of either the 1887 incident with Martí or his subsequent role in Carmen's departure from New York, scrupulously avoiding both matters in his memoir of the revolution. Enrique Trujillo, *Apuntes históricos: propaganda y movimientos revolucionarios en los Estados Unidos desde enero de 1880 hasta febrero de 1895* [Historical Notes: Propaganda and Revolutionary Movements in the United States from January 1880 to February 1895] (New York: El Porvenir, 1896).

111. Sarabia, *La patriota*, 50.

112. Tablada, 107, 187.

113. *JMOC*, 4:262.

114. Ibid.

115. Sarabia, *Noticias*, 121, 124–125.

116. Spain, Anexo al despacho no. 119 [Annex to report no. 119], October 11, 1891. Serie de Ultramar, Archivo del Ministerio de Asuntos Exteriores, Madrid.

117. Ibid.

118. Ibid.

119. Ibid.

120. Spain, Despacho no. 114 del Ministro Plenipotenciario de S. M. al Excmo. Señor Ministro de Estado en Washington [Dispatch no. 114 of the Plenipotentiary Minister to the Honorable Minister of State in Washington, DC], September 18, 1891. Ministerio de Ultramar, Archivo del Ministerio de Asuntos Exteriores, Madrid.

121. Hidalgo Paz, *José Martí 1853–1895*, 143–144; Sarabia, *Noticias* 124–126.

122. C. Neale Ronning, *José Martí and the Emigré Colony in Key West: Leadership and State Formation* (New York: Praeger, 1990), 19–38; Louis A. Pérez, "Cubans in Tampa: From Exiles to Immigrants 1892–1901," *Florida Historical Quarterly* 57 (October 1978), 129–140.

123. Hidalgo Paz, *José Martí 1853–1895*, 144–145.

124. Rodriguez-Silva, 256–257.

125. *JMOC*, 1:272.

126. *JMOC*, 4:279.

127. Ibid., 269.

128. Ibid., 276–279.

129. Rodríguez-Silva, 257–258.

130. *JMOC*, 4:284.

131. Ibid., 287.

132. Gary R. Mormino and George E. Pozzetta, *The Immigrant World of Ybor City 1885–1985* (Urbana: University of Illinois Press, 1990), 50–55; Ronning, 20.

133. *JMOC*, 1:275.

134. Ibid., 276.

135. Manuel Deulofeu y Lleonart, *Héroes del destierro: la emigración, notas históricas* [Heroes of Exile: Historical Notes on Emigration] (Havana: M. Mestre, 1904), 153.

136. Spain, Despacho no. 72, Sección V del Cónsul de España en Cayo Hueso, Pedro Solís, al Excmo. Señor Ministro Plenipotenciario de S. M. en Washington [Dispatch no. 72, section 5 of Pedro Solís, Spanish Consul in Key West, to the Honorable Plenipotentiary Minister in Washington, DC], December 26, 1891.

137. Rodríguez-Silva, 260; Hidalgo Paz, *José Martí 1853–1895*, 147.

138. *JMOC*, 20:397.

139. Ronning, 24–25.

Chapter Twelve. New York (4): The Final Push

1. Epigraph: *JMOC*, 2:362.

2. Hidalgo Paz, *Incursiones*, 124.

3. Ramón Roa, *A pie y descalzo de Trinidad a Cuba, 1870–1871: recuerdos de campaña* [On Foot and Shoeless from Trinidad to Cuba, 1870–1871: Memories of the War], 1890 (reprint, Miami: Club del Libro Latinoamericano, 1977).

4. In García Pascual, 271–272.

5. Ibid., 273.

6. For the origins of the nickname "Cristo Inutil," see Mañach, 123–124. For the history of the "Capitán Araña" slur, see Carlos Ripoll, *José Martí: notas y estudios* [José Martí: Notes and Studies] (Miami: Dos Ríos, 1999), 172–174.

7. *JMOC*, 1:293.

8. Quoted in Rodríguez-Silva, 270.

9. In García Pascual, 275–276.

10. Ronning, 22.

11. *JMOC*, 1:297.

12. Carlos Ripoll, *Patria: El periódico de José Martí* [*Patria*: José Martí's Newspaper] (New York: Eliseo Torres, 1971), 4–5.

13. Ibid. See also Sarabia, *Noticias*, 131–132.

14. Rodríguez-Silva, 272–273.

15. Hidalgo Paz, *Incursiones*, 125–126.

16. Ibid., 127–128.

17. Ibid.

18. Tablada, 127. For a full list of Martí's known travels during 1894–1895, see Hidalgo Paz, *José Martí 1853–1895*, 286–298.

19. *JMOC*, 1:466.

20. Ibid., 301.

21. Ibid., 404.

22. Ibid.

23. *JMOC*, 20:502.

24. Rodríguez-Silva, 278–280; Hidalgo Paz, *José Martí 1853–1895*, 154–156.

25. *JMOC*, 2:85–89.

26. Ibid., 43–44.

27. Ibid., 93–97.

28. Rodríguez-Silva, 280–281; Hidalgo Paz, *José Martí 1853–1895*, 158.

29. Sarabia, *Noticias*, 134–141.

30. Spain, Despacho no. 56 al Ministro de Estado en Madrid y al Encargado de Negocios de España en Washington por Luis Felipe Sagrarioz de la legación española en Washington [Dispatch no. 56 to the Minister of State in Madrid and to the Agent for Spanish Affairs in Washington, DC, from Luis Felipe Sagrarioz of the Spanish Delegation in Washington, DC], August 8, 1892.

31. Ibid.

32. *JMOC*, 2:119.

33. Ibid., 121, emphasis in the original.

34. Surveillance reports dated August 31 and September 8 mistakenly place Martí somewhere in Florida, "probably in Key West." Spanish agents did not discover Martí's presence in the Dominican Republic or his meeting with Gómez until September 20, nine days after they met. Spain, Anexo al Despacho no. 66 del Cónsul General de España en Nueva York, Arturo Baldosano y Topete, al Ministro Plenipotenciario de España en Washington [Annex to Dispatch no. 66 of Arturo Baldosano y Topete, General Consul of Spain in New York, to the Plenipotentiary Minister of Spain in Washington, DC], September 6, 1892; and Spain, Anexo al Despacho no. 66 del Cónsul de España en Cayo Hueso, Pedro Solís, al Ministro Plenipotenciario de España en Washington [Annex to Dispatch no. 66 from Pedro Solís, Consul of Spain in Key West, to the Plenipotentiary Minister of Spain in Washington, DC], September 12, 1892. See also Emilio Rodríguez Demorizi, *Martí en Santo Domingo* (Havana: Ucar, García, 1953), 333.

35. Hidalgo Paz, *José Martí 1853–1895*, 159.

36. Quoted in Luis F. Del Morál, *Serafín Sánchez: un carácter al servicio de Cuba* [Serafín Sánchez: A Man of Character in the Service of Cuba] (Havana: Luis J. Botifoll, 1955), 24.

37. Rodríguez-Silva, 284–285; Hidalgo Paz, *José Martí 1853–1895*, 160.

38. Rodríguez-Silva, 286–287; Hidalgo Paz, *José Martí 1853–1895*, 162.

39. Spain, Despacho no. 56.

40. Hidalgo Paz, *José Martí 1853–1895*, 163.

41. Ibid., 164–169; Rodríguez-Silva, 287–289.

42. Hidalgo Paz, *José Martí 1853–1895*, 168.

43. Ibid.

44. Sarabia, *Noticias* 160.

45. Ripoll, *La vida íntima*, 73–77.

46. Sarabia, *Noticias*, 160–161; Tablada, 112–114.

47. Sarabia, *Noticias*, 161.

48. Hidalgo Paz, *José Martí 1853–1895*, 169–170.

49. *JMOC*, 2:467.

50. Thomas, 303.

51. *JMOC*, 2:216.

52. Rodríguez-Silva, 299.

53. Sarabia, *Noticias*, 163; Hidalgo Paz, *José Martí 1853–1895*, 170.

54. Rodríguez-Silva, 299; Hidalgo Paz, *José Martí 1853–1895*, 170.

55. Ibid.

56. Rodríguez-Silva, 299–301.

57. Spain, Despacho no. 45 de Laureano Pinero, Teniente Alcalde de Velasco, Holguín, al Alcalde Municipal de la Ciudad de Holguín [Dispatch no. 45 from Laureano Pinero, Lieutenant Mayor of Velasco, Holguín, to the Municipal Mayor of the City of Holguín], April 26, 1893, Archivo del Museo de Historia La Periquera, Holguín, Cuba.

58. *JMOC*, 2:314–316.

59. *New York Times*, "Cuban Patriots Surrender," May 4, 1893.

60. *JMOC*, 2:321.

61. Thomas, 303.

62. Ibid., 303–304.

63. José Lubiano Franco, *Antonio Maceo: Apuntes para una historia de su vida* [Antonio Maceo: Notes toward a History of His Life] (Havana: Editorial de Ciencias Sociales, 1989), 2:75.

64. *JMOC*, 2:335–349.

65. Hidalgo Paz, *José Martí 1853–1895*, 176.

66. Rodríguez-Silva, 302; Hidalgo Paz, *José Martí 1853–1895*, 176.

67. *JMOC*, 2:299.

68. *Patria*, "El delegado en viaje" [The Delegate Abroad], 2.63 (May 27, 1893) and 2.69 (July 8, 1893). This was a column regularly published by *Patria* staff during Martí's travels.

69. *JMOC*, 2:387.

70. Rodríguez-Silva, 303; Hidalgo Paz, *José Martí 1853–1895*, 177.

71. *JMOC*, 2:359–360.

72. Ibid., 358.

73. Ibid., 367.

74. Ibid., 385–391.

75. Hidalgo Paz, *José Martí 1853–1895*, 181–182.

76. Ibid., 183–184.

77. See, for example, *JMOC*, 2:433–435.

78. Ibid., 422.

79. Ibid., 418.

80. Thomas, 304; Burrows and Wallace, 1041.

81. Ronning, 28–29.

82. L. Glenn Westfall, *Key West: Cigar City U.S.A.* (Key West: Historic Florida Keys, 1984), 44–45.

83. Thomas, 304–305.

84. *JMOC*, 3:32.

85. Ibid., 36.

86. Ibid., 49.

87. Ibid.

88. Ibid., 50–51.

89. John C. Appel, "The Unionization of Florida Cigarmakers and the Coming War with Spain," *Hispanic American Historical Review* 36.1 (February 1956): 44–45.

90. Deulofeu y Lleonart, 84. Estimates of the Cuban population in Key West are conflicting and not terribly reliable, as the island's proximity to Cuba made for a fluid and partly undocumented population. Census counts thus are especially unreliable. That said, sources estimate the early 1890s Cuban population on Key West as fluctuating between 1,000 and 10,000, out of a total count of 18,000–21,000 inhabitants. See Ronning, 20.

91. *JMOC*, 3:69.

92. Ripoll, *Martí y el fin*, 36–43.

93. *JMOC*, 4:321–326.

94. *JMOC*, 3:89.

95. Enrique Loynaz del Castillo, *Memorias de la Guerra* [Memories of the War], 1901 (reprint, Havana: Editorial de Ciencias Sociales, 1989), 69–73.

96. De Baralt, 47.

97. *JMOC*, 3:173.

98. Ibid., 214.

99. Ibid., 227.

100. Ibid., 178.

101. Ibid., 186.

102. Ibid., 208–210.

103. Hidalgo Paz, *Incursiones*, 182–195.

104. *JMOC*, 3:188.

105. Ibid., 190.

106. Ibid., 208.

107. Spain, Despachos no. 7 and no. 8 del Vice Consul de España en Panamá, L. A. Fernández, al Capitán General de la Isla de Cuba [Dispatches no. 7 and no. 8 from L. A. Fernández, Vice Consul of Spain in Panama, to the Captain-General of the Island of Cuba], June 23, 1894.

108. Hidalgo Paz, *José Martí 1853–1895*, 190–198. Pages 294–295 present Martí's full itinerary from May 12 to September 1, 1894.

109. *JMOC*, 3:239. Underlined in the original.

110. Hidalgo Paz, *José Martí 1853–1895*, 294–295.

111. *JMOC*, 3:269.

112. Ibid., 291–199; Hidalgo Paz, *José Martí 1853–1895*, 200–201.

113. *JMOC*, 3:333–334.

114. Ibid., 263–266.

115. Ibid., 264.

116. Ibid., 335–340.

117. Antonio Rafael de la Cova, "Fernandina Filibuster Fiasco: Birth of the 1895 Cuban War of Independence," *Florida Historical Quarterly* 82.1 (Summer 2003), 20.

118. Hidalgo Paz, *José Martí 1853–1895*, 200–202.

119. Sarabia, *Noticias*, 199.

120. De la Cova, 17.

121. Ibid., 18–19; Rodríguez-Silva, 311.

122. *New York World*, "Off on a Secret Cruise," January 11, 1895, 2; *Savannah Morning News*, "Held Up by Uncle Sam," January 16, 1895, 8.

123. De la Cova 22–23; Hidalgo Paz, *José Martí 1853–1895*, 202–203.

124. *JMOC*, 4:17.

125. *New York World*, "Off on a Secret Cruise"; *Savannah Morning News*, "Held Up by Uncle Sam"; *Florida Times-Union*, "Took Arms by Thousands," January 16, 1895, 1.

126. *Florida Times-Union*, "Bagged by Baltzell," January 13, 1895, 1.

127. De la Cova, 26.

128. George L. Baltzell, Report of George L. Baltzell to the United States Secretary of the Treasury, January 19, 1895, RG 36, Bureau of Customs, Letters Sent 1891–1912, Fernandina, Fla., entry 1997. http://latinamericanstudies.org/1895/RG-36.pdf.

129. *Florida Times-Union*, "Bagged by Baltzell" and "Took Arms by Thousands."

130. *New York Herald*, "Arms Consigned to Mr. Borden," January 15, 1895, 12; *Florida Times-Union*, "All Filled with Arms," January 15, 1895, 1.

131. De la Cova, 34–36; Hidalgo Paz, *José Martí 1853–1895*, 203–207.

132. *JMOC*, 4:19.

133. Ibid.

134. Ibid.

135. Ibid., 41–42.

136. Luis Rodolfo Miranda, *Reminiscencias cubanas de la guerra y la paz* [Cuban Reminiscences of War and Peace] (Havana: P. Fernández, 1941), 158–159; de Baralt, 46.

137. De Baralt, 62–63.

138. Sarabia, *Noticias*, 202.

139. Miranda, 46.

Chapter Thirteen. Farewells and Rowboats

1. Epigraph: Spain, Despacho al Cónsul General de España en Santo Domingo, March 31, 1895.

2. *JMOC*, 20:212.

3. Ibid., 234.

4. *JMOC*, 4:52.

5. Rodríguez-Silva, 331; Hidalgo Paz, *José Martí 1853–1895*, 209.

6. Ibid.

7. Hidalgo Paz, *José Martí 1853–1895*, 209.

8. Rodríguez-Silva, 333; Sarabia, *Noticias*, 204.

9. *JMOC*, 4:70.

10. Ibid.

11. *JMOC*, 20:474.

12. *JMOC*, 4:65.

13. Enrique Collazo, *Cuba independiente* [Independent Cuba] (Havana: La Moderna Poesía, 1900), 51. More than one close observer of Martí during his final years noted his irregular eating habits. See, for example, Horatio Seymour Rubens, *Liberty: The Story of Cuba* (New York: Brewer, Warren, and Putnam, 1932), 32–33. See also Tablada, 188–191.

14. *JMOC*, 19:200.

15. Ibid., 203.

16. Ibid., 203–204.

17. Ibid., 204–205.

18. *JMOC*, 16:100.

19. Hidalgo Paz, *José Martí 1853–1895*, 209.

20. Collazo, 82–83.

21. Rodríguez-Silva, 333; Hidalgo Paz, *José Martí 1853–1895*, 209.

22. Joseph E. Wisan, *The Cuban Crisis as Reflected in the New York Press: 1895–1898* (New York: Columbia University Press, 1934), 41.

23. Hidalgo Paz, *José Martí 1853–1895*, 209.

24. Francisco (Panchito) Gómez Toro, *Papeles de Panchito* [Papers of Panchito], ed. Bladimir Zamora (Havana: La Abríl, 1988), 51.

25. *JMOC*, 2:353.

26. *JMOC*, 19:195.

27. Collazo, 83.

28. Ibid.

29. Hidalgo Paz, *José Martí 1853–1895*, 211.

30. *JMOC*, 20:235.

31. For Martí's letters of March 12 and 20 about his arrangement with Dellundé, see *JMOC* 4:86 and 88–89, respectively.

32. *JMOC*, 20:475.

33. *JMOC*, 4:105.

34. Rodríguez-Silva, 335; Hidalgo Paz, *José Martí 1853–1895*, 211.

35. *JMOC*, 4:87.

36. Thomas, 307–308.

37. *JMOC*, 4:101. Pages 112–114 have Martí's letter of March 28, 1895, to Gonzalo de Quesada.

38. Rodríguez-Silva, 335–336; Hidalgo Paz, *José Martí 1853–1895*, 211–212.

39. Sarabia, *Noticias*, 214–215.

40. Ibid., 216; Hidalgo Paz, *José Martí 1853–1895*, 212.

41. Gerardo Castellanos, *Los últimos días de Martí* [Martí's Final Days] (Havana: Ucar, García, 1937), 132; Hidalgo Paz, *José Martí 1853–1895*, 213.

A Narrow Escape—and One Last Letter for His Patria

1. Valentín Tejada, *Martí a su paso por Santo Domingo* [Martí's Travels in Santo Domingo] (Guantánamo, Cuba: M. Medrano S. en C., 1935), 74–76; Tablada, 135–136.

2. Sarabia, *Noticias*, 218.

3. *JMOC*, 4:121–122.

4. Gómez, *Diario*, 124.

5. Ibid., 125.

Chapter Fourteen. "My Life for My Country"

1. Epigraph: *JMOC*, 4:167.

2. Gómez, *Diario*, 276.

3. Wisan, 48.

4. Gómez, *Diario*, 276.

5. Martí famously ends Poema III of *Versos sencillos* with a call to "Tell the blind bishop, / the blind Spanish bishop / To come, to come later / To my temple, to the mountain!" For the full text of the poem in Spanish, see *JMOC*, 16:66–69. For an excellent English translation, see *Versos sencillos/Simple Verses*, 24–26. Gómez also makes two references in his war diary to the cave he christened *el templo*, one each on April 11 and April 13. Gómez, *Diario*, 277.

6. *JMOC*, 19:215.

7. Two theories exist for the origins of the term *mambi*. One credits as the inspiration for the term a black Spanish officer, Juan "Eutimio" Mamby or Mambi, who joined the insurgents fighting Spanish rule in Santo Domingo in 1818. Another theory is that *mambi* stems from an indigenous word for those who first resisted Spanish rule in the fifteenth and sixteenth centuries. See Gabriel Cardena and Juan Carlos Losada, *Nuestro hombre en La Habana* [Our Man in Havana], 2nd ed. (Barcelona: Planeta, 1988), 27–28.

8. The ya-ya, Cuban majagua, and cupey are all native Cuban flora that Martí was seeing for the first time in nearly sixteen years. The jutía (*Capromys pilorides*) is a large rodent native to Cuba, typically measuring about eighteen to twenty-four inches and weighing as much as fifteen pounds. The jutía has been a staple of the Cuban country diet for centuries. For useful entries on these and other Cuban flora and fauna, see Eduardo Saumell, *Fauna y flora cubanas* (Miami: Laurenty, 1989).

9. *JMOC*, 19:212–213.

10. Ibid., 213.

11. Gómez, *Diario*, 278.

12. *JMOC*, 19:217.

13. The yagua (*Genipa americana*), which Martí here calls *jagua*, is a tree that bears a mangolike fruit and is native to Cuba. Saumell, 136.

14. *JMOC*, 19:217 and 4:124–130, respectively. Martí's diary entry for April 15 served as a draft of the account he sent Quesada and Guerra, which despite its date he did not complete until the next day. See also Hidalgo Paz, *José Martí 1853–1895*, 215.

15. *JMOC*, 19:216–217. Gómez's one-sentence diary entry for April 15 confirms that it

was a day of relative calm in the camp: "The 15th, in camp, dispatching communications and orders to various points, even to New York via Baracoa" (278).

16. *JMOC*, 4:124.

17. Ibid., 127.

18. The quotation is from an untitled commentary on the front page of the May 17, 1895, issue of *La Discusión*, a Havana newspaper of the time. For an analysis of the commentary in *La Discusión* as an example of a broader strategy designed to discredit and embarrass Martí, see Miguel Fernández, *La muerte indócil de José Martí* [The Indocile Death of José Martí] (Miami: Editorial Nueva Prensa Cubana, 2005), 12.

19. *JMOC*, 4:128.

20. *JMOC*, 19:218. For other Martí references to Cicero, see *JMOC*, 8:156, 21:256–257, and 25:107–108.

21. In an interview conducted in August 1898, Gómez conceded that had Martí lived he easily would have won the hearts and votes of the assembled representatives to serve as Cuba's first president:

> Este momento de alegría, a mí me da miedo. . . . Ahora Martí hubiera podido servir a la Patria; este era su momento. Martí reconocía todo esto, convencía a los recalcitrantes y animaba a los retardados. Como orador era formidable. El que lo oía no tenía ya voluntad propia, y estaba dispuesto a seguirlo. La Asamblea hubiera sido el.

In Orestes Ferrara, *Mis relaciones con Máximo Gómez* [My Relationship with Máximo Gómez] (Havana: Molina, 1942), 215.

22. *JMOC*, 19:218.

23. Martí notes the Spanish pursuit in his April 20 diary entry: "A rider brings news from Imía that they have come after us along the Jobo." *JMOC*, 19:220.

24. Martí's discussions of race, most famously in his 1893 essay "Mi raza" (My Race) but also in pieces such as "Los cubanos de Jamaica en el Partido Revolucionario" (The Cubans of Jamaica in the Revolutionary Party), stress the importance of a race-blind movement in combating the Spanish strategy of undermining solidarity by raising fears among whites of a race war. This strategy had proven successful during the Ten Years' War and was a political weapon that Martí was keen to deny Spain in the struggle at hand. *JMOC*, 2:298–300 and 21–26, respectively. See also Ada Ferrer, *Insurgent Cuba: Race, Nation, and Revolution, 1868–1898* (Chapel Hill, NC: University of North Carolina Press, 1999).

25. Martí records in his April 21 diary entry that "Maceo was wounded in a plot by [Spanish General] Garrido's Indians" and that Maceo's brother José "slayed Garrido with his machete." *JMOC*, 19:220.

26. Ibid. Crombet died instantly, shot through the head. For a fuller account of Crombet's death and José Maceo's narrow escape, see Franco, 2:104–105.

27. *JMOC*, 19:219.

28. Ibid., 223.

29. *JMOC*, 19:223.

30. *JMOC*, 20:226.

31. Hidalgo Paz, *José Martí 1853–1895*, 219.

32. Among the journalists who interacted with the insurgency, George Eugene Bryson and Grover Flint enjoyed the most substantial contacts; Flint spent four months with Gómez's army in 1897 and published a graphic book that sharply criticized Spanish tactics. By then, Spain had turned against the U.S. press and started expelling and occasionally imprisoning correspondents suspected of sympathizing with the rebels. Wisan, 195–196. For more on Bryson's 1897 expulsion due to his championing of Cuban prisoner Evangelina Cisneros, see Wisan, 324–331, and especially 329n59. For Martí's and Gómez's co-written letter to the *Herald*, see *JMOC*, 4:151–160.

33. Antonio Maceo's May 3 letter sets their meeting at Bircoey, a nearby and secure but not easily accessed location. In his reply the next day, Martí changed the venue in a postscript: "After consulting with José [Maceo] and scouts, that we may meet sooner instead of going to Bircoey, we will take the trail to Zamora and will be with you earlier." Antonio Maceo, *Ideología política: cartas y otros documentos* [Political Ideology: Letters and Other Documents], Havana: Sociedad Cubana de Estudios Históricos e Internacionales, 1950), 1:238. See also *JMOC*, 4:162.

34. *JMOC*, 4:161.

35. Gómez, *Diario*, 280.

36. *JMOC*, 19:228; Gómez, *Diario*, 281–282.

37. Neither Gómez's nor Maceo's diary contains any information regarding the content of their private conversation, likely for fear of their plans falling into enemy hands should they be captured or killed. Martí notes his exclusion from this initial phase of the discussion: "Maceo and G. speak nearby, in low voices." *JMOC*, 19:228.

38. Ibid., 228–229.

39. Ibid.

40. Ibid.

41. Gómez, *Diario*, 280.

42. José Galvez was Spain's appointed minister of the Cuban autonomous government. Juan Gualberto Gómez, trained like Martí as an attorney, was among the most prominent Afro-Cubans involved with the revolution. Aline Helg, *Our Rightful Share: The Afro-Cuban Struggle for Equality, 1886–1912* (Chapel Hill: University of North Carolina Press, 1995), 53–54, 120–122. See also Franco, 2:110–113.

43. *JMOC*, 19:236–237, underlining in the original.

44. Ibid., 238.

45. Gómez, *Diario*, 283–284.

46. *JMOC*, 19:237–243. Gómez's diary entries during the same period make no mention of weather or any other such factors. Gómez, *Diario*, 283–284.

47. Martí mentions Gómez's illness only once, near the end of his May 12 letter to Maceo, by way of excusing the general's not having co-signed the letter, which he usually did in the case of official correspondence. Gómez in his diary did not mention feeling ill, although he did so at length elsewhere in his diaries; given the general's state of vexation and impatience with Maceo by this point, perhaps Martí was simply covering for Gómez's refusal to address Maceo at all. *JMOC*, 4:165.

48. Philip Sheldon Foner, *The Spanish-Cuban-American War and the Birth of American Imperialism*, vol. 1: *1895–1898* (New York: Monthly Review, 1972), 28–30.

49. *JMOC*, 4:167.

50. *JMOC*, 19:238.

51. Gómez, *Diario*, 283.

52. *JMOC*, 4:167.

53. Ibid., 168.

54. Ibid., 167. For the Old Testament account of David's battle against Goliath, see 1 Samuel 19–54.

55. For the Old Testament account of Jonah's defiance, punishment, and deliverance, see Jonah 1–4.

56. *JMOC*, 4:169.

57. Foner, 17–20, 28–30.

58. Martí notes in his May 19 letter to Gómez that Masó's men, "despite lacking useful animals, would have wanted to follow you in your search for the convoy: but they feared that the comings and goings might cause confusion rather than serve any useful purpose." *JMOC*, 19:170.

59. Hidalgo Paz, for example, sees the May 18 letter in precisely this way, calling it "the letter known as [Martí's] political will." *José Martí 1853–1895*, 224.

60. Gómez, *Diario*, 284.

61. José Miró, "La tragedia de Dos Ríos" [The Tragedy of Dos Ríos], *La Discusión*, September 2, 1911, 1–13.

62. Gómez asserts in his May 19 diary entry that the Spanish suffered seven casualties at Dos Ríos, while Martí was the only Cuban killed in the battle, a count supported by historians and independent observers at the time. On the other hand, in his report on the battle, Spanish Colonel Ximénez de Sandoval claimed that aside from Martí the Cubans suffered "fourteen visible dead and many wounded. . . . On our side five dead and seven wounded." Other witnesses on each side reported figures ranging from five to seven dead on the Spanish side and between a single death (Martí's) and up to fourteen among the Cubans. Gómez, *Diario*, 284–285; Ximénez de Sandoval, "Memoria de Dos Ríos," *La Discusión*, September 9, 1911, 2–8. For a further discussion of the range of conflicting casualty counts, see M. Fernández, 120–121 and 125n19.

63. Gómez, *Diario*, 284–285. For a book-length argument along these lines, see Florencio García-Cisneros, *La muerte de José Martí: versiones y discrepancias de Máximo Gómez* [The Death of José Martí: Versions and Discrepancies of Máximo Gómez] (New York: Noticias de Arte, 1993). See also M. Fernández, 29–44.

64. The absence is especially glaring in José Lubiano Franco's otherwise exhaustive, three-volume biography of Antonio Maceo. Franco devotes more than four pages to a single battle on May 13, an important victory at Jobito, then jumps to May 20 and Maceo's reaction to news of Martí's death the previous day. The narrative thus skips over the entire period of Maceo's operations with Masó. Franco, 2:118–122.

65. Rolando Rodríguez, *Dos Ríos: a caballo y con el sol en la frente* [Dos Ríos: On Horseback and Facing the Sun] (Havana: Centro de Ciencias Sociales, 2001), 4.

66. Gómez claimed in his May 19 diary entry (285) to have ordered Martí to stay out of the fight, and Miró's account confirmed the general's final words to the civilian leader: "When the Cubans departed for battle, Gómez charged the Master with these words: 'Martí, stand down. This is not the place for you.'"

67. This is Jorge Mañach's claim in *Martí, el apostol* (221). Those confiscated papers apparently have not survived, for there is no record of their contents having been published or of their being placed in any archive.

68. Willis Fletcher Johnson, *The History of Cuba* (New York: B. F. Buck, 1920), 4:16. For a slightly less elaborate variation on the same story, see Enrique Piñeyro, *Como acabó la dominación de España en América* [How the Spanish Domination of America Ended], 1908 (reprint, Paris: Garnier Hermanos, 1925).

69. Gonzalo de Quesada y Miranda, *Alrededor de la acción de Dos Ríos* [Regarding the Incident at Dos Ríos] (Havana: Seoane, Fernández, 1942); the full text of Sandoval's letter to de Quesada is on pages 13–26.

70. See, for example, various editions of *Historia de Cuba* (Havana: Pueblo y Educación, 1989–1995). For an example of these textbooks' Cuban American counterparts, see Carlos Márquez Sterling, *History of Cuba: From Christopher Columbus to Fidel Castro* (New York: Las Américas, 1969). A textbook that stirred considerable controversy by deviating from the exile community's view of Cuban history and contemporary condition is Alta Schreier's *Vamos a Cuba* [Let's Go to Cuba] (Portsmouth, NH: Heinemann, 2000).

71. This is invariably the role to which Martí's biographers have relegated de la Guardia, most famously in Mañach (218). But later studies of Martí's death have also neglected Ángel de la Guardia. See, for example, Cintio Vitier, "Hallazgo de una profecía" [Fulfillment of a Prophesy], *Casa de las Américas* 158 (September–October 1986): 30–38; and Guillermo Cabrera Infante, *Mea Cuba* (Barcelona: Plaza y Janés, 1992), 157–189. Miguel Fernández offers a useful overview of these and other recent studies on Martí's death (9–60). It is worth noting, however, that even Fernández's otherwise laudable book hardly mentions de la Guardia's role at all.

72. Gómez, *Diario*, 285.

73. Enrique Gay-Calbó, *Ángel de la Guardia, el compañero de Martí en Dos Ríos* [Angel de la Guardia, Martí's Companion at Dos Ríos] (Havana: Academia de la Historia de Cuba, 1957), 13.

74. Ibid., 14–15.

75. Ibid., 15–17.

76. Calixto García was a close friend of de la Guardia's father, Miguel; besides the other commanders' concerns, this gave García further incentive to guard the life of his young officer. Gay-Calbó, 16. García included the news of de la Guardia's mortal wound received in battle on August 29, 1897, and of his death the following day, in his September 3, 1897, letter to Gómez. For the text of García's letter to Gómez, see Gay-Calbó, 25–30.

77. Ibid., 17.

78. Ibid., 11.

79. For a sampling of the letters that Ángel de la Guardia Rosales, the young colonel's son, donated to the *academía*, see Gay-Calbó, 21–30. Gay-Calbó's acknowledgment of the donation appears on page 21.

80. Ángel de la Guardia's only other written reference to Martí's death occurs in a May 13, 1897, letter to his family in which he assumes that they have heard of the event and his own subsequent promotion: "You will already know about Dos Ríos, I was promoted there to lieutenant and received a strong embrace from Gen. Gómez." Ibid., 21–22.

81. Reports of the number of Spanish troops vary from 600 to more than 1,100. Ibrahim Hidalgo Paz estimates that Sandoval's troops numbered more than 600, significantly fewer than Gómez's claim of more than 800. Hidalgo Paz, *José Martí 1853–1895*, 224.

82. Gómez, *Diario*, 284–285.

83. Gómez asserts in his May 19 diary entry (285) that Martí's death occurred because Martí "refused to obey" an order and that in having to lead his forces into battle, Gómez was forced to leave Martí behind. Fermín Valdés Domínguez writes in his August 29, 1896, diary entry that Gómez actually blamed Masó for Martí's death. According to Valdés, Gómez accused Masó of having left the civilian leader alone with de la Guardia, whom he called "a madman," and of keeping himself out of danger rather than following the other two into battle (2:136–137).

84. According to Dominador de la Guardia's eyewitness account as cited in a 1911 book, Martí and Ángel de la Guardia were roughly fifty meters ahead of the rest of the Cuban troops when Martí was killed. In Enrique Ubieta, *Efemérides de la revolución cubana* [Ephemeralities of the Cuban Revolution] (Havana: Molina, 1911), 2:290.

85. Gómez and Masó Parra had long loathed each other, so much so that Gómez later sought to have Parra tried and executed on charges of desertion. The charges were dismissed, but Parra eventually did abandon the *mambi* cause and join the Spanish side, taking about three hundred troops with him. Gómez then accused several Cuban officers of having colluded in Masó Parra's defection and sought to have them tried and executed. Ubieta, 3:289–290; José Masó Parra, letter to Captain Juan Maspon Franco, June 25, 1895, Fondo Donativos, box 244, no. 40, Archivo Nacional de Cuba, Havana.

More interesting than Gómez's apparent vendetta against Masó Parra is his interest in having his file—which included the letter in question—sealed with the aim to *salcocharlo* (cook it), an obvious euphemism for its destruction. Such an act would not have been beyond Gómez, whom some have suspected of destroying the missing May 6 entry from Martí's war diary. Loynaz del Castillo, 508; M. Fernández, 36–37.

86. In Ubieta, 2:288.

87. Masó Parra, letter.

88. De la Guardia used the term *prefectura* to refer to the area of the camp itself. In Ubieta, 2:288.

89. *JMOC*, 10:25.

90. Ibid.

Epilogue

1. Carlos Ripoll, *Nuevas páginas sobre Martí* [New Writings on Martí] (New York: Dos Ríos, 2004), 180.

2. Ripoll, *Nuevas páginas*, 179.

3. Quoted in Carlos Ripoll, "La autopsia de José Martí" [The Autopsy of José Martí], November 4, 2001, 1, http://eddosrios.org/marti/Article-30/autopsia.htm, accessed August 2, 2013.

4. Ibid., 2–3.

5. Ibid.

6. Rodríguez-Silva, 346.

7. In Charles I. Bevins, ed., *Treaties and Other International Agreements of the United States of America 1776–1949*, vol. 6: *Canada–Czechoslovakia*, U.S. Department of State Publication #8549, 1116. The full text of the Platt Amendment is on 1116–1119.

8. Tomás Estrada Palma, letter to Gonzalo de Quesada, March 14, 1901, in *Archivo de Gonzalo de Quesada*, ed. Gonzalo de Quesada y Miranda (Havana: Ciencias Sociales, 1948), 1:151–152.

9. López, *José Martí*, 21–23.

10. Ibid.

11. Ibid., 44–45.

12. Ibid.

13. Fidel Castro, *La historia me absolverá* [History Will Absolve Me], 1954 (reprint, Madrid: Júcar, 1976), 117.

14. *JMOC*, 20:236.

Works Cited

Aguirre, Carlos. "Cárcel y sociedad en América Latina: 1800–1940" [Prison and Society in Latin America: 1800–1940]. In *Historia social urbana: Espacios y flujos* [Urban Social History: Ebbs and Flows], ed. Eduardo Kingman Garcés, 209–252. Quito, Ecuador: 50 Años FLACSO, 2009.

Altamirano, Ignacio. *Obras completas* [Complete Works]. Vol. 21: *Epistolario (1850–1899)*. Mexico City: Consejo Nacional para la Cultura y las Artes, 1992.

Appel, John C. "The Unionization of Florida Cigarmakers and the Coming War with Spain." *Hispanic American Historical Review* 36.1 (February 1956): 38–49.

Arenas Guzmán, Diego. *El periodismo en la revolución mexicana, 1876–1908* [Journalism during the Mexican Revolution, 1876–1908]. 2 vols. Mexico City: Biblioteca del Instituto Nacional de Estudios Históricos de la Revolución Mexicana, 1966.

Avrutin, Eugene M. *Jews and the Imperial State: Identification Politics in Tsarist Russia*. Ithaca, NY: Cornell University Press, 2010.

Baeza Flores, Alberto. *Vida de José Martí: el hombre íntimo y el hombre public* [Life of José Martí: The Private Man and the Public Man]. Havana: Comisión Nacional Organizadora de los Actos y Ediciones del Centenario y del Monumento de Martí, 1954.

Ballester, Ana Cairo. *José Martí y la novela de la cultura cubana* [José Martí and the Novel of Cuban Culture]. Santiago de Compostela, Spain: Universidad Santiago de Compostela, 2003.

Baltzell, George L. Report of George L. Baltzell to the United States Secretary of the Treasury, January 19, 1895. RG 36, Bureau of Customs, Letters Sent 1891–1912, Fernandina, Fla., entry 1997. http://latinamericanstudies.org/1895/RG-36.pdf.

Balzac, Honoré de. *Traité des excitants modernes* [Treatise on Modern Stimulants]. 1845. Reprint, Paris: Edicions de Boucher, 2002.

Baudelaire, Charles. *Les paradis artificial, opium et haschisch* [The Artificial Paradise: Opium and Hashish]. Paris: Poulet-Malassis et de Broise, 1860.

Bello, Antonio Martínez. *La adolescencia de Martí* [Martí's Adolescence]. Havana: P. Fernández, 1944.

Bevins, Charles I., ed. *Treaties and Other International Agreements of the United States of*

America 1776–1949. Vol. 6: *Canada–Czechoslovakia.* U.S. Department of State Publication #8549. Washington, DC: Government Printing Office.

Bowen, Wayne H., and José E. Alvarez. Introduction to *Military History of Modern Spain,* ed. Bowen and Alvarez, 1–14.

———, eds. *A Military History of Modern Spain: From the Napoleonic Era to the International War on Terror.* Westport, CT: Praeger, 2007.

Boyer, Richard Everett. "Mexico City and the Great Flood: Aspects of Life and Society, 1629–1635." PhD diss., University of Connecticut, 1973.

Brigham, William Tufts. *Guatemala, the Land of the Quetzal: A Sketch.* London: T. Fisher Unwin, 1887.

Brion Davis, David. *The Problem of Slavery in Western Culture.* Ithaca, NY: Cornell University Press, 1966.

Bristowe, Lindsey W., and Philip B. Wright. *The Handbook of British Honduras for 1888–89.* Edinburgh, Scotland: William Blackwood and Sons, 1888.

Broderman, Nohely S. *José Martí: patriota y poeta* [José Martí: Patriot and Poet]. Havana: Ediciones Geminis, 1973.

Browne, Daniel Jay. *Letters from the Canary Islands.* Boston: G. W. Light, 1834.

Burgues, Paul. *Justo Rufino Barrios: Una biografía.* Guatemala City: Editorial del Ejército, 1971.

Burrows, Edwin G., and Mike Wallace. *Gotham: A History of New York to 1898.* Oxford, England: Oxford University Press, 1999.

Cabrera Infante, Guillermo. *Mea Cuba.* Barcelona: Plaza y Janés, 1992.

Cadalso y Manzano, Fernando. *Estudios penitenciarios: presidios españoles, escuelas clásica y positiva y colonias penales, con un breve compendio de la legislación, costumbres jurídicas y prácticas penitenciarias que rigen en los establecimientos* [Penitentiary Studies: Spanish Prisons, Classical and Positivist Schools, and Penal Colonies, with a Brief Compendium of the Legislation, Juridical Customs, and Penitentiary Practices That Govern These Establishments]. Madrid: F. Góngora, 1893.

Caldwell, Robert Granville. *The López Expeditions to Cuba.* PhD diss., Princeton University, 1915.

Camp, Roderic Ai. *Mexican Political Biographies, 1884–1935.* Austin: University of Texas Press, 1991.

Cañizares-Esguerra, Jorge. "Racial, Religious, and Civic Creole Identity in Colonial Spanish America." *American Literary History* 17:3 (2005): 420–437.

Cardena, Gabriel, and Juan Carlos Losada. *Nuestro hombre en La Habana* [Our Man in Havana]. 2nd ed. Barcelona: Planeta, 1988.

Casanovas, Joan. *Bread or Bullets: Urban Labor and Spanish Colonialism, 1850–1898.* Pittsburgh, PA: University of Pittsburgh Press, 1998.

Caselli, Graziela, Jacques Vallin, and Guillaume Wunsch. *Demography: Analysis and Synthesis.* New York: Academic Press, 2006.

Castellanos, Gerardo. *Los últimos días de Martí* [Martí's Final Days]. Havana: Ucar, García, 1937.

Castro, Fidel. *La historia me absolverá* [History Will Absolve Me]. 1954. Reprint, Madrid: Júcar, 1976.

————. *José Martí: El Autor Intellectual*. Centro de Estudios Martianos. Havana: Editora Política, 1983.

Centro de Estudios Martianos. "Documentos sobre José Martí" [Documents Regarding José Martí]. *Anuario del Centro de Estudios Martianos* 2 (1979): 35–49.

Céspedes, Carlos Manuel. *De Bayamo a San Lorenzo* [From Bayamo to San Lorenzo]. Havana: Ministerio de Educación, 1944.

Chaffin, Tom. *Fatal Glory: Narciso López and the First Clandestine U.S. War against Cuba*. Baton Rouge, LA: LSU Press, 2003.

Chassen de López, Francie R. *From Liberal to Revolutionary Oaxaca: The View from the South, Mexico 1867–1911*. University Park, PA: Penn State University Press, 2004.

Christiansen, E. *The Origins of Military Power in Spain*. Oxford, England: Oxford University Press, 1967.

Cockroft, James D. *América Latina y Estados Unidos: historia y política país por país* [Latin America and the United States: History and Politics Country by Country]. Mexico City: Siglo XXI, 2001.

Collazo, Enrique. *Cuba independiente* [Independent Cuba]. Havana: La Moderna Poesía, 1900.

Colón, Cristóbal. "Carta de Cristóbal Colón a Sr. Rafael Sánchez" [Letter from Christopher Columbus to Mr. Rafael Sánchez], April 25, 1493. In *Viajes de Cristóbal Colón: Con una carta* [Travels of Christopher Columbus: With a Letter], ed. Fernández de Navarrette, Martín. Barcelona: Calpe, 1922. 201–209.

Corbitt, Duvon C. "Mercedes and Realengos." *Hispanic American Historical Review* 19 (1939): 262–285.

Cruz, Mary. *El hombre Martí* [The Man Martí]. Havana: Centro de Estudios Martianos, 2007.

Cunningham, Michele. *Mexico and the Foreign Policy of Napoleon III*. London: Palgrave Macmillan, 2001.

Cupull, Adys, and Froilán González. *Creciente agonia* [Growing Agony]. Havana: Editorial José Martí, 2009.

Dana, Richard Henry. *To Cuba and Back: A Vacation Voyage*. London: Smith, Elder, 1859.

de Baralt, Blanca Z. *El Martí que yo conocí* [The Martí I Knew]. Havana: Trópico, 1945.

de la Cova, Antonio Rafael. "Fernandina Filibuster Fiasco: Birth of the 1895 Cuban War of Independence." *Florida Historical Quarterly* 82.1 (Summer 2003): 16–42.

Del Morál, Luis F. *Serafín Sánchez: un carácter al servicio de Cuba* [A Man of Character in the Service of Cuba]. Havana: Luis J. Botifoll, 1955.

Delgado, Gloria, and Harim B. Gutiérrez. *Historia de México*. 2 vols. New York: Pearson, 2006.

Desmond, Lawrence Gustave. *Yucatán through Her Eyes: Alice Dixon Le Plongeon, Writer and Expeditionary Photographer*. Albuquerque: University of New Mexico Press, 2009.

Deulofeu y Lleonart, Manuel. *Héroes del destierro: La emigración, notas históricas* [Heroes of Exile: Historical Notes on Emigration]. Havana: M. Mestre, 1904.

Díaz del Castillo, Bernal. *Historia verdadera de la conquista de la Nueva España* [True History of the Conquest of New Spain]. Madrid: Emprenta del Reyno, 1632.

Dobson, John M. *Bulls, Bears, Boom, and Bust: A Historical Encyclopedia of American Business Concepts.* Santa Barbara, CA: ABC-CLIO, 2007.

Dunlop, Robert Glasgow. *Travels in Central America: Being a Journal of Nearly Three Years' Residence in the Country: Together with a Sketch of the History of the Republic, and an Account of Its Climate, Productions, Commerce, Etc.* London: Longman, Brown, Green, and Longmans, 1847.

Ellem, Warren A. "The Overthrow of Reconstruction in Mississippi." *Journal of Mississippi History* 54.2 (1992): 175–201.

Engerman, Stanley L. "A Population History of the Caribbean." In *A Population History of North America,* ed. Michael R. Haines and Richard Hall Steckel, 483–528. Cambridge, England: Cambridge University Press, 2000.

Escobedo, Jaime Hugo Talancón. *Benito Juárez: la educación y el estado* [Education and the State]. Mexico City: Universidad Nacional Autónoma de México, 2006.

Estrade, Paul. *José Martí: los fundamentos de la democracia latinoaméricana* [José Martí: The Foundations of Latin American Democracy]. Madrid: Casa de Velasquez, 2000.

———. "La Pinkerton contra Martí" [Pinkerton versus Martí]. *Anuario del Centro de Estudios Martianos* 1 (1978): 207–221.

Farwell, Byron, ed. *The Encyclopedia of Nineteenth-Century Land Warfare: An Illustrated World View.* New York: W. W. Norton, 2001.

Fernández, Miguel. *La muerte indócil de José Martí* [The Indocile Death of José Martí]. Miami: Editorial Nueva Prensa Cubana, 2005.

Fernández-Armesto, Felipe. *The Canary Islands after the Conquest.* Oxford, England: Oxford University Press, 1982.

Ferrara, Orestes. *Mis relaciones con Máximo Gómez* [My Relationship with Máximo Gómez]. Havana: Molina, 1942.

Ferrer, Ada. *Insurgent Cuba: Race, Nation, and Revolution, 1868–1898.* Chapel Hill: University of North Carolina Press, 1999.

Fildes, Valerie A. *Breasts, Bottles, and Babies: A History of Infant Feeding.* Edinburgh, Scotland: Edinburgh University Press, 1989.

Florescano, Enrique, and Susan Swan. *Breve historia de la sequia en México* [Brief History of Drought in Mexico]. Veracruz, Mexico: Universidad Veracruzana, Dirección Editorial, 1995.

Foner, Philip S., ed. *Our America: Writings on Latin America and the Struggle for Cuban Independence.* New York: Monthly Review, 1977.

———. *The Spanish-Cuban-American War and the Birth of American Imperialism.* Vol. 1: 1895–1898. New York: Monthly Review, 1972.

Fowler, Will. *Gobernantes mexicanos: 1821–1910* [Mexican Heads of State: 1821–1910]. Mexico City: Fondo de Cultura Económica, 2008.

Fraga, Luis Ricardo. *Latino Lives in America: Making It Home.* Philadelphia: Temple University Press, 2010.

Franco, José Lubiano. *Antonio Maceo: apuntes para una historia de su vida* [Antonio Maceo: Notes toward a History of His Life]. 3 vols. Havana: Editorial de Ciencias Sociales, 1989.

García, Neftali G. *The Mexican Revolution: Legacy of Courage.* Mexico: Xlibris, 2010.

García-Cisneros, Florencio. *La muerte de José Martí: versiones y discrepancias de Máximo Gómez* [The Death of José Martí: Versions and Discrepancies of Máximo Gómez]. New York: Noticias de Arte, 1993.

García Cubas, Antonio. *Mexico: Its Industry, Trade, and Resources.* Trans. William Thompson. Mexico City: Mexico, Departamento de Fomento, Colonización y Industria, 1893.

García del Pino, César. "*El Laborante*: Carlos Sauvalle y José Martí" [*The Laborer*: Carlos Sauvalle and José Martí]. *Revista de la Biblioteca Nacional José Martí* 60.2 (May–August 1969): 165–194.

———. El Laborante *y otros temas martianos* [*The Laborer* and Other Martí Topics]. Havana: Unión, 2006.

García Guatas, Manuel. *La Zaragoza de José Martí* [José Martí's Zaragoza]. Zaragoza, Spain: Institución Fernando el Católico, 1999.

García Martí, Raúl. *Biografía familiar* [Family Biography]. Havana: Cárdenas, 1938.

García Pascual, Luis. *Destinatario José Martí* [Letters to José Martí]. Havana: Abril, 2005.

Garner, James Wilford. *Reconstruction in Mississippi.* New York: Macmillan, 1902.

Garner, Paul. *Porfirio Díaz.* Profiles in Power. White Plains, NY: Longman, 2001.

Gay-Calbó, Enrique. *Ángel de la Guardia, el compañero de Martí en Dos Ríos* [Ángel de la Guardia, Martí's Companion at Dos Ríos]. Havana: Academia de la Historia de Cuba, 1957.

Gaya Nuño, Juan Antonio. *Historia del Museo del Prado: 1819–1976* [History of the Museo del Prado: 1819–1976]. León, Spain: Everest, 1976.

Gómez, Máximo. *Diario de Campaña 1868–1899* [War Diary 1868–1899]. Havana: Instituto del Libro, 1968.

———. Interview. *New York Herald*, June 11, 1895, 2–3.

Gómez Toro, Francisco (Panchito). *Papeles de Panchito* [Papers of Panchito]. Ed. Bladimir Zamora. Havana: La Abríl, 1988.

Guerard, Albert León. *France: A Modern History.* 2nd ed. Ann Arbor: University of Michigan Press, 1969.

Handy, Jim. *Gift of the Devil: A History of Guatemala.* Boston: South End, 1984.

Hart, John Mason. *Revolutionary Mexico: The Coming and Process of the Mexican Revolution.* Berkeley: University of California Press, 1987.

Harter, Jim. *World Railways of the Nineteenth Century: A Pictorial History in Victorian Engravings.* Baltimore, MD: Johns Hopkins University Press, 2005.

Hays, J. N. *The Burdens of Disease: Epidemics and Human Response in Western History.* New Brunswick, NJ: Rutgers University Press, 2010.

Hazard, Samuel. *Cuba in Pen and Pencil.* Hartford, CT: Hartford, 1871.

Healy, David. *James G. Blaine and Latin America.* Columbia: University of Missouri Press, 2000.

Helg, Aline. *Our Rightful Share: The Afro-Cuban Struggle for Equality, 1886–1912.* Chapel Hill: University of North Carolina Press, 1995.

Henein, Michael Y. *Valvular Disease in Clinical Practice.* Berlin: Springer, 2008.

Herrera Franyutti, Alfonso. *Martí en México: recuerdos de una época* [Martí in Mexico: Remembrances of an Era]. 1933. Reprint, Mexico City: Consejo Nacional para la Cultura y las Artes, 1996.

Hidalgo Paz, Ibrahim. *Incursiones en la obra de José Martí* [Incursions in the Work of José Martí]. Havana: Centro de Estudios Martianos, 1989.

———. *José Martí 1853–1895: cronología*. 2nd ed. Havana: Centro de Estudios Martianos, 2003.

Hill, S. S. *Travels in Peru and Mexico*. 2 vols. London: Longman, Green, Longman, and Roberts, 1860.

Historia de Cuba. Textbook series. Havana: Pueblo y Educación, 1989–1995.

Holden, Robert H., and Rina Villars. *Contemporary Latin America: 1970 to the Present*. Hoboken, NJ: John Wiley, 2012.

Hoy, Suellen. *Chasing Dirt: The American Pursuit of Cleanliness*. London: Oxford University Press, 1996.

Huish, Robert L., and W. George Lovell. "Under The Volcanoes: The Influence of Guatemala on José Martí." *Cuban Studies* 39.1 (2008): 25–43.

Hutton, Patrick H., Amanda S. Bourque, and Amy J. Staples, eds. *Historical Dictionary of the Third French Republic, 1870–1940*. New York: Greenwood, 1986.

Iconografía del apóstol José Martí. Secretaría de Instrucción Pública y Bellas Artes. Havana: El siglo XX, 1925.

Izaguirre, José María. "Martí en Guatemala." *Revista cubana: homenaje a Martí en el centenario de su nacimiento* [Cuban Journal: Homage to José Martí on the Centennial of his Birth], 332–342. Havana: Ministerio de Educación, Dirección General de la Cultura, 1953.

James, William D., Timothy G. Berger, and Dirk M. Elston. *Andrews' Diseases of the Skin: Clinical Dermatology*. Amsterdam: Saunders Elsevier, 2006.

Johnson, Willis Fletcher. *The History of Cuba*. 4 vols. New York: B. F. Buck, 1920.

Keane, Augustus Henry. *Central America: The West Indies and South America*. London: E. Stanford, 1878.

Klein, Herbert S. *The Atlantic Slave Trade*. Cambridge, England: Cambridge University Press, 1999.

Knapp, Frank Averill. *The Life of Sebastián Lerdo de Tejada, 1823–1889: A Study of Influence and Obscurity*. Austin: University of Texas Press, 1951.

Komlos, John. *Stature, Living Standards, and Economic Development*. Chicago: University of Chicago Press, 1994.

Lapunzina, Alejandro. *Architecture of Spain*. Westport, CT: Greenwood, 2005.

Lens, Sidney, and Howard Zinn, eds. *The Forging of the American Empire: From Revolution to Vietnam, A History of U.S. Imperialism*. Human Security Series. London: Pluto, 2003.

Lewis, Paul H. *Authoritarian Regimes in Latin America: Dictators, Despots, and Tyrants*. Lanham, MD: Rowman and Littlefield, 2006.

Lizaso, Félix. *Martí, místico del deber* [Martí, Dutiful Mystic]. Havana: Losada, 1952.

Lloyd, Christopher. *The Navy and the Slave Trade*. London: Longmans Green, 1949.

Loaeza, Guadalupe. "La puerta falsa/El poeta suicida" [The False Door/The Poet's

Suicide]. *Fondo de Cultura Económica*, January 6, 2008. http://www.fondodecultura economica.com/editorial/prensa/Detalle.aspx?seccion=Detalle&id_desplegado =12610. Accessed July 16, 2012.

López, Alfred J. "Hugo Meltzl and That Dangerous American Supplement; or, A Tale of Two 1877s." Special issue, *The Americas, Otherwise*, ed. Lois Parkinson Zamora and Silvia D. Spitta. *Comparative Literature* 61.3 (Summer 2009): 220–230.

———. *José Martí and the Future of Cuban Nationalism*. Gainesville: University Press of Florida, 2006.

Lovell, W. George. "The Century after Independence: Land and Life in Guatemala, 1821–1920." *Canadian Journal of Latin American and Caribbean Studies* 19.37–38:243–260.

Lowry, Richard S. *"Littery Man": Mark Twain and Modern Authorship*. Oxford, England: Oxford University Press, 1996.

Loynaz del Castillo, Enrique. *Memorias de la guerra* [Memories of the War]. 1901. Reprint, Havana: Ciencias Sociales, 1989.

Maceo, Antonio. *Ideología politica: cartas y otros documentos* [Political Ideology: Letters and Other Documents]. 2 vols. Havana: Sociedad Cubana de Estudios Históricos e Internacionales, 1950–1952.

Mañach, Jorge. "La hermana de Martí" [Martí's Sister]. Part 1 of 2. *Diario de la Marina*, January 11, 1924, 1–3.

———. *Martí, el apostol* [Martí, the Apostle]. Madrid: Espasa-Calpe, 1933.

María y Campos, Alfonso. "Porfirianos prominentes: orígenes y años de juventud de ocho integrantes del Grupo de los Científicos, 1846–1876" [Prominent Porfirians: Origins and Childhood of Eight Members of the Group of Scientists, 1846–1876]. *Historia Mexicana* 34.4 (April–June 1985): 610–661.

Márquez Sterling, Carlos. *Biografía de José Martí*. Barcelona: Manuel Pareja, 1973.

———. *History of Cuba: From Christopher Columbus to Fidel Castro*. New York: Las Américas, 1969.

———. *Martí, ciudadano de América* [Martí, Citizen of America]. New York: Las Américas, 1965.

Martí, José. *Epistolario* [Letters]. 2 vols. Ed. Gonzalo Quesada y Miranda. Havana: El Siglo XX, 1948.

———. *José Martí: Epistolario*. 3 vols. Ed. Luis García Pascual y Enrique H. Moreno Pla. Havana: Ciencias Sociales, 1993.

———. *Obras completas de José Martí* [Complete Works of José Martí]. Havana: Centro de Estudios Martianos, 1985.

———. *Obras completas de José Martí* (JMOC). Havana: Centro de Estudios Martianos, 2001.

———. *Versos sencillos/Simple Verses*. 1891. Reprint with translation and introduction by Manuel A. Tellechea. Recovering the U.S. Hispanic Literary Heritage. Houston: Arte Público, 1997.

May, Robert E. *John A. Quitman: Old South Crusader*. Baton Rouge, LA: LSU Press, 1995.

Mazzotti, José Antonio. "Epic, Creoles, and Nation in Spanish America." In *A Companion to the Literatures of Colonial America*, ed. Susan P. Castillo and Ivy Schweitzer, 480–499. New York: Wiley-Blackwell, 2005.

Meltzl de Lomnitz, Hugo. "Present Tasks of Comparative Literature." 1877. In *Comparative Literature, the Early Years: An Anthology of Essays*, ed. Hans-Joachim Schultz and Philip H. Rhein, 56–62. Chapel Hill: University of North Carolina Press, 1973.

Mendive, Rafael María. *Poesias de Rafael María de Mendive*. 3rd ed. Havana: Miguel de Villa, 1883.

Mercado, Manuel. *Discurso inaugural pronunciado en la Academia de Jurisprudencia Teórico-Práctica el día 19 de enero* [Inaugural Lecture Given at the Academy of Theoretical-Practical Jurisprudence on January 19]. Mexico City: Ignacio Cumplido, 1860.

Mews, Constant, ed. and trans. *The Lost Love Letters of Héloïse and Abelard: Perceptions of Dialogue in Twelfth-Century France*. Basingstoke, England: Palgrave Macmillan, 2001.

Miranda, Luis Rodolfo. *Reminiscencias cubanas de la guerra y la paz* [Cuban Reminiscences of War and Peace]. Havana: P. Fernández, 1941.

Miró, José. "La tragedia de Dos Ríos" [The Tragedy of Dos Ríos]. *La Discusión* (Havana), September 2, 1911, 1–13.

Montero, Oscar. *José Martí: An Introduction*. London: Palgrave Macmillan, 2004.

Morales, Salvador. *Martí en Venezuela, Bolívar en Martí* [Martí in Venezuela, Bolívar in Martí]. Caracas: Ediciones Centauro, 1985.

Morales y Morales, Vidal. *Iniciadores y primeros mártires de la revolución cubana* [Initiators and First Martyrs of the Cuban Revolution]. 3 vols. Havana: Moderna Poesía, 1901.

———. Introduction to *Poesias de Rafael María de Mendive*, by Mendive, iii–xxxiv. 3rd ed. Havana: Miguel de Villa, 1883.

Mormino, Gary R., and George E. Pozzetta. *The Immigrant World of Ybor City 1885–1985*. Urbana: University of Illinois Press, 1990.

Muller, Daila Antonia. "Cuban Emigrés, Mexican Politics, and the Cuban Question, 1895–1899." PhD diss., University of California–Berkeley, 2007.

The National Cyclopedia of American Biography. Vol. 10. 1880. Reprint, New York: J. T. White, 2012.

Navarro García, Luis. *Las guerras de España en Cuba* [Spain's Wars in Cuba]. Madrid: Encuentro, 1998.

The Numismatist. "Miguel García Granados." Obituary. Vol. 63 (1950): 145.

Núñez y Domínguez, José de Jesús. *Martí en México*. Mexico City: Mexico, Secretaría de Relaciones Exteriores, 1933.

Nyrop, Richard F. *Guatemala: A Country Study*. 2nd ed. Washington, DC: Department of the Army, 1984.

Olavarría y Ferrari, Enrique de. *Reseña histórica del teátro en México, 1538–1911* [Historical Summary of the Theater in Mexico]. 1914. 3 vols. 3rd ed. Mexico City: Porrúa, 1961.

Ortiz Monasterio, José. *México eternamente: Vicente Riva Palacio ante la escritura de la historia* [Mexico Forever: Vicente Riva Palacio before the Structure of History]. Mexico City: Fondo de Cultura Económica, 2004.

O'Shaughnessy, Edith. *Diplomatic Days*. New York: Harper and Brothers, 1917.

Oviedo, José Miguel. *La niña de New York: una revisión de la vida erótica de José Martí*

[The Girl from New York: A Revision of the Erotic Life of José Martí]. Mexico City: Fondo de Cultura Económica, 1989.

Page, E. Legh. "Notes on a Journey from Belize to Guatemala, and Return by the River Polochic in 1834." *Journal of the Royal Geographical Society of London* 8 (1838): 317–327.

Payne, Stanley G. *Politics and the Military in Modern Spain*. Stanford, CA: Stanford University Press, 1967.

Peraza, Nicanor Bolet. *Venezuela a Martí* [Venezuela to Martí]. Havana: Lex, 1953.

Pérez, Louis A. Jr. *Cuba: Between Reform and Revolution*. New York: Oxford University Press, 1988.

————. "Cubans in Tampa: From Exiles to Immigrants 1892–1901." *Florida Historical Quarterly* 57 (October 1978): 129–140.

Pérez Galdós, Victor. *José Martí: visión de un hombre universal* [José Martí: Vision of a Universal Man]. Barcelona: Puvill, 1999.

Pérez Nápoles, Rubén. *José Martí: el poeta armado* [José Martí: The Armed Poet]. Madrid: Algaba, 2004.

Phillips, William D. Jr., and Carla Rahn. *A Concise History of Spain*. Cambridge, England: Cambridge University Press, 2010.

Pí y Margall, Francisco, and Francisco de Pí y Arsuaga, eds. *Historia de España en el siglo XIX: sucesos políticos, económicos, sociales y artísticos* [History of Spain in the Nineteenth Century: Political, Economic, Social, and Artistic Events]. 8 vols. Madrid: Segui, 1902.

Picó, Fernando. *El día menos pensado: historia de los presidiarios en Puerto Rico (1793–1993)* [When Least Expected: A History of Prisoners in Puerto Rico (1793–1993)]. Río Piedras, Puerto Rico: Huracán, 1994.

Pierson, Peter. *The History of Spain*. Westport, CT: Greenwood, 1999.

Piñeyro, Enrique. *Como acabó la dominación de España en América* [How the Spanish Domination of America Ended]. 1908. Reprint, Paris: Garnier Hermanos, 1925.

Pirala, Antonio. *Anales de la guerra de Cuba* [Annals of the War in Cuba]. 4 vols. Madrid: Felipe González Rojas, 1898.

Ponce de León, N., trans. *The Book of Blood: An Authentic Record of the Policy Adopted by Modern Spain to Put an End to the War for the Independence of Cuba (October 1868 to November 10, 1873)*. New York: N. Ponce de León, 1873.

Portuondo, José Antonio. *Martí y el diversionismo ideológico* [Martí and Ideological Diversionism]. Havana: Centro de Estudios Martianos, 1974.

Preston, Julia, and Samuel Dillon. *Opening Mexico: The Making of a Democracy*. London: Macmillan, 2005.

Prieto, Alejandro, and R. Piatkowski. *Ideas generales sobre el ferrocarril interoceánico de Guatemala* [General Ideas Regarding the Interoceanic Railroad of Guatemala]. Guatemala City: Taracena e Hijos, 1880.

Quesada y Miranda, Gonzalo de. *Alrededor de la acción de Dos Ríos* [Regarding the Incident at Dos Ríos]. Havana: Seoane, Fernández, 1942.

————, ed. *Archivo de Gonzalo de Quesada*. 2 vols. Havana: Ciencias Sociales, 1948–1951.

————. *Iconografía martiana*. Havana: Oficina de Publicaciones del Consejo de Estado, 1985.

———. *Martí, hombre* [Martí, the Man]. Havana: Seone, Fernández, 1940.

———, ed. *Papeles de Martí* [Martí's Papers]. 3 vols. Havana: Academia de la Historia de Cuba, 1933.

Rable, George C. *But There Was No Peace: The Role of Violence in the Politics of Reconstruction*. Athens: University of Georgia Press, 2007.

Riley, James C. *Low Income, Social Growth, and Good Health*. Berkeley: University of California Press, 2007.

Ripoll, Carlos. "La autopsia de José Martí" [The Autopsy of José Martí]. November 4, 2001. http://eddosrios.org/marti/Article-30/autopsia.htm. Accessed August 2, 2013.

———. *Escritos cubanos de historia, política y literatura* [Cuban Writings on History, Politics, and Literature]. Miami: Dos Ríos, 1998.

———. *José Martí: letras y huellas desconocidas* [José Martí: Unknown Letters and Traces]. Miami: Eliseo Torres, 1976.

———. *José Martí: notas y estudios* [José Martí: Notes and Studies]. Miami: Dos Ríos, 1999.

———. *José Martí: nuevas obras completas* [José Martí: New Complete Works]. Miami: Dos Ríos, 2001.

———. *Martí y el fin de una leyenda* [Martí and the End of a Legend]. New York: Dos Ríos, 2007.

———. "Martí y Francia" [Martí and France]. *Trazos de Cuba* 14 (1996): 18–19.

———. *Nuevas páginas sobre Martí* [New Writings on Martí]. New York: Dos Ríos, 2004.

———. *Patria: el periódico de José Martí* [Patria: José Martí's Newspaper]. New York: Eliseo Torres, 1971.

———. *La vida íntima y secreta de José Martí* [The Intimate and Secret Life of José Martí]. Miami: Dos Ríos, 1995.

Rives, Timothy. "Grant, Babcock, and the Whiskey Ring." *Prologue: Quarterly of the National Archives and Records Administration* 32.3 (Fall 2000). http://www.archives.gov/publications/prologue/2000/fall/whiskey-ring-1.html. Accessed June 30, 2012.

Roa, Ramón. *A pie y descalzo de Trinidad a Cuba, 1870–1871: recuerdos de campaña* [On Foot and Shoeless from Trinidad to Cuba, 1870–1871: Memories of the War]. 1890. Reprint, Miami: Club del Libro Latinoamericano, 1977.

Robinson, Albert G. *Cuba Old and New*. 1915. Reproduced, Project Gutenberg, 2004. http://gutenberg.org/ebooks/11464.

Robles Pozo, José. *Derecho procesal de España . . . : las leyes y la jurisprudencia vigentes del enjuiciamiento criminal* [Procedural Law of Spain . . . : The Laws and Jurisprudence of Criminal Prosecution]. Madrid: Revista de Legislación, 1890.

Rodas Chaves, Germán. *José Martí: aproximación a sus primeros 20 años de vida* [José Martí: Overview of His First Twenty Years of Life]. Quito: Abya Yala, 2001.

Rodríguez, Raúl. *Los escudos invisibles: un Martí desconocido* [The Invisible Shields: An Unknown Martí]. Havana: Capitán San Luis, 2003.

Rodríguez, Rolando. *Dos Ríos: A caballo y con el sol en la frente* [Dos Ríos: On Horseback and Facing the Sun]. Havana: Centro de Ciencias Sociales, 2001.

Rodríguez Demorizi, Emilio. *Martí en Santo Domingo*. Havana: Ucar, García, 1953.

Rodríguez-Silva, Delfin. *Cronología martiana: la ruta apostólica de José Martí 1853–1895* [Martí Chronology: The Apostolic Route of José Martí 1853–1895]. Miami: Ediciones Universal, 1996.

Roig de Leuschsenring, Emilio. *Martí en España* [Martí in Spain]. Havana: Cultural, 1938.

Ronning, C. Neale. *José Martí and the Emigré Colony in Key West: Leadership and State Formation*. New York: Praeger, 1990.

Ross, Delmer G. "The Construction of the Interoceanic Railroad of Guatemala." *The Americas* 33 (January 1977): 430–456.

———. *Development of Railroads in Guatemala and El Salvador, 1849–1929*. Lewiston, NY: Edwin Mellen, 2001.

Rotker, Susana. *Fundación de una escritura: las crónicas de José Martí* [Foundation of a Genre: The Chronicles of José Martí]. Havana: Casa de las Américas, 1992.

Royet, Paul, and Patrice Mériaux. *Surveillance, Maintenance, and Diagnosis of Flood Protection Dikes: A Practical Handbook for Owners and Operators*. Versailles: Quae, 2007.

Rubens, Horatio Seymour. *Liberty: The Story of Cuba*. New York: Brewer, Warren, and Putnam, 1932.

Salinas Álvarez, Samuel. *Historia de los caminos de México, época prehistórica, época colonial* [History of the Roads of Mexico, Prehistoric Times, Colonial Times]. Mexico City: Banco Nacional de Obras y Servicios Públicos, 1994.

Sánchez Gávez, Samuel. *Martí ciñó el mandil: prueba documental de su filiación masónica* [Martí Wore the Apron: Documented Proof of His Masonic Affiliation]. Havana: Biblioteca Nacional José Martí, Ediciones Bachiller, 2007.

Sande, Luis Toledo. *Cesto de llamas: Biografía de José Martí* [Basket of Flames: Biography of José Martí]. Havana: Editorial de Ciencias Sociales, 1996.

Sandoval, Ximénez de Sandoval. "Memoria de Dos Ríos." *La Discusión*, September 9, 1911, 2–8.

Sanz Delgado, Enrique. "Disciplina y reclusión en el siglo XIX: criterios humanizadores y control de la custodia" [Discipline and Imprisonment in the Nineteenth Century: Humanizing Criteria and the Control of Custody]. *Anuario de Derecho Penal y Ciencias Penales* 55 (January 2002): 109–201.

Sarabia, Nydia. *Noticias confidenciales sobre Cuba 1870–1895* [Confidential Reports on Cuba 1870–1895]. Havana: Editora Política, 1985.

———. *La patriota del silencio: Carmen Miyares* [The Silent Patriot: Carmen Miyares]. Havana: Ciencias Sociales, 1990.

Saumell, Eduardo. *Fauna y flora cubanas*. Miami: Laurenty, 1989.

Schreier, Alta. *Vamos a Cuba* [Let's Go to Cuba]. Portsmouth, NH: Heinemann, 2000.

Seematter, Mary E. "The St. Louis Whiskey Ring." *Gateway Heritage*, Spring 1988, 32–42.

Semple, Ellen Churchill. *American History and Its Geographic Conditions*. San Francisco: Houghton Mifflin, 1903.

Shaw, W. A. *The History of Currency 1251–1894: Being an Account of the Gold and Silver Moneys and Monetary Standards of Europe and America, Together with an Examination of the Effects of Currency and Exchange Phenomena on Commercial and National Progress and Well Being*. 1896. Reprint, New York: G. P. Putnam's Sons, 1967.

Shirer, William L. *The Collapse of the Third Republic*. New York: Simon and Schuster, 1969.

Shubert, Adrian. *A Social History of Modern Spain*. London: Routledge, 1990.

Simmons, Donald C. Jr. *Confederate Settlements in British Honduras*. Jefferson, NC: McFarland, 2001.

Smith, Gene. *Maximilian and Carlota*. New York: William Morrow, 1974.

Smorkaloff, Pamela María. *Readers and Writers in Cuba: A Social History of Print Culture, 1830s–1990s*. London: Taylor and Francis, 1997.

Soto-Hall, Máximo. *Martí y el general Justo Rufino Barrios*. Guatemala City: Biblioteca de Cultura Popular, 1952.

Soto Paz, Rafael. *Antología de periodistas cubanos* [Anthology of Cuban Journalists]. Havana: Empresa Editora de Publicaciones, 1943.

Staten, Clifford L. *The History of Cuba*. New York: Palgrave Macmillan, 2005.

Steiner, M. "Postpartum Psychiatric Disorders." *Canadian Journal of Psychiatry* 35 (1990): 89–95.

Stephens, John Lloyd. *Incidents of Travel in Central America, Chiapas, and Yucatan*. New York: Harper and Brothers, 1871.

Stewart, James Brewer. *Wendell Phillips: Liberty's Hero*. Baton Rouge, LA: LSU Press, 1998.

Suárez Suárez, Reinaldo. *José Martí contra Alphonse Karr, en defensa de la vida, contra la pena de muerte* [José Martí versus Alphonse Karr, in Defense of Life, against Capital Punishment]. Biblioteca Jurídica Virtual. Mexico City: Instituto de Investigaciones Jurídicas, Universidad Nacional Autónoma de México, 2006.

Tablada, Ricardo Hodelín. *Enfermedades de José Martí* [Illnesses of José Martí]. Santiago, Cuba: Oriente, 2007.

Tarragó, Rafael E. *Experiencias políticas de los cubanos en la Cuba española: 1512–1898* [The Political Experiences of Cubans in Colonial Cuba: 1512–1898]. Barcelona: Puvill, 1996.

Tejada, Valentín. *Martí a su paso por Santo Domingo* [Martí's Travels in Santo Domingo]. Guantánamo, Cuba: M. Medrano S. en C., 1935.

Tejera, Emiliano. "Gobernadores de la Isla de Santo Domingo, siglos XVI–XVII" [Governors of the Island of Santo Domingo, Sixteenth–Seventeenth Centuries]. 1915. *BAGN: Boletín del Archivo General de la Nación*. http://www.bagn.academiahistoria.org.do/boletines/boletin18/BAGN_1941_No_18-04.pdf.

Terrero, Roberto. "Apuntes para una biografía: Manuel Mercado, íntimo amigo de José Martí" [Notes toward a Biography: Manuel Mercado, Intimate Friend of José Martí]. Havana: Universidad de Ciencias Pedagógicas Blas Roca Calderío, September 27, 2011.

Thomas, Hugh. *Cuba; or, the Pursuit of Freedom*. 1971. Updated ed., New York: DaCapo, 1998.

Thurtle, V. "Post-Natal Depression: The Relevance of Sociological Approaches." *Journal of Advanced Nursing* 22:3 (1995): 416–424.

Tobar Cruz, Pedro. "Crónica de la conspiración de Antonio Kopesky en 1877 y el gobierno liberal de Justo Rufino Barrios" [Chronicle of the Conspiracy of Antonio

Kopesky in 1877 and the Liberal Government of Justo Rufino Barrios] *Antropología e historia de Guatemala* 1 (1979): 127–137.

Trujillo, Enrique. *Apuntes históricos: propaganda y movimientos revolucionarios en los Estados Unidos desde enero de 1880 hasta febrero de 1895* [Historical Notes: Propaganda and Revolutionary Movements in the United States from January 1880 to February 1895]. New York: El Porvenir, 1896.

Tucker, Spencer, ed. *The Encyclopedia of the Spanish-American and Philippine-American Wars: A Political, Social, and Military History*. Santa Barbara, CA: ABC-CLIO, 2009.

Tuñon de Lara, M. *La España del siglo XIX* [Spain of the Nineteenth Century]. Barcelona: Laia, 1977.

Ubieta, Enrique. *Efemérides de la revolución cubana* [Ephemeralities of the Cuban Revolution]. 4 vols. Havana: Molina, 1911.

Valdés Domínguez, Fermín. *Diario de soldado* [Soldier's Diary]. 4 vols. 1895. Reprint, ed. Hiram Dupotey Fideaux, Havana: Universidad de Havana, Centro de Información Científica y Técnica, 1972.

———. "Ofrenda de hermano" [Brother's Offering]. 1908. Reprint, *Opus Habana* 7.1 (2003): 1–8.

Vega, Bernardo. *Memorias de Bernardo Vega: Contribución a la historia de la comunidad puertorriqueña en Nueva York* [Memoirs of Bernardo Vega: A Contribution to the History of the Puerto Rican Community in New York]. Ed. César Andreu Iglesias. Rio Piedras, Puerto Rico: Ediciones Huracán, 1977.

Vela, David. *Martí en Guatemala* [Martí in Guatemala]. Guatemala City: Guatemala, Ministerio de Educación Pública, 1954.

Velázquez de la Cadena, Mariano. *A Dictionary of the Spanish and English Languages*. New York: D. Appleton, 1877.

Vincent, Charles. *Black Legislators in Louisiana during Reconstruction*. Carbondale, IL: SIU Press, 2011.

Vitier, Cintio. "Hallazgo de una profecía" [Fulfillment of a Prophesy]. *Casa de las Américas* 158 (September–October 1986): 30–38.

Wagner, Regina. *The History of Coffee in Guatemala*. Bogotá: Villegas y Asociados, 2001.

Walford, Cornelius. *The Famines of the World, Past and Present*. Manchester, NH: Ayer, 1970.

Walton, Gary M., and Hugh Rockoff. *History of the American Economy*. 2nd ed. Boston: South-Western College, 2010.

Wang, Andrew, and Thomas M. Bashore, eds. *Valvular Heart Disease*. Contemporary Cardiology. Berlin: Springer, 2009.

Westfall, L. Glenn. *Key West: Cigar City U.S.A.* Key West: Historic Florida Keys, 1984.

Wisan, Joseph E. *The Cuban Crisis as Reflected in the New York Press: 1895–1898*. New York: Columbia University Press, 1934.

Wise, George Schneiweiss. *Caudillo: A Portrait of Antonio Guzmán Blanco*. New York: Columbia University Press, 1951.

Zéndegui, Guillermo de. *Ámbito de Martí* [Martí's World]. Bogotá: Departamento de Publicaciones, Sociedad Colombista Panamericana, 1954.

Index